# LEADERS OF REFORM

# LEADERS OF REFORM

Progressive Republicans in Kansas
1900-1916

ROBERT SHERMAN LA FORTE

THE UNIVERSITY PRESS OF KANSAS
*Lawrence/Manhattan/Wichita*

© 1974, 2020 University Press of Kansas
All Rights Reserved
First Published 1974. Reissued 2020.

The text of this book is licensed under a Creative Commons Attribution-NonCommercial-NoDerivatives 4.0 International Public License (https://creativecommons.org/licenses/by-nc-nd/4.0).

Published by the University Press of Kansas (Lawrence, Kansas 66045), which was organized by the Kansas Board of Regents and is operated and funded by Emporia State University, Fort Hays State University, Kansas State University, Pittsburg State University, the University of Kansas, and Wichita State University.

Open access edition funded by the National Endowment for Humanities and the Andrew W. Mellon Foundation Humanities Open Book Program.

Typographical errors may have been introduced in the digitization process.

Library of Congress Cataloging in Publication Data
La Forte, Robert Sherman, 1933–
Leaders of reform: progressive Republicans in Kansas, 1900–1916.
Bibliography: p.
ISBN 978-0-7006-0124-0 (cloth : alk. paper)
ISBN 978-0-7006-3160-5 (paper : alk. paper)
ISBN 978-0-7006-3105-6 (ebook)
1. Kansas—Politics and government—1865–1950. 2. Republican Party. Kansas. I. Title.
Classification: LCC: F686.L16  DDC: 320.9'781,03 74-961
LC record available at https://lccn.loc.gov/74000961.

The paper used in this publication is acid free and meets the minimum requirements of the American National Standard for Permanence of Paper for Printed Library Materials Z39.48-1992.

TO

**FRANCES, MARK,
GEOFFREY, AND RUSSELL**

# CONTENTS

Kansas Open Books Foreword, Charles Delgadillo
**ix**

Acknowledgments
**xiii**

1
Prologue: The Progressive Republicans of Kansas
**1**

2
Factional Beginnings: Of Boss-Busters
and Political Machines, 1900–1903
**13**

3
Transitional Factionalism: The Kansas Republican League
and Reform, 1904–1906
**31**

4
Growing Dissidence: Mainly Railroads, 1906
**51**

5
From Civic Leaguers to Square Dealers:
Kansas Politics, 1906–1908
**67**

6
Bristow and the Birth
of the Progressive Republican Faction, 1908
**89**

7
The State and Governor Stubbs, 1909–1911
**111**

8
Taft and the Kansas Insurgents, 1909–1910
**135**

9
The Republican Primary of 1910 and Its Aftermath
**163**

10
With Roosevelt to Armageddon, 1912
**185**

11
A New Party, a Parting of Old Friends, 1913
**209**

12
The Year They Really Stood at Armageddon, 1914
**229**

13
Epilogue: How Things Can End
**247**

Notes
**263**

Bibliography
**297**

Index
**307**

# KANSAS OPEN BOOKS FOREWORD

*Leaders of Reform* was published in 1974, at the culmination of the dramatic social and political upheaval of the 1960s and 1970s. The book was written at a time when America was reshaped by major protest movements, and the same was true about the Progressive movement that thrived in the United States from around 1900 to 1920. Scholars are products of their times, and it is not surprising that historians who matured professionally during the 1960s and 1970s would be interested in the Progressive Era. Groundbreaking works such as Robert Wiebe's *The Search for Order, 1877–1920* (1967) and Lawrence Goodwyn's *Democratic Promise: The Populist Moment in America* (1976) reconstructed the way the Progressive and Populist movements were born, grew, and developed. Historians writing during the 1960s and 1970s were naturally interested in social movements and change, and the elite-led reform of the Progressive Era offered an interesting contrast with the grassroots movements of the sixties.

*Leaders of Reform* earned a largely positive reception upon its release. In his June 1975 review of the book in the *Journal of American History* David Thelen highlighted the work as "one of the best monographs on the political and legislative activities of a state's progressive leaders." Lewis Gould praised La Forte in the *Southwestern Historical Quarterly* for having a "balanced view of his actors. He is aware of the mixed motives of both progressives and conservatives" (July 1975, 79:108–109). And LeRoy Ashby, writing in the *Pacific Northwest Quarterly*, credited the work as a meaningful contribution to the history of the Kansas progressive movement. The work was criticized as well, primarily for its lack of statistical analysis. Thelen stated that the main problem with the book was that it lacked explanatory power and that the author "just does not care about popular attitudes." One reviewer was more specific, arguing that the author should have analyzed roll-call votes or dissected electoral results by demographic group. *Leaders of Reform* was a fine local study, the reviewer stated, but "such studies . . . need to be methodologically more sophisticated and intellectually more rigorous than *Leaders of Reform*." (Theoharis 1975, 199–200).

*Leaders of Reform* was published at another moment of transition: the movement toward social history. The book was a work of standard political history recounting the way in which a cast of seventy Kansas progressive Republican reformers—including businessmen, newspapermen, politicians, and social leaders—built the Progressive movement in their state. That is, the work focused on a community of white male political elites at a time when the trend among historians was moving away from political history and toward social history. This explains why reviewers criticized the work's lack of statistical analysis, a key method used by social historians to establish generalities about communities. Although it suffered from bad timing, *Leaders of Reform* was true to its title: it was about the leaders of progressivism in Kansas, not the rank and file. The historiographical trend since *Leaders of Reform* was published has been decidedly toward examining social groups and marginalized communities. More recent studies of the Progressive movement have focused on the reform impulse in marginalized communities, such as women and the poor, and the Progressives' reputation has particularly suffered as scholars have more closely examined the Progressive record on race. Recent events have also continued to spur lines of inquiry regarding the Progressives. The end of the Cold War increased interest in the international context that birthed the American Progressive movement, and the War on Terror provoked studies focusing on the role violence and terrorism played in shaping Progressive political discourse.

Recent political developments have driven a resurgence of interest in political history, and it is timely that *Leaders of Reform* receive a second look. The work reconstructs how the Kansas reform movement took root in the state Republican Party, how reformers were able to capture the organization, and the ways in which their reform project succeeded or failed. Understanding the path Kansas progressive Republicans used to take control of their state party in the early twentieth century gives us perspective on how the progressive Democrats or Trumpian Republicans are working to take or maintain control of their parties today. There are lessons for modern reformers in the story of how Kansas Progressives struggled to address a system that they believed was engineered to keep control in the hands of the establishment. Progressive reformers encountered successes and failures as they sought to advance their cause, and reformers today would do well to studiously examine the Progressives' record. *Leaders of Reform* is a valuable work that was appreciated in its day, and it has tremendous potential to help educate and inspire historians and would-be reformers alike on a continuing basis.

Charles Delgadillo<br>
Corona, California<br>
March 2020

# ACKNOWLEDGMENTS

Anyone who has written or is writing a book knows the debt an author owes to others. I should like to acknowledge an obligation to the staffs of the Library of Congress and the libraries of the University of Kansas, Kansas State College of Pittsburg, North Texas State University, and East Texas State University, and, most importantly, to the excellent group of archivists and librarians at the Kansas State Historical Society. I should like to thank the following colleagues and friends who contributed advice or concern, or in some other way helped to bring this study to completion: Professors Francis Schruben of Pierce College (Los Angeles); Elmo Richardson, formerly of Washington State University; A. Bower Sageser and Homer Socolofsky of Kansas State University; Michael J. Brodhead of the University of Nevada (Reno); O. Gene Clanton of Washington State University; Robert J. Chasteen of East Texas State University; and Jack B. Scroggs of North Texas State University. Dean Burton J. Williams of Central Washington State College and Virginia Seaver of the University Press of Kansas were of assistance in divers ways. More than a decade ago I had the honor of studying under the supervision of two of the best-informed men ever to work in Kansas history: Professors James C. Malin and the late George L. Anderson. I should also like to thank Professors M. Elizabeth Cochran and Dudley T. Cornish of Kansas State College of Pittsburg for having led me to the study of history. My dear friend Edward J. Coomes, Jr., was a constant source of encouragement and positive criticism. I am especially grateful to the man who made it possible for me to call myself historian, Professor Donald R. McCoy, scholar, teacher, and gentleman.

# 1

## PROLOGUE: THE PROGRESSIVE REPUBLICANS OF KANSAS

Progress and reform were probably the most overused words in the vocabulary of the Kansas politician during the late nineteenth and early twentieth centuries. Political leaders then were as aware as scholars are today that this was an Age of Discontent, marked by prohibition, populism, and progressivism, as well as a host of lesser reform movements. To the degree that a common bond existed among reformers during those years, it existed in their views of government, society, and the economy. Disaffected with the economy, resentful of the arrogance of power, possessing a view of the "more perfect" society, reformers agreed only on general goals.

Government, they felt, needed to play a more positive role in regulating businesses that had grown too powerful during the Gilded Age. The people, disenfranchised by the politics of money, needed to have a larger role in determining the men and laws that governed them. Public welfare needed to be promoted by benign social policies, and the morality of the populace needed statutory protection from temptations. On specifics these reform groups disagreed. In part this difference existed because of conviction; in part because of location in time and space. Each movement was led by different people, and to a lesser degree each was composed of a different constituency. Dissatisfaction with the status quo was their primary characteristic, and it was the main reason reform was popular.

In the following pages one aspect of early-twentieth-century reform is discussed—the progressive movement and, more particularly, its influence upon the leadership of the Republican party of Kansas. Because so much has been written about early-twentieth-century reformers and because some writers have discussed Kansas politics of this period, several observations relative to these other views seem necessary as an introduction. For example, historians find it hard to agree when Kansas political leaders launched a progressive reform movement. The point of departure in this work is 1900, a date chosen because it marks the beginning of a period of intense factional fighting among Kansas Republicans that resulted in rhetoric and achievements described by some scholars as "progressive." This period is considered here as a time of preprogressive factionalism, lasting from 1900 to 1906; it is discussed briefly in chapters two and three. This is done because a relationship exists between political alignments during the preprogressive period and those of the progressive-Republican era from 1906 to 1916.

What most historians know but tend to forget is that the majority of progressives were involved in politics years before they became interested in reform. In Kansas this was particularly true of progressive Republicans who had begun their careers as opponents of populism. The motivation of the young progressives, upon entering the political field, appears to have been power, prestige, and pelf. If a Republican handled his affairs properly in the 1880s and 1890s, when these men became active, he could look forward to at least a local reputation, a moderate income, and a meaningful role in determining local policies. The Kansas politician would have easily appreciated Alfred Adler, with his stress on individual achievement.

These same men turned to reform because by the first decade of the twentieth century the political climate was changing nationally. The speeches of Theodore Roosevelt, Robert La Follette, and William Jennings Bryan were unsettling to Kansans, who were recovering from the revelations of Populists. Despite prosperity, or maybe because of it, successful politics meant getting in line with change. As the new emphasis developed, genuine metamorphosis began to occur in the thinking of Republican leaders who were destined to be called progressives. They began to see economic injustices, political inequalities, and growing immoralities, not because it was expedient to do so, but because the discrepancies had become apparent. Popular government did seem to be threatened by plutocracy; agricultural Kansas was being cheated by the industrial East; liquor was still being consumed despite the state's constitutional ban on the manufacture, distribution, and sale of alcoholic beverages. It was comforting to know that by 1908 one could oppose what was wrong in Kansas and still control the state's government. In fact, unless the mantle of progressivism graced the shoulders of a Republican, his chances of retaining power and office were seriously jeopardized.

One of the finest specimens of the progressive Republican was Kansas' most famous editor, the man from Emporia, William Allen White. He had entered politics as a foe of Populists. His editorial "What's the Matter with Kansas?" had not only excoriated the People's party, it had also helped to elect a president and bring White a national reputation. A protégé of the leaders of his Grand Old Party, he allegedly began to receive printing contracts from federal officers and to have his voice heard in Republican councils. White evidenced satisfaction with party activities until the early years of Roosevelt's presidency; then he began to change. Later in life he described his transformation by noting: "I met Theodore Roosevelt. He sounded in my heart the first trumpet call of the new time that was to be."[1] In becoming a progressive, White retained his importance in the Republican party, increasing it briefly from 1908 to 1912. His national fame was well established by then, and though his wealth was moderate, he was far from the struggling farm-town journalist he had been. By the middle of the decade he had become a true believer in reform; he would later write that he had joined up because he realized that the millenium had not yet arrived and that the "continuous orderly growth of human institutions" required that the "highest caliber" of leaders be involved. In this way, he believed, conditions could be improved.[2]

Whether White and his associates were responsible for improved conditions in Kansas is, of course, a moot question. They were not the only group that was contributing to the passage of reforms. Democrats, regular Republicans, and a few Socialists helped to fashion these laws. Moreover, those who opposed specific changes often forced progressive Republicans to compromise their views, thus diluting their legislation. The law that established the Public Utilities Commission was an example of compromise; it was replaced later by an enactment creating the Kansas Corporation Commission. Moreover, laws that fulfilled the reformers' goals did not always work. The Bank Deposit Guaranty Law insured deposits, but it did not last. Financial difficulties in the late twenties caused the legislature to repeal it. In this instance the failure of progressivism was not absolute, since the Kansas system served as a link

3

between uninsured bank deposits and the Federal Deposit Insurance Corporation of 1933.

White's characterization of the progressive Republican as the "highest caliber" of leader, one who was interested in improving conditions, is also open to question. A good many reformers in Kansas acted in a disinterested manner, but an equally large number profited from the changes that they encouraged. For example, their support of the direct primary resulted in part from their inability to gain power through the convention system. But their disinterestedness was most questionable in economic matters. Twenty out of thirty-five major reform laws that they passed were related to the economy of the state. In almost every instance these enactments favored those who supported the progressives. In national politics the progressives were as concerned as old-line Republicans in promoting Kansas interests. Controversies over tariffs and railroad rates in the Sixty-first Congress, 1909–1911, demonstrated as much. Richard Abrams, in his excellent study of Massachusetts during the Progressive Era, correctly observed that "although insurgent leaders usually assumed a moral rhetoric, the 'evil' they condemned in many cases was merely the greater power or advantage of their competitors."[3] Of course, Kansans were among the leaders of the insurgency, and they were understandably interested in ways of affecting the distribution of benefits in order to favor their home state.

Contemporaries of the progressive Republicans often questioned White's notion that the reformers represented the "highest caliber" of leadership. None put his objection as colorfully as Albert T. Reid. With a few inaccurate statements, he wrote:

> Arthur Capper twice tried to connect with the state printer "graft," as his paper now refers to the old arrangement. He was beaten by Henry Allen who made an air-tight arrangement with George Clark, and they split the pot. Will White had a nice little side line also. An arrangement under the Roosevelt administration made it necessary to ship all the pension vouchers to Emporia for Bill White to print. Somewhat expensive, impractical, and occasioned much delay, but Bill was one of the "ring" in those days. Well, one day Cy Leland who became pension commissioner, kicked this arrangement upside down, brought the printing to Topeka and gave it to Arthur Capper, who was also quite "regular." Then White went after Cy, who was henceforth an "undesirable." . . . Also there is Bristow—"the lean and hungry" one who wanted Senator Long to get him an easy job with a good salary, so he could loaf around Kansas and look after the interest of the "ring." Gentlemen, we are saved![4]

That Kansas progressives were not perfect will surprise no one. The question to be resolved is how imperfect were they? From observations that have been made about reformers in other states, they seem to have been about average; not as high-minded as some, but then not as opportunistic as others.

Fortunately, a number of thoughtful studies of progressivism have been done in the last several decades, and they provide a basis for comparison of Kansas progressive-Republican leaders and their movement with those in other states. These studies generally reveal that reform was something different in each state. However, certain common aspects have been shown to exist. For example, George Mowry, in his admirable study of California, determined that the progressive movement there began in Los Angeles and San Francisco and later worked its way upwards to the state level.[5] Some scholars have found that this urban origin of the movement existed elsewhere; Hoyt Warner used his detailed inquiry into Ohio to chronicle this paradigm of progressive reform.[6] In Kansas the model is not valid. Kansas progressive Republicanism began at the state level and later influenced change in local government. Moreover, Kansas progressives did not draw their major support from the state's one metropolitan area, Kansas City, as did other state progressives operating in California, New Jersey, Tennessee, and Ohio.[7] Nor did progressivism thrive in the semiurban towns of 10,000 to 30,000 people, which possessed the nearest thing to industrial populations in a primarily rural state. The portion of Kansas with the fewest industries—that is, the western two-thirds—voted most consistently for progressive Republicans in party primaries, while the more populous, industrialized eastern third often failed to return progressive-Republican majorities.

As a general rule, the progressives lost Wyandotte, Shawnee, Sedgwick, Crawford, Cherokee, Leavenworth, and Montgomery counties. Many Kansas manufacturing and mining interests and one out of every four of the state's 1.6 million inhabitants were located in these seven counties in 1910. Democrats, Socialists, and antiprogressive Republicans were the leading political forces there. This was true because until 1910 progressive Republicans included in their program very few measures that appealed to the working class. In that year, however, the progressives did incorporate a number of labor-oriented planks into the Republican platform. But by then the progressive Republicans had become known as prohibitionists, and this fact circumscribed their appeal to the industrial laborers, who almost to a man were "wets." Moreover, Socialists and reform Democrats constantly emphasized the conservative nature of the progressive leadership in the Republican party. In so doing, they not only negated the progressives' appeal to the laborer but also touched upon a central fact of progressive Republicanism in the state.

In general, like the middle western movement discussed in the works of Russell Nye, Theodore Saloutos, and John D. Hicks,[8] Kansas progressive Republicanism was a moderate reform impulse in comparison to alternative ones offered earlier by Populists and to those being offered during the period by Socialists and radical Democrats. Kansas progressivism resembled the American reform tradition in general. Kansas progressives were not men interested in violently upsetting the existing order of life in their state or in disturbing the good within its heritage. They were not as sophisticated as the reformers that Robert Wiebe describes, who, having witnessed the disintegration of their established community, sought to recreate a new order through bureaucratic means.[9] They were conservative in their outlook, somewhat simplistic, and certainly not revolutionary. They planned moderate experimentation with government rather than destruction and upheaval.

If the progressives were radicals, as some of their contemporaries maintained and as David Thelen has recently suggested,[10] in Kansas they were conservative radicals who were interested in practical solutions to specific problems. This pragmatic approach was well summarized in 1916 by Kansas' Chief Justice William A. Johnston when he told an audience of Grangers that "Kansas had led in progressive legislation . . . [and had] kept pace with the evolution of society." He added:

> No one need fear that Kansas law-makers will imperil property rights, arrest progress or injure the institutions of our state. . . . The people . . . are naturally fair minded and would rebel at once if any man or legislature should by statute or otherwise undertake to do that which would cripple business, sacrifice property rights or unduly encroach on the personal rights or liberties of any one.[11]

In the same conservative vein, Kansas' most important progressive-Republican governor, Walter Roscoe Stubbs, said in 1905: "I would not have you confuse, in any sense whatever, the honest, sterling banker, merchant, corporation, or business man, who has grown rich out of legitimate profits . . . with these greedy, money-mad, lawless concerns. The one is a necessity and a blessing to a community, the other a law breaker and a menace to the perpetuity of popular government."[12]

Kansas progressives were not, however, conservative in the same sense that this term is used by Gabriel Kolko in describing the national movement. They could not enact laws to rationalize markets and thus aid businesses, as Kolko says national reformers did. Kansans certainly did not approve of the established economic relationships that Congress was allegedly promoting. Kolko is probably correct in suggesting that state progressives were more liberal than their counterparts in Washington.[13] Kansas reformers were also not conservative in the manner that Virginia's progressives were, according to Raymond Pulley's discussion of the latter.[14] Unlike the Old Dominion, Kansas had had no "ideal" period in its history to which its progressive Republicans wished to return. Thus, no Bourbon restoration was taking place on the Great Plains in the early twentieth century.

Kansas reformers were akin to what has become the progressive prototype, described best by George Mowry. They were young men of northern European stock who were born either in Kansas or in the Midwest. Most had Protestant backgrounds, had attended college, and held at least a middle-class niche in the economic structure of the state. They had been anti-Populists and had been moderately important in Republican politics during the nineties. Of the seventy progressive Republicans whose backgrounds were traced during this study, most conformed to this general description.

The meaning of this composite character is unclear. An analysis of the backgrounds of forty-five regular Republican and thirty-two Democratic leaders shows that they also conformed to this description. That is, they were young, "well fixed," educated Anglo-Saxon Protestants who came from families with leadership traditions in Kansas. One thing does seem clear: in choosing their political spokesmen, Kansans normally selected men who represented the general character of the state's population, or ones who possessed characteristics that the voters thought were ideal.

In their backgrounds, Kansas progressives differed somewhat from their predecessors in reform, the Populists. Although O. Gene Clanton has pointed out the middle-class nature of the major Populist leaders in his book on that movement,[15] many local Populist leaders were farmers. Such was not the case with local progressives. Yet despite their middle-class background, Kansas progressives do not substantiate the general opinion about progressives that was presented by Richard Hofstadter in his seminal work, *The Age of Reform*,[16] and was endorsed by Warner in his Ohio study. Unlike their progressives, Kansas' counterparts were not frustrated political leaders of a traditional ruling middle class who were losing power to newer groups in American society. They were, of course, the late-nineteenth-century nabobs of Kansas Republican affairs, but generally they felt secure in their positions and did not launch a progressive reform movement in order to maintain their social status.

Another interpretation of the cause of the progressive movement, which has some validity in the case of Kansas, but which can be exaggerated, is that it was a continuation of populism.[17] Having come on the heels of the Populist movement, progressive Republicanism bore a programmatic resemblance to the earlier reform movement. Issues that were popularized by the People's party of Kansas later became essential parts of Republican platforms written by progressives. This caused a number of former Populists to draw attention to the similarity between progressivism and populism.

In 1910, for example, Judge Frank Doster, one of the founders of Kansas populism, ruefully suggested that progressives had sandbagged his movement in broad daylight. "Our pockets," he complained, "have been rifled of the last political penny we possessed . . . by men who for twenty years had been professing lofty scorn of our political possessions." The theft of these issues, he declared, "is the boldest and most defiant piece of political buccaneering ever perpetrated." Populist reform proposals that were taken by the progressives included, according to Judge Doster, downward revision of the tariff, antitrust legislation, the direct primary, the direct election of senators, a postal savings bank, the graduated income tax, and the initiative, referendum, and recall.[18]

Had the judge wished, he could have extended this list to include laws favoring the improvement of working conditions for the Kansas labor force; laws regulating public utilities, especially railroads; and laws concerning three constants in Kansas politics—governmental economy, bigger pensions for veterans, and irrigation projects for the western half of the state. In 1910 and 1912 progressive Republicans had written all of these into their platforms.

But had Judge Doster stressed the similarity between Populists and progressives too much, he would have been guilty of obscuring three outstanding features in the development of progressive reform goals that were largely unrelated to populism. First of all, Republicans for quite some time had supported a number of these reforms. From late 1870 onward they had backed laws designed to revise the Kansas tax structure, regulate Kansas railroads, control monopolies, and improve the conditions of industrial labor. They had favored tariff reciprocity from the mid nineties, switching to tariff revision in 1906. They also supported the three stand-bys—irrigation, economy, and pensions.

Secondly, overemphasis on the relationship obscures the fact that, in essentials, progressive Republicans drew upon a reform tradition that had existed in Kansas long before the People's party was created. James C. Malin, in recognition of this, has convincingly argued that by the 1880s the mainstream of the Kansas reform tradition was well established. According to Malin, the Prohibition party of 1872 and 1876 and the Labor Reform party of 1872 "were leaders in the advocacy of reform." He has written: "This applies to reform unique to the years closely related to 1872, but more important, it applies also to reforms that became central to social change of the next forty years. Whatever was not comprehended in those three platforms, with very few exceptions, was added by the Greenback platform of 1880."[19]

The third way in which exaggeration of the relationship between progressives and Populists misinterprets progressive development is in underestimating the impact of early-twentieth-century events on the progressives. For example, in 1914 the Kansas Progressive party supported a number of changes in existing legislative and political-party practices as a result of Speakers Joseph G. Cannon's and James Beauchamp ("Champ") Clark's management of the House of Representatives. The Kansas Progressives in 1914 wanted party caucuses at the congressional level to be open to the public. They demanded that votes taken in standing committees or in committees of the whole be indicated by member in the journals of the Senate and House. They also supported the discharge of bills from committees. They hoped in this way to secure popular legislation by making it possible for a majority of the members of either congressional body to vote to discharge bills from committees. Moreover, the Kansas Progressives promised in their 1914 platform to release "all persons elected as Progressives in the state from any demands made by party organization in making appointments, in administering laws, and in performing the duties of office."

Another way in which the Kansas Progressives reacted to new realities in twentieth-century America was by demanding in 1914 that additional impartial scientific commissions be established in the state. Having already created a public utilities commission, they favored the establishment of similar nonpartisan scientific bodies to manage the state's economy and its charitable endeavors. They also hoped to replace elective officers with these commissions; and they supported the short ballot, which presumably would have retained only the governor and lieutenant governor as elected officials. In three important ways, then, an overemphasis on populism as the progenitor of progressivism obscures the true relationship between them. A connection was not entirely absent, but it was not the central factor.

There was another significant difference between populism and progressivism. Populism, as Raymond Miller has demonstrated, was an economically based movement, supported by financially depressed farmers.[20] Farm families who voted for progressive-Republican candidates were no longer part of an economically deprived class. What one former Populist called McKinley Prosperity had turned Kansas into a materially well-to-do state by 1900. Other than during the panic of 1907, the state's enterprises boomed throughout the next decade. There were, of course, pockets of poverty, such as the coal fields in the southeastern part of Kansas and the oil fields of the south central section following a period of overproduction in 1903 and 1904. But despite these exceptions, the Kansas economy grew at a rate greater than the national average. Almost all indicators of growth between 1900 and 1910 reveal that Kansans sat atop America's economic ninth wave. Table 1 clarifies this point. What seems un-

TABLE 1. ECONOMIC GROWTH

|  | Year and Amount | Year and Amount | Percentage Increase |
|---|---|---|---|
| *Agriculture:* | | | |
| Value of Farm Property | 1900 | 1910 | |
| U.S.A. | $20,439,901,164 | $40,991,449,090 | 100.5 |
| Kansas | 864,100,286 | 2,039,389,910 | 136.0 |
| Value of Crops Sold | 1899 | 1909 | |
| U.S.A. | 2,998,704,412 | 5,487,161,223 | 83.0 |
| Kansas | 113,522,693 | 214,859,597 | 89.3 |
| Value of Animals Sold for Slaughter | | | |
| U.S.A. | 912,423,557 | 1,833,175,487 | 100.9 |
| Kansas | 70,460,808 | 137,923,252 | 95.7 |
| *Industry:* | | | |
| Capital Invested | | | |
| U.S.A. | 8,975,256,000 | 18,428,270,000 | 105.3 |
| Kansas | 59,458,000 | 156,090,000 | 162.5 |
| Value of Products | | | |
| U.S.A. | 11,406,927,000 | 20,672,052,000 | 81.2 |
| Kansas | 154,009,000 | 325,104,000 | 110.9 |
| *Mines, Wells, Quarries:* | | | |
| Value of Products | 1902 | 1909 | |
| U.S.A. | 771,486,926 | 1,175,475,001 | 52.4 |
| Kansas | 9,526,060 | 18,386,812 | 93.0 |

SOURCE: Compiled from *Thirteenth Census of the United States, 1910*, 5:78–79, 525, 545; 8:542–543; 11:318.

believable is that agricultural Kansas ranked fourteenth among the forty-eight states in the value of industrial goods produced. It was tenth in coal production, seventh in petroleum output, and third in lead and zinc mined. As was to be expected, farming was still the main economic activity in Kansas. In value of agricultural lands, it ranked sixth; and in value of farm crops produced, seventh. Kansas was also one of seven states to register an increase of more than $100 million in the value of its crops between 1900 and 1910. The average income of a Kansas farm had been $650 in 1899; it was $1,200 a decade later. Only in population growth did the state fall behind the national average. The population of the United States rose 21 percent during the decade, while that of Kansas increased only 15 percent. Yet these data were deceptive, since for Kansans the 15 percent contrasted markedly with the paltry 3 percent during the nineties.[21]

The economic good fortune of Kansas was not lost on her leaders. Edward W. Hoch, governor from 1905 to 1909, described the state's growth in an article that he entitled "Advancement and Prosperity of Kansas."[22] Charles M. Harger, newspaper editor and free-lance writer from Abilene, told the readers of *Review of Reviews* that Kansas farmers were not only better educated than during Populist days; they were more affluent. Farmers who had voted for Jerry Simpson and John Breidenthal, he wrote, were now satisfied investors holding stock in "hundreds of country banks." "The keynote of the west to-day," he added, "is optimism. It has such a tremendous amount of business heaped up, such expansive plans for the future."[23] In 1908 John Mumford, writing in *Harper's Weekly*, capped the rejoicing by labeling the place that had formerly been viewed as "Hell burnt over" as "This Land of Opportunity."[24]

Historians, once conditioned to accept reform movements as companions of economic depression, wondered about progressivism. Occurring as it did during a time of abundance, the progressive movement offered an endless challenge not only to those who sought to ascribe events to economic causes but also to those who accepted nonmaterialistic explanations. The Kansas movement was created by a number of forces, including rising economic expectations and a desire, by developing smaller economic interests, to have a larger share of the marketplace. But just as important in creating unrest were party factionalism, ambition for office, and a sincere interest in furthering democratic idealism. This idealism was what most progressive Republicans used in order to explain why their reform movement occurred. "Kansas has solved the problem of bread and butter," said Walter R. Stubbs in 1905. He continued:

> It is now for our people to determine whether to be a Kansan shall be greater than to be a resident of any other state in the Union. . . . Correct plans, wise policies, noble purposes and high standards for our state government and institutions, together with a general public demand for absolute integrity . . . will answer these questions as they should be answered.[25]

It would be dramatic, but too simple, to close this introduction on a note suggesting that Stubbs's challenge had caused inspired young men of noble purpose to rise to a public demand for absolute integrity and wise policies. As will become apparent, the history of Kansas progressive Republicans, like the story of every man, is much more complex and much less certain.

# 2

## FACTIONAL BEGINNINGS: OF BOSS-BUSTERS AND POLITICAL MACHINES, 1900–1903

The progressive movement within the Kansas Republican party grew to maturity in a political soil fertilized by factional unrest. Beginning in the nineteenth century, Kansas Republicans splintered into feuding groups, because the spoils of office were too few to satisfy all party leaders. The factionalism that contributed to the disorder that aided the rise of progressivism, however, dated from 1900, when a group known as the Boss-Busters began a systematic campaign to remove national committeeman Cyrus K. Leland and his "machine" from power. A fight within the Republican party made little sense at that time. William Jennings Bryan, who had dragged Kansas into the Democratic column in 1896, was still active in the affairs of his party. He seemed assured of renomination when the national convention met at Kansas City in July. Moreover, Populists, Democrats, and Silver Republicans had formed a coalition in the state. To be sure, Republicans had won off-year elections in 1898, when about 45,000 fewer voters had gone to the polls. But the Fusionists of 1898 had demonstrated a cohesion not evidenced before; and although some Democrats and Populists were pessimistic after the elections, others, such as John Breidenthal of Topeka, looked forward to getting reformers back to "first principles" so that they could win the state in 1900. Complacency did not seem to be the order of the day for Republicans; from the standpoint of party interest a factional fight was unwarranted. Nonetheless, they had one under way as the new century began.[1]

Cy Leland of Troy, the source of factional unrest, had dominated Republican affairs in the state during the decade when Populism waxed strong, and as a result he had created a potent group of enemies within the party. He was unable to satisfy the demands of all important members, and thus, unintentionally, he had created a combination of anti-Leland Republicans. In 1899 these dissatisfied leaders founded the Boss-Busters League. The aim of the organization was as simple as the cause of factionalism itself. The Boss-Busters planned to remove national committeeman Leland and his friends from office. In this way they believed that they could construct a firm foundation of party unity. Like participants in other antiboss movements occurring throughout the United States in those years, they claimed to oppose "boss rule" on principle and to desire the establishment of political leadership under democratic tenets. Their reform rhetoric disguised an opportunistic reality. The Boss-Busters were factionalists, not idealists.[2]

Whether one believes that Cy Leland bossed the Republican party of Kansas to the extent his opponents charged depends largely upon one's conception of bossism. Certainly his opinions were significant in the decisions that Republicans made regarding policy, patronage, and state candidacies. But that he alone controlled these questions, as the Boss-Busters maintained, is undeniably false. From the time that he became national committeeman in 1884 until 1900 he always shared, or was forced to share, the prerogatives of power. Indeed, even in the years of his greatest strength, he had to accept the candidacies of men he did not like.

On certain occasions, however, Leland could be unbending. As the Boss-Busters knew, some politicians never received his help and were always thwarted by him. The reasons for his opposition varied, but in many cases they related to things that men had done to displease him in the past. Leland, like most Kansas Republicans, was a hardened factionalist. He had been "trained," as William Allen White, renowned editor of the *Emporia Gazette,* expressed it, in a definite Republican camp in the 1860s; and to enemies of this group he remained permanently hostile. Only when no alternative was possible would he work with these traditional opponents, and then they always had to remember that Leland's aid came out of necessity, not choice, and that at the first opportunity he would turn against them. Certainly, this attitude made him appear untrustworthy, but in the context of Kansas affairs it made him no more vicious than the typical party leader.

To some people who knew Leland intimately there was much to admire about him. White, who enjoyed his friendship for more than twenty years, approvingly viewed "Uncle Cy" as "a man who would stay in the game of politics, protect his ante, and play his cards, even after he had lost his major stake."[3] The most favorable comment concerning Leland came from William A. Johnston, chief justice of the Kansas Supreme Court. At Leland's sixtieth birthday celebration Johnston asserted that Leland was "too brave to be aroused by power, too generous to be moved by revenge, too level-headed to be moved by flattery, and too manly and honorable to ever break a promise or desert a friend."[4]

Leland agreed with these evaluations. In his reminiscences, published in 1913, he claimed that he had never lied, welshed, or used money to buy votes or offices during his long career. He had, he said, depended for his success upon a private platform which was to "work in politics and keep everlastingly at it."[5]

If Leland had been all that he and Johnston claimed, trouble would have found him anyway in contentious Kansas politics. That many Republicans did not agree with these views made opposition to him more certain. E. N. Morrill, governor from 1895 to 1897, appraised his one-time friend as a man who "would scruple at nothing." "He would," Morrill charged, "disregard all pledges, all friendships, all principles of honor and right to work out his favorite plans."[6] The most graphic assessment of Leland came from attorney William P. Hackney, a bombastic orator from Winfield. "A dog he is," Hackney said, "he was born a whelp."[7]

Actually, there was little in Leland's physical appearance to suggest that he could be passionately disliked or admired. He possessed a strong, leonine face, but often graced it with a smile, a twinkling expression. He was five feet, six inches tall, of medium weight, had a ruddy-brown complexion, and in his later years wore a well kept, grayish beard and mustache. He was friendly, though quiet in conversation, and had a keen, agile mind, with an elephantlike memory. Like most state politicians, he was never known as a man of profound intellect. He reportedly walked with a slight swagger, but in general he might easily have been one of a number of well dressed, locally important politicians in Kansas at the turn of the century.

That Leland was not is obvious. Although he never reached the pinnacle of an all-powerful boss, as his opponents maintained, he did hold important positions of power within the Republican establishment. Not only was he national committeeman for sixteen years, in 1900 he was recognized as President William McKinley's and Senator Mark

15

Hanna's most trusted aide in the southwestern United States. He had been given this unofficial recognition after helping to secure McKinley's presidential nomination and election in 1896. Officially, McKinley appointed him commissioner of the richest and most powerful federal office in Kansas, the Missouri Valley pension agency.

Earlier, under President Benjamin Harrison, Leland had held another important federal office as collector of internal revenue for Kansas. But though his federal connections had helped him in the scramble for leadership, his reputation as a boss stemmed from a clever move that he engineered in 1894. That year he won the gubernatorial election for Morrill, a highly respected banker from Hiawatha and a member of one of the better-known political families in America. Although the nineties were not good years for the Republican party, in 1894 its Populist and Democratic opposition appeared to be on the verge of dividing their successful Fusionist organization because of internal disagreement. Leading Fusionists did, however, make a serious attempt at reconciliation early in 1894. At this juncture Leland supposedly managed to have disaffected Democrats produce a nominee of their own for governor. By splitting the opposition, he succeeded in electing Morrill with only 49 percent of the vote. He and his friends never let Kansas Republicans forget this maneuver. They recalled it on all appropriate occasions.

But there were other sources of Leland's power during the nineties. Like many successful Kansas politicians, he worked closely with powerful economic-interest groups in the state, especially the Atchison, Topeka and Santa Fe Railway Company. With the help of one of its capable general solicitors, George Peck, Leland first became a major force within the Republican party. In 1900, however, Peck had become chief attorney for the Chicago, Milwaukee and St. Paul Railroad Company in Illinois, and the Santa Fe purportedly had withdrawn from state politics. Furthermore, other Kansas railroads, once neutral or friendly towards Leland, now opposed him.[8]

Although the Boss-Busters paraded a form of antiboss idealism, the major reason for their opposition to Leland was his failure either to recommend their friends for office or to deal with them as political equals. For example, he angered Marcus A. Low, general attorney for the Rock Island, and J. R. Richards, state solicitor for the Missouri Pacific, by refusing to recommend one of their associates, Judge Albert Horton, for the federal bench in 1899. Leland opposed Joseph R. Burton of Abilene as a senatorial candidate on several occasions, and he blocked the Topeka banker David Mulvane from becoming Republican national committeeman. Unwisely, he kept General Joseph K. Hudson, publisher of the *Topeka Daily Capital,* from being appointed consul to Mexico in 1898. A. W. ("Farmer") Smith, a former Republican gubernatorial candidate, felt that Leland had double-crossed him and caused his defeat in 1892; while Patrick Henry Coney, an official of the Kansas G.A.R., disliked Leland for his alleged mismanagement of the pension office as well as for his opposition to Coney's friend Congressman Charles Curtis.[9]

Since many leaders of the Boss-Busters League were politicians from Topeka, its first meeting was held there in the summer of 1899. Initially the Boss-Busters were concerned with offsetting a campaign against Charles Curtis which was being waged by Leland and his protégé Congressman Willis J. Bailey.[10] Although Curtis had spent three terms in the House of Representatives, he had served the First Congressional District, composed of northeastern Kansas counties, for only one year. He had represented the Fourth Congressional District in east central Kansas until a Fusionist redistricting measure had gone into effect in 1898. To foment trouble, the Fusionists had placed Curtis's home county, Shawnee, in Leland's First District. Before this time Leland and his friends had ruled the area unchallenged. When Curtis announced in 1898 that he would seek the nomination in his new district, Lelandites recognized the threat that this posed to their power.

Leland therefore picked his most popular adherent to oppose Curtis at the 1898 nominating convention in Horton, Kansas. He chose the amiable, intelligent banker from Nemaha County, Willis J. Bailey. Leland could not persuade Case Broderick, the incumbent of the old First District, to step aside. Broderick's presence in the contest limited the support for Bailey, since both men had been members of the same faction. By the time Republicans met at Horton, it was apparent that Leland could not secure the nomination for Bailey. Nevertheless, a reported 701 ballots were taken before Leland compromised with Curtis's backers. In one of the strangest exchanges in political history, Leland, with Bailey's knowledge, gave Curtis the Republican nomination in the district. In return, Bailey was to have Curtis's support in 1898 at the Republican state convention for the nomination as congressman-at-large. These men further agreed that two years later, in 1900, Curtis would run at-large and Bailey would seek the district position. This arrangement was called the Horton Agreement. Only part of it was kept.

In 1898 both men were nominated and elected as planned. But in 1899 Curtis, now well established in his new district and nearly certain of renomination, decided to break the agreement. When he repudiated it, he insisted that only Marcus A. Low had been authorized to operate as his official representative at Horton and that because Low had made no agreements in 1898, he, Curtis, was not bound by what others might have done in his name. Among those who signed the Horton Agreement were two of Curtis's staunchest supporters, David Mulvane and Judge Horton.[11]

Leland and Bailey were furious when it became apparent in 1899 that Curtis did not intend to fulfill the bargain. They planned to repay his treachery by demolishing him, but in their haste they miscalculated. They mounted a systematic attack on Curtis midway in 1899, thus causing the reaction that gave birth to the Boss-Busters League. Then they failed to appreciate the strength of the league. In letters to one of their confederates in Washington, Joseph L. Bristow, they derided the "clubs" of "old fossils" formed against them, and they scorned the league's "brass band campaign." A few weeks before the First District convention, however, some of Leland's associates began to grow uneasy, and a few of them defected to the Boss-Busters. Leland's "farobank style of politics" would not work this time, reported one friend. Curtis was renominated by the convention in February; he was subsequently reelected.[12]

Curtis's candidacy called the Boss-Busters League into existence, then tested its strength. The success of the league caused its founders to expand their goals. In late 1899 Joseph Burton joined some of his friends who were already active in the league, thus giving the organization a statewide purpose. Burton decided that through the Boss-Busters he could demonstrate that he, not Leland, was the major political force in the Republican party. In this way he could further his ambition of replacing Lucien Baker when Republican legislators met in January 1901 to elect or reelect a U.S. senator. Because other Boss-Busters hoped to increase their political influence through a statewide campaign against Leland, they supported Burton under the Busters' banner.

Joseph R. Burton, who determined the course of Boss-Buster affairs from February to May of 1900, had been a tireless worker within the Republican party for the past twenty years. He was an extremely handsome man, with a finely chiseled nose, deep-set eyes, and a bushy mustache; only extra large ears marred his otherwise classic visage. He spoke eloquently, with the trained voice of an actor, had an excellent command of the language, and could memorize lengthy speeches after one or two readings.

During the 1880s he became a leading member of the antiprohibitionist wing of the Republican party. He wrote the first Kansas antitrust law in 1889. Earlier, he was instrumental in securing the first legislation regulating Kansas railroads. Misfortune befell him in 1889, when he was accused of accepting a bribe in connection with the passage of a bill allowing insurance companies to appeal decisions of the superintendent of insurance to state courts. According to his testimony, he was innocent of the charge. He had been employed by Topeka insurance interests, but only after the close of the session that passed the bill. Whether he told the truth in this instance is now an academic question; thereafter, his reputation suffered, although his career bloomed.[13]

In his bid for Congress in 1892 Burton was defeated by the Populist-Democratic organization. He first sought nomination to the Senate in 1894, when Lucien Baker, a compromise candidate promoted by Leland, defeated him. Two years later, Burton managed to carry the Republican caucus, but William Jennings Bryan's campaign had swept a majority of Fusionists into the state legislature, which elected a Democrat, William A. Harris. At the Republican state convention in 1898 Burton served as permanent chairman, but he was not strong enough to displace Leland in the party.[14] In the next two years his political power increased considerably.

By the time of the 1900 state convention Burton reportedly numbered two-thirds of the delegates among his supporters. At the Boss-Busters caucus on May 15, over 353 delegates were present, and 200 others who were due to arrive at the convention were pledged to oppose Leland.[15] Burton's purpose at the state meeting was to defeat Leland's forces and demonstrate his power within the party. Through the Boss-Busters he hoped to control the Kansas delegation to the national convention and to have it choose one of his friends as national committeeman. If his candidates made a good showing in the state convention, county leaders would be impressed, and Burton believed that they would influence state legislators to vote for him in the Republican legislative caucus that would select the U.S. senator in 1901. Legislators would also be watching affairs at Topeka so that they could catch any political bandwagons that started rolling there.

The major problem that Burton faced in fulfilling his ambitions resulted from the aspirations of an extremist wing of the Boss-Busters, which was determined to disgrace Leland. Although Burton disliked the "boss," he did not want a fight to develop that would leave Republicans divided in November. His dilemma was resolved in an unusual way. Recognizing that the Boss-Busters would control the convention, Leland diverted attention from the magnitude of his defeat by claiming that the "real contest" was the one concerning the Republican state chairmanship. In reality, this position was not in question. According to traditional methods, there was no way that Leland's close associate Mort Albaugh could be removed. Under the Kansas political system, the governor named the state chairman; Governor William E. Stanley, first nominated with "the machine's" help in 1898 and certain to be renominated, would undoubtedly retain Albaugh. Taunted by Leland, the extremists among the Boss-Busters threatened to remove Albaugh by breaking tradition and carrying the selection of state chairman to the convention floor.[16]

They probably could not have done this; but if they had tried, a fight would have developed that no one could have controlled. Understandably, Burton could not allow this to happen. He informed the Boss-Busters that the question of the state chairmanship was so disruptive to Republican harmony that he had to meet with Leland's friends and discuss a compromise. In a caucus just prior to the beginning of the convention, Burton and the Lelandites worked out an understanding. Stanley would name the state chairman; Burton would decide the Republican delegation to the national convention. Silas Porter, an ally of Leland's, would be temporary chairman of the convention, but Burton would choose the permanent chairman. This agreement was enforced to the letter on May 17.[17]

The 1900 state convention, though viewed differently by some writers, was a defeat for Leland and a complete success for Burton, albeit extreme Boss-Busters were dissatisfied with Burton's conciliatory maneuvers. Not only did Burton's friends control the national delegation, which later elected Mulvane as national committeeman; Burton capped his convention victory in January 1901, when he easily carried the Republican legislative caucus. Later in the month he was elected to the Senate. Of Leland's machine, Albaugh continued as state chairman, and Stanley was reelected governor. These developments kept Leland's defeat from being total.

The selection of Porter had disturbed A. W. ("Farmer") Smith, one of the extreme anti-Lelandites, but the retention of Albaugh threw him into a rage. Leland's defeat was less complete than Smith had expected. "I get madder and madder," he wrote an ally, "to think that we allowed ourselves to be misled and deceived by a lot of fellows that we ought to have known better than to have trusted."[18] "Every mistake that was made at the convention," he added, "is traceable to the Burton camp or influence. Instead of Burton coming there and working with us, he . . . [ran] a little side show of his own."[19]

After the 1900 state convention the Boss-Busters League fell into temporary inactivity. It was revived briefly in late 1901, when Leland came up for reappointment as the Missouri Valley pension agent. In the fight over reappointment the Boss-Busters were again instrumental, helping to prejudice President Theodore Roosevelt against Leland. Roosevelt had asserted earlier that he was honor-bound to reappoint Leland, since McKinley had intended to do so. But Burton named his own candidate, Wilder Metcalfe, to oppose Leland; and Roosevelt, who had refused several other recommendations of Burton's, did not want to further aggravate him.[20]

Although Roosevelt made much of Leland's reputation, there is reason to believe that this had little to do with his decision not to reappoint the one-time boss. It may be, as John Blum maintains, that Leland was removed because of his close association with Senator Hanna, whom Roosevelt feared would contest his 1904 nomination.[21] Although Blum does not document his assertion, in August 1901, the month before McKinley's assassination, Roosevelt seemed favorably disposed towards Leland. Then he wrote William Allen White that he was "particularly struck" by what he had heard of Leland and that he wanted to meet him. "If he decides for me," added the ambitious vice-president, "I want to take [him] . . . into my innermost councils and have him as one of the men who shapes the whole course of events."[22] Something or someone changed the president's mind; Metcalfe was appointed.

Leland's defeat removed him from the center of political agitation in Kansas, allowing him an opportunity to regroup. During early 1902, like the mythical Phoenix, he began quietly to arise from the ashes. Before 1901 he had begun to cultivate members of the less fanatical opposition among the Boss-Busters, such as Marcus Low, whose support Leland had acquired in the pension-agency fight. Low had gone to Washington, where he met with the president and tried to persuade him to reappoint Leland.[23]

Leland's opportunity to regain stature within the party came in a much different and more secure fashion. In 1902 and early 1903 two of his former lieutenants, Willis J. Bailey and Congressman Chester I. Long, won important nominations and elections. Bailey, whom Leland had groomed for Congress, was nominated by the Republicans in May as their candidate for governor, and he easily defeated his Democratic opponent, W. H. Craddock, in November. Then, in January of 1903, after months of fighting, Long emerged as the victor in a scramble for William Harris's senatorial seat. Leland was only a nominal factor in both elections, but these victories, coming to men closely associated with him, improved his political standing immensely. When another antimachine fight was mounted in 1904, Leland was still important enough to be included as a machine leader. By then, however, Leland was not the main target, Governor Bailey bore the brunt of the so-called reform activities.

Bailey had been an active Republican during the last two decades of the nineteenth century. From 1888 to 1900 he had continuously sought public office. He had been a state representative, but had been defeated three times in his efforts to obtain nomination in the First Congressional District. He served as the congressman-at-large from 1899 to 1901. In late 1901 he began to build support throughout Kansas for his nomination as governor, and by January 1902 he was a serious contender.

Some politicians believed that Bailey's candidacy would end in a failure because of his close connections with Leland. Leland at first tried to dissuade him from seeking the nomination; but once Bailey became committed, Leland started to work covertly for him. In January the former boss persuaded Low and his Rock Island friends to remain neutral during the gubernatorial struggle. Their neutrality indicated that railroad interests would not oppose Bailey. Leland now felt secure, and he began to work openly. He tapped sources that had made him powerful before Boss-Busterism. In the Second Congressional District, for example, he and a prominent newspaper friend, Billy Morgan, reportedly ran over their opposition and packed the district convention with "Bailey's crowd."[24] In county after county, Bailey won old-time Leland supporters to his standard. But Bailey's candidacy received its most significant boost from other sources. Congressman Long and his campaign managers, C. S. Jobes and Mort Albaugh, decided early in 1902 that Bailey's success in the gubernatorial race was indispensable to Long's senatorial fight at a later date.[25] Cooperation with Bailey and the election of Bailey would give Long and his friends the gubernatorial prestige and patronage that they needed for victory in January 1903.

To be doubly sure that in supporting Bailey he was backing a winner, Long told Bailey to line up the railroads. Their neutrality, which was implied by Low's actions, was not good enough. Long felt that the railroads could be brought to Bailey's side if Bailey became the "people's candidate." Thus, Long advised Jobes and Albaugh to whip up grassroots support for Bailey and make him the "popular and leading candidate" before the state convention.[26]

In Albaugh and Jobes, Long possessed allies who were unwilling to chance the whims of a fickle public to convince railroad officials that

Bailey was their man. They preferred a more direct method. In April they arranged a meeting in St. Louis between Bailey and the general counsel of the Missouri Pacific, Alexander G. Cochrane. Cochrane was an active factor in Kansas politics; he served in part as a "political broker" between state politicians and the financial interests that owned western railroads.[27] He could control Missouri Pacific support, and he could influence other railroad officers to support certain candidates.

It was at the conference between Cochrane and Bailey that the future governor of Kansas convinced the Missouri Pacific attorney that he would serve Cochrane's interests better than other candidates could. In a letter to Congressman Long, Jobes explained the importance of the Bailey-Cochrane meeting, noting that Cochrane had promised all of the Missouri Pacific's political strength to Bailey. Cochrane also promised to keep other railroads from opposing Bailey. At the same time, Albaugh, fearful of an unexpected slip, arranged for the Union Pacific to support Bailey. He promised the general attorney of the Union Pacific, N. H. Loomis, that C. C. Coleman, a personal friend of Loomis's, would receive the Republican nomination for attorney general of the state if Albaugh's friends controlled the forthcoming convention in Wichita.[28]

At about the time that Jobes and Albaugh struck their agreements with railroad officials, George Cole, a popular political figure who had been spoken of as the "railroad candidate," withdrew from the gubernatorial race to become a staunch supporter of Bailey. With Cole's withdrawal, only one obstacle appeared to remain in Bailey's path to the statehouse. The followers of Senator Burton, with some exceptions, were backing James A. Troutman of Topeka as their candidate. Troutman was a well-known politician and a leading member of the prohibition wing of the Republican party. Troutman could have been a threat to Bailey. But to Bailey's and Long's relief, three other candidates, who would take votes from Troutman, entered the race. Moreover, Troutman was receiving very little actual support from Burton and his lieutenants.[29]

It is difficult to believe that Burton lacked a reason for his inactivity in 1902, but no evidence exists to explain his motives. He did not seem particularly concerned with the outcome of the gubernatorial nomination. Apparently, Burton was not interested in committing himself to a fight that might hurt his continued control of the national apparatus of the Kansas Republican party. As a Republican senator, he was now publicly responsible for the welfare of the party and was outwardly an avowed opponent of factionalism. The senator had another possible reason for being noncommittal in 1902. He was a favorite of the railroads, as was

George Cole at first. But Burton personally despised Cole and was not interested in helping him. Later, when the Missouri Pacific and the Union Pacific decided to support Bailey, Burton could not openly oppose their decisions, even though Bailey was a Lelandite.

Burton's major problem in 1902 stemmed from an earlier promise to help Charles Curtis's senatorial candidacy in 1903. If Curtis failed to make a strong political showing at the Wichita convention, it could be interpreted as weakness on Burton's part. If the Burtonites worked vigorously to defeat Bailey and then Bailey won, this, of course, would not only eliminate Curtis, it would also harm Burton's prestige. On the eve of the state convention the *Topeka Daily Capital,* a sometime Burton organ, carried a variety of anti-Bailey stories, which seemed to indicate that Burton might fight the Leland-backed gubernatorial candidate.[30] By late May, however, a compromise slate of Republican candidates had been arranged, and Bailey was the predetermined choice for governor. Burton willingly acceded to the nomination of Bailey in return for other positions for Burtonites on the ticket. In this fashion he again averted a struggle between the factions.[31]

The slate of candidates that Mort Albaugh prepared in conjunction with Burton's friends was eventually nominated, and the state convention was carried off as planned. Although the *Daily Capital* continued to publicize the magnitude of the struggle between Bailey and Troutman, on the final tally Bailey easily defeated the Topeka prohibitionist, by 561 votes to 217. And though the newspapers stressed the depth of the factional struggle at Wichita, on the day of the meeting the *Daily Capital* admitted that the 1902 gathering "was one of the most harmonious conventions ever held in the state."[32]

Charles Curtis received a tremendous ovation when he addressed the convention, though he had said that he might naturally have felt sore over events that transpired at Wichita. He, as all other politically aware individuals, recognized that Long's senatorial candidacy received a tremendous boost because of Albaugh's deft management of affairs. Nevertheless, Curtis promised that he was leaving Wichita as a dedicated member of a Republican party "united and harmonious for a great victory."[33]

Harmony also served as Senator Burton's theme. But the attention of the state convention in 1902 centered on Chester I. Long. When the permanent chairman finished his introductory remarks on Republican affairs, the delegates began to chant "Long, Long, Long"; and Long, responding, appeared on the convention stage. Though the would-be senator spoke briefly, he emphasized that most of his time at Wichita had been spent arranging "business of much interest to himself." The convention understood his meaning and cheered wildly.[34]

In retrospect it appears that Chester I. Long's decision to tie his candidacy to the success of Willis J. Bailey, thus controlling the state convention of 1902, was one of the wisest moves that he made as a Kansas politician. After the convention there was little question that Long was the man to beat in the senatorial race. His showing at Wichita impressed numerous local leaders, and many were certain that at the convention they had witnessed a preview of Long's eventual victory.[35] Not only did Long prove his statewide power to local politicians, he also won the temporary devotion of Bailey. This would mean that he could eventually draw upon the power and prestige of the governor's office. Leland was also impressed, and he was thankful for Long's help. Although he remained publicly committed to Governor William E. Stanley and his senatorial aspirations, he privately endorsed Long. Leland's decision to remain publicly with Stanley, so Long said, was based on a fear that Stanley's supporters might switch to Curtis should the governor prove too soon to be a weak candidate.[36]

But the election of Long, though it seemed probable in May of 1902, was no sure thing. Curtis, who would be his main opponent in January, still had the support of Burton and was in his own right no political lightweight where nominations were concerned. Furthermore, at the outset of the senatorial contest, Curtis seemed to be favored by at least three of the most powerful railroads in the state; and in senatorial fights many Kansas political leaders believed that the railroads determined who won. Thus, in 1902 Long was pressed to break what he felt was Curtis's stranglehold over the railroads. Stated simply, Long needed to win the backing of these lines.

As a political leader, Chester I. Long possessed more than the common gift of knowing when and how to get things done. He became involved in Republican politics in the late 1880s, when he was elected to the state senate, and for the eight years after 1892 he faced Jerry Simpson in four "Big Seventh" congressional races. During his battles against the "Sockless Socrates of the Plains," Long took a typically western-Kansas Republican stand in favor of the subtreasury idea, paper money, free silver, the tariff, overseas expansion, and imperialism. He won half of his contests against Simpson, defeating the versatile Populist in 1894 and 1898.[37]

From 1900 onward, as a veteran Republican congressman, Long cautiously planned for the 1903 senatorial election. It was not until April

1902 that his chances improved substantially. Then, his first important contacts with powerful railroad leaders were made. In April, when Albaugh and Jobes arranged the conference between Alexander Cochrane and Bailey, Cochrane had expressed a desire to meet with Long. He told Jobes that, generally speaking, Long seemed to be a man who "should have the support of the Missouri Pacific for United States Senator." In May, after discussions with Long in St. Louis, Cochrane decided that his assumption had been correct. Subsequently, Missouri Pacific efforts were directed towards election of Long.[38]

During the next few months both Cochrane and Long continued to cultivate railroad officials, until by December of 1902 all five major Kansas railroads supported Long's candidacy. The account of how Long won solid support from the railroads in 1903 is one of the most intriguing chapters in Kansas Republican affairs and one that is most often misrepresented by Kansas scholars. After the backing of the Missouri Pacific had been secured, Cochrane persuaded Lyman Parker, the general solicitor for the Frisco Railroad, to arrange it so that his railroad would use its political power in Kansas to support Long.[39] Together, Cochrane and Parker convinced E. D. Kenna to use Santa Fe's strength in Long's behalf. But Kenna was an uncertain quantity, since Santa Fe policy did not allow its general attorney to make the final decision in questions as important as a U.S. Senate race. Some better way had to be found to assure Long that the Santa Fe would not oppose him.[40]

Likewise, the Union Pacific and Rock Island, both political titans in Kansas, needed to be won over to Long. This could have proven doubly difficult, since the local attorneys for these roads were supporters of Burton and Curtis. Albaugh had managed to persuade Loomis of the Union Pacific to support Bailey, but he had had less success with Loomis in respect to the senatorial race. Low of the Rock Island could only be made to support Long if higher officials in the Rock Island forced him to do so. But there was a way in which all of these lines could be brought to support Long.

William C. Beer of New York had once served the New York Life Insurance Company as a "national political expert," but at the beginning of the twentieth century he joined his former New York Life employer, George Perkins, in the House of Morgan. With Perkins, Beer was instrumental, as a Washington lobbyist, in securing the Bureau of Corporations Act in 1902.[41] Through Perkins, Beer had connections with the managers of the Union Pacific, the Rock Island, and the Santa Fe. Aware of Beer's political talents,[42] Long contacted C. S. Jobes in June of 1902 and asked Jobes to request Charles S. Gleed, formerly general solicitor for the Santa Fe and then publisher of the *Kansas City Journal,* to secure active support for Long's candidacy from "Mr. Beer and his friends."[43] Gleed refused to do so, because he opposed Long.[44]

Undaunted, Long sought other ways to secure Beer's support. Having already returned to Kansas, he used Fourth Assistant Postmaster General Joseph L. Bristow as his contact with Beer in Washington. On September 16 Long received a coded telegram from Bristow. Deciphered, it read: "Beer telephoned that Perkins had talked with the Rock Island and Santa Fe people, and they have assured him that their interests will support you. He asks that I find out what their local people are doing and let him know. Give me situation as to attitude of M. A. Low and others."[45] On the next day, Bristow, who had established a reputation as a reformer by uncovering corruption in the Cuban post office during American occupation of the island, wrote:

> Our New York friends seem to have made the request suggested. I had a telephone message yesterday stating that on Tuesday Mr. Perkins had a talk with the gentlemen controlling the interests referred to, and was assured that their interest would be in favor of your election. If this is correct it makes a sure thing; but it will not do to neglect the smallest detail and I am anxious that the local fellows out there be sounded to see whether they are in accord with the wishes of their superiors; so I telegraphed you as I did.[46]

Although Long and Bristow failed to broach the problem of Union Pacific backing at that time, Winslow S. Pierce, general counsel for the railroad, wrote Long from New York in December, advising him that the Union Pacific management had decided to join the already great armada of railroads that supported him.[47] This decision had been temporarily delayed by Loomis, the attorney for the Harriman line in Kansas. Cy Leland, in his recollections, remembered that in 1903 New York financiers sent George Beer to Kansas to superintend Long's election campaign, and he recalled that Loomis had been whipped into line. In 1906 a *Topeka Daily Capital* reporter recalled that during the 1903 senatorial election Loomis, who had "lobbied for weeks," had been "a most energetic factor" in Long's victory.[48]

Not only did the legal departments of the great railroads assist Long through activities such as Loomis's; reportedly the lines also made large donations to the senator's campaign fund. In a 1907 polemic on what he styled "the commercial community of interests," Burton claimed that

Long received $67,000 from New York financiers so that he "might be enabled to make sure of the ratification by the Kansas Legislature of his election." According to Burton, who was forced to resign from the Senate in 1906 because of a bribery conviction, Long was elected on "the 9th day of December, 1902, in the Equitable Building in New York."[49] William Allen White stated in 1912 that Long had received $30,000 from the Missouri Pacific to use in his election.[50]

As senator, Long did several things that indicated his subservience to railroad interests. He tried, unsuccessfully, to secure an appointment to the United States Circuit Court for Cochrane. He did convince the federal government to revise a bridge-building contract for a subsidiary of the Missouri Pacific when it was unable to meet a previously arranged schedule. Thus the subsidiary was not required to pay a time-forfeiture penalty. In February of 1904 he and Senator Joseph W. Bailey of Texas managed to force two bills through Congress that allowed the Santa Fe to exchange certain of its holdings for Indian reservation lands.[51]

Working with railroad officials was not always easy, as Long discovered in late 1902. Because of the power that the Speaker of the Kansas House could wield in the legislative caucus selecting a senator, Long needed a Speaker who was favorable to his candidacy. In arranging this, Long, Albaugh, and Leland chose J. T. Pringle. The Burton leaders in the legislature quite naturally opposed Pringle, who was closely identified with Leland. Either because of this or because he sincerely disliked Pringle, Low of the Rock Island threatened to begin an open political battle with Long. Low, who had an inflated view of his political power, apparently believed that Long could be forced to support whomever the attorney suggested. On the advice of Leland, Long brought pressure from eastern sources on Low, thus preventing disruption of his plans during an important period. Pringle was eventually chosen Speaker, and according to one statehouse reporter, "Pringle's victory . . . went a long way towards determining that Charles Curtis would not be elected United States Senator in 1903."[52]

A number of other arrangements had to be made in January 1903 in order to satisfy Long and his campaign managers that there would be no slip-ups at the Republican caucus. To increase his political strength in the Fourth and Fifth Congressional Districts, Long, with the help of Leland and Albaugh, secured the support of Henry J. Allen and George Clark. Clark and Allen were both candidates for state printer in 1903, but the favorite in the race was Edward W. Hoch of Marion. Clark, who published a newspaper at Concordia, was a force in the Fifth District;

and Allen, from his *Ottawa Evening Herald* offices, had wide contacts in the Fourth District. Together, the supporters of Clark and Allen outnumbered Hoch's friends. It fell to Albaugh and Leland to arrange a trade between Allen and Clark. If both of them would work for Long's election, Clark was to receive the state printership, but he was to allow Allen to take half of the fees paid to the state printer during his term. All public printing was done by contract with private firms at that time. According to allegations, kickbacks on fees were common, and usually state printers used their own shops to print state materials. When the state-printership deal was consummated and when Clark was elected, a howl arose across the state. Fortunately for Long, the protest was directed at Leland and Governor Bailey, not at the interests that benefited from the arrangement.[53]

The thing that bothered Long most in preparing for his senatorial candidacy was his fear that Governor Stanley would not eventually withdraw from the race as Leland had promised he would. Stanley was serious about his candidacy. Leland and other supporters of Stanley, however, knew that the governor could not command enough strength to win the nomination. If Stanley withdrew from the race too early, chances were that half of his friends would then vote for Curtis at the caucus in January. Leland believed that the wisest policy was for Stanley to continue in the contest until the balloting began at the caucus; then, in a dramatic switch, Leland and Long's managers would carry the majority of Stanley's votes to Long. This maneuver would keep most of Stanley's friends in line.[54]

On 21 January 1903 the Republican legislative caucus convened at Topeka to name its choice for the U.S. Senate. As Leland had planned, Stanley's voting power represented the difference between victory and defeat for Curtis or Long. For six ballots Stanley continued his candidacy, and then on the seventh roll call he switched his votes to Long. Long was easily nominated on that ballot.[55] A few days later his election to the Senate was certified by the legislature, where Republicans greatly outnumbered Democrats.

One result of Stanley's switch was his appointment to the Dawes Commission of the Five Civilized Tribes in Oklahoma. This act prompted some Kansas Republicans to remark that Long, like a faithful political leader, honored his political debts. Stanley only reluctantly accepted the position and then remained but a short time on the commission.[56] It seemed to him a rather thankless reward. His failure to capture the senatorial race in 1903 virtually eliminated him as a leader in the state party.

The demotion of one factional leader from a position of importance within the Republican party was only a minor result of the Long-Bailey elections. In 1902 Republicanism had a chance to recover from the Boss-Buster movement of two years earlier. Senator Burton, in office and free of reelection concerns, had become party conciliator. His new attitude allowed Leland and his friends to regain stature and offices within the party. The coalition that defeated the boss seemed to have been dissolved permanently, and the Kansas Republican party superficially appeared to be "reformed" by 1902.

Leland's amazing recovery, however, had given power to his friends, and it made some leaders realize that they needed to undertake a new reform movement to eliminate the machine. In 1903, when a number of scandals implicating high officials of the Leland faction became known to the public, rank-and-file Republicans also demanded a change. Consequently, factional fighting resumed, and a number of minor but potentially important Republicans were hurt by it.

# 3

## TRANSITIONAL FACTIONALISM: THE KANSAS REPUBLICAN LEAGUE AND REFORM, 1904–1906

On 18 January 1904 Republican state chairman Mort Albaugh reported on party affairs to Senator Chester I. Long. Like earlier summaries sent from Topeka to Washington by Albaugh, this message dealt with problems confronting Long's friends in the factionalized Kansas Republican organization. This letter, however, contained a greater sense of urgency and anxiety. On January 13 a reform association, which called itself the Kansas Republican League, held a rally at Topeka;[1] and Albaugh, after a few days of waiting, concluded that this group posed a threat to the welfare of his political allies.

Although the alleged purpose of this organization was to lead an antimachine reform movement, Albaugh realized that it represented a combination of Kansas railroad attorneys, some supporters of Senator Joseph R. Burton, and a few sincere reformers. Four years earlier a somewhat similar coalition, the Boss-Busters, had dethroned Cy Leland. It had taken two years for Leland, Albaugh, and others to recoup their losses, and then they had succeeded because the earlier movement crumbled from want of zeal. There was, so it seemed to Albaugh, no lack of ardor this time. The league, he wrote Long, has "a degree of frenzy in it akin to the old Pops . . . and I want to say frankly . . . I think it will take every possible effort . . . to stem this tide and even then we may fail."[2]

The leaders of the Kansas Republican League had called the mid-

31

January meeting at Topeka as the first step in a concerted drive to capture county conventions that were being held throughout the state during the second half of the month. Counties were selecting delegates to attend the Republican State Convention in March. The leaders of the Republican League knew that if they controlled enough county delegations, they would in turn control the Republican party at the state convention and would eventually control the state. Two years earlier, preparations for the county conventions and for the state convention had been relatively undramatic, but since 1902, events had transpired that insured that the preconvention period would be hectic in 1904.

From mid 1903 onward the governor's office had come under sporadic attack from "reformers." Governor Willis J. Bailey spent an undistinguished year as chief executive of Kansas, but revelations of petty graft during his first few months in office aroused the ire of certain leading Kansas newspapers and gave opponents of the so-called Leland machine a rallying cry. During the regular session of the legislature in 1903 men close to Bailey were implicated in a number of small-scale scandals, and the governor unfortunately failed to disassociate himself from charges that he was implicated in these money grabs.

Like Bailey's administration, the legislature of 1903 was commonplace. It enacted laws making the Kansas railroad commission elective, and it prepared a constitutional amendment that would make the office of state printer subject to popular vote. It sent a delegation to the St. Louis World's Fair. It did not reapportion the state's congressional districts, reorganize the state treasury system, or create a state tax commission, as many citizens had demanded. Some newspapermen commended the legislators for having kept their work unusually free of the normal blackmail practiced against Kansas business interests. Blackmail had been kept at a minimum, so one writer said, because Republican bosses exercised strong control and kept legislators in line.[3]

But like Banquo's ghost, the thing that would not stay down in 1903 was the charge of abuse of public funds, and before the end of the year the distinguishing feature of the legislature was not honesty but petty larceny. According to a veteran reporter who covered the legislature, nothing regarding charges of dishonesty was exaggerated by the press. In a column appearing at the close of the session, Jay House charged that "everybody who had sufficient pull was put on [the state payroll] by one or the other of the bodies. If there was no position open a new one was created."[4]

Allegedly, the elevators at the state capitol were operated by a force of men that was sufficient to keep them going around the clock in six-hour shifts, with six or seven assistant operators ready to spell regular crews should they tire. Likewise, each window in the legislative chambers was said to have an assistant sergeant-at-arms to raise and lower it.[5] Not everyone agreed with the complaints of newspapermen. For example, Albaugh wrote that he thought newspaper criticism was essentially unfair regarding petty graft and that "a better and cleaner House had never been assembled in Kansas."[6]

Nevertheless, the opinion that the state was being plundered by petty chiselers persisted, and it was turned into a political weapon against Governor Bailey. Initially, the old Republican boss, Cy Leland, was the object of the attack, since supposedly he "ran the House of Representatives," where most of the dishonesty occurred. But by the close of the 1903 session and thereafter, Bailey replaced Leland as the main target of scorn. In November of 1903, in order to allay criticism of his administration, Bailey announced that he and Attorney General C. C. Coleman were meeting to discuss what steps were needed in order to remedy irregularities and to discuss whether it was necessary to have an investigation of the charges of dishonesty. Apparently it was not, since no further actions were reported from the governor's office.[7]

So far as evidence does exist relative to the scandals in Bailey's administration, the governor appears to have had nothing to do with the small raids on state funds. But his unwillingness or his failure to stop such affairs did seem to support charges that he was protecting petty chiselers for political reasons. These charges hurt him substantially in 1904. They even prompted an old friend to attack him. William Allen White, a member of the Leland-Bailey faction, editorialized in July 1903 that Kansas was in dire need of a governor who would attack corruption no matter whom he injured and no matter what position he touched. "Kansas needs," White wrote, "a man with a jaw—not the jawbone of an ass; not a jawsmith full of wind and wonders, but a man with a firm jaw who can set it by time lock and go after the petty-larcenists."[8]

But White was not seriously interested in seeing Bailey removed from the governor's office at the end of his first term. During most of the anti-Bailey campaign he defended the governor. In doing so, he followed the lead of his factional confederate, Henry J. Allen of Ottawa, who attacked members of the Republican League. If the Republican party needed reforming, Allen wrote—and White agreed—it would be by Kansans of good faith and not by men angered because of "somebody's defeat for the Senate or somebody's failure to become State Printer, or somebody's desire to organize and control a legislature."[9]

During the campaign against the governor, Bailey and his friends defended his administration by dismissing Republican League charges of corruption and by repeating Allen's statement that the reform organization was "built on resentment and personal disappointment," because of defeats suffered in the 1903 senatorial race, in the contest over the office of state printer, and in the past legislative session. Bailey used this defense sincerely, since he believed that the league was seeking revenge for his having helped Long's candidacy in late 1902 through the contests for the speakership and the office of state printer.[10]

Many local politicians did consider Bailey's actions at that time reprehensible. Judge Nelson I. Case of Oswego, for example, claimed that he was terribly angered when Bailey and Leland arranged the speakership and when Clark resorted to "unlikely methods" in squeezing out E. W. Hoch for the job of state printer. Hoch, in Case's opinion, was eminently suited for the office of state printer and would "easily have been elected had ordinarily fair methods been observed."[11]

Corruption, the fight over the job of state printer, and the speakership struggle contributed only in part to Governor Bailey's woes in 1903. The so-called Leland machine in November of 1903 won a struggle with Senator Burton and attorneys of Kansas railroads over the position of federal district judge that became vacant when William C. Hook resigned to accept a place on the United States Circuit Court of Appeals. Burton and the railroads favored Topeka attorney Charles Blood Smith, while Leland, Long, and Albaugh backed their own associate, Judge John Pollock of Winfield. After they had fought for months, President Roosevelt appointed Pollock, because of Long's endorsement and because the president disliked Burton by this time.[12] Bailey had little to do with the outcome of the fight, but as the first friend of Long's and Leland's to stand for reelection, he bore the brunt of the hostility that was aroused by Pollock's victory. Bailey displeased railroad officials in other ways. J. R. Richards of the Missouri Pacific, which supported Bailey in 1902, had the following to say of the governor in early 1904:

> From the very instant that Governor Bailey was elected he has shown an unfriendly spirit towards us, without the least disposition to reciprocate what we have done for him and his friends. It has given me deep pain, after we have exhibited in so many ways to Governor Bailey . . . such a friendly spirit. . . . What else could be expected than that I and my friends . . . fight in self-defense?[13]

Publicly, the struggle against Willis J. Bailey was based upon a number of vague but high-minded principles. The speakership, the election of a state printer, the appointment of Pollock, and railroad animosity remained sub rosa issues during the Kansas Republican League's campaign. Edward W. Hoch, who became governor as a result of the movement, set the tone for the anti-Bailey crusade in January of 1904, stating that the league was motivated by aims higher than mere personal dislike of certain officials:

> It is a movement widespread and intense and impersonal. . . . It grows out of unwise leadership; of unfair standards of Republicanism; of factional intolerance; of the multiplicity of useless offices; of extravagance in public expenditures; of enormous increase in the burdens of taxation; . . . of the trafficking in public trusts to subserve private and factional ends. In a word, it is a culminating protest against the skull and cross bones in politics.[14]

Although the Kansas Republican League claimed to be an anticorruption, antiextravagance reform organization, much like its predecessor, the Boss-Busters, it included men with a variety of motives. The initial leaders of the league were Burtonites and railroad officials, whose reputations as reformers remained dubious. Other politicians whose reform images were less tarnished included Edward W. Hoch and Walter R. Stubbs, both former friends of Burton's. By early 1904 these men had become independent of all factions and seemed to be genuinely interested in change.

Neither Hoch nor Stubbs took part in the Boss-Busters campaign of 1900. As individuals they were fundamentally different in character and circumstances. Stubbs, a millionaire contractor from Lawrence, was energetic, strong-willed, and relatively new to public affairs. Hoch was a moderately well-to-do newspaper editor. He was easy-going and quiet and was a veteran politician. He had purchased the Marion *Record* in 1872. During the decade of populism he had remained a staunch Republican, playing a significant role as a state legislator.[15] Claiming to be a moderate, he was one of the strongest supporters of prohibition in the Republican party. His prohibitionist ideas incorporated most of what James H. Timberlake has established as the progressive framework in this area. Hoch held the antiliquor ideal to be "a great benefit morally, educationally and financially."[16]

Walter R. Stubbs, the other reform leader, was a markedly different man. His meteoric rise in Republican affairs led writers to stress his amateur political status. A wealthy railroad builder, he did not seek public office until 1902, and by 1904 he was Republican state chairman. He was an able practitioner of the art of politics. He fared well under the convention system, but with the adoption of the statewide primary in 1908 his multicolored talents shone forth in splendor. He reportedly spent a fortune advancing his political aspirations, purchasing newspapers and spending freely for publicity and party organization.[17]

In 1902 a local political leader induced Stubbs to run for state representative. Though inexperienced, he was easily nominated and elected. He remained unnoticed until 6 March 1903, when, according to one observer, he "broke loose" and joined the reform bandwagon that was under way in the house. In a maiden speech Stubbs announced that henceforth he should be known as a reformer who would help to free the state legislature of the dictations of Republican party bosses. His debut caused quite a stir in the *Kansas City Star*. One week after Stubbs's announcement the *Star* noted that the representative from Lawrence was "a new member who commanded marked attention" and that Stubbs always had "something to say which was to the point," even though his speeches were not well organized.[18]

Since the personal papers of Walter R. Stubbs are not available, there is no sure way of knowing why he joined the antimachine group. Two explanations are usually put forth concerning his motives. According to one group of writers, Stubbs witnessed the role that New York financial interests played in the election of Senator Long in 1903 and was angered by it. He was also dismayed by extravagance during the same legislative session. Another theory, not as widely accepted, claimed that Stubbs became a reformer as a result of a double cross by the Leland-Albaugh machine. The machine, wishing to demonstrate its power to the fledgling state representative, was said to have diverted funds from the appropriations of the University of Kansas in order to finance a road-building project between the state penitentiary at Lansing and the federal penitentiary at Leavenworth. Stubbs, unimpressed by this and angered because he felt that he represented the university, retaliated by joining the campaign to remove bossism from the legislature.[19] Whatever Stubbs's motives, he was a leader of the Kansas Republican League by early 1904.

The Kansas Republican League itself supposedly originated in 1903 during the regular session of the state senate, when, as George P. Morehouse, one of the founders of the league, expressed it, "a little antimachine club" called the Lodge was formed to stop legislative boodling. In a letter written about a year later to the head of the Kansas State Historical Society, Morehouse claimed that before the senators returned home from the 1903 session in March, the Lodge invited Republicans from over the state to a semisecret meeting at Topeka. There they organized the Kansas Republican League and elected Morehouse, who was from Council Grove, president of the organization. Morehouse also wrote that in the months after March the league worked effectively and quietly to remove Bailey from the governor's chair, sending hundreds of letters and much antimachine propaganda into all corners of Kansas. The league supposedly held a public meeting in May, its only rally of any importance until 13 January 1904.

Morehouse maintained in his letter that from the first there were two goals set for the league. The first was to make certain that Bailey was not renominated in 1904; the second was to champion Theodore Roosevelt for the presidential nomination.[20] Evidence regarding its activities in 1903 seems to indicate, however, that during the first year the idea of helping to secure the nomination for Roosevelt was not really an aim of the organization. This objective appears to have resulted from Hoch's insistence in January 1904 that nomination of Roosevelt be a goal. Of course, Roosevelt was a popular figure in Kansas, and his name attached to any reform group could only add to its popularity.

According to observers wise in the ways of the Republican party, the decision to have Hoch oppose Bailey in 1904 was made in the final analysis by the friends of Senator Burton. At first, Burtonites such as National Committeeman David Mulvane and Rock Island attorney Marcus A. Low opposed Hoch, but by January 1904 they had reversed their positions and were supporting him. Rumor had it that Hoch would have announced as a candidate in late 1903 if Mulvane and Low had approved and that he would not have entered in 1904 had they not untimately sanctioned his candidacy.

Stubbs and Thomas Bent Murdock encouraged Hoch to announce for the gubernatorial race in late 1903. They planned a Hoch-for-Governor rally at Topeka in December, but it failed to materialize. Stubbs also circulated petitions across Kansas, which numerous people signed, indicating that they favored Hoch for the nomination. At a January 5 meeting called for the purpose of having Hoch announce his candidacy, he still would not commit himself. During the following week Mulvane reportedly informed Hoch that Hoch would have Mulvane's and Low's support. As a result, a letter from Hoch, which "virtually announced his candidacy," was read to the meeting of the Kansas Republican League in Topeka on January 13. Hoch's formal announcement came in late

January. His candidacy united Stubbs, Murdock, the Burtonites, and important railroad officials in the Kansas Republican League.[21]

In the campaign to oust Bailey and nominate Hoch, the effective politicking was carried on by members of the Kansas Republican League. Although they organized county conventions throughout the state, in retrospect their victory in Reno County proved to be the key to Bailey's defeat. Situated in the most populous part of west central Kansas, Reno County virtually dominated the political affairs of the areas adjacent to it. During the few years preceding 1904, Billy Morgan, a leading lieutenant of the Leland-Long-Albaugh coalition, controlled it. Morgan, who preceded George Clark as state printer, was also editor and publisher of the *Hutchinson News*. Articulate, though cautious as a political manipulator, he had previously had little trouble within his political bailiwick. This was not to be true in 1904.

Metropolitan dailies from Kansas City and Topeka had been criticizing Morgan's faction since early 1903, but he felt that their influence was nominal. Then, in January of 1904, Hutchinson attorney W. Carr Taylor, vice-president of the Kansas Republican League, began to recruit anti-Bailey precinct committeemen for the Reno County convention. Morgan fought back, but with too little, too late. On January 24 Taylor and his friends controlled the Reno County convention, electing a delegation to the state convention that endorsed Hoch.[22] Immediately, Sumner County followed suit. Then county after county in central and western Kansas joined the Hoch bandwagon.[23] By January 26, two days after the Reno County convention, Bailey's supporters were ready to surrender. On that day Albaugh recognized that the "Hoch epidemic" had spread so rapidly that all was lost. "I thought," he wrote Senator Long, "that the victory in Jackson [County] might check [Hoch] . . . but when the boys lost out in Reno, I knew, beyond a question of doubt, that it was impossible to check it. Everything has gone to pieces, and I feel sure the governor will get out of the race."[24]

On January 30 Bailey withdrew from the campaign. The assault in mid January took its toll on his sagging confidence; and with the defeat in Reno County, he saw no alternative except withdrawal. Kansas governors normally served two terms; Bailey served one. In his announcement that he would not seek renomination he stressed that though he felt that he deserved the usual second term, he was quitting because he believed the party was paramount to his personal ambitions. He said that his continued presence in the race could only injure the party irreparably.[25] Such solicitude for Republican welfare seemed unreal, but no better explanation for Bailey's avoiding an intraparty fight exists. He, of course, would not have withdrawn had he not recognized that defeat was imminent. The immediate results of 1904 were that Bailey was finished politically and Leland temporarily took a back bench in the party leadership. So did Albaugh, who resigned as state chairman when Bailey withdrew.[26]

Immediatey prior to Albaugh's resignation and Bailey's decision not to seek renomination, another event rocked the Republican party. On January 23 Senator Burton was indicted by a federal grand jury in St. Louis. He was charged with accepting money from the Rialto Grain and Securities Company in violation of an act forbidding senators and congressmen from using their influence to prejudice the outcome of investigations by the post-office department. The securities company was trying to regain mailing privileges that had been revoked as a result of the firm's alleged use of the mails to commit fraud.[27]

In late 1903 United States District Attorney Joseph W. Folk raided the office of the Rialto Company in search of evidence in connection with another case he was prosecuting. While he was seizing the Rialto records, Folk discovered letters that incriminated Burton in a conspiracy with the firm concerning the post-office investigation. Folk presented this evidence to Attorney General Philander Knox, who, in turn, passed it on to President Roosevelt. Together they ordered a full investigation of Burton's activities, and on the basis of the inquiry they sought an indictment.[28]

Burton's problems naturally had repercussions in Kansas. The genesis of the case against Burton, which became public on January 23, was hotly debated by the various factions. Fourth Assistant Postmaster General Bristow was accused of having initiated the proceedings at the eleventh hour to ease the fight that was then coming to a climax against his political confederate Governor Bailey. If Burton, who had connections in the Kansas Republican League, were disgraced, this would naturally damage the reputation of the league as a champion of honesty. Furthermore, Bristow was known to have senatorial ambitions of his own, which could be advanced only if Burton's seat were vacated.

As a Lelandite of long standing, Bristow made an ideal suspect. But Bristow seems to have had little to do with the indictment. In a letter to a friend in the faction, Senator Long stated that President Roosevelt had informed him that Attorney General Knox, in conjunction with Folk, had decided to begin legal proceedings. Burton initially had suspected Bristow, but later he came to believe that President Roosevelt, rather than the assistant postmaster general, was the cause of his woes.[29]

From the time of his presentment onward, Burton never did deny that he had been on the Rialto payroll, nor did he deny that he had worked for the company through postal officials. He said that in this respect he had not violated any federal statute and that in appearing before the department he had only followed examples set by legislators older and more experienced than he. David Graham Phillips tried to prove this in his famed *Treason of the Senate*. Burton agreed that his actions might have seemed indiscreet, but he did not think they were either morally or legally wrong.[30]

The jury that convicted Burton in April of 1904 disagreed. They maintained that letters exchanged by Burton and officials of the Rialto Company indicated that he had received payments from the firm; they also maintained that his statement in one letter that he intended "to attend to matters" in Washington made him guilty of using his influence as a senator to prejudice a post-office investigation. For two years the senator fought the conviction through federal courts. On 21 May 1906, however, the United States Supreme Court ruled against him. A few months later he resigned from the Senate, on the eve of proceedings to expel him, and was imprisoned for a short term.[31]

Burton's indictment in January 1904 injected an element of confusion into the activities of the Kansas Republican League. Although Burtonites were only moderately active at this time, they were exceedingly powerful in the league, and the senator's arrest did upset the power structure of the league and modify its emphasis. Burton and his friends had become members of the league in order to increase their political power, which had been curtailed in 1902 by their role as harmonizers. Because railroad men figured prominently as supporters of Burton, his group had a conservative influence on league activities. When Burton's followers became uncertain of their future after the senator had been indicted, reformist elements headed by Stubbs and Hoch increasingly set the tone for the organization. This caused a number of Kansas railway officials to become apprehensive about it. Before this time, they had believed that the "Methodist purification" talk used by Stubbs and Hoch was just demagogic fare, designed to gain support. As Hoch and Stubbs increased their influence, officials of the Santa Fe and the Rock Island began to have second thoughts about the league.

During the first week of February, both Low of the Rock Island and A. A. Hurd, general attorney for the Santa Fe, told Balie Waggener, a Democrat and the Missouri Pacific representative, who had opposed Hoch and Stubbs all along, that perhaps they had created a monster and that maybe the election of Hoch would prove worse for corporate interests in Kansas than even the election of the most extreme Populist in the state. Waggener agreed, saying "[Hoch] is known to be antagonistic to railroad interests. . . . His nomination . . . will bring about a worse condition of affairs than . . . during the Populist legislature of 1897."[32]

As far as leaders of the Republican machine were concerned, dissension within the Republican League was grist for their political mill. Although Governor Bailey, Mort Albaugh, and Leland could find little solace in Burton's troubles, others of their confederates, especially politicians close to Senator Long, were elated over Burton's defeat and the dissension within league ranks. Senator Long and his associates recognized that if the Kansas Republican League were successful, it would constitute a threat to them at a future date. Thus, when the league began to split into warring groups, Billy Morgan happily advised the senator to avoid any agreements with league members until a complete rupture had occurred. In this way, Morgan believed that Long could improve his standing in the party.[33]

Morgan's certainty that a division would come was based on a number of accurate observations concerning the nature of the league's leadership. Aware of railroad influence, he suspected that neither Stubbs nor Hoch could be restrained by these interests for long. Moreover, he felt that Stubbs, Hoch, and Mulvane all had senatorial ambitions, which would conflict when Burton resigned. He was certain that Mulvane, even if he were not primarily interested in a Senate seat, would not want Hoch or Stubbs to become powerful within the Republican party. On the basis of these opinions, Morgan decided that Mulvane would soon seek an understanding with Long. Morgan felt that Mulvane and his friends would make useful allies. He was not alone in this view; Albaugh, as well as Morgan, suggested that Long should at the moment avoid any alliance with Mulvane but that he should do everything possible to encourage a split in the Republican League.[34]

Considering the way in which the old machine group in the Republican party was affected by the campaign of the Kansas Republican League in 1904, it becomes imperative at this point to note that between 1901 and 1904 a significant shift in power occurred within the ranks of the so-called Leland machine. As has previously been noted, Leland never completely regained the position that he had lost by his defeats in 1900 and 1901. During 1902 and 1903 the important leaders within the Leland alliance were Bailey, Long, and Albaugh. The withdrawals of Bailey and Albaugh in late January 1904 eliminated them as factional strongmen, although

Albaugh remained an advisor to Long. By February, Senator Long was the supreme power in "the machine." For many politicians who remained loyal to the faction, Long was now looked upon as the man who should make the major decisions concerning the activities of the faction.

In February, then, Long rendered his first judgment as boss of the faction. He agreed with Morgan's and Albaugh's suggestions that the differences within the Republican League should be exploited. He, too, felt that the time was not yet propitious for a union with Mulvane and his supporters, that watchful waiting should be the policy of the machine faction. The senator believed that the time to act would be at the state convention in 1904, where Long's supporters could cleverly promote disharmony in the ranks of the Republican League by backing its reform wing on certain points and by upholding the railroad group and Mulvane on others. In this way they would demonstrate to each wing the essential incompatibility of various elements in the membership of the league. In the long run, the senator expected a factional understanding with Mulvane.[35]

Although the Republican State Convention at Wichita in March of 1904 offered Long's faction the hoped-for opportunity to divide the Republican League, what happened there did not completely destroy it. Long's cohorts used their votes to help nominate a slate of candidates that was arranged by the railroad group of the Republican League, but they also helped to write a reform platform that was not to the liking of the railroad following. Their best single chance to demonstrate the fallacy of perpetuating an organization that included Mulvane, railroad attorneys, Stubbs, and Hoch came over the question of the state railroad commission.[36]

Stubbs and Hoch had promised a place on the commission to J. S. George, president of the powerful Kansas Federation of Commercial Interests. The federation was one of Stubbs's main supporters in 1904, and at one point it demanded all five Republican nominations to the commission. With Hoch's help, Stubbs apparently convinced George to accept a more moderate reward; but at the state convention, because of railroad opposition and because of the votes provided by the Long faction, even this recompense was denied George. In spite of his defeat, George was not alienated from Stubbs and Hoch, but he was at the time angered by Republicans in general and the Republican League in particular.[37]

Having lost the struggle over the railroad commission and having seen the railroad favorites dominate the state ticket, Stubbs and Hoch salvaged what they could at the convention by incorporating their reform ideas into the party platform. They were responsible for anticorruption and economy planks in the platform. They wrote the part of that document calling for equalization and minimization of state taxes. With others they endorsed the old McKinley program of trade reciprocity, and they encouraged a wider use of the Sherman Antitrust Act. After a bitter struggle they placed a "radical" railroad plank in the platform, by which the Republicans promised to enact amendments to existing laws in order to eliminate discrimination, inequality, and extortion in rate-making and to require adequate facilities for customers of all lines operating in Kansas. Waggener's fears regarding Hoch's antirailroad bias seemed to be coming true.[38]

A few days after the state convention the Republican state committee convened to select a chairman for the party. At this meeting, Long and his backers irreparably splintered the Kansas Republican League. Prior to the committee meeting, Mulvane and railroad officials agreed that State Treasurer J. R. Burrows of Smith County should be the next Republican state chairman. Stubbs already had declined the support proffered by Hoch, and Hoch subsequently decided to support newspaperman Tom McNeal of Topeka. Stubbs, in turn, endorsed a friend, State Representative Jonathan N. Dolley of Maple Hill. But Hoch opposed Dolley, and Stubbs would not support McNeal. Thus, to keep the reform wing intact, Stubbs was forced back into the chairmanship race.

Mulvane hoped to eliminate Stubbs from the contest by getting the Republican League to endorse Burrows. Knowing that his supporters could control a league caucus, Mulvane called a meeting just before the state committee was to vote for state chairman. At the caucus Mulvane nominated Burrows, and Hoch entered Stubbs as a candidate. With the help of his railroad associates, Mulvane easily defeated Hoch and Stubbs in the voting, and Burrows received the endorsement.

Hoch was angered, of course, by this turn of events. He claimed the traditional right of the party's gubernatorial nominee to name the state chairman. When the Republican League delegates returned to the state committee meeting, Mort Albaugh, acting for the Long faction, requested a temporary adjournment. During the intermission he contacted Hoch and informed him that Senator Long was interested in seeing Republican tradition upheld and that the senator's friends would vote with Hoch. Convinced that he should name the state chairman, Hoch accepted the support of his recent enemies. With this information, Albaugh next met privately with Burrows and informed the state treasurer that he must withdraw from the race. The state committee then reconvened. Hoch nominated Stubbs, and with the help of Long's friends the Douglas County millionaire was elected. Apparently Mulvane did not know about Albaugh's agreement with Hoch, because when Burrows declined to stand for the office prior to the nomination of Stubbs, Mulvane hurriedly conferred with the treasurer and then stomped violently from the hall where the committee was in session.[39]

This bit of political melodrama delivered the blow that Long's backers had anticipated. The Kansas Republican League was permanently split, and its last meeting was held in the form of the caucus during the session of the state committee. Henceforth, more groups would be operating in the Kansas Republican party.

The proliferation of factions, however, was no longer destined to be the central theme of Kansas politics. The mainstream of Republicanism was shifting as both the times and the men in party affairs began to create a new Republican character, one that was more responsive to issues and less devoted to personalities and friendships. The solace found in the old uncomfortable factional arrangement was now to be shattered as Republicans became issue-oriented and even less unified. From 1900 to 1904 crude forms of antibossism, anticorruption, and harmony campaigns dominated Republican discussions and attracted the majority of public attention. Because of these less essential concerns, fundamental questions about Kansas government were brushed aside.

After 1904 some Kansas Republicans began to react to social, economic, and political problems in line with a pattern being established across the United States, and they began to demand an active role on the part of the state government. In their response these new Republicans were guided by a traditional Kansas reform attitude, which had been established as early as the 1870s, as well as by a number of problems that matured in the early twentieth century. What they would demand after 1904 would be government operated under the utilitarian plan of the greatest good for the greatest number. In the process they would increase the tempo of change and release reform energies hitherto misdirected towards antibossism.

The first burst of reform lawmaking came in 1905, assuaging some old grievances and temporarily resolving some immediate problems. Hoch, freed from the restraints of the nonreform element in the Kansas Republican League, increased the number of changes he sought beyond those included in the 1904 platform. Having easily defeated the Democrat David M. Dale in November, he appeared before the state legislature in January 1905 with an extensive reform program.

As was expected, he demanded in his initial legislative message that the corruption of the previous session not be repeated. He requested that a modified civil-service system be created in order to supply personnel for state charitable institutions, that a state printing plant be built, and that new methods be developed to eliminate the practice of depositing state money in favored Topeka banks. Having enumerated reforms to correct the issues that had been part of the reason for creating the Kansas Republican League, Hoch recommended laws to regulate the exploitation of Kansas gas and oil wealth. He asked for the enactment of railroad laws that would fulfill the promises of the 1904 platform. And, he urged that juvenile courts be created. The governor recommended that the archaic property-tax structure in Kansas be revised by the establishment of a state tax commission. His message also stressed the need to bolster existing prohibition laws.

Hoch, who was a reluctant supporter of female suffrage, proposed a limited municipal franchise for women. He then noted that reapportionment of Kansas congressional districts was needed because of the population changes reported in the 1900 census. In an unexpected move he insisted that a direct-primary law be enacted. He concluded his message with the usual requests for the construction of better roads and for laws promoting the irrigation of arid lands.[40]

Hoch's address was a comprehensive underscoring of the new temper of Republican politics in Kansas. It surpassed any previous gubernatorial message in breadth of aim and understanding of problems. It incorporated the whole of the 1904 platform and added ideas that Hoch had emphasized independently during the campaign. The governor had once told a crowd of supporters that party platforms were "sacred," like personal promises and business contracts. Now the governor added that he intended to keep Republican pledges.[41]

Ed Hoch was not known as a political battler, but when Republican legislators seemed reluctant to accept his suggestions, he forced much of his program through the legislature with the help of Stubbs, who was elected Speaker of the House. He withheld patronage, made lavish job promises, used special messages, and appealed to the public in order to achieve his goals. Before Hoch's objectives were realized, a number of acrimonious fights took place among Republicans, and ultimately Hoch's reform measures caused a split between the governor and Stubbs.[42]

Hoch was unable to keep his pledge of less governmental spending during the 1905 session, but no one charged that there was corruption as a result of increased state appropriations. The *Kansas City Star,* evaluating the legislature at the close of the session, listed as the main achievements of Hoch's administration the plan to construct a printing plant, the election of a state printer, the establishment of a regulated, diversified system for depositing state funds, and the reorganization of the Kansas eleemosynary system. The biggest shortcomings of the legislature, according to the *Star*, were its unwillingness to create a tax commission and its failure to pass the proposition for a statewide primary.[43]

These reforms, important as they were, were not the big news of the 1905 legislature. That body was destined to be remembered as the one that tried to establish a state oil refinery in Kansas. "Monopoly," Hoch had said during his electioneering in September of 1904, "threatens to rob our people of the chief benefits of this great [oil] endowment! How can we save this wealth to the state and to its people?" The way, of course, seemed clear to him—enact laws to curb the activities of the Standard Oil Company.[44]

Most Kansans, and certainly Governor Hoch, believed that Standard Oil was using its position as the only large oil refiner in the state to lower the price paid for crude oil purchased from independent Kansas producers. "We must," Hoch said at the Kansas Day Club meeting in 1905, "take that monster the Standard Oil Company by the throat and compel it to be decent."[45]

Whether Standard Oil was being decent or indecent in 1905 remains a moot question. Allan Nevins has argued that overproduction caused Standard to cut prices in the Kansas oil fields in 1904 and 1905. He wrote: "In Kansas alone the Standard had lost millions in falling prices on the huge quantities it had too generously bought. Even when prices were steady, the carrying charges on . . . stored oil were heavy, while losses by fire, evaporation, and leakage added to the bill."[46] To compensate for losses, or for potential losses, price cuts were made.

Of course, Standard Oil could easily endure its losses, since it operated on an international scale and was able to offset income deficits in one area by higher prices in another. Kansas independents could not shift their burden of lower prices. They were also unwilling to accept the classical idea of supply and demand as the root of the difficulty. They understood that behind impersonal market factors lurked live men. In the case of the Standard Oil Company, they felt that the men were sinister individuals who were interested in squeezing every independent out of business and in monopolizing the oil market further. The Kansas attitude was cogently expressed again by Governor Hoch, writing in the *Independent* in 1905: "The Standard Oil Company is a national and an international monopoly. It has for years carried on a systematic absorption of the oil interests of this country and of foreign countries. It has been the cause of bankruptcy to many small investors and threatens to bankrupt all of them who oppose its greedy ambitions." He added that it worked locally to reduce the price of crude oil, so that Standard could gain possession of other people's properties.[47]

The fact that Standard was actually preparing to leave Kansas in favor of the Indian Territory, where new wells were springing up, seems to have escaped the notice of many Kansans. Rather than acquiring more holdings in the state, the company was actually interested in reducing its commitments.[48] Nevertheless, the complaint that Standard intended to seize all oil holdings remained the major source of criticism against the New Jersey organization.

Charges directed against Standard Oil Company took three forms in 1905. Independent producers complained that Kansas railroads were giving rebates to the company, that Standard was purchasing crude oil at different prices from various producers, and that it held too powerful a position in the Kansas oil market. Standard Oil did dominate oil refining in the state. To make matters worse, it used its position in an authoritarian fashion. Whenever a Kansas producer sold oil to the company, the latter did all the business involved in the transaction. It measured and tested the oil, fixed the price paid, paid whatever royalties were due landowners, and distributed the profit from the sale to the producer's stockholders according to their holdings. This naturally angered the managers of independent companies that were doing business with the New Jersey corporation.

Many independents believed that Standard Oil Company punished producers who at times sold crude oil to independent refineries by refusing to accept the oil of these independents during the crisis of 1904–1905.[49] Standard Oil further contributed to suspicion of its methods when in 1903 it devised a new program for classifying crude oil. It divided Kansas oil into three gravitation categories and paid different rates for each grade. Although from a scientific viewpoint its method made sense, the practice angered a number of local producers who complained that "Standard Oil gaugers . . . marked crude oil lower than it ought to be."[50]

The most damaging charge against Standard concerned discrimination in railroad rates. Standard's rise to greatness as a result of railroad rebates was well known, and Kansans assumed that the same method of tampering with freight rates was being used again. According to a reporter for a national magazine, the company in 1902 and 1904 conspired with the

Santa Fe to raise rates on shipments of crude oil from Kansas in order to deter independents from using this means of escaping Standard. For its cooperation the Santa Fe supposedly received a 10 cent per barrel royalty on all oil shipped through Standard's Sugar Creek pipeline. Although the conspiracy charge was never proven, Santa Fe rates were raised in 1904. Moreover, Charles Gleed, a director of the Santa Fe, was in close touch with Standard officials during this period. Another railroad operating in Kansas—the Missouri, Kansas and Texas Railway Company—had John D. and William Rockefeller as members of its board of directors. It is easy to understand why many independents assumed complicity between Standard Oil and the railroads.[51]

If Standard did make clandestine arrangements with railroads, its actions in this respect were fundamentally different from those of the independent producers. While Standard Oil secretly fought to gain an advantage in the marketplace, Kansas producers were publicly attempting to secure the same thing. In January 1905 they formed the Kansas Oil Producers Association and planned to use it as a vehicle to promote their interests in the oil fields. Their objective was to induce the state to act as a countervailing force to Standard Oil.

At their organizational meeting on January 19 the oil producers outlined what the Kansas legislature should do to promote their interests. To stop discrimination in freight rates, they asked for a law granting a maximum tariff on oils and for a law making Standard's Sugar Creek pipeline a common carrier. They requested legislation forbidding anyone to undersell a competitor in order either to ruin him or to recoup losses suffered in another area. They also wanted a board of supervision that would grade and inspect oils. The keystone of their program, as they saw it, was a demand that the state build and operate its own oil refinery. They assumed that a refinery large enough to compete with Standard could be built and operated efficiently enough to raise the price of crude oil.[52]

Four of the five requests made by the oil producers became law in 1905, with only the resolution asking for a board of supervision being defeated. Of the laws enacted, the measure to establish a state oil refinery met the stiffest opposition. It was easy to find support for the other three measures, since no actual expenditure of state funds was involved, but a refinery would be costly. Moreover, state regulation differed considerably from state ownership. In the refinery law the oil producers were challenging the foundations of free enterprise. Speaker Stubbs said, "The public policy and constitutional laws of this state . . . are opposed to the government engaging in a commercial business."[53] For this reason Stubbs, although he favored economic regulation, fought the refinery proposal and temporarily kept Hoch from giving it his unqualified endorsement.

Hoch had not realized how much a refinery would cost when he initially approved the idea. When he found out the expense involved, he modified his views on what type of refinery should be built. Rather than a plant that would compete with Standard Oil's, Hoch suggested a pilot refinery, so the state could get some idea of the cost of refining oil and then take steps to see that Standard paid an honest price for crude oil.[54]

Hoch's revised opinion was unacceptable to the Kansas public and to the oil producers. Public pressure always bothered Ed Hoch. He was a man whose nerve fiber was more that of the democrat than was his colleague Stubbs's. If Stubbs believed his ideas correct, he never yielded in regard to them. Hoch was sensitive to criticism, and he allowed his attitude to be influenced by popular demand. After having switched in January from the idea of a competitive refinery to the idea of a limited pilot plant, he did another about face in February. He returned to the original concept of a competitive refinery, and he used his influence to force a measure providing for its construction through the Kansas legislature. His second reversal won him the gratitude of the oil producers and the public, but it cost him Stubbs's support and led to charges that he was a devotee of socialism and populism.

Hoch answered these charges in a special message to the legislature and in an article in the *Independent*. The gist of his tortured logic in answering these complaints was that a state refinery constituted the antithesis of socialism. "True," he noted, "it has the semblance of socialism, but its soul is that of competition." He said that socialism attempts to negate property rights; whereas the refinery law negated no rights of the Standard Oil Company to own property. No one planned to drive Standard from Kansas, or to deny it a legitimate profit. He added that if free competition were possible, there would be no need for a state refinery; but such was not the case, "on account of the greatest Socialistic corporation now doing business on earth, the Standard Oil Company."[55]

In March the State Refinery Law was passed. It provided that an oil refinery be constructed at Peru in Chautauqua County, where it would be operated by inmates of a proposed branch of the state penitentiary. An appropriation of $410,000 was passed in the form of bonds to be sold by the state treasurer and by the warden at Lansing. Governor Hoch immediately ordered that the reserve school fund not be used to purchase these securities. This announcement caused potential buyers of the bonds to wait and wonder. If the state were reluctant to buy its own bonds, private investors would do well to discover the cause of this reluctance. At about the same time the state treasurer and the warden refused to sell the bonds. Attorney General Coleman then requested a writ of mandamus to force the treasurer and warden to act. In a hearing on this request the State Supreme Court ruled not only that the mandamus was unwarranted but that the refinery law was unconstitutional, since it intended to create a state-owned business in competition with private capital.[56]

The struggle against Standard Oil in Kansas occasioned a national investigation of the corporation in 1906. During the agitation for a state refinery, Congressman Philip P. Campbell of southeastern Kansas presented a resolution to the House of Representatives, asking that the Bureau of Corporations be instructed to inquire into the activities of the Standard Oil Company. The next year, bureau chief James R. Garfield headed such an investigation.[57]

Kansas Republicans had come a long way during the oil fight. In 1890 J. G. Blonecker, president of the state's Republican League, had said that he had little fear of monopolies, because the laws of supply and demand would always right such situations. He added that if a man was driven out of business, he would just have to seek another occupation. Fifteen years later a Republican governor, Edward Hoch, was convinced that "man's cupidity needed some sort of curb." The problem, Hoch said during the struggle with Standard, was to find a way in which capital and talent could have the widest latitude, while the interests of the people were still protected against selfishness.[58]

The oil legislation of 1905 set the tenor for the legislature of that year. The fight for the passage of administrative measures kept the prairie fires of reform, which the Kansas Republican League had lighted, aglow. One perceptive observer wrote that perhaps the country had witnessed "the definite starting-point of a victory for fair play that will mark a new era in government."[59] The first burst of legislative activity carried important changes into operation, but not all demands for reform were met. The oil question was exhausted, but Standard's alleged allies, the railroads, still provided fuel for the fires of reform. As in the days of populism, Kansas reformers began to turn their attention towards unfair railroad activities. During the remainder of the decade the Santa Fe, the Missouri Pacific, and others of the great transcontinental lines were to become the symbols of the need for change.

# 4

## GROWING DISSIDENCE: MAINLY RAILROADS, 1906

The activities of the 1905 legislature and the Kansas Republican League were only two manifestations of unrest among Kansas voters in the early years of the century. Like most historical phenomena, the roots of steadily increasing dissidence were grounded in many factors, with factionalism and oil problems, previously discussed, only partial causes. Among the more important reasons for dissatisfaction were events that transpired largely beyond the borders of Kansas. For example, the actions of Theodore Roosevelt were not the result of initiatives taken in the Sunflower state, but they were responsible for creating in Kansas a sentiment favoring a "Square Deal" that supposedly would initiate honesty in government and righteousness in socioeconomic practices. The publications of Muckrakers were not the products of Kansas writers, except for William Allen White, but they, too, attracted attention.

In the home area of Charles Monroe Sheldon one need not explain that the Church, with its emphasis on the "Social Gospel," was creating conditions favorable to reform. Equally apparent as causes of unrest were the lingering ideals of the Populists and the activities of a number of former Populists who were anxious to see the public accept their beliefs. "There seems little left," wrote a minor official of the defunct People's party to White, "that we Populists of fifteen years ago can do except to bid you God speed."[1] Of course, populism's 1896 spokesman,

William Jennings Bryan from nearby Nebraska, influenced the state's Democrats directly and its Republicans indirectly.[2]

Kansas also had an idealism of its own—other than populism—which appeared regularly in the news journal with the largest circulation in the state, the *Kansas City Star*. From its headquarters in Missouri the publisher of the *Star*, Colonel William Rockhill Nelson, consistently encouraged civic and state reform of a noneconomic sort. A man of feudalistic temperament, Nelson was an advocate of honest government and, as such, contributed to public dysphoria.[3]

But Nelson's ideals, Roosevelt's "Square Deal," populism, the Social Gospel, and other elements of voter restlessness were far less important in contributing to the growth of discontent after 1905 than the hostility occasioned by the economic and political malpractices of Kansas railroads. In 1910 an anonymous Kansan, writing in the *Outlook* magazine, explained how he had become a progressive. He had been, so his article stated, a ruling member of the Kansas Republican machine from 1895 onward. But in 1906 he was converted to progressivism, because he could no longer stomach the activities of Kansas railroads.

The anonymous Kansan related that his family had been loyally Republican since Lincoln, and from his school days on, he had fought for regular Republicanism. Like his associates, he considered politics primarily a game to be won or lost without concern for the consequences of victory or defeat. He knew that railroad corporations governed Kansas through the Republican party, but that did not matter. He felt that this was their way of protecting themselves against crazy anarchists who were trying to drive railroads out of business. Roosevelt, as president, had first caused him to begin to inspect the Republican way of doing things. He had begun to realize that freight rates were discriminatory, and this recognition had encouraged political skepticism.

The rates, he noted, "were fixed to favor Kansas City as a jobbing center. Our mechants could buy stuff more advantageously from a Kansas City jobber than from the factory in the East, because of the discriminatory freight rates, combined with the rebates that the big shipper always got." Under conditions such as these, railroad rate-making had once more become a major issue in the state. At the 1906 Republican State Convention the anonymous Kansan had first realized the implications of having the railroads arrange slates of candidates and control the party platform. "I saw," he stated, "they [the railroads] were in politics so that they could run things as they pleased. After that convention I stopped calling myself a Republican." The Hepburn railroad bill fight,

Senator Robert M. La Follette, and the *Kansas City Star*, he added, had all contributed to his increased bitterness towards railroads, and this feeling had grown, encompassing others, until a "Great Awakening" had taken place in Kansas. People in the East, the progressive concluded, wondered why Kansans, who were now prosperous, had become insurgents. "They miss the point. We've really been converted. We had never thought much about the consequences involved in our course of letting the railways run things. . . . But we have got our eyes open now."[4]

Precisely why large numbers of Republican voters had had their "eyes opened" midway through the first decade of the century can be understood within the context of a continual suspicion of railroads in Kansas that began in the 1870s. In 1867 the state legislature had established maximum charges for passenger and freight traffic. In the 1870s the first of a series of reform movements demanding closer supervision of the railroads had developed, and by 1883 Kansas had copied a number of other states in creating a Board of Railroad Commissioners. In the 1890s Populists and Democrats, convinced that the Kansas commission was unable to regulate the railroads adequately, had replaced it with a Court of Visitation. They had given the court full power to determine reasonable rates and establish classifications for all intrastate freight. They had also allowed the court to order railroads to make necessary physical improvements.

To insure the court the power to enforce its decrees, the Populists and Democrats had given its judges the authority to seize railroad properties and operate them through receiverships if companies refused to comply with court orders. At the same time, the Court of Visitation Law had established the office of solicitor, which provided that the attorney who served in this capacity would argue shippers' cases before the tribunal. Since litigation with railroads had been costly under the old commission law and had caused numerous complaints to be deferred, the Populists and Democrats had made railroads bear the cost of cases that the railroads lost and had made the state liable for the expenses of cases that the railroads won. In late 1899 and early 1900, the United States District Court of Kansas and the Kansas Supreme Court had ruled the Court of Visitation Law unconstitutional. They said that it violated "constitutional limitations designed to protect owners of property against oppressive action by the states." The Court of Visitation, in the opinion of the district court, combined judicial, legislative, and executive power in a way that represented oppression of property rights and thus contravened the law of the land and of Kansas.[5]

For more than a year Kansas was without a body to regulate railroads. In 1901, however, a second Board of Railroad Commissioners was created. This body, composed of three men appointed by the governor, was given basically the same powers as the first commission. It could hear complaints lodged by shippers against the railroads, and it could decide what actions to take. It could, after such hearings, order specific rate changes; and it was to enforce whatever maximum rate laws were enacted by the legislature. The 1901 law allowed any shipper to come directly to the commission with charges against railroads. The notable deficiencies of the 1901 law, according to shippers, were that the commission could not initiate rate actions on its own, that the commission could not classify freight unless complaints were made, and that the high cost of the litigation would have to be borne by the shipper if he lost his case.[6]

Thus, Kansas shippers continued to seek revisions in the state railroad law. Assuming that appointive bodies were not as responsive to public demands as ones elected by the people, the shipping interests succeeded in making the commission elective in 1903. A year later, although they failed to nominate their friends as commissioners on the Republican ticket, they managed to get a stringent railroad plank incorporated into the Republican platform, and as a result in 1905 they were rewarded by a railroad law that came close to satisfying some of their demands. The 1905 statute gave the attorney for the railroad board the power to initiate cases involving unfair practices without complaints having been lodged. It required railroads to file rate books with the commission, and it also allowed the board to advise the Interstate Commerce Commission on interstate rates charged in Kansas that the state board considered unreasonable but could not litigate because of the *Wabash* case in 1886.[7]

Assured by political leaders that this advisory power would have an influence on interstate rates, the group that spearheaded railroad reform in the early twentieth century—the Kansas Federation of Commercial Interests—placed its imprimatur on the 1905 law, believing that long-sought relief was at hand. This was done despite the fact that the law fell somewhat short of the stronger measure that the federation had advocated and despite the fact that most federation officials realized that their main complaints were occasioned by discrimination in interstate rates.[8]

At first the new legislation seemed to be capable of accomplishing the shippers' demands. In late 1905 the railroad commissioners, following a series of hearings, presented Kansas railways with a long list of lower tariffs, designed to offset interstate discrimination. In January 1906, however, when the new rates were to become effective, four of the largest railroads in Kansas—the Santa Fe, the Union Pacific, the Rock Island, and the Missouri Pacific—responded by filing restraining orders against the commission's decree. As a result, a Kansas district court issued injunctions suspending the new rates. During 1906 other commission decisions to lower rates were challenged by the railroads, but in January 1907 the commission, in a special session, succeeded in persuading the railroads to lower rates on the interstate shipment of wheat, coal, and grain products and on the intrastate movement of corn, groceries, and paper.[9]

The railroads had accepted the lower rates, hoping in early 1907 to quiet criticism while the Kansas legislature was in session. The 1907 legislature was considering a law that would establish a flat rate of two cents per mile for passenger traffic and a law that would make it illegal for anyone other than railroad employees to accept free transportation over the lines. This latter provision was supposed to help remove railroads from Kansas politics.[10]

The lower rates established in early 1907 did not silence critics of railroad malpractices, and late in the year the railroads decided to raise their rates. They justified the increases by arguing that they, too, should profit from the affluence of the Kansas economy in the early twentieth century. This decision assured the continuation of an already steady stream of criticism against them. Since 1903 complaints regarding unfair railroad rates had been commonplace. In 1903, for example, the *Southwestern Grain Journal,* a prominent agricultural magazine, summed up the feelings of wheat farmers by stating that the Kansas legislature had failed to secure uniform low rates from the railroads and that it had not been able to enforce existing laws, which required that more be charged for long hauls by the lines than for short hauls.

The *Journal* also noted that each harvest found the railroads unable to supply the needed number of boxcars for Kansas millers. It suggested that not only was honest rate regulation needed, but that legislation to make railroads fulfill their obligations of adequate service to shippers was also necessary. While it touched upon the main theme of dissatisfaction—high tariffs—this article also illustrated that other railroad practices helped to nurture militant antirailroad sentiment. The disaffected included not only members of the Kansas Federation of Commercial Interests, but also leaders of such powerful organizations as the Kansas Chamber of Commerce, the Kansas Improved Stock Breeder's Association, the Kansas chapter of the United Commercial Travelers of America, numerous local commercial clubs, farmers' organizations, and the combined salt manufacturers of Kansas.[11]

Complaints against the railroads that created the antirailroad persuasion of 1906 can be grouped into three general areas. There were those dealing with rates, those concerned with inadequate service, and those stemming from the involvement of railroads in Kansas politics.

Despite laws to the contrary, discrimination was the single most characteristic feature of railroad rate-making in the years before 1906. Having been "the result of experience; of contact with shippers; of conference and compromise," as President E. P. Ripley of the Santa Fe explained, discrimination understandably existed. Ripley noted that, to complicate matters more, rates were also "the result of competition between railroads—between railroads and waterways—between markets and between individuals—and lastly, they [were] . . . due to legislation and national laws."[12]

The problem in Kansas, although it was affected by the numerous reasons given by Ripley, was essentially one resulting from competition between markets. In the formative years of railroad service, Kansas City, Missouri, had been given favorable rates. Its aggressive civic leaders and its ideal location on the Missouri River had made the city the leading metropolitan area for Kansas. As such, Kansas City became the gateway through which products to and from the eastern seaboard entered Kansas, and, naturally, large jobbing houses arose in the city. By the late nineteenth century, Kansas jobbers, interested in expanding their own enterprises and weary of competing on an unequal basis with Kansas City, began to demand an end to discriminatory rates. Having failed in their early agitation, they continued their campaign for favorable rates into the Progressive Era. Under the leadership of J. S. George, the Kansas Federation of Commercial Interests directed most of the vocal aspects of the rate-making struggle.

George, who kept in constant touch with state officials, amassed an impressive array of evidence of unfair rate-making over the years. He spurred Kansas officials to initiate a number of cases before the I.C.C. in an attempt to secure better rates. According to George, railroads established rates on what was called the "Missouri River Basing Line"; and while this gave Atchison and Leavenworth advantages on freight charges, it laid the commerce of "the principal cities of Kansas, such as Lawrence, Topeka, Salina, Wichita, Coffeyville, Independence, Arkansas City, and Hutchinson . . . under tribute principally to Kansas City." "From the beginning," George wrote, "Kansas has been a tribute payer to other states, while her commerce has built at least one great city in another state, she has none worthy of the name within her own borders." There was a time during the 1890s when George had been interested in making his home town of Hutchinson into the one great Kansas metropolis, but the years had hardened him, and he no longer possessed such grandiose plans. He was now willing to settle for a rate structure that would allow him to improve his wholesale business in a much more limited way.[13]

George's complaints against railroad rates were not limited to general assertions. Time and again he produced long lists of tariffs on various commodities in order to illustrate the magnitude of discrimination under which interior jobbers operated. Although rate books were complex things with multitudes of schedules, it seems useful to cite from one of George's more lengthy portrayals of existing freight charges from St. Louis to Kansas City in comparison to similar levies from St. Louis to Wichita.

Agricultural implements, for example, bore tariffs of 16.5 mills per mile when shipped from St. Louis to Wichita, but when the same goods were sent from St. Louis to Kansas City whey were assessed 15 mills per mile. According to George, numerous articles were treated in a similar fashion. The following are a few products of the many he mentioned, and the percentages are the rates that Wichita wholesalers paid in excess of Kansas City jobbers: paper roofing, 128 percent; asphalt, 114 percent; starch, 103 percent; bags and bagging, 97 percent; paint, 95 percent; cotton piece goods, 75 percent; packing house products, 71 percent; cereal food products, 52 percent; iron and steel articles, 42 percent; general rates by goods on all classes, 13 percent; class three and class five goods (the most commonly used classes by Kansas shippers) 42 percent. Thinking of his own home area, he noted that Hutchinson had a lower rate, compared with goods shipped from St. Louis to Kansas City, in only one commodity, sugar. This advantage had resulted from an I.C.C. judgment of a few years earlier.[14]

George was not the only Kansan to muster detailed evidence of rate discrimination in the period. In 1906 a future United States senator, Joseph L. Bristow, criticized the railroad practice of using Kansas City as a basing point, citing numerous instances of how Kansas interests were being mistreated. For example, in a political handbook circulated during the year, he wrote:

> The rate on wheat from Salina [Bristow's home] to Kansas City, a distance of 185 miles, is 15 cents per hundred pounds, while the rate from Kansas City to Chicago, a distance of nearly 500

57

miles, is only eight cents per hundred pounds. The export rate from Salina to Galveston is 26½ cents per hundred, while the export rate from Kansas City to Galveston is only 11½ cents per hundred pounds. Wheat shipped from Salina to Galveston does not go to Kansas City but directly south to Galveston and the distance is not as far as it is from Kansas City to Galveston. The wheat producers of central Kansas are therefore required to pay the freight from Salina to Kansas City though the service is never performed.[15]

Evidence of this sort was commonplace and does not need to be belabored. The suggestions of how discrimination could be ended, however, were important in molding public opinion, and they help to explain why the protest became involved in state politics.

Nonpolitical remedies had been put forth prior to 1906, such as Charles Harger's recommendation that the entire western part of the Mississippi Valley reroute its products, sending them to the Gulf Coast for overseas shipment, rather than to eastern ports. The ports of Galveston and New Orleans were considerably closer than those on the Atlantic Coast, and thus the cost of transportation to them would be lower. The problem involved in Harger's suggestion revolved around the unwillingness of the railroads to establish lower rates to these southern ports, since business of this type constituted a "one-way haul." Cars sent eastward could be returned to the West laden with goods produced in the factories of New England or the Middle Atlantic states, but southern industry was almost nonexistent, and cars returned from there loaded with ballast.[16]

Because conditions such as those noted in the above Bristow quotation predominated, Harger's solution was out of the question. Moreover, a hope that railroads would help solve the problem of discrimination by their own action was fruitless. Even railroad officials who were favorable to Kansas shippers, such as H. W. Mudge of the Santa Fe, admitted that it was impossible to give favorable rates to Kansas towns, noting that "Kansas City would boycott [the Santa Fe] . . . to the extent of its ability . . . and wherever possible . . . route freight over other lines" if the Santa Fe were to attempt such a move.[17]

Even if this had not been the case, it would have been illogical for the railroads to give Kansas towns rates that were comparable to those of Kansas City. Kansas City possessed a mature market by the turn of the century, and the volume of railroad business into Kansas City was far greater than that to smaller Kansas communities; this naturally excused the use of lower rates. By all axioms of sound economic practice, this larger volume justified lower rates, because numerous shipments of large quantity cost the railroads less to handle. Furthermore, railroad men were also imbued with the prevailing opinion that good, sound, steady customers should receive the advantage of special rates. Kansas civic leaders were not, of course, interested in rational economic arguments, and despite the logic of the railroad case, they believed that they should receive rates equal to those received by Kansas City.

Thwarted in their attempts to secure nonpolitical redress, these leaders naturally turned to the government for relief. Their goal was simply to get lower rates, and their idea of how this could be achieved was not unique. By controlling state and national lawmaking bodies, they hoped to secure legislation that would end rate discrimination and force railroads to charge the lowest possible rates practicable.

Their opinions of how rates should be established differed substantially from those of railroad managers. The dominant sentiment among railroad officials was that the cost of doing business and the value of service should be used as the criteria on which rates were decided. According to the proponents of government regulation, the value of railroad property should be used. The shippers hoped to write laws that would enable state and national regulatory bodies to evaluate the roads, and then they hoped to arbitrarily establish a proper annual revenue for each. The precise percentage of profit for each railroad would vary, but quite often 5 and 6 percent were suggested as ideal margins of profit.

The great majority of Kansas railroad reformers favored eliminating the right of railroads to make appeals to federal courts with regard to decisions made by regulatory bodies. Most of these men had lost faith in the existing legal system, and they favored drastic measures, because they felt that the dangerous state of affairs justified them. On one occasion George wrote Governor Stubbs as follows:

> The greatest evil that this country is suffering is that of discrimination on the part of railroads. . . . Surely a system of rate making that will give all sections of this country full advantage of their natural locations would tend . . . to give . . . every individual the full opportunity that should accrue to him or them from their location. Anything less is UnAmerican and I believe a national menace.[18]

But rate discrimination and high tariffs were only two of the reasons for unrest in Kansas concerning railroads. Almost as significant were complaints about poor railroad service and about the cavalier fashion in which railroads often treated shippers and passengers. Service, wrote H. L. Resing of the Wichita Chamber of Commerce, "has become so slow in the matter of moving practically all articles of freight . . . [that it] menaces the commercial welfare of this section of the state." Resing suggested that the Kansas, or the Interstate, Commerce Commission be allowed to fix rules and regulations placing time limits on shipments in relation to the size of loads and the distance of hauls. If fixed schedules were not kept, then offending railroads were to be fined on the basis of the delay occasioned and the loss caused in a firm's business.[19]

There were also complaints made by shippers and travelers about the lack of cars at harvest time and about the poor conditions of freight depots, passenger terminals, and rolling stock. One of many unjust practices of railroads was reported to Stubbs after he became governor in 1909. According to W. S. Cochrane of the Midland Brick Company of Peru, Kansas, railroads required industrial concerns wishing transportation connections to pay for sidetracks and spurs to mainlines. The railroads then forced these industries to deed the appendages to them free of charge.

Cochrane, realizing that railroads did this to protect themselves from businesses that would not contribute enough traffic to pay for the cost of a spur, suggested that a more equitable practice than the one being followed could be developed. He maintained that companies wishing sidetracks should be required to make them pay, but that railroads should construct the trackage, while forcing the company to offer a bond that would be forfeited in case the spur failed to pay for itself. In this fashion, railroads would lose nothing, but would not be able to have customers build spurs and then force them to donate the spurs to the railroads. Cochrane also complained about what he said was the common practice of forcing companies that constructed spur lines to sign "cutthroat contracts" whereby the shipper promised to give all his incoming and outgoing freight to one railroad.[20]

Complaints of this nature were frequent. The point is that both rates and services, as well as arbitrary railroad practices, contributed to public unrest in the state. There was, however, one view expressed by certain reformers which denied that rates and other actions such as those noted above were significant as a cause of dissidence. This attitude was advanced by William Allen White, for example, when he wrote to George Nicholson of the Santa Fe in 1906 that tariffs and services were not the real root of the complaint against railroads, but that the fundamental source of dissatisfaction was the role played by their legal departments in Kansas politics. As long as railroad officials tried to run the Republican party, White said, there would be dissatisfaction with them. Thus, he later wrote to Thomas J. Norton, also of the Santa Fe, that it was not passenger fares or maximum freight-rate charges that sparked a rising clamor against his company in Kansas, but instead it was attempts by railroad officials to "boss our politics."[21]

There is no doubt that railroad attorneys played important parts in Kansas politics until at least 1908. Senator Long and Governor Bailey felt that their political futures depended upon the aid of railroad lawyers in 1902 and 1903. Although White was correct in suggesting that public concern over the political role of railway officials contributed to popular disapproval of the lines, he was probably deliberately making an incorrect statement when he said that rates and other facets of the controversy were unimportant. Since railroad attorneys played a significant role in causing the rising dissidence, it seems well to explore briefly the source of their political power and to suggest the modifications in their relationships to politics that resulted from the protest against them during the Progressive Era.

According to many who were wise in the ways of Kansas Republicanism, railroad officials were able to influence affairs from 1875 onward because they granted free transportation to politicians who could control conventions and influence votes in legislative proceedings. "It isn't courtesy," an editor wrote in 1900, "that prompts a railroad company to give free transportation to judges, legislators and other officials with their raft of political helpers and kin; it is to keep them 'good.' "[22] Eight years later, after Kansas had outlawed the free pass, Judge Nelson Case, who accepted free transportation in his time, wrote:

> The pass system was the most effective measure for corrupting the local politician that has ever been inaugurated. A free ride on the railroad for himself whenever he wanted to go to the state capital . . . and occasionally a free ride for his family and for some of his local political associates, and always a free ride to the party convention for all workers, who would line up for whatever measure or candidate the special interests wanted to put through, was as much of a compensation as any local machine politician expected or thought he could reasonably ask for. . . . By means of this system the railroads were nearly always able to secure a majority in the legislature who would favor no law against which they protested.[23]

In 1913 Cy Leland, who had used free passes with relish in controlling delegations to Republican conventions during his heyday, admitted that "when it came to the convention, unless it happened to be some man who was strong or who had had only one term . . . it was necessary to get the railroads on your side, or else you wasn't [sic] in it for a minute." In 1902 Kansas City banker C. S. Jobes wrote to one railroad attorney that above all else he "wished again to emphasize the importance of having the matter of transportation for the delegates of the State Convention arranged for." According to *Topeka Daily Herald* writers in 1903, railroads were themselves opposed to free travel over their lines, but rather than face political hostility, they chose to use it as a means of protecting themselves.[24]

Politicians were not the only group to profit from the practice of granting free transportation. Almost all newspaper editors and star political reporters carried systems passes and were presumably influenced by this fact. At least William Allen White felt this to be true. Although White did not return his own transportation largess until 1907, he informed Stubbs in 1904 that he believed in his own case, he, White, could be more conscientious in the pursuit of justice for railways if he did not have their transportation in his pocket.[25]

The major pressures applied against newspapers were not through free passes, but rather through advertising and through the purchases of newspapers. It was commonly believed, for example, that Charles Gleed's *Kansas City Journal* was owned by the Santa Fe. Gleed was an important official in the Santa Fe organization. Throughout his career as a publisher he maintained that he was not biased in favor of the Santa Fe, but even a cursory reading of the *Journal's* columns indicates that this was not the case.[26]

An excellent instance of the way in which the financial power of the railroads coerced certain newspaper publishers is supplied by the relationship between Gleed and Ermi Zumwalt, publisher of the *Bonner Springs Chieftain*. Zumwalt purchased the Bonner Springs newspaper with funds lent to him by Gleed, and as late as 1910 Zumwalt had not retired his obligation. In 1910 he supported a railroad reformer, Alexander Mitchell of Lawrence, for the United States House of Representatives. Mitchell opposed the incumbent congressman, Charles F. Scott, in the Republican primary. Scott, a protégé of Speaker Joseph G. Cannon's, was also a friend of Gleed's and of railroad interests in Kansas. During the campaign, Zumwalt received a letter from Gleed, informing Zumwalt that Gleed was "chagrined to feel that [he was] . . . giving financial support to a paper . . . fighting a life long friend." Although Gleed suggested that he did not intend to make Zumwalt stop supporting Mitchell, his letter was a thinly disguised threat, as were others that he sent later. Needless to say, Zumwalt withdrew his editorial backing of Mitchell's candidacy.[27]

During the height of the protest against railroad practices, a serious effort was made by railroad men to buy the *Topeka Daily Capital,* one of the most powerful critics of the railroads. On that occasion its publisher, Arthur Capper, refused to sell. Capper, however, remained financially dependent upon railroads, since many advertised in the *Capital* and other Capper publications. In 1910 Capper noted that while most railroads used his ad columns, the Santa Fe was boycotting his papers and had been doing so for a number of years.[28] Sometime between 1910 and 1914 the Santa Fe had begun an account with Capper publications; in return, Capper yielded his independent stand relative to the Santa Fe.

Capper, who had previously shunned the pressure of advertisers, as in the case of the Long-Critchfield Corporation in 1907, altered the tone of his editorial policy regarding railroads after 1914. Capper was a candidate for governor at the time, and this may have made him amenable to pressure. In April 1914 he received complaints from the Santa Fe regarding editorials that were then appearing in the *Capital,* and late in the month he held meetings with representatives of the line to discuss their grievances. Although his correspondence does not indicate what transpired at these meetings, two years later, on 23 August 1916, L. M. Jones, a Santa Fe official, commended Capper for having redirected the newspaper's editorials and noted how the *Capital's* whole policy had improved since the 1914 meetings. Charles Gleed, who disliked Capper, often said that he did not believe Capper was sincerely hostile to the Santa Fe and that he thought Capper would run "the Capital in whatever way would make him the most money."[29]

There were times when advertising was so necessary to railroads that they could not withdraw their accounts from hostile journals. In the case of the nationally famous *Life* magazine, Santa Fe President E. P. Ripley was angered because his railroad could not stop advertising in its columns. Despite the fact that *Life* was, to Ripley's way of thinking, a "socialistic periodical," he did not feel that it was practical to withdraw Santa Fe advertising from it. In a letter to Gleed, Ripley wrote, "I do not believe . . . we can immolate ourselves on the altar of our principles to the extent of refraining from the use of this advertising medium unless our neighbors will do the same thing." Ripley had tried to have other railroads join a boycott of *Life.*[30]

Cooperation among the railroads ultimately supplied the means for them to exert influence after their supposed demise as political powers.

Before discussing how they cooperated after 1908, we should take note of two other sources of power that the railroads exercised in the days before progressive Republicanism stopped them from being overt political agents. W. R. Smith, general attorney for the Santa Fe in 1907, claimed that his company employed forty full-time local attorneys in Kansas and that these men were all politically active. The activities of these attorneys, or so reformers claimed, caused most of the antirailroad sentiment. In 1906 the work that Ned Loomis of the Union Pacific did in Charles Curtis's senatorial contest caused the *Capital* to remark that Loomis hurt the best interests of his railroad by being open in his machinations. Harking back to when George Peck had controlled Santa Fe politics, the *Capital* stated that Peck had shown regard for public opinion, but that under Loomis "the Union Pacific's part in politics is open and undisguised and without any attempt at dignity."[31] One can cite numerous cases of interference on the part of railroad attorneys during the pre-1908 period.

Another source of railroad power was the use of their deposits in local banks. In 1911, for example, Gleed informed the treasurer of the Santa Fe that the Fourth National Bank of Wichita should be given Santa Fe deposits. "B. F. McLean, president of the Fourth," Gleed wrote, "has been and is an enormous shipper over the Santa Fe and is perhaps the most effective man in Wichita in public affairs. He fights for his friends and his fighting is always effective. He is locally very popular and very strong." McLean and the Fourth National received Santa Fe deposits.[32]

Cooperation among railroad officials representing the main lines in Kansas came in two ways after 1908. First they joined together to sponsor campaigns to improve the public image of their enterprises. Then in 1913 they combined to present a single well-financed lobby at the legislative session that year. The idea of an "education campaign" to improve the public image of the railroads dated back to 1905, when W. R. Smith became general attorney for the Santa Fe and A. A. Hurd became its "special attorney." According to Ralph Faxon, administrative assistant to Senator Long, Smith and Hurd were promoting such developments in the hopes of reinstituting the days of George Peck.[33]

In 1910 the *Santa Fe Employees' Magazine* noted that all raliroads had joined together to try to win the gratitude of the public by a campaign in various population centers to promote the idea of the usefulness of the railroads and to give proper information concerning freight rates. They began to use statements by scholars in order to justify their tariffs. For example, they circulated material compiled by Logan Grant Mc-

Pherson, a railroad economist and lecturer at Johns Hopkins University, to show how little the cost of transportation added to the price of articles. At about the same time they explored the possibility of hiring Professor E. B. Cowgill of the Department of Economics of the University of Kansas to create a Bureau of Economic Discussion.

Gleed wrote to Santa Fe freight agent J. R. Koontz that Cowgill's plan was "to secure from recognized authorities on economics, strong, terse, timely and sound discussion of various phases of economics and sociology for publication in such manner as to affect the convictions of the people in favor of the railroads." Koontz vetoed the idea, not because he disliked it, but because he discovered that Cowgill intended to resign from the university faculty once he had started the economics bureau, and Koontz could not see "that his line of work, if detached from the University, would be any improvement upon the field now covered by Mr. Jarrel and others associated with me." J. F. Jarrel was a reporter for various Topeka newspapers during this period. With the development of publicity campaigns, railroad attorneys could claim, as they did, that rather than trying to influence politics through direct participation, as in the past, they were involved in an acceptable democratic tradition of educating voters and that they were, as Missouri Pacific attorney Balie Waggener said, "trusting to the fairness of the people."[34]

This did not mean that railroad officials were not still involved with politicians and state legislatures. In 1912 Loomis of the Union Pacific contacted the general counselors of the Santa Fe, the Rock Island, the Missouri Pacific, and the M.K.T. railroads to "suggest the propriety of making a change in the manner of looking after legislative matters in . . . Kansas." He explained that in the past, each railroad had had representatives from its law department on hand at every session of the legislature, but this system worked at odds for the common interests of the railroads and caused the railroads to receive adverse publicity because of the large number of lobbyists. He recommended that a single lobby with ample funds be created in order to eliminate the inefficient old way of doing business.[35]

His suggestion was received favorably by each of the general attorneys, and in December 1912 Loomis chaired a meeting in Topeka at which representatives of the railroads agreed to have a single lobby and chose two Union Pacific attorneys to head it. They selected R. W. Blair and Paul Walker, both of whom had had experience in lobbying. Blair and Walker immediately set about their task by defining the common areas of railroad interests. To defeat attempts by railroad unions to improve safety requirements and to write wage-and-hour legislation, they called railway laborers from their jobs in order to oppose union leaders at legislative hearings. They entertained key legislators and devised other ways to affect votes on antirailroad bills.[36]

At the end of the session, after some trying experiences, Blair proudly reported that of 150 punitive measures aimed at the railroads, only 23 had passed and only 5 of these were at all dangerous. He was exceedingly satisfied with his accomplishments, and he suggested that at last the railroads had found an adequate way to protect themselves. He might well have been elated, since even a former critic of railroad meddling in the legislative process, the *Daily Capital,* congratulated the companies for having developed a new method "in marked contrast to the methods followed . . . not many years ago." According to the *Capital,* the lines had operated without subterfuge and had argued valiantly for their points. Such was not entirely true, but the *Capital,* by its comments, was illustrating a change that had taken place in Kansas between 1906 and 1913.[37]

In reality, the *Capital* was not evidencing a tolerance of railroad practices that were based upon the nature of those practices per se. It was demonstrating rather that the lethargy that caused the Kansas public to become unconcerned with railroad affairs affected the editors of the *Capital* as well. By 1913 other factors had replaced the rates, services, and political machinations of the railroads as the main causes of public unrest. Antirailroad sentiment had helped to bring about a reform movement in Kansas, creating the necessary voting strength to put new Republicans in office. These men then passed laws that many people believed would put an end to railroad abuses as a live issue. Complaints about railroad malpractices were the primary cause of reform in 1906, but by 1913 the railroad question was secondary. Once they were in office, reformers solved the railroad problem to the public's satisfaction by creating the utilities commission and by passing other laws regulating railroad conduct. Having done this, they turned their attention elsewhere.

Before this metamorphosis occurred, a number of crucial reform waves aimed at abuses by the railroads swept the state. The rivulets of unrest joined with the mainstream of discontent caused by Kansas railroads in 1906. The first breaks in the dam of traditional Republicanism had come in 1904 and 1905. These holes enlarged in 1906, and during the next two years the whole traditional political structure gave way to the crushing tide of progressive reform.

# 5

## FROM CIVIC LEAGUERS
## TO SQUARE DEALERS:
## KANSAS POLITICS, 1906–1908

Antirailroad agitation in Kansas, which became intense after 1905, was helped by President Theodore Roosevelt's willingness to support national demands for reform of the railroads. Late in 1904 he requested regulations that seemed to correspond to what the Kansas Federation of Commercial Interests (K.F.C.I.) and other shippers had been demanding since the days of populism. In response to the president's message, the Esch-Townshend bill and the Hepburn bill, among others, were introduced into Congress. The more stringent Esch-Townshend measure died in the Senate during the session, and in 1905 Roosevelt had to ask again for a railroad law, specifically requesting the enactment of the Hepburn bill.

Believing that the President would need help during the 1905–1906 session to overcome the supposedly strong bloc of railroad congressmen, the K.F.C.I., spearheaded by Wichita business leaders, organized the Kansas Civic Voters League. It was hoped that the league would be able to pressure reluctant Kansas congressmen into aiding Roosevelt, something a majority of Kansans wanted.[1] The league could also do other things. It could help to improve Kansas railroad laws, and it could concentrate on eliminating railroad influence from Republican politics by controlling the state convention in 1906.

The initiative in forming the Kansas Civic Voters League came from the Wichita Chamber of Commerce, which issued a call to over two thousand Kansas business leaders, asking them to attend a meeting at Toler Auditorium in Wichita on 10 January 1906. There, according to the invitation, a war against the railroads for "a better and more equitable tariff than is now charged" would commence.[2] Plans for the meeting were developed in late 1905, and an impressive group of national reformers, including Congressman Irving Lenroot of Wisconsin, Governor George Van Sant of Minnesota, and author Ray Stannard Baker, were to be present. These national dignitaries were to provide the keynote oratory for the meeting. Lenroot was to discuss the redemption of Wisconsin under Robert M. La Follette, and Van Sant was to speak in behalf of Roosevelt's program for reforming the railroads.

The main purposes of the meeting were to form the Civic League and to adopt resolutions explaining the aims of the organization. For more than two decades, Kansas shippers and Wichita business leaders had tried to adjust freight rates and services to their advantages. They felt that they had been largely ineffective. They had used political pressure in the past through the K.F.C.I., which, despite its activities, had accomplished little. A tightly organized group encompassing major Kansas shipping interests as well as important Republican political leaders had never been tried.

The purpose at Wichita was to establish such an organization, which would be structured in a manner similar to the political parties in the state. As it was outlined at the Wichita meeting, the Kansas Civic Voters League was to have ward, township, and county societies, formed primarily from the memberships of local associations of merchants, farmers, and stock raisers. Periodically, the county organizations were to send delegates to statewide rallies. Between state meetings, an executive committee, composed of leading business and political figures from each of the congressional districts and from the state at large, was to conduct league affairs.

Because the founders of the league understood the nature of political power in Kansas, they decided to forswear help offered by some Democrats at Wichita, choosing to use only Republicans in the leadership of their organization. Although the league elected J. S. George, the top official of the K.F.C.I., as chairman, other prominent places were assigned to such leaders of the Republican party as Speaker of the House Walter R. Stubbs and former Fourth Assistant Postmaster General Joseph L. Bristow.

During 1905 a number of Republican politicians had demonstrated sympathy towards the demands of shippers. They were naturally viewed as logical allies for the league. Only Bristow, among those friendly to the shippers, showed reluctance about being closely associated with the league, but he attended the Wichita meeting despite his reservations. At the time, Bristow was preparing to announce his candidacy for the United States Senate seat that would be open in January 1907. He was uncertain in early 1906 whether the prorailroad following of Senator Chester I. Long would endorse his candidacy. He had attacked railroad abuses, but he did not believe that he would lose Long's support as a result, because they had worked together politically since 1902. Initially his need for Long's help probably prompted Bristow to oppose the political activist program of the Kansas Civic Voters League. His attitude brought forth a blast from C. L. Davidson, president of the Wichita Chamber of Commerce, who argued that the railroads were in politics. "If we fight the railroads effectively," he told Bristow, "we must get into politics . . . the field where the enemy is." How else, he asked, could lower rates be realized? Why else hold a meeting at Wichita, if not to form a politically active group?[3]

That the K.C.V.L. was political in purpose could not be doubted. That it planned to help nominate Republicans who would be favorable to its cause and that it hoped to pressure other governmental officials to support its resolutions in 1906 were equally obvious. Since the success of the league depended upon its political clout, it had to be enmeshed in the political process. Whether it could unify its forces for the 1906 Republican State Convention was problematic early in the year. It could, however, easily indicate the policies that its candidates would have to advocate. Thus, several important resolutions were passed at the Wichita meeting, including support for the position taken by Roosevelt on the regulation of railroads in his annual message to Congress in December 1905.[4]

Specifically, the league endorsed the idea of giving the Interstate Commerce Commission the power, on its own motion or upon complaints by shippers, to amend rates, rules, regulations, schedules, or classifications as established by railroads if these were unjust, unreasonable, or discriminatory. This power was to be subject to judicial review. The president was to be authorized to appoint an assistant attorney general who would register and prosecute complaints. Other resolutions opposed the granting of free transportation by the railroads to favored individuals and supported a law to set maximum passenger fares.

The league advocated the use of uniform bookkeeping procedures by railroads and the investigation of railroad expenses and accounts, as well as the enactment of laws to halt the overcapitalization of railroads. Because railroads had played dominant roles in the Kansas convention system, the league endorsed a party primary that would include candidates for the United States Senate. As a final suggestion, a resolution asking for a downward revision of the national tariff was agreed upon.[5] This last objective was the only nonrailroad aspiration mentioned by the league's leadership.

Newspaper reaction to the K.C.V.L. varied. William Allen White's *Emporia Gazette*, which during 1905 had become a reform journal, greeted the league as an organization designed to secure more equitable railroad rates and "better legislation . . . [while] sending men to the legislature who are not controlled by a corporation."[6] In its news columns the *Topeka State Journal* accorded fair coverage to the meeting, but editorially it warned reformers to beware of such leaders as Stubbs and State Representative James A. Troutman of Topeka. "In the past," the *State Journal* noted, "they have both been railroad favorites."[7]

The most belligerent attitude towards the Civic League was taken by the *Kansas City Journal*, which was influenced by the Santa Fe. The *Journal* initially labeled the Wichita meeting a "rejuvenated Farmers' Alliance movement," calling it a pro-Populist gathering attended by former leaders of the People's party. Later it chided the organization for being a "fake agrarian movement," stating that the Wichita conference had been dominated by greedy jobbers from central and western Kansas and by political opportunists. This senseless agitation was bad, wrote the *Journal's* editor, because "it disturbs business conditions, creates bad blood, and sets back the clock of progress."[8]

Since the K.C.V.L. intended to extend its power through Republican politics, which meant an active role in the state convention, the reactions of the leading Republican in the state, Senator Chester I. Long, as well as those of his followers, were extremely significant. During the Wichita rally, Troutman had singled out Long as one of the men in Congress who needed to be criticized because of his favorable disposition towards railroads. By inference, Troutman charged the senator with advancing the interests of the railroads to the detriment of those of Kansas. Long, who was a protégé of the railroads, was not anxious to run afoul of the league, because of its potential political influence and because of its apparent emotional effectiveness.[9]

Walter R. Stubbs's connection with the Wichita rate convention (as the meeting that formed the league was generally called) did, however, complicate Long's relationship with the Civic League. Although the action that the senator had taken in 1904 to dissolve the Kansas Republican League had been a clever move at the time, Long and his faction in the process had advanced the political career of Stubbs, who had been chosen Republican state chairman. During the 1905 session of the legislature, Long instructed State Representative Billy Morgan, his spokesman in Topeka, to support Stubbs, who had become Speaker of the Kansas House.

In late 1905 Stubbs repaid Long's help by launching a concerted attack on the senator. Apparently the Speaker was angered by Long's early equivocations on the Hepburn bill and by the senator's obvious collaboration with railroad officials. Whatever Stubbs's reasons, reports began to reach Long in December 1905 to the effect that Stubbs was "constantly pointing to [Long's] . . . defection from the cause of the people." One correspondent wrote to the senator, "He is very sorry . . . that you are against the people of Kansas and while he says you will get on the 'bandwagon' he says you cannot fool the people of Kansas."[10] After receiving reports of this nature, Long, who naturally was sensitive to such charges, decided that the time had arrived for him to oppose the state chairman and to consummate an alliance with National Committeeman David W. Mulvane. During 1906, as Stubbs became closely involved with Civic League activities, his major political antagonists became Long and Long's supporters in Kansas.[11]

His opposition to Stubbs was only one of Long's reasons for becoming an opponent of the K.C.V.L. The emphasis that league officials placed on the establishment of a direct-primary system that would include candidates for the Senate indicated to Long that a movement was under way within the league to replace him in Congress. Although his reelection would not come until 1908, he believed that it was necessary to block the primary, because he believed that he was nearly invincible, within the existing party structure. Not only was Long hostile towards the Civic League because of its insistence on a party primary; but Civic Leaguers, once they had discovered his position on the primary, became disenchanted with him.[12]

The political power of the K.C.V.L. received its first test in May 1906 at the Republican State Convention. By then the league's program and its political plans had become so entwined with the destinies of individual politicians who had joined it that their setbacks were naturally considered defeats for the league. The failures of the league's major political leaders at the state convention were attributable far more to personal political maneuverings between January and May than to any ideological shortcoming of the league itself. As usual, Kansas politicians hoped to demonstrate their prowess at the state convention and to secure as many offices as possible for their friends. In 1902 Long had helped his senatorial candidacy this way, thereby engineering the nomination of Governor Bailey.

In 1904 the Kansas Republican League completely dominated the state ticket, forcing the incumbent, Governor Willis J. Bailey, to announce prior to the state convention that he would not seek a second term. The Republican League nominated Edward Hoch; but after the convention the K.R.L. split. The wing that included National Committeeman Mulvane and the old following of Senator Joseph R. Burton, as well as several prominent railroad attorneys, parted company with Governor Hoch and Stubbs. During the 1905 session of the legislature Stubbs alienated more members of the Republican League, especially the so-called Senate Lodge. Then the Speaker split sharply with Hoch over the state oil-refinery law and over Hoch's appointment of John Q. Royce as Kansas bank commissioner.[13]

There were other developments that increased the Stubbs-Hoch schism. In spite of Hoch's commitment to prohibition, churchmen throughout Kansas were highly critical of his first administration, claiming that he failed to enforce antiliquor laws adequately. In defense of the governor, the *Topeka Daily Capital* argued that Hoch was the only chief executive since John A. Martin's time, back in 1885, to try actively to stop the sale of alcohol. Nevertheless, Hoch did not satisfy the drys, who were friendly towards Stubbs.[14]

Furthermore, Governor Hoch became involved in a suit between the Missouri, Kansas and Texas Railroad Company and the federal government over land previously granted to the line. He used the state's prestige in presenting a case in favor of the M.K.T. In 1905, no matter what the merits of a railroad's position, any attitude favorable towards one of them was politically dangerous. Stubbs, of course, wanted to avoid any complaint that might possibly link him even indirectly with the "Katy." In addition to the M.K.T. affair, corruption reminiscent of Bailey's administration cropped up during Hoch's first term. In late 1904 State Treasurer T. T. Kelley, a Republican Leaguer of the Mulvane wing, was charged with negligence or fraud in managing the state's school fund. In 1905 Hoch inherited the situation. He hired a Chicago firm to investigate the allegations, but he failed to pursue the case with the vigor that many Kansans expected. A cloud of distrust remained over the treasurer's office, and Kelley's troubles affected Hoch's reputation.[15]

The most sensational smear of the governor came a few days before the 1906 state convention, when he allegedly made improper advances towards Mrs. William E. Stanley, the wife of Kansas' governor from 1899 to 1903. The story circulating at that time claimed that Hoch had attempted to make love to Mrs. Stanley during an official visit by her to the governor's office in connection with the administration of the Kansas Board of Charities, on which she served. The tale, of dubious accuracy, seems to have been fashioned as a last-minute attempt to convince Republicans that Hoch was unworthy of renomination. According to insiders, the rumor was probably started by Hoch's factional opponent, Henry J. Allen.[16] For the above reasons Stubbs was indifferent over the question of Hoch's renomination in 1906.

Other political changes under way during 1905 and 1906 that conditioned the outcome of the 1906 state convention included the impending imprisonment of Senator Burton. With Burton preparing to enter a federal prison, National Committeeman Mulvane assumed leadership of the Burton faction. Mulvane, before becoming a stalwart in the Burton crowd, had been one of Congressman Charles Curtis's staunchest friends, and he had remained moderately interested in the congressman's political success thereafter. In 1905 Mulvane resumed a working friendship with Curtis in order to help him secure the soon-to-be-vacated senatorial seat of Burton. Mulvane was able to retain most of Burton's former adherents when he switched his loyalty to Curtis.

By early 1904, as has previously been noted, a metamorphosis within the "machine," as Leland's one-time supporters were called, had taken place. Senator Long, a leading lieutenant of the machine, was recognized by then as the new leader of the organization. His assumption of control, however, created a number of changes among the "machine's" leadership. Leland, still active in Republican affairs, was playing a lone hand politically in 1906, sometimes supporting Stubbs and the K.C.V.L., sometimes working with Mulvane and Curtis. Another former Lelandite, William Allen White, having dropped his allegiance to the "machine" when Long took control, became committed to reform politics and found himself regularly in agreement with Stubbs. White's friend Henry J. Allen, although he left the Leland organization at the same time that White withdrew, refused to support Stubbs and the reformers. Allen was as yet unreconciled to Stubbs, who, as Speaker of the Kansas House, had been responsible for removing Allen from the Board of Charities.[17]

The political switch in 1906 that was destined to have the greatest impact on Kansas Republicanism was Joseph L. Bristow's split with the Long faction. Bristow had been the only intimate friend of Cy Leland's to cast his fortunes with Senator Long. He had helped to arrange railroad support for Long in the senatorial election in 1902; he ranked just behind Morton Albaugh as a leader of Long's forces. In 1905 Bristow became interested in filling the senate seat that Burton was to vacate. Bristow naturally expected Long's help, since according to the unwritten rules of the factional arrangements in Kansas, Long was indebted to Bristow.

Unfortunately for Senator Long, he was in no position to help Bristow then. For a number of reasons Long, even if he had wanted to, could not afford to aid his lieutenant. Many of Long's Kansas supporters were opposed to Bristow's candidacy, especially Albaugh. Moreover, by helping Bristow, Long would not increase his own strength and would probably incur the hostility of the Curtis-Mulvane group. Long was, of course, interested in an arrangement with Curtis and Mulvane. In 1906, therefore, Long followed an unusual course. He allowed Albaugh, Billy Morgan, and others among his political friends to combine with Mulvane and Curtis in order to control the Republican State Convention; but publicly he refused to endorse Curtis's senatorial candidacy. In this way he could pretend, as he did, not to be using his prestige to defeat Bristow. Although Bristow was not deceived by Senator Long's maneuver, he did not force Long to admit that Long's actions were paving the way for an eventual Curtis victory.[18]

The arrangement between Senator Long's supporters and the Mulvane-Curtis faction to control the 1906 state convention was worked out primarily by Long's faithful representative in Kansas, Morton Albaugh. Albaugh was the one Kansas political leader in the early twentieth century who was able to approach politics as a game of offense, to be won or lost in line with the actions that he devised. Rather than allowing events to develop, Albaugh, when he could, sought to master affairs and make things happen. A political manipulator of enormous ability, he would arrange nominations in advance of state conventions, and then, with a powerful array of support for his slate, he would present it to the convention for ratification.

In 1902 he had done this well and thus had contributed to Long's eventual election to the Senate. Two years later the Kansas Republican League had upset his stratagems. Since reform movements disturbed party equilibrium and hampered Albaugh's brand of politics, he was constitutionally opposed to such developments. Thus, in 1906 he systematically organized the forces that were capable of defeating the Kansas Civic Voters League and his factional enemy, Walter R. Stubbs.

To accomplish his aims Albaugh needed the support of Mulvane and Curtis. It was relatively easy to secure their help, since both of them wanted help from him in the impending senatorial struggle. Even if Curtis had wished to do so, he could not have cooperated actively with the K.C.V.L., because he wanted to retain the railroad support that had been promised to him earlier. Rumors were also afloat that Stubbs was the Civic League's candidate for the Senate. Long's faction was the most logical source of power available to Curtis, even though Long insisted publicly that the combination that Albaugh was arranging was not to be construed as a group that would endorse Curtis's senatorial ambitions. Nevertheless, Curtis knew that the popular assumption would be that Long was in favor of his nomination and election to the Senate.[19]

Public statements issued by Civic League officials in early 1906 indicated that the league would come to the state convention prepared to force its men and its program upon the Republican party. As events developed, such was not the case. The K.C.V.L., despite its boasts, did not succeed in unifying the members of a number of sympathetic groups. Furthermore, until the day before the state convention, the league's delegates to the convention had no specific plan of action. Grass-roots sentiment seemed to favor the reformers, but the lack of planning and the generally unresponsive nature of Kansas Republicanism doomed the league's political forces to defeat at the state gathering. Lt. Gov. W. J. Fitzgerald, a member of the Curtis-Long combination, wrote: "If we have a delegate convention, . . . we can beat Mr. Stubbs bad. If we have a primary nomination . . . he will 'mop the earth' with us."[20]

Fitzgerald's prophecy was fulfilled at the state convention on May 2. Stubbs, the main political figure in the K.C.V.L., in cooperation with Bristow and Leland, succeeded in maintaining a short-lived supremacy, nominating and electing the temporary chairman of the convention.[21] Then, the Curtis-Long coalition ground out its victory. It nominated a slate of candidates, arranged earlier by Albaugh, for every state office except the positions of attorney general and one of three railroad commissioners. In those places, two popular political figures allied to Stubbs and the Civic League were selected. Fred S. Jackson of Eureka was nominated for attorney general, and George W. Kanavel of Sedgwick was selected for the position on the railroad commission.[22]

Otherwise, the convention went as planned by Albaugh, resulting in a rout for the reformers and Stubbs. Edward W. Hoch, who was to have been ditched by Stubbs and the league if they carried the convention, was easily renominated as the gubernatorial candidate; and the 1906 platform was distinctly antileague in its wording. The platform was silent on such issues as the primary-election law, a law to control the granting of railroad passes, and a law to establish a two-cent-per-mile passenger fare.

The biggest failing of the platform, from the point of view of the reformers, was the railroad plank. Although the platform supported the Hepburn bill, which had already passed the House of Representatives with nearly unanimous approval, it did not deliver a ringing declaration in favor of national laws that would make it possible to establish rates on the basis of railroad evaluation and that would forbid overcapitalization by the lines. Republican reformers were particularly suspicious of the platform, because it had been written primarily by railroad politicians and others who were opposed to the Civic League. They understood that this meant the continuation of regular Republicanism. The *Topeka Daily Capital* expressed its disdain by labeling the platform an "old-fashioned, point-with-pride, pledge nothing, offer nothing" program.[23]

A jubilant *Kansas City Journal* probably added to the reformers' distrust by announcing that Stubbs had been "riding for a fall" and at last had received his due.[24] The capstone of suspicion was supplied by W. R. Smith, a former justice of the Kansas Supreme Court who was general solicitor for the Santa Fe railroad. Gloating over the "evaporation" of Stubbs and the league, Smith remarked that Stubbs's "last attempt to fan . . . the extinct embers of Populism had failed miserably."[25] Smith, though he was competent as a spokesman for the Santa Fe, was woefully short-sighted as a political prognosticator. Despite their dismal showing at the state convention, within two months Stubbs and the Civic League reformers were again active in Republican affairs, this time with a new organization and new methods for promoting their program of reform.

During May and June the Kansas Civic Voters League remained relatively inactive at the state level, while its local organizations continued to hold meetings to discuss possible action in late 1906. Then, on July 18, in response to letters sent by Thomas ("Bent") Murdock of El Dorado, forty officials of the Civic League gathered at the National Hotel in Topeka. Their purpose was to reorganize the league and to secure finances for a new campaign designed to commit the Republican party to the goals that the K.C.V.L. had outlined at the January meeting.[26]

To accomplish this, a new body, popularly known as the Square Deal Republican Club, was formed. Its official name—the Kansas Republican

League or the State Republican League—was only incidental. The important aspect was the intention of its leaders to capitalize on President Roosevelt's inspiring campaign slogan of 1904 and to stress its Republican orientation. When the Square Deal Club was organized, S. C. Crummer, who replaced Stubbs as Republican state chairman in 1906, denounced the movement and warned all Republicans who wished to remain in good standing with the party to avoid becoming members of the splinter group.[27]

Republicans, nevertheless, composed the entire membership of the organization, with east central Kansans dominating it. State Senator J. H. Stewart of Wichita was chairman of the July 18 meeting, and two others from that city—Congressman Victor Murdock and C. L. Davidson, president of the Chamber of Commerce—were elected as members of the club's executive committee. Three prominent Topeka Republicans, State Representative J. A. Troutman, publisher Arthur Capper, and editor Harold Chase, were also named committee members, with Troutman serving as permanent chairman of the organization. Other leading Republicans on the executive committee were Stubbs; his confederate from Maple Hill, State Senator Jonathan N. Dolley; Bristow; and two ardent friends of Bristow's, State Senator Fred Quincy and J. L. Bishop of Salina. Two of William Allen White's political friends from Emporia, State Representatives C. A. Stannard and George Plumb, son of former U.S. Senator Preston B. Plumb, were also members of the executive committee.[28]

An impressive Republican leadership was one aspect of the new organization. Another was a plan to publish a handbook that would indicate how much support Republican candidates running for office in the November elections intended to give to Square Deal ideals. This tactic, which was designed to commit Republican candidates to reform, had been unsuccessfully initiated in early July by some members of the Civic League who circulated letters requesting office seekers to announce their positions on specific reforms. At the Square Deal meeting in July, the club endorsed a separate plan to send questionnaires to all Republican candidates for office and then to publish their answers in a campaign handbook. The questionnaires, in the form of petitions from the constituencies of candidates, asked the nominees to state their positions on the proposed primary law, the anti-pass law, a two-cent passenger-fare law, and a law to create a Kansas tax commission that would reevaluate railroad property and then tax it on the same basis as other Kansas property.

The questionnaires were sent to 185 Republicans during August and September. A total of 119 replied. Then, on 23 October 1906, the results were published by Arthur Capper's Mail Printing House in Topeka. According to plan, the volume, which was called *The Square Deal Hand Book*, was sent to Republican voters throughout the state. Promoters of the booklet claimed that every Republican in Kansas received a copy, but a more realistic statement said that "as many as possible" were circulated to party members at the county level.[29]

The handbook caused an immediate uproar in Republican ranks; for the first time since the days of populism, a divided Republican party entered a general election. Those Republican candidates who refused to answer the questionnaires denounced the handbook as a "rabbit book," charging that only political cowards and opportunists had answered the inquiry. Earlier, while the questionnaires were circulating, the *Kansas City Journal* suggested that the real purpose of the handbook was to create a following that would be capable of electing Walter R. Stubbs to the Senate in 1907.[30]

This complaint, foreseen by Square Dealers, had been previously rebuked. William Allen White, reacting to a similar charge earlier, had stated that the idea for a list of questions to be sent to candidates for office had originated at the January rate convention in Wichita. The plan was revived in June by the Emporia branch of the Kansas Civic Voters League. The prime movers behind the handbook, according to White, were the nonpolitical members of the Civic League. Stubbs's role in the handbook affair and in the formation of the Square Deal Republican Club was merely that of a worker for the shipping interests of Kansas and against the railroad cause. The intention of the Square Deal reform movement, White added, was assuredly not that of pacemaker for the senatorial candidacy of Stubbs or anybody else.[31]

Bent Murdock, one of the founders of the Square Deal Club, did not agree. Although he refused to say that Stubbs was necessarily the candidate that the Square Dealers would support, he claimed that the organization would try to control the state legislature in January 1907 in order to elect a senator who was favorable to railroad reform. Murdock, who had been one of the earliest advocates of the *Square Deal Hand Book*, was usually informed on the inner working of the reform body.[32]

The most serious complaint raised against the handbook and the Square Deal Club was the charge that Square Dealers by their activities would cost Republican candidates numerous votes in 1906. Contradicting this assertion, Walter R. Stubbs maintained that an endorsement by the handbook would be worth thirty or forty thousand votes for Republican candidates. James A. Troutman, Square Deal chairman, countered accusations that he and his organization were working against the interests of Republicanism by claiming that the reformers were averting a mass exodus by voters from Republican ranks.

"While the masses of the party were passing resolutions," Troutman said, "the fixers were setting up delegations for the purpose of disregarding the popular will." A few selfish and malignant men had created a situation that had caused widespread discontent and threatened revolt; and the Square Deal Republican Club had arisen to placate this feeling and to keep the "people of Kansas, Republican by tradition and education," within the party. The aim of Square Dealers, Troutman concluded, was to correct a dehorned platform and to elect Republicans by making the party responsive to the public will. To add to the impression that the Republican party of Kansas was a reform-oriented party, Square Deal leaders brought Wisconsin's reform senator, Robert M. La Follette, to Kansas in 1906.[33]

Despite the fears of some candidates, Republicans were once again returned to office in the November elections. This time, however, their majorities showed slight declines when compared to an average of votes cast for Republican candidates from 1898 to 1904. Compared to the Republican returns of 1904, when a popular presidential candidate headed the ticket, the decrease was even larger. In 1906, E. W. Hoch received the lowest percentage polled by a successful Republican gubernatorial candidate in any general election in Kansas between 1890 and 1912. He received 48.2 percent of the vote, while his Democratic opponent, former Senator William A. Harris, received 47.6 percent. Obviously, this was not a normal midterm swing.[34]

Before the election a number of Republicans informed Hoch that they would not vote for him, because they believed that he allowed corporate influences to dominate the 1906 Republican State Convention and, consequently, the Republican party. William Allen White, who had been a staunch Republican until 1906, wrote Hoch's opponent after the election, "I could not see my way clear to advise people to vote for Hoch . . . and yet I did not want the Democratic party as a party to win in Kansas."[35]

In appraising the causes for the poor Republican showing, the reform press listed as prime reasons the hostility to corporate influences associated with the party and the popularity of the former Fusionist senator, William A. Harris, who headed the Democratic ticket. The *Kansas City*

*Journal* felt that Hoch's poor showing was the result of less support having been given to his candidacy by Wichita, Topeka, and Kansas City newspapers, all of which were nominally Republican journals.[36]

Considering the voting statistics from 1898 through 1912, it becomes clear that the election in 1906 marked the beginning of a steady decline in Republican majorities, which by 1912 had dropped sufficiently to allow a number of reform Democrats to win office in Kansas. An immediate consequence of the 1906 election, however, was the return of the usual Republican majority to the state legislature. This fact assured the election of a Republican to the United States Senate in 1907, and it meant that the Republican caucus in the state legislature would determine which Kansas politician would next journey to Washington.

Despite the earlier statements by Bent Murdock, by late 1906 various Square Deal personalities were disclaiming any intention of using their club to organize the senatorial caucus and thus choose a candidate for senator. No doubt, Square Dealers who were seeking the senatorial position would have welcomed the endorsement of their candidacies by the club. The fact that three men who were important in the movement were involved in the race precluded this possibility. Moreover, other candidates, including Curtis, Congressman Philip P. Campbell, Senator A. W. Benson, and James F. Getty, a relatively unknown state senator from Kansas City, had all written acceptable replies to the handbook questionnaire.

The Square Dealers were thus neutralized. If it wished to demonstrate its reform character, the organization could not single out any of the candidates to endorse. The leading Square Dealers who were seeking the office—Stubbs, Bristow, and Congressman Victor Murdock—were unable to reach a compromise in support of the candidacy of one of them. Consequently, the man least acceptable to the reformers, Charles Curtis, won the nomination of the Republican legislative caucus, and therefore the election, in 1907.

Regardless of the lack of a well-organized opposition, the selection of Curtis was no simple matter. The struggle for the Senate seat had begun months before Senator Joseph R. Burton resigned in June 1906 to enter a federal prison. Initially, Bristow and Curtis were the only Republicans discussed as candidates. When Burton resigned, some people, unaware of the Stubbs-Hoch rift, speculated that the governor would appoint Stubbs to fill Burton's seat until the legislative session in 1907. This would have given Stubbs an edge when the regular selection was made.

At the time, Stubbs was not avowedly a candidate, but many politicians considered him as such.

Hoch, angered by reports that Stubbs had actually tried to stop his renomination at the state convention and still smarting over their differences of opinion on the refinery law, did not intend to appoint Stubbs. To avoid becoming involved in this intraparty struggle, the governor decided to select a candidate who was not associated with any wing of the party. In the atomized Republican organization in Kansas such a resolve proved difficult to keep. Hoch finally found an ideal person to appoint in F. D. Coburn, a man widely acclaimed for his work as secretary of the Kansas Department of Agriculture. But Coburn, having reached old age, declined the offer. Then Hoch, apparently willing to incur Stubbs's ire, delivered what Charles Sessions, the governor's private secretary, considered a "solar plexus blow" to Stubbs. Hoch chose Judge A. W. Benson of Ottawa, a resident of Stubbs's home congressional district, to replace Burton.[37]

If Stubbs had not been a candidate for the Senate prior to the appointment of Benson, as his close friends claimed, it became apparent thereafter that he wanted the position. Stubbs's chances of being elected in January 1907 were decidedly hurt by the interim appointment of Benson. The fact that he did not undertake a concerted effort to win the nomination of the Republican caucus until December of 1906 further aggravated his situation. From June until November little public attention was directed towards the senatorial contest, because the Square Deal movement and then the general elections occupied the attention of the press.

The first important development in the race came in December, when Senator Long, who had previously refused to endorse Curtis, quietly told his friends not to help any candidate for the Senate other than Curtis. Actually, there was no need for Long to give definite instructions to support Curtis, since most of his followers were doing so already. Nevertheless, he chose a strange way to state his position. He did not instruct his friends to help Curtis, but rather he told them not to help anyone else. Long's support of Curtis probably indicated that by December the Topekan had received the final approval of the major Kansas railroads for his elevation to the Senate.[38]

Other developments in connection with the senatorial race during December were interesting if not particularly important in determining the outcome. Bristow, unaware of Long's advice to his supporters, still sought Long's aid, writing a number of supplicating letters to Long's associates. A rumor during the month had it that Bristow, Murdock, and

Stubbs had finally agreed upon a single candidate. Another maintained that Stubbs, though working hard for the position, really planned to withdraw from the campaign and back Murdock. None of these contingencies developed. Nor did the proposed candidacy of former Governor Willis J. Bailey. In early December, Bailey indicated that he would enter the senatorial contest. His statements to this effect prompted William Allen White to write Bailey that not only would his candidacy hurt their mutual friend Joseph Bristow, but that it would help elect their common enemy Curtis.[39]

In spite of White's concern, and although the Emporian managed to keep Bailey from seeking the nomination, Curtis could not be defeated in 1907. Professional political observers at the Republican caucus claimed that Long's support ultimately carried Curtis into office, since the congressman "was not particularly strong in the . . . legislature" that elected him. The disorganized nature of the opposition to Curtis, according to this view, had made Long's delegation the deciding factor. By working through legislators who were allied with the Long faction, Albaugh arranged for the election of J. S. Simmons of Dighton as Speaker of the Kansas House on January 7. "The speakership fight," Albaugh later asserted, "won the Senatorial fight." There were a number of candidates for the Speaker's chair, including Simmons, Cy Leland, J. W. Creech, and C. A. Stannard, the Square Deal candidate. Simmons won because of the votes of representatives belonging to the Long and the Curtis-Mulvane factions.[40]

The men who voted for Simmons gave Albaugh, who was handling arrangements for Curtis, a nucleus of strength for the senatorial race four days later. Having managed to secure cooperation among these representatives in the Simmons election, Albaugh had little trouble in commanding their support for Curtis on January 11. Because there were 125 representatives and only 36 senators in the caucus, the nucleus of House members that Albaugh controlled was nearly a majority. In spite of this, the selection of Curtis did not come on the initial ballot. A number of men favorable to Curtis had been instructed to cast their first votes for other candidates. According to Albaugh, he and F. Dumont Smith, the leader of support for Curtis among state senators, agreed that these legislators should first vote for the other candidates and then, on the second or third ballot, switch their support to the Topekan.

The final agreement was that the deadlock would be broken on the third tally, with legislators favorable to Curtis switching when the teller reached the C's. The break developed as planned, but Curtis still lacked a majority and was not nominated until the fourth ballot was cast. His election later, on January 22, which was a formality, gave him the remaining term of Burton and another six years beginning in March. Republican tradition had been for caucuses to make the nominations unanimous, but in 1907 that tradition was broken. Stubbs, who was a member of the House, refused to vote for Curtis.[41]

The election of Curtis should not have come as a surprise to the disorganized reform group, which was strong on rallies and resolutions but shy on effective preparations in crucial elections. Although Albaugh's contribution must be considered, Curtis was a highly competent politician in his own right. During his unsuccessful senatorial campaign in 1903, a *Topeka State Journal* reporter wrote this glowing account of Curtis's effectiveness as a politician:

> Charles Curtis . . . is undersize and does not approach the schoolgirl's dream of a statesman. He has hair as black as the darkest night, a nut-brown skin with the glow of health upon it, and eyes which possess the power of looking straight through a representative. There is no man in Kansas who knows so much about every one. For instance, this is the way Mr. Curtis greets a short grass statesman, who has just arrived in Topeka: "Why, hello, Jim how are you? How are the folks? And your uncle, old Fred Siftings, who lived down in the bend in the creek, how is he? And Jerry, your youngest boy; how is he doing in school this year? I understand that he still tops his class. Your wife was looking especially well when I last saw her, and I hope she is still hearty and good looking." And he goes on this way until he has threshed over the pedigree of the whole family, and all the time he is holding on to the representative's hand and looking into his eyes with that piercing gaze, which could convince a stone image of his sincerity. When Mr. Curtis finally does let go of the hand that man is pretty apt to leave with the resolution that he will vote for Curtis if he can ever get out from under his instructions.[42]

In the day of indirect election of senators, informality and a wide acquaintance with state legislators were good senatorial politics.

Moreover, Curtis was not the *bête noire* that William Allen White described him as being in his highly imaginative autobiography. The senator was susceptible to popular pressures and often worked for objectives that the majority of Kansas Republican voters approved of. He was unwilling to stake his political future on the whims of reformers, and in this sense he was an opponent of reform. Nevertheless, he was a moderate opponent during most of the Progressive Era. His election in

1907, despite charges made by reformers, was less a victory for the railroads than Long's election in 1903 had been; and if corporate interests significantly influenced the 1907 legislature, Curtis received their support because he offended them less than the other candidates. The railroads backed him by default rather than by design.[43]

Considering the nature of the laws enacted by the 1907 legislature, it is hard to find absolute proof that corporations dominated it. Nevertheless, they did seem to manage the session to some degree. Charles Gleed, who was the publisher of the *Kansas City Journal,* a director of the Santa Fe, and a biennial corporation lobbyist in Topeka, responded to complaints from Chicago financial groups concerning the reforms of the 1907 legislature by defending that body. Gleed argued that the legislature, rather than having attempted to destroy property or make radical changes, had tried to correct inequalities and irregularities. He added, "As a matter of fact, . . . I personally have very pleasant recollections of the session that . . . has just passed."[44] Gleed was never pleased by meaningful reforms.

In 1907 Governor Hoch had gone before the legislature to request all of the laws that he had endorsed in *The Square Deal Hand Book* and other reform legislation that was being tested or enacted throughout the United States. Specifically, Hoch asked for a primary law, an anti-pass law, a two-cent passenger-fare law, and a law to create a Kansas tax commission. To better enforce prohibition, the governor requested that a board of control be created. He also sought extension of the powers of the railroad board, asking that telephone and telegraph companies be brought under its control and that added funds be appropriated so that the tax commission could reassess railroad property.[45]

Stung by his poor showing in the general election, Hoch hoped to refurbish his image by having his second legislative session be as productive as his first. The Kansas legislature, performing in its usual fashion, moved too slowly for the governor, and in late February he appeared before the body a second time. Criticizing the lawmakers for only bothering with "local legislation," he urged them to respond to the demands then engulfing Kansas. "The people believe," Hoch said, "that free railroad transportation is a species of favoritism which . . . tends to corrupt politics. . . . I think this legislature will not adjourn until it . . . abolishes the free pass." Fearful that other laws recommended in his annual message would not be enacted, he repeated his earlier requests almost to the letter. The primary law, he stressed, was exceedingly important. In March, he appeared once more before the Kansas House to demand that a primary law be passed.[46]

By then most of his earlier proposals had been enacted into law. A tax commission had been created, and an anti-pass law and a law establishing maximum freight rates had been passed. The legislature had enacted a two-cent passenger-fare law, but not in a form that completely satisfied the governor or the reformers. A party-primary law had failed.

The Anti-pass Law enacted by the Kansas legislature was the result of criticism from 1900 onward of the railroad practice of granting free transportation to politicians and newspapermen and to their families. According to popular opinion, railroads managed to control state politics in this fashion. Nelson I. Case, a local politician from southeastern Kansas, considered the pass "the most effective measure for corrupting . . . local politicians ever inaugurated."[47] The *Kansas Knocker,* a magazine published briefly in Topeka in 1900, remarked, "It isn't courtesy that prompts a railroad company to give free transportation to judges, legislators and other officials."[48]

Actually, by 1907 railroads no longer favored the granting of free passes, although they claimed that they were forced to continue the practice that had once been advantageous to them. By then the railroads had developed subtler ways of influencing judges and legislators, and they frowned on having to be criticized for using an obsolete practice. According to one newspaper account, the railroads had encouraged the enactment of the law that forbade free transportation. Many regular Republicans fought the bill, but in spite of their efforts, it became law, effective 1 January 1908. Hearty congratulations from railroad officials to state officials greeted its proclamation then.[49]

The other important piece of legislation enacted in 1907 was that creating the Kansas State Tax Commission. The most immediate reason for its passage was Square Deal agitation for the reassessment of railroad holdings and the taxing of them on the same basis as other Kansas property. In 1905, in his message to the legislature, Governor Hoch had mentioned the need to revise the Kansas tax structure, but the idea for a tax commission had originated much earlier.

In the 1880s State Treasurer Samuel T. Howe had recommended a commission in his annual report. In 1901 a special commission was appointed by the legislature to investigate inequities in Kansas taxes and to suggest how they could be eliminated. In 1902 this body filed a lengthy report with the legislature, but the tax commission that it recommended was not created. In 1907, when railroad problems abetted other reform sentiments, proponents of the commission were able to have such a body established.⁵⁰

In consequence, a three-man tax commission headed by former Treasurer Howe was constituted. In 1907 it reassessed Kansas property, increasing taxable assets in the state by two billion dollars, from 0.5 billion to 2.5 billion; but it also lowered the mill levy in Kansas from 8.5 to 4.5 per dollar value. Although in reassessing the property of the railroads, the commission raised their assessments and taxes, the railroads wound up contributing less than previously to the total sum collected from the property and real estate tax. This situation was the result of even greater increases in assessments and taxes on other properties. Although many politicians expected immediate complaints due to the commission's work in 1907, criticism of its operation was slight.⁵¹

Not only was Governor Hoch active during the 1907 legislative session, but after the session closed in March, he supported other objectives favored by reformers. With the help of Attorney General Fred Jackson and two members of the legal department of the Kansas State Temperance Union—John Marshall and J. K. Codding—he began a "vigorous campaign" to enforce the state's liquor laws. This campaign, Attorney General Jackson claimed, drove the open saloon from Kansas, although liquor was still being dispensed illegally from homes and drug stores.⁵²

The governor's most popular action in 1907 was the Two-cent Passenger Fare Law. The legislature, compromising with railroad attorneys, passed a watered-down version of the bill that reformers wanted. The law provided for the sale of mileage rate books issued in two forms, one for five hundred and one for twenty-five hundred miles of railroad transportation at $10.00 and $50.00, respectively. The former could only be used on one line, while the latter could be used interchangeably on all railroads crossing Kansas. This met the demand of a vocal pressure group, the United Commercial Travelers of America. The majority of those who wanted to reform the railroads, including most Square Dealers and, in this instance, Governor Hoch, were not impressed by the law.

In mid 1907 the reformers began to urge Hoch to call a special session of the legislature so that a law could be enacted to set a flat fare of two cents per mile. Hoch opposed the idea of an extra session, preferring instead another method to secure the reduction in passenger rates. Other states had passed two-cent-fare laws and had found them blocked by railroad actions in federal courts. Hoch decided that the desired results could best be secured by having the Kansas Railroad Commission issue a decree forcing the lines to provide fares of two cents per mile. On

August 22 he asked the commission to take this action. After two weeks of hearings, the commission ordered the reduction, but the railroads warned that they would not obey the order when it became effective in October.[53]

In response to their challenge, Hoch indicated that perhaps a special session would be necessary to deal with the recalcitrant lines. Reporters covering the exchanges between the governor and railroad attorneys claimed that Hoch's statement regarding his convening of the legislature caused the political friends of Senator Long to flock to the Topeka headquarters of the railways. Long and his supporters feared a special session, since it might enact a primary law. Supposedly, they pleaded with railroad officials to accept the new fare in order to avoid the action that the governor threatened. On October 2, perhaps as a result of pressure from their friends, railroad leaders allowed the commission's order to go into effect, but they immediately filed suit against the new rates in the United States District Court at Kansas City. This suit dragged on for years, and in 1914 it was settled in favor of the railroads.[54]

The two-cent-fare victory was universally cheered by the reform press in 1907. Yet even this accomplishment did not quiet criticism that had been present in reform journals since the close of the regular session of the legislature. Dissatisfied, in spite of the fact that many of their ideas had become law, reform editors demanded that a primary election be held in 1908. Like their reform allies, they feared that without the primary their opponents would continue to control the Republican party and the key positions on the Republican ticket. In the reformers' minds one office—that of U.S. Senator—had become extremely important as a symbol of a successful future for their beliefs. In 1908 Senator Long stood for reelection. If the reformers could defeat him, victory in Kansas would seemingly be theirs. If Long won, chances were that the reform impetus would stall. Long's position was so secure within the established party framework that reform leaders believed that he could be defeated only in a primary election. Chances for a primary seemed poor in late 1907.

The Square Deal movement itself had begun to flounder midway through the year. Immediately after the legislature had adjourned, there had been a good deal of activity among local clubs, and a state executive meeting had been held in April. Jonathan N. Dolley replaced James A. Troutman as chairman of the executive committee, but a statewide reform rally was deferred until Senator Robert M. La Follette could be secured as a speaker. Talk of a Square Deal slate of candidates for 1908 was dismissed as ineffectual until a primary law could be passed. After April, little public attention was given to the Square Dealers.[55]

The Square Deal movement, then, and reform in general had come to rest on one issue. Either a primary would be held, which would allow reformers a chance to elect their candidates, or the forces of conservatism would continue to prevail in the state. Governor Hoch momentarily held the key to the future of reform. Only he could call a special session of the legislature at which a primary law might be enacted. In late 1907, White, Stubbs, Bristow, and a host of others began to demand that the governor convene a special session of the legislature to consider a primary bill.

# 6

## BRISTOW AND THE BIRTH OF THE PROGRESSIVE REPUBLICAN FACTION, 1908

"The grotesqueness of our conference rose in my mind. . . . Here was a pleasant, kindly spoken, innocuous, elderly gentleman [Joseph L. Bristow], . . . another boisterous, well meaning person [Walter R. Stubbs], . . . you and I . . . we four and no more sitting in a calm state making a Governor and Senator."[1] Thus did William Allen White, small-town newspaper publisher, companion of presidents, spokesman of "uplift" Republicanism in the Middle West, describe a small, secret meeting in Topeka that gave birth to the powerful progressive faction within the Republican party of Kansas.

In a more immediate and tangible sense, however, the conference that White was recalling to *Topeka Daily Capital* editor Harold Chase resulted in an agreement between two leading Republican reformers, Walter R. Stubbs and Joseph L. Bristow. According to the understanding reached in Topeka, Bristow, a former fourth assistant postmaster general, would run as the reform candidate in the 1908 senatorial primary, while Stubbs, a former Republican state chairman and former Speaker of the Kansas House of Representatives, would seek the gubernatorial nomination.

The need for the secret gathering arose in early 1908, after reform forces had secured the long-desired party primary as part of the state's political system. Certain that only division within the ranks of the reformers could defeat their cause in a contest before the voters, White had labored assiduously since mid 1907 to unify the powerful groups headed by Stubbs and Bristow. Initially, neither man had demonstrated much of an inclination to compromise on the 1908 senatorial election, although a similar split had hurt the reformers' chances in the senatorial caucus in January 1907, which Charles Curtis won. Fortunately for the reform faction, Stubbs began to recognize early in 1908 that he could not remain a political force in Kansas if he, too, did not help to foster unity. Thus he yielded the senatorship to the ever-adamant Bristow and accepted what he felt was the less desirable opportunity—to be governor of Kansas.[2]

The popularity of reform, the fear of defeat, and the establishment of the party primary made it easier for White and Chase to accomplish the difficult task of bringing Bristow and Stubbs together. The party primary, which supplied the linchpin of unity in this case, was an issue that Kansas reformers had championed from 1904 onward. But in the last few months of 1907, because they understood that the public favored reform, the primary had become the absolute route to victory. The primary would allow reformers to overcome the stranglehold that conservatives had held on the state-convention system.[3] Obviously, they did not wish to waste the primary by continuing to be divided within their own ranks.

Republicans first endorsed the statewide primary in their 1904 platform. In the legislative sessions of 1905 and 1907 they had failed to enact a primary law, mainly because Senator Chester I. Long and his supporters had opposed it. At the time of the 1906 state convention, when the senator managed to stop the party from reendorsing the idea of a primary, he wrote that he was interested in blocking it as a statewide affair because two classes of men—demagogues and the very rich—would otherwise have special advantages in Republican affairs. "I do not belong to either class," he noted, "although it is not from a personal standpoint that I object to the state primary." His opposition, or so he said, stemmed from the fact that the primary would be unfair to western Kansas.[4]

Long knew, of course, that his own strength in Republican politics lay in that part of the state. When it appeared that a primary law might pass during the 1907 legislature, he claimed that he did not fear going before the voters to seek reelection. "But," he added, "if the representatives of the small western counties have any regard for their interests, they will never consent to such a proposition. It would take from [these] . . . districts their present power in the legislature in the nomination of a senator, but they would still be expected to furnish the votes to elect him." This he thought was wrong, because the Republicans who elected the officials should be the ones who nominated them. "They ought not," he concluded, "be compelled to take the instructions of the people of the large eastern counties."[5]

Long thus opposed the primary because of its impact upon western Kansas and because it would harm his own interests. By 1907 the Long faction, in alliance with supporters of Curtis, controlled the existing party machinery; and in a struggle for delegates under the convention system, their combined forces seemed certain to renominate Senator Long. But many Republicans who opposed the primary law had less to lose than Long had, and they offered complaints that were less selfishly motivated. Charles Gleed, a conservative railroad and telephone official in Kansas, feared it as an overextension of democracy. "My opinion," he once remarked, "is that the people should not be asked to vote on any matters they know nothing about." Regarding the primary, he stated:

> I am against any law which restricts United States Senators to those who nominate themselves and go from door to door describing their fitness for the position. The result of that method will always be found to give us men like Jeff Davis of Arkansas. I stick to the principle that this is a representative form of government and when it ceases to be such I hope for a first-class monarchy. Any pure democracy has always meant trouble.[6]

A more graphic denunciation of the primary was rendered by attorney William P. Hackney of Winfield, who called the law "a fraud designed by wealth and intelligence in order to eliminate Republicans and Negroes from Politics." "Oh! the ghouls," he added, "how mercilessly they torment the great souls of Washington, Hamilton, Marshall, Lincoln, and . . . all the other great men."[7]

The advocates of the primary had their arguments as well, and they were able to approximate the temper of the early twentieth century far better than their opponents. They favored the primary because it increased democracy, that hoary tenet which they said had influenced the aims of the Founding Fathers and all American development since 1776. Their main contention was that the primary improved the quality of men who sought office and that it eliminated corruption and the opportunity for corruption. "I cannot now tell you," wrote progressive Republican J. N. Dolley, "how corrupt, how vicious, how high-handed, how subversive of good morals, how rotten, the old convention system was!" He added:

> The inside workings of state conventions and midnight conclaves leading up thereto have never been told. . . . It may suffice to say that cliques and cabals representing the corporations, the special interests and those who have fattened at public expense had manipulated caucuses, county conventions and state conventions, legislatures and congresses and traded and dickered and trafficked in political candidacies and policies for a generation, and the people had no remedy. . . . The natural leader of men, the man of character, the man who stands for something, will count for more under the new dispensation than ever.[8]

To a man, Stubbs, Bristow, White, and other leaders of the Square Deal movement agreed with this appraisal. But their advocacy of the measure had a more practical reason. Having won public confidence, they needed a method to translate public support into political power. The primary law, passed in late January 1908, gave them this opportunity.[9]

The special session of the state legislature that enacted the primary law was called by Governor Edward W. Hoch after intense pressure from various groups had forced him to act on their demand. Initial agitation for the session started during the controversy over the two-cent passenger rate in mid 1907. But action by the railroad commission negated this reason. Then, late in the year, Stubbs, White, and their allies opened a campaign for an extra session at which a primary law might be enacted. As late as 20 December 1907, Governor Hoch opposed the idea, noting that invariably such sessions were failures.[10]

There were suggestions that the Republican state committee issue a call for a statewide primary when the state committee met on 28 December 1907. Stubbs, Daniel R. Anthony, Jr., and others supported this idea. But Mort Albaugh, Billy Morgan, and David Mulvane blocked the proposal at the meeting.[11] The only alternative available after this was the special session. During the first week of January 1908 pressure on Hoch became intense; with all other avenues closed, the governor gave in and issued a call for the legislature to convene at Topeka on 16 January.

Reformers who supported the primary law were not the only people who were trying to force the governor to act. The bank panic of 1907 made itself felt in the state late in the year, and beginning in November, a number of Kansas bankers requested a special session, in which a law to guarantee bank deposits might be enacted. For more than a decade, "radicals" in Kansas had supported such a measure, and more recently, nearby states had begun to consider similar proposals. Not until the panic of 1907, however, did moderate Republicans champion the guaranty plan. Then worry over financial conditions in the state brought them to the idea; and the panic, rather than quieting the clamor for a special session as Senator Long had predicted it would, increased it. Albaugh, the senator's right-hand man, had been sure that this would happen, since "radical agitators" would invariably blame economic misfortune on the railroads, Wall Street, and various other intangible octopi.[12]

But so-called radicals were not the only ones who were interested in the session because of the banking crisis; as letters to the governor indicated, the country banker and his small-town business associates were the "agitators" in this instance. In a letter typical of those received by Governor Hoch, Belleville banker M. C. Polley wrote: "It seems to me that the recent panic has caused a stagnation in business and a lack of confidence in depositors." This lack of faith, Polley suggested, would be overcome if the state legislature reconvened and quickly passed a law to guarantee bank deposits.[13]

Hoch had a number of proposals to make to the special session, which met from January 16 to January 30; but the main parts of his message dealt with the primary law and the bank-deposit guaranty law. And although the legislature enacted some of his other suggestions, they spent the major part of their fourteen days considering the two proposals that Hoch stressed. Despite the governor's efforts, the deposit guaranty law was not enacted.[14]

The primary law was the major question raised in the session. In his message Hoch stressed the need to have a direct statewide primary that would apply in 1908. "All the people of Kansas," he said, "should decide if the progressive movement for good government in the state is to go on." Rumors that Senator Long's friends planned to pass a measure that would not be operative until 1910 caused the governor to warn that the law should take effect immediately.[15]

Ironically, although Hoch, White, Bristow, and Stubbs were the men most responsible for the enactment of a primary law in Kansas, they could not claim credit for its wording. The bill, which finally was passed in late January, was fashioned largely by the friends of Senator Long, although they did not defer its operation, as it had been rumored that they would.

On January 15 Long publicly endorsed the measure in a letter to the *Topeka Daily Capital*. Albaugh had informed him a few days earlier that the bill would pass. Characteristically, after he had been informed that the primary law would undoubtedly be passed, Long set about to determine its final form so that his own interests might be helped. First, he recommended that the primary election be held late in 1908, in

August, after the Republican National Convention. In this way he felt that his candidacy would be enhanced, because, as he wrote Albaugh, the national party would undoubtedly nominate "William H. Taft or some candidate for President . . . classed in the public mind as . . . conservative." "The platform," he added, "will then be known and I think the people will realize that the things Mr. Stubbs stands for are in fact in the Democratic platform rather than in the Republican."[16]

Another stipulation that Long made to his followers in the legislature was that the law be worded so that the senatorial nomination would be based on the majority or plurality of legislative districts in the state. In this way, western Kansas, though less populous than the eastern section, would dominate the senatorial primary. Long also instructed his supporters to insist on the provision that delegates to the national convention continue to be selected in the traditional way at state and congressional conventions.[17]

The primary law that was passed by the special session was a simple arrangement somewhat similar to those adopted by forty-four other states during this period. It provided that all candidates for state and congressional offices were to be nominated on the basis of a majority or plurality of votes at the August primary. The candidate for senator was to be chosen, as Long had instructed, by the votes cast in legislative districts. Long also recommended that the people be allowed to express their choice for senator later, at the November election, and the primary law made this possible. It provided that each candidate for the state legislature could register his preference for senator at the time of the general election. In this way the candidates were to be pledged to vote for the man they endorsed. It was assumed that the senatorial candidate who received the most endorsements would be the victor at the party primary, but legally the legislators were not bound by the choice made by the voters in the primary. Only their honor committed them to the senatorial candidate chosen in the primary.[18]

In spite of the fact that desirable features for a primary law had been debated extensively, there were defects in the law that was passed. For one thing, the secret ballot was not made mandatory. For another, there were no provisions for registering voters in a specific party, so that a voter could choose whichever party ballot he wished. In 1908 Republicans in Kansas could see few advantages in the "open primary." Prior to the election, Fred Jackson, the progressive Republican who was serving as attorney general of the state, decided that a voter could be forced to file an oath attesting to his party affiliation if he were challenged. Jackson added that the oath was not legally binding on the voter, but that it was a moral obligation that each person undertook. Hoch summed up the fear that Republicans had of the "open primary" when he said that it would damage party solidarity and perhaps eliminate parties entirely.[19]

In the eyes of most of the proponents of the primary law, the legislation passed in 1908 was flawless. For the reformers it meant that they would control the Republican party and that their leaders would be elevated to important public offices. Almost as soon as Governor Hoch signed the bill, the leaders of the Square Deal movement were able to agree on candidates for senator and governor. Because of William Allen White's persistence and Stubbs's realism, Bristow was approved as the reformer who would seek the senatorial nomination. According to these men, the contest would be the premier struggle between reform Republicanism and the forces of conservatism. Bristow's adversary in the race, Chester I. Long, had hoped that both Bristow and Stubbs would oppose him. He found solace in the selection of Bristow since he believed that Stubbs would be a far more formidable opponent. Nevertheless, he did expect a difficult and distasteful contest with his former ally.[20]

The opinions of Long and his followers about Bristow as a reformer conditioned their belief that he would be easier to defeat than Stubbs. Despite earlier claims that Bristow was an up-to-date version of the former Populist senator William A. Peffer, neither Long nor his supporters felt that Bristow, their one-time associate, was a sincere advocate of change. In their view he was a political fortune hunter, one who was interested in office for the office's sake alone; and, as such, they were certain that he could be discredited publicly.[21]

They based this belief on Bristow's correspondence with Long in early 1906. Unable to secure Long's support in the senatorial race that was unfolding that year, Bristow wrote the senator that without the aid of Long's friends, his only hope for victory was "to make a crusade throughout the state against the railroads and corporations." Adding that although he did not want to do this, as affairs stood, he felt compelled to do so.[22]

Bristow had the reputation of being cool and aloof, which also indicated to Long's associates that Long would beat him. Although they admitted that Bristow could be an effective stump speaker who would sway some voters, they felt that his inability to project a warm, compassionate image hurt him as the self-styled "popular candidate." One opponent had written on an earlier occasion that Bristow had admirers but few supporters.[23]

In 1908, however, personality defects that might normally have ended the career of a man like Bristow were to work to his advantage. In a number of middle western states, revolts against traditional, glad-handing Republican politicians were under way, and earnest, humorless men were replacing them. Bristow was essentially one of these dour characters, having been described by a friend as a man whose earnestness was almost tragic, a man who became unspeakably pathetic when he tried to assume a light and jovial manner.[24]

Bristow was a newspaper publisher in his early years, but after 1895 his career as a journalist was frequently interrupted as he became involved in Republican politics at the state level. In 1894, when he had been an unsuccessful candidate for the Fifth Congressional District nomination, he became connected with Cy Leland, who promoted him to secretary of the Republican State Central Committee. In 1895 Governor E. N. Morrill appointed Bristow as his private secretary. But it was during the free-silver campaign in 1896 that he made his biggest political advance. That year, while serving as secretary to the Republican State Central Committee, he helped to plan the presidential campaign in Kansas. He met William McKinley and apparently became friendly with the future president. His acquaintanceship served him well, because in 1897, when McKinley was filling minor federal offices, he appointed Bristow to be fourth assistant postmaster general, reportedly over Senator Mark Hanna's opposition.[25]

Bristow gained national prominence for his work in the postal service. In 1900 he was sent to Cuba to investigate charges of fraud in the postal system established there after the Spanish-American War. During his investigation he reportedly ran afoul of Senator Hanna, since Hanna had placed a number of his friends in the Cuban office, and Bristow had accused them of fraud. Hanna pressured McKinley to have Bristow removed, but the president, wishing to upgrade the quality of public life on the island, stood staunchly by Bristow. Hanna's appointees were subsequently jailed.[26]

Bristow's effort received widespread attention in the national press and particularly in Kansas. He earned a reputation for being a fearless investigator and a simon-pure politician. Thus, when the hint of scandal arose again in the Post Office Department in 1903, he was chosen to investigate it. When President Theodore Roosevelt appointed him, he told Bristow to seek "the whole truth." He said that he "cared not a rap who [was] hit."[27]

But Roosevelt was a politician as well as a crusader; therefore, when

Bristow's investigations showed that a number of important congressmen were implicated, thus interfering somewhat with Roosevelt's presidential plans in 1904, Roosevelt had had enough. He decided that corruption had been eliminated from the postal service, and although he commended Bristow for his excellent work, he condemned him for being overzealous. Roosevelt wrote to the postmaster general, Ethan Allen Hitchcock, that Bristow had been so carried away that the post-office inspectors under Bristow had "proceeded upon the assumption that there was fraud everywhere and made reports that were not backed up by the facts, with the result that it was both humiliating and harmful."[28]

In January 1905 Bristow resigned from the Post Office Department under pressure from Congress and the president. He later said that he had not wished to leave office but had felt compelled to do so. Feeling that Bristow had been misused, another Kansas appointee in Washington wrote home: "One day they're it, and the next day nowhere."[29] In a letter to Senator Long, Roosevelt later denied that he had forced Bristow to resign, stating that it was absurd to pay heed to such stories.[30] After he had resigned, Bristow was appointed to a commisson that was investigating the handling of contracts for the construction of the Panama Canal. In the course of his inquiries he journeyed to the Canal Zone, where he wrote a number of reports regarding affairs there. After having completed his work in Panama, he returned in late 1905, hoping to secure another federal appointment. He made an unsuccessful bid for the Senate in 1906.[31]

Bristow's campaign in 1908 was conditioned by the antirailroad fever that was running high then. Politicians all over Kansas had to "get right" on the railroad issue. Among other things, "getting right" meant supporting President Roosevelt in his advocacy of the Hepburn bill. Senator Long was the first important Kansas officeholder to feel the need to do this.

In late 1905 the Wichita Chamber of Commerce, as well as other commercial clubs in Kansas, asked Long to state his position on railroad reform. Apparently caught unprepared by the request, Long marked time by claiming that out of courtesy he should not make a statement while the Senate was conducting hearings on the question of amending the Interstate Commerce Commission Act. His answer displeased Kansans. Other senators were stating their opinions, the president of the Wichita Chamber of Commerce told him, adding that he didn't think that "'senatorial courtesy' (whatever that may mean) demands silence from a man when his constituents are asking for him to speak on a public question of this kind."[32]

Long avoided making a statement until he could find out what attitudes some of his leading supporters—primarily Kansas railroad attorneys—were expressing regarding the proposed legislation. Because they appeared to be opposed to the Hepburn bill, Long found it necessary to return to the state and convince them that widespread support for stronger railroad regulation necessitated his favoring it. Long's friends reminded him of what he well knew, that since 1903 it had been "whispered about that 'the allied money power' supplied [him] . . . with the 'sinews of war' when [he] . . . was elected." "You should be careful," one friend added, "and do nothing that would tend in any way to confirm that suspicion."[33] On 9 November 1905 Long met quietly with attorneys Marcus A. Low of the Rock Island and N. H. Loomis of the Union Pacific and received their approval for his support of a compromise version of the Hepburn measure.[34]

Railroad officials were changing their opinions regarding possible regulation in November of 1905. The Esch-Townshend bill, which died in the 1904-1905 session of Congress, would have allowed the Interstate Commerce Commission to set new "reasonable rates" after I.C.C. hearings and make them effective after a period of thirty days. Aware that some form of legislation would pass, officials of most railroads decided that they should support a measure that would not be "radical" but would serve their interests. Thus, they supported the law that bore Colonel Pete Hepburn's name.

Before the measure passed Congress, it was amended to suit the wishes of railroad officials. In this way it became a different law from the one that Roosevelt had initially suggested. He had favored a form of restricted judicial review that would have allowed courts to consider I.C.C. decisions only on the basis of procedural due process. He had also supported immediate implementation of I.C.C. orders. Senator Long "got right with Roosevelt" by engineering the so-called compromise between the president's initial position and that of railroad spokesmen in Congress. His compromise gave the railroads the "broad" judicial review that they had sought. It allowed appeals from I.C.C. opinions on both substantive and procedural due process. Moreover, the "compromise" allowed railroads to delay the implementation of I.C.C. decisions until they had exhausted all appeals to federal courts.[35]

Believing that his compromise would satisfy the complaints of Kansas reformers, Long wrote: "I hope that what has happened here can be utilized to good effect in the state in preventing Mr. Stubbs from . . . assuming to represent the people and the President."[36] Roosevelt had already told Long that "my position now is exactly yours." He added that in the recent compromise they had gone as far as was possible at the time.[37]

Roosevelt's acceptance of the Long compromise disgusted a number of Kansas railroad reformers, but they did not publicly express their feelings since Roosevelt was extremely popular in the state. Privately they agreed with A. A. Richard's judgment that "if the railroads did not write the [Hepburn] law the fellows who got it up did just as good a job for the railroads as the best railroad attorney could have done."[38]

By 1907 Long was fully aware of the strength that reformers had developed in Kansas. His role during 1906 in Congress did not impress the "Square Dealers," and his support of Curtis in the 1907 senatorial race and his opposition to the primary law made him their main adversary. At first he believed that he could mollify some reformers by seeming to support their ideas on railroad reform. The others, his supporters informed him, were part of the traditional opposition, which was centered in the old Populist counties and in areas that were consistently anti-Long.[39] He seemed to be sure that he would be renominated.

But in April, Long began to view affairs differently; he started worrying about a strenuous reelection fight, and he decided to make a more direct appeal to the public. He wrote Senator Curtis that "the situation in the state is so serious that it will require some very careful attention." To offset the Square Deal movement he suggested that Curtis and he form Taft Clubs. In this manner they could both demonstrate their support of William Howard Taft for the presidency and show that they adhered to Roosevelt's wishes. Taft was Roosevelt's choice for the presidential nomination in 1908.[40] But Taft Clubs such as Long wanted failed to materialize when Curtis proved reluctant and when Long discovered that Republicans of every persuasion supported Taft's nomination. The presidential question was settled at the December 27 meeting of the state committee, with all factions favoring Taft. A Taft delegation was elected just as easily at state and congressional conventions in 1908.[41]

Thus, presidential politics did not affect the first Kansas primary, which was one of the liveliest and most vicious campaigns in the recent history of the state. It began quietly in April, when Long's friends tried to coax Governor Hoch and former Governor Willis J. Bailey into the race in order to offset some of Bristow's appeal in eastern Kansas. At first Long allowed political appointees to handle his campaign, while he remained in Washington. Mort Albaugh established Long's election headquarters in Topeka in February, and in March the senator's private secretary, Ralph Faxon, was sent to manage it.[42]

Billy Morgan was named as campaign chairman. By writing letters and by sending political agents around the state, he created Long organizations at the county level. Kansas City banker C. S. Jobes was entrusted with raising funds, although traditional contributions, such as those given by Long's appointees, were sent directly to the senator. Long indicated that he would not ask for nor expect funds from corporations, but he did accept donations from railroad attorneys. Moreover, railroad officials indicated that they were working for his reelection, and at least one of his personal representatives used a free railroad pass to travel about Kansas on political business.[43]

Until mid May there was nothing extraordinary about Long's campaign. There were, of course, numerous complaints from his managers. Bristow began an extensive speaking tour in late April, and some of Long's supporters felt that Long should do something spectacular to counter its effects. They suggested that he make a speech of "grandstand magnitude" in the Senate so that copies might be distributed to Kansas voters. Furthermore, they wanted him to make it abundantly clear that he supported the so-called Roosevelt policies in Washington as well as in Kansas. Long's backers were worried about charges that he felt so certain of reelection that he did not intend to become involved in stump appearances and other ritualistic actions expected of campaigners. They warned him that affairs were not "as they ought to be" in Kansas and that he had better get home to take care of business on his own. "Frankly," Albaugh wrote, "I cannot get away from the feeling that there is danger ahead."[44]

But Long was receiving other advice, indicating that developments were not as bad as his campaign managers said they were. Marcus Low informed the senator on May 16 that "the situation here looks quite favorable . . . for yourself." Charles Gleed had noted earlier that prospects for a good harvest were keeping the people "in a general way good natured." "I do not believe," he added, "they will get sufficiently excited over . . . Bristow or anybody else to beat you." Long's anxiety about crusade-minded Wichita was quieted by Morgan, who noted that all political workers in the city favored Long. The only opposition came from the city's commercial club, which was gradually being drawn towards Long's camp.[45]

Then, during the third week of May, William Allen White, who was

Bristow's manager and the mastermind of his campaign, unloaded a political bombshell. He sent a selected list of Long's voting record in the Senate to three metropolitan dailies—the *Kansas City Star*, the *Topeka Daily Capital,* and the *Wichita Eagle.* The list, which included Long's votes on private and public bills, on unimportant and important measures, was said to indicate that the senator did not represent the people of Kansas. To a degree it proved that Long allied himself with corporate interests and voted against measures that since 1900 had come to be identified with "the people."[46]

Long's lieutenants, already disturbed, became frantic. They reported that everywhere they were encountering bad effects from White's attack and that Long must return to Kansas to refute the Emporian's charges. "There is no question," Albaugh wrote the senator, "that the White article . . . hurt badly. It is one of those indefinite things where he simply gives pages of the Congressional Record together with the absolute statement that your vote was for Wall Street and against the interest of the people of Kansas. He raises . . . doubt." Because Long's friends were not familiar with his stands on specific laws listed in White's charges, Albaugh suggested that Long frame a reply that would turn the affair to their advantage.[47]

Long knew what to do. Charles Gleed told him to reply "by stating facts and giving the explanation of every vote. Dwell . . . particularly on those votes in which you were co-operating with the President. If I were you I would avoid every indication of trying to dodge the issue."[48] Long planned to do even better. He would go to Emporia, have White beside him on a public platform, and then and there explain away the voting record. White had given him an opening that he could exploit, and the senator happily announced that he "accepted it with full confidence that [he would] . . . be successful."[49]

Emporia's illustrious publisher had become involved in the senatorial campaign of 1908 years before it started. He had been a close friend of Long's when both men belonged to the Leland organization, and in 1901 he had claimed that Long was "a clean, square, honest, brave, intelligent public man." At that time White wrote: "If you need me, . . . wire me and I will come any place you say or . . . [do] any thing you please." Two years later White suggested that the senator assume control of the Kansas Republican party and that he then stamp out factionalism and backbiting. Between 1902 and 1906, however, White became a close friend of President Roosevelt's and, to a lesser degree than he later claimed in his *Autobiography,* an idealistic advocate of the Square Deal. Thus, during 1906, when Senator Long failed to respond properly to the antirailroad crusade in Kansas and when he supported Charles Curtis for the Senate, he became a pariah in White's eyes.[50]

During 1906 and 1907 White became a devotee of what he and a few other Kansans were calling progressivism. He was dissatisfied with the political leadership in the state, and he often lamented the lack of progressive accomplishments. He deplored the fact that Kansas lagged behind Massachusetts, New York, Texas, Oregon, and Ohio in progressive legislation, and after hastily considering her history, he argued that "Kansas ought to become one of the leaders of this new movement."[51] To correct this lack of progressive leadership, he spent 1907 quietly trying, with Stubbs, to arrange for Bristow's candidacy. On 27 January 1908 he opened the "Bristow Boom" with an article in the *Gazette* that placed the former postal inspector in line with "Rooseveltian policies" and pictured him as a leader of the Stubbsian crusade in Kansas. White claimed that although Bristow was not then a candidate for the Senate, he was ready to respond to a grass-roots call. Whether or not the grass roots spoke is a moot question, but on February 6 the fateful conference between Stubbs and Bristow was engineered by White, and Bristow left the meeting as a senatorial hopeful.[52]

White immediately set to work to elect his candidate. He developed the rudiments of county organizations, started a publicity campaign, began to raise funds, and scheduled speeches by important national reformers who supported Bristow. He brought Senators Robert M. La Follette and William E. Borah into the state. La Follette, who was deservedly considered by White as America's leading Republican reformer, came because he loathed Long. Borah, a former Kansan who had become prominent as an Idaho reformer, spoke for Bristow to repay a political debt that he owed to White.[53]

Long returned to Kansas, and on June 10 he appeared on the stage of the Emporia Opera House with White. Considerable ballyhoo accompanied Long's arrival, and a circuslike atmosphere prevailed on the night of the meeting. Each man had his own claque present, but during the course of the evening, Long gained the better of the match. He had discovered 3 mistakes in White's 35-point indictment, and he hammered away at these, forcing White to admit his errors. The senator implied that the 3 mistakes only illustrated White's greater error in opposing him. He inferred that none of the charges brought by White was accurate, and he denounced the Emporian for having included only 35 of the 699 roll-call votes that Long had cast during his congressional career.

White could not adequately give and take with a man who had held his own in debates with "Sockless Jerry" Simpson. But White had his newspaper, and the next day he loosed a general barrage of charges against Long that easily erased any ground lost the previous night. White complained that the senator was still a willing tool of the special interests. Privately, White held the same opinion, although he admitted that Long was a good citizen except for being ideologically committed to corporation views.[54]

The June encounter neither improved nor hindered Long's campaign, but it did make it livelier. The senator's record was not his major weakness. His main political mistakes were his unwillingness to discuss most current issues and his desire to stress the shortcomings in the personality of his opponent. Long refused to mention Bristow during the Emporia meeting, hoping to show that White was the impressario of the opposition. This, he felt, would make Bristow appear to be incompetent and incapable of conducting his own campaign. It would indicate that Bristow was weak politically, thus causing professional politicians to withdraw their support from him. The senator was also helping to circulate a rumor that he had made a "deal" with the former postal inspector. He hinted that if Bristow were defeated, Long would try to induce Taft to appoint Bristow postmaster general. He intended to make Bristow appear to be a half-hearted candidate.[55]

When Bristow left no doubt by his campaigning that he was a serious candidate, Long recognized the fact and introduced a letter that Bristow purportedly had written to Long in 1905, asking the senator to secure a soft federal job for him. Bristow reportedly had told Long that with a job that would not necessitate his leaving Kansas, he could take care of the senator's interests in the state. The letter was used to demonstrate Bristow's opportunism, with Long's supporters claiming that Bristow would never have become a reformer if he had received such an appointment. When the two candidates appeared in a joint debate in Topeka at the close of the campaign, Long was still avoiding most issues and discussing Bristow's opportunism.[56]

One issue that Long did not avoid, though he might have profited by evading it, was the regulation of railroads. Long would not advocate expanded power for the I.C.C., and he would not support the setting of rates on the basis of railroad valuation. His biggest mistake in rate-conscious Kansas was his position on discrimination in rates for long and short hauls. Hoping to gain an edge over Kansas City, Missouri, the reformers supported rates based on the mileage system, a position that Bristow advocated in 1908 and later in the Senate.

Long, however, favored discriminatory rates and opposed rates based on mileage. He argued correctly when he said that "if the railroads had not been permitted to make special rates on grain and other products produced by the farmers of the Mississippi Valley, these farmers would never have been able to compete with the farmers of New York and New England." With special rates for a long haul, they could and did drive farmers from the eastern United States out of business. The stopping of special rates on manufactured goods sent to large population centers in the West, which the reformers wanted, would invite the end of favorable rates on grain shipped east. Long therefore opposed the demand for rates based on mileage and favored differentials for long and short hauls. He seemed to be motivated by the state's interests, but his explanation was too involved, and, more importantly, it did not satisfy the small-town jobbers in Kansas, who were hungry for favorable rates.[57]

On other issues the senator fared no better. He would not take specific stands on many measures. After the national convention he repeatedly said that he supported the Republican platform, a document widely criticized for its conservative character. Moreover, he was constitutionally opposed to yielding to the meaningless generalities of the reform clamor in the state, stating that "if the people of Kansas want the kind of Senator that is always ready to take extreme positions against corporations and attack them, . . . then evidently I do not fill the bill and the sooner I retire . . . the better they will be satisfied."[58]

When asked if he backed the principles promoted by Taft in his presidential acceptance speech, Long refused to answer because he was uncertain of their meaning, and on at least one occasion he stated frankly that he would not pledge himself to support all of "Roosevelt's policies." When pressed by his managers to ask Roosevelt for a statement to the effect that the senator had generally supported the president, Long answered: "If the people of Kansas are not convinced that I was in accord with the President on the important questions . . . then nothing . . . he will say could change the situation."[59]

Roosevelt never did repudiate claims made by Long's friends that he and Long had normally been in close agreement on issues. Nor did he comment on a letter circulated by Long in which the President praised him for his work on the Hepburn Act. In later years Long came to believe that he was not reelected to the Senate because he failed to advocate Roosevelt's policies in 1908. Whether he was making the distinction between advocacy and support is unclear, but his failure to convince the voters either way during the campaign hurt him.[60]

The impression that Long was unfriendly to Roosevelt's policies was created largely in one way, but it was disseminated in a number of ways. The precise meaning of the term "Roosevelt's policies" was never clear, but it was used generally to mean opposition to "predatory wealth" and "special interests." In this way, when Long was called a "railroad senator," it meant that he favored special interests and thus opposed Roosevelt's ideals. This type of logical confusion was presented to the public through many reform newspapers in Kansas and by *Collier's* magazine in a July article carrying the provocative title "Long of Kansas: The Third in a Series of Studies of Senate Undesirables."

In the article, Long was described as a "railroad senator" who had not been bought by the lines, because "the point of view of the railroads is his own point of view." The role that railroads had played in his election in 1903 was elaborated upon, and his attempt to place Missouri Pacific attorney Alexander Cochrane on the Circuit Court was noted. Much of the criticism in the article related to Long's voting record; this indicated that William Allen White probably wrote the story, despite the by-line of J. M. Oakison. White, of course, was a personal friend of the editor of *Collier's*, Norman Hapgood.[61]

Campaign circulars, such as the one entitled "The Line-up of Long: For Delegates and Dollars vs. People and Popular Government," were also used to create the impression that Long was a man of the "special interests" and would, as the circulars said, be denouncing Roosevelt as a wild Populist if he were not a popular president. "Where did Long get his money for the 1908 campaign?" it asked. "Can a legislator accept munificent sums, or small for that matter, for his campaign expenses from special interests . . . and be honest?"[62]

The remaining Square Dealers in Kansas were not to be left out in the assault on Long. Long had failed to answer their questionnaire in 1906, and their former chairman, James A. Troutman, was interested in having his say about the senator. Troutman contributed one of several circular letters that compared Long and Bristow and their careers. Troutman charged that Long was conservative, cowardly, and a tool of corrupt influences, while Bristow was brave, progressive, and a man of parts. "Bristow has a backbone," he exclaimed, "Long is an invertebrate!"[63]

Bristow's speeches also helped to fashion the impression that Long was not a true Rooseveltian. White decided early in the campaign that this approach would be good politics, and Bristow agreed. Bristow, however, was moderate in his denunciations of Long, withholding malicious charges and condemnations of the variety that White and Troutman developed. This lack of fire distressed White, who believed that much could be accomplished by acrimony. On a number of occasions White became extremely upset with his candidate. In mid June he wrote, "Oh Lord, . . . if it was only Victor Murdock." Much of White's concern stemmed from his beliefs that Bristow's campaign lacked vigor and that it was not reaching enough people. "You make a loud noise," he informed Bristow, "and the roaring in your head makes you think there is something doing, but there isn't!"[64]

Actually, Bristow's campaign, in the days before the wide use of motor cars, was a gigantic endeavor. He spoke in seventy-one counties, delivering seventy-two formal addresses during fifteen weeks. He traveled by horse and buggy, appearing in little halls and country schoolhouses, at farm picnics and old soldier's reunions. He condemned the boss of the United States Senate, Nelson Aldrich; spoke against railroad corruption; and opposed stock and grain gambling in the East. His campaign might have seemed meek and mild to White, but to his opponents it seemed as if the spirit of Mary "Yellin" Lease had returned. Albaugh wrote that Bristow operated his campaign on the same theory "that the crusaders used to work up their cohorts to retake the holy land." Bristow later claimed that he had found it hard to cover a state as large as Kansas and that the young men had been easier to influence than the middle-aged voters. "The old soldier and the young man were usually . . . enthusiastic," he wrote, "the old soldier because you could arouse in him a patriotism and the young man because he was full of ambition and new and progressive ideas."[65]

Bristow's speeches were filled with progressive idealism. He supported La Follette's program to regulate rates on the basis of railroad evaluation; he asked expanded powers for the I.C.C., including the right to investigate rates on its own initiative; and he favored limiting the capitalization of railroads to their actual cost. He advocated the conservation of coal lands and revision of the Dingley tariff. He opposed the Aldrich currency bill and "any other bill by that man!" "While I am an ardent Republican," he said on one occasion, "I am not an ultra partisan. I will cooperate with . . . any political party in behalf of measures that are for the best interest of my constituents."[66]

Bristow closed his campaign with a series of debates with Long. At first he tried to avoid such encounters, but despite Long's reputation as a debater, White pressed Bristow to accept. White argued that Long would give Bristow exposure; unless Bristow failed miserably, he would profit from the crowds that Long would draw. The general opinion that prevailed after the debates was that despite Long's magnificent style, Bristow had had the better of the matches. Bristow later wrote that the debate at Sterling, Kansas, had turned voter momentum in his favor. He noted: "The time was right but the need was the current to start the thing running. Long went into the Sterling debate with absolute confidence in his ability to wipe me off the earth, but he did not. . . . The people present seemed to feel I had the best of it."[67] Bristow closed his campaign in Topeka, sharing the platform again with Long. Once more Bristow bested the senator, as the public mocked Long constantly about his voting record. A reporter for the *Topeka State Journal* wrote that the audience had badgered Long continually and that "the Senator looked like a beaten man."[68]

On August 4, Kansans cast their first vote in a senatorial primary, giving Joseph L. Bristow a victory margin of more than six thousand votes, 63,115 to 56,839. In the all-important legislative districts he won with a majority of nine senatorial and representative districts. Bristow's greatest strength was in central Kansas, where support for railroad reform had taken deep root. In the center of the state he carried twenty-one of the twenty-five counties, losing one by a single vote. In western Kansas he fared almost as well. Despite the fact that Long resided in that area, Bristow won thirty-one of the fifty-four counties. Only the semi-industrial eastern part of the state did not support him. There he carried only nine of twenty-seven counties, losing ten by extremely wide margins. He believed that he lost the southeastern corner partly because he did not campaign enough there. Other factors also worked against him. Lead, coal, and oil producers were not tariff revisionists; nor were the small businessmen of the area interested in ending discrimination by the railroads, since they paid the same tariffs as businessmen in Kansas City, Missouri. Moreover, Bristow was linked with Walter R. Stubbs, the reformers' gubernatorial candidate, and in the heavy-drinking mining districts Stubbs's prohibitionist ideas did not sit well. Bristow's poor showing in the northeastern corner of Kansas can be explained in much the same manner, but there an added factor hurt him. Cy Leland, Stubbs's opponent in the gubernatorial contest, had once led a powerful political machine in that area, and remnants of it were still intact, fighting the reformers in 1908.[69]

The primary race between Leland and Stubbs was a side show compared to the main attraction that was being staged by Bristow and Long.

Leland never seriously challenged Stubbs, since, as one biased journalist put it, "everyone knew Stubbs accomplished more for the good of Kansas in four year in politics than the venerable warrior of Troy had in forty years."[70] Leland could do little to counteract his reputation as a political manipulator, and Stubbs did little to gain the nomination. Compared to his campaigns in 1910 and 1912, Stubbs's 1908 effort was a minor one. The reform press, spearheaded by the *Topeka Daily Capital*, supported him, and only his antilabor, antiliquor reputation hurt him anywhere. He carried ninety-one of the one hundred and five Kansas counties, but he lost some populous semi-industrial areas in the southeastern and northeastern parts of the state. He won every county that Bristow carried save antiprohibitionist Sedgwick. He received 70,977 votes to Leland's 53,046.[71]

The reform press was jubilant over Stubbs's and Bristow's victories, claiming that defeat of their opponents signaled the redemption of the Republican party from the hell of corporate control and machine domination. Reflecting upon his success, Bristow attributed it to the people's weariness with paying exorbitant freight rates on goods shipped into the area and on their opportunity to express a choice for senator directly through the primary. He felt that the eastern press emphasized Senator La Follette's role in the election too much, but he admitted that the senator had helped. To Taft, the party's presidential nominee, Bristow wrote: "The nomination of Mr. Stubbs is a fortunate one, and the fact that Senator Long is not on the Ticket is also fortunate. . . . He simply has failed to convince the people of his . . . sympathy with the 'Roosevelt policies,' and as a result, thousands of them are exceedingly hostile to him."[72]

Long's opinion about why he had been defeated differed substantially from Bristow's appraisal. "I was defeated by Democrats and independents calling for Republican tickets," he wrote Congressman Edmond H. Madison. "I have been defeated twice before by such votes at general elections, but this is my first experience with the members of other parties participating in a Republican contest determining the results."[73] Long remained bitter after his defeat, avoiding Bristow and making no move to appear conciliatory towards the new Republican candidate. This caused a great deal of worry for Bristow, who feared that the candidates of a divided party might not be able to win at the general election.[74]

Three weeks after the primary election, Republicans met in Topeka to write their party platform. Before the adoption of the primary system, they had written the platform at the state convention. But in 1908 and thereafter, a party council, which was composed of candidates for office, as well as state and county political leaders, was convened for this purpose. Thus, on August 25, the Republican council gathered in the capital city. Bristow and Stubbs, having won the recent elections, were in control of the meeting, and they kept it a moderately tame affair. Their friends were selected to important offices on the council, and their opinions were written into the state platform. The two men had already agreed on specific provisions that were to be included in the platform. At the council, by requiring a two-thirds majority to amend the report of the resolutions committee, they succeeded in pushing their ideas past all opposition.

Bristow wrote the national portions of the platform, incorporating the major issues of his recent campaign into it. The segment dealing with state affairs was composed by Stubbs, who committed the party to support laws dealing with conservation, railroads, education, and unfair business practices. Specifically, this part of the platform called for laws that would forbid unregistered lobbyists, require publication of campaign expenditures, and make the Kansas State Tax Commission elective. A law to guarantee bank deposits was promised, as was a "Blue-Sky" investment law and a law limiting the indebtedness of railroads. In all, the platform was what could have been expected, considering the nature of the primary in 1908.[75]

If a person had judged the Kansas Republican party on the basis of disaffection of certain leaders with the organization after the primary, he would probably have concluded that in November none of the party's important candidates would win. Superficially, 10 to 15 percent of the voting strength of the organization seemed to be ready to bolt the major candidates. But beneath the apparent discord a reconciliation was being forged, with the reformers in the unfamiliar role of conciliators. Following the party council, the caucus of the state committee allowed the reformers a chance to pacify a number of their opponents. Nonreform Republicans were given positions of leadership on the state committee, and letters from conservatives after this meeting indicated that intraparty disagreement was being resolved.[76]

During October the deepest divisions were healed, and by the time of the general election a nearly unified Republican effort was possible. As in the past, Republican candidates won most of the elections. Stubbs handily defeated his Democratic opponent, Jeremiah Botkin, by 196,692 to 162,385 votes. He polled 40,000 more votes than Hoch had in 1906, and 10,000 more than Hoch had in 1904, despite greater interest on the part of voters in the previous presidential year. Taft carried the state, and all eight Republican candidates for Congress were elected. A Republican majority was returned to both the Kansas House and Senate. This fact assured Bristow's election by the legislature the following January.[77]

The Republican victory in Kansas illustrated a trend in middle western states that year. In areas where progressives dominated the party, Republican majorities were returned; but in states where conservatives continued in control, Democrats took office. In Kansas, reformers captured almost all of the party machinery and gained the positions of governor and U.S. senator. At last they were given an opportunity to try to translate their ideas into laws. This work they set about doing in Topeka, with the convening of the legislature in January 1909, and in Washington, when a special session of Congress met in March. The reformers understood that unless their new strength bore legislative results, they would be politically doomed. Their first test came in Kansas, but eventually they were destined to stand or fall on the basis of their national performance.

# 7

## THE STATE
## AND GOVERNOR STUBBS, 1909-1911

After Walter R. Stubbs left the governor's mansion in 1912, William Allen White remarked that he thought Stubbs had been the best governor in Kansas history. Stubbs had secured important reforms and had furthered the cause of honest government. He had been successful, White concluded, despite a stubborn, impolitic nature and an attitude that undoubtedly marked him as a crank.[1]

Although Stubbs's personality was a hindrance to him as a reform governor, equally burdensome was the opposition of many of the most adroit legislators in both political parties. He was never able to master the intricacies of the legislative process, but he salvaged much of his program by taking advantage of the popularity of reform. In this way he forced reluctant legislators to support his goals. The governor's choice of men to manage the administration's programs in both the 1909 and 1911 state legislatures was poor, and only by his dynamic personal intervention midway through each session was Stubbs able to save what better floor leaders should have accomplished.

His legislative managers were inexperienced, while his opposition came from older Democratic and Republican leaders who were wise in the ways of parliamentary rules. Characteristically, he lost some of the "old guard" support because he would not play the game of provincial politics. He vetoed unimportant but expensive local bills. He shunned legislators socially, when invitations to the governor's mansion might have won additional votes for issues that he was vitally interested in. Although on a few occasions he acted as a hardened dispenser of patronage, he usually refused to make purely political appointments. He was incapable of the comradery that was typical of politics even in this era of reform. But Stubbs's apparent weaknesses were actually his greatest strengths. Because he was unorthodox, because he refused to yield to temptations that normally govern political relationships, he earned the respect of reputable men and of Kansas voters. "He is awfully square and fine and true," White wrote in 1911, "but he is not a friendly man. I have come to admire him deeply. . . . [He] is a man who is essentially strong and brave and wise, if not always just and sympathetic."[2]

During the 1908 campaign Stubbs had paid little attention to various Republican primary contests for the state legislature. He had entered none of the local fights on the side of progressive candidates, as White had wanted him to do, and after his nomination and election he had come to Topeka without any detailed plans for organizing the reform forces in the 1909 legislative session. The success of the reform campaign of 1908, he assumed, would help his program through the legislature, since he proposed to ask for little more at the session than Republicans had promised in their state platform. He indicated that the speakership of the Kansas house should be given to his close supporter, Representative Jonathan N. Dolley, who had been chosen as Republican state chairman. When Dolley's election as Speaker was easily secured at the Republican caucus in January, Stubbs apparently felt that little more needed to be done to prepare for the session.[3]

The governor's first concern upon taking office was to arrange for appointees to fill positions vacated as a result of the change of administrations. In jobs closely associated with the governor's office, Stubbs placed his personal friends; but in positions where ability was most important, he allowed competent officials to remain, or he engaged men who were qualified by experience and training to fill them. His attitude regarding patronage was one of his biggest problems, and certainly one that contributed to some of his legislative woes.

He tried to keep men who smoked or drank off the state payroll; and as a governor dedicated to economy, he cut agency staffs as much as possible. He believed that many people were employed by the state simply to satisfy political needs. Once in office, he eliminated sinecures that might have been used to achieve his legislative ends. To one of the many supplicants who had worked loyally for his election, he wrote:

"There has been a large reduction in the number of employees in some of the departments and will be less patronage under this administration than . . . under the former one. But, this is simply carrying out the policy which was outlined publicly before my nomination and election."[4] His determination to adhere to campaign promises did not satisfy the needs of county leaders, and many local politicians complained bitterly about his parsimonious distribution of state offices and funds related to them.[5]

Of course, Stubbs made exceptions in the use of the appointive power. The case of Thomas ("Bent") Murdock serves as a notable example of Stubbs's yielding to the spoils system. Murdock had been a leader of the Republican "railroad ring" in the late nineteenth century, but after 1906 he had become a prime mover of reform. In 1908 he had supported Stubbs, and after the election he had appeared in Topeka, looking for a job. He reportedly asked to be named to the proposed public-utilities commission, an appointment that his past experience made impossible. To avoid the distasteful task confronting him, the governor asked Senator Joseph L. Bristow to recommend Murdock to President William Howard Taft for the position of commissioner of the Missouri Valley pension agency in Topeka. But Bristow, at odds with Senator Charles Curtis regarding federal appointments in Kansas, could not help.[6]

Pressured by Murdock's long-time friend William Allen White, Stubbs settled the matter by naming "Bent" fish and game commissioner, a position that Murdock seemed qualified to fill. Justifying the appointment and excusing the governor for making it, White wrote: "It does not require executive or administrative ability. Murdock will have direct charge of no funds and will be responsible for no policy, and he could do the work admirably without the slightest danger of error." Presumably, anyone could, but State Treasurer James Nation later complained about Murdock's performance.[7]

Although appointments such as Murdock's could not improve the quality of executive government in the state, Kansas laws were administered better under Stubbs than ever before. In some ways the governor alone was responsible for this improvement, but in others he was helped by highly competent, energetic men who had been elected to minor state offices. For example, a dispute in 1911 between Stubbs and John R. Dawson, the attorney general, concerning the proper enforcement of prohibition obscured the fact that both men did outstanding work in enforcing antiliquor laws in areas that were notorious for their violations of them. The 1909 session of the legislature passed a "bone-dry" liquor law, forbidding the sale of intoxicating beverages anywhere in Kansas, including drugstores, which had previously been exempt. At the 1911 session the governor was given the power both to remove county officials who failed to enforce state laws and to call special elections in order to replace them.

Armed with these enactments, Stubbs moved into Kansas City and Wichita and into Crawford and Cherokee counties, the heartlands of moonshining and bootlegging. In the southeastern section—soon to become known as the Little Balkans because of its turbulent immigrant population—Kansans operated illegal distilleries twenty-four hours a day in abandoned coal mines, and liquor was dispensed freely from taverns. A shocked temperance officer, J. K. Codding, describing what confronted him when he crusaded in one of the towns in that area in 1905, wrote to a friend:

> The conditions there beggar description. Twenty-two saloons, one saloon for every 131 inhabitants, and one saloon for every 34 miners. Little boys in knee pants buy and drink liquor over the bar, playing cards in the saloons until away into the night; a thirteen year old girl as bar tender; mothers setting their babies down on the floor and rushing across with a pail and getting beer. All being poisoned and degraded by the liquor traffic. The first thing you ought to do, before you attempt to make a speech or send a dollar to the Hindu missions, is to go to Frontenac . . . and spend a night, and you will be so filled with the necessity of the right kind of work in Kansas, that you will not have any peace of mind, until you can do something to help these men in their immoralities.[8]

Understandably, Stubbs would say that he intended to go after lawbreakers in Crawford County "roughshod." "I trust," he added, "we shall be able to accomplish some good there." At first he brought the Crawford County sheriff to Topeka to warn him that he would be removed if he continued to be dilatory in his enforcement of the prohibition law; then he told representatives from the area that the state militia would be sent to both counties if the liquor laws were not properly enforced. He used a $10,000 contingency fund, $6,000 higher than that of his predecessor, to send special investigators to the southeastern part of the state and prosecute violators of the law.[9]

The illegal open saloon gradually disappeared from the area, although clandestine sales of "deep-shaft" whiskies continued. Stubbs's effectiveness was underscored in a number of ways, but the most dramatic was in threats sent to him by one tavern owner who promised to assassinate him if ever he ventured into the mining district. The governor announced, with some justification, in 1912 that the state had been cleared of liquor-law violators, albeit a few distilleries remained in operation, and a few drinking parlors sold whiskey on the sly.[10]

Stubbs had not carried the southeastern corner of Kansas in the 1908 election because of his prohibitionist sentiments, but an antiunion, antilabor reputation had hurt him there also. As governor, he had a number of opportunities to correct this impression, and he proved that he was neither antiunion nor antilabor. He helped to secure laws that were favorable to laborers, and he enforced legislation that was designed to improve working conditions in the coal fields. He was one of a very few Kansas chief executives who heeded complaints from miners that safety regulations were not being properly enforced. Working with Erasmus Haworth, a professor at the University of Kansas, he ordered investigations into mining operations, and he directed the attorney general to use the courts to make mine operators meet the comprehensive safety standards that had been provided in the 1890s by Kansas legislatures.[11]

His most impressive actions, however, were taken during a labor walkout in May 1910. In the past, the Southwestern Interstate Coal Operators Association had greeted strikes by Kansas miners with appeals to the state for protection from riotous, unruly unionists. In 1910 the same pattern was used after a general shutdown resulted from contract failures in the coal fields. After he had received a number of pleas for state troops, the governor dispatched an assistant attorney general to southeastern Kansas to check on conditions there and to make recommendations with regard to future state action. The investigation resulted in a report that denied that there was violence and concluded that a low standard of living among the workers was the cause for labor troubles.[12]

When the operators' association wrote Stubbs again, the governor delivered a stinging reply. "I regret," he retorted, "the tone of your letter. It has given me the impression that your association is not as keenly alive to the importance of conciliation and arbitration . . . as it is to the use of the state's military force in the coercion of your employees." He added that the state would not send troops to force men to accept wages that were "unreasonably low and entirely insufficient to maintain themselves and their families." If conditions did not improve in the area, he threatened to use troops in the way that Roosevelt had planned to do in Pennsylvania during 1902.[13]

Stubbs was also responsible for labor laws that in his day were considered radical social legislation. He supported an employers' liability law and a workmen's compensation act. Both measures had been endorsed by the 1910 Republican platform and included in the governor's message to the legislature in 1911. Passage of them would have been easy had not the liability law angered the railroads and the compensation act frightened small businessmen and Kansas farmers.

In hearings before the senate, three railroads sent their chief attorneys to protest the liability law on the grounds that it was a punitive measure that would provide unnecessary protection for workingmen. The two features that the railroads disliked were the regularization of legal procedures in order to stop the railroads from shifting court jurisdictions and the elimination of contributory negligence as a defense. The bill did provide for comparative negligence, which allowed juries to reduce payments for damages according to how much the employee had contributed to his own injury. In this form the bill passed.[14]

The workmen's compensation act proved to be a more difficult proposition to carry. Two key groups of supporters of the progressive Republicans—small-town merchants and big farmers—opposed the idea of state compensation for injuries, at least in the form that the bill initially took. To make the legislation acceptable to the powerful mercantile and farm groups, Stubbs reluctantly had to amend it so that firms with fewer than fifteen employees would be exempt from its provisions and so that employees and employers could decide if they wished to be included in the compensation program. Labor-union officials, who supported the bill at first, denounced it in this form, noting that farm leaders were once again displaying a total disregard for the masses and were supporting the vested interests. Nonetheless, the bill, as amended, passed.[15]

Among the many complaints voiced against Stubbs during his political career was the claim that he created major issues out of minor problems. To a degree this charge was correct. Stubbs did, for example, magnify the importance of liquor-law violations at an exclusive Topeka men's club in 1909, when he threatened to use the state militia to close it if the club's officers did not stop their "boozing"![16] In some instances, however, his spectacular activities were aggravated by real problems and real malpractices that justified vigorous reactions. In some respects Stubbs's friends were more interested in crying wolf than he was. Two cases can be cited to illustrate this fact.

Under George Gould's presidency the Missouri Pacific had become what Santa Fe spokesman Charles Gleed believed to be the worst-managed railroad in the country. Much of its rolling stock was old and inferior, while some depots, freight houses, and road beds were decrepit and dangerous. In late 1909, service along the central branch of the Missouri Pacific became so poor that Franklin S. Adams, Mayor of Waterville, Kansas, appealed to Stubbs to do something about the line. Adams was joined by other civic leaders in the area, and together they formed the Railroad Improvement Agitation Association. By consistently pushing their case, they forced Stubbs to act in November. After sending a well-publicized telegram to Gould, threatening state action if the railroad was not improved, Stubbs began a series of talks with the vice-president of the company, C. S. Clarke.

The governor's position was that if the road were not improved with "reasonable speed," it was "the duty of the state to ask for a receiver of the property and improve the road-beds, the depots, the equipment and the service on its own account." The Missouri Pacific needed no further prodding. It began a costly reconstruction program along the line, which quieted most of the agitation in that locality. The publicity that was given to Stubbs in the affair snowballed, and a large number of letters requesting improved facilities all over Kansas were sent to his office. Had he wished, he could have started a popular campaign against all the railroads to improve their equipment, but he chose to do otherwise. Since he was uncertain of the charges, he asked the board of railroad commissioners to investigate complaints before he acted. Consequently, he never developed a crusade for railroad improvement.[17]

The other example of Stubbs's moderating the demands of his friends in order to avoid a potentially spectacular campaign resulted from the alleged existence of a creamery trust in Kansas in late 1911. Antitrust views were almost universally popular in the state, and in this instance William Allen White desired that antitrust action be taken. White had been given a list of complaints from western Kansas farmers who claimed that a dairy trust was operating in that part of the state. Elmer Peterson, editor of the *Cimmaron Jacksonian*, a Republican reform journal, had collected the charges, which in essence alleged that an agreement existed among big dairies so that low prices could be paid for milk purchased from farmers and high prices could be extracted from retailers and consumers. The evidence presented by Peterson was largely hearsay, but White and he were absolutely certain of its validity. To meet their demands the governor dispatched an investigator to western Kansas to check the charges.

In February 1912, T. B. Armstrong toured the area and reported that the trouble stemmed from a "personal affair" in Cimmaron, but that agreements might possibly exist in nearby Dodge City. He discounted any widespread collusion. Other inquiries also revealed that Peterson and White were wrong about a conspiracy. Had he been so inclined, Stubbs could have ballooned Peterson's charges into a major reform activity. He chose to heed the state dairy commissioner, who maintained that nothing should be done since the charges seemed baseless. The entire agitation collapsed when the governor did not intervene.[18]

Stubbs was not averse to creating or taking part in highly publicized events that cast him in a favorable light. At times his self-aggrandizement was helped by opponents who mistakenly gave him opportunities to champion popular causes. The railroads, for example, decided to raise rates throughout the West on the eve of congressional consideration of what became the Mann-Elkins Act in 1910. Stubbs, an advocate of lower freight rates, was among the first to protest the increase, and despite President Taft's success in delaying the hikes, Stubbs used the controversy to his political advantage.

He decided to hold a regional protest meeting in Topeka, inviting dignitaries from surrounding states, and he arranged to make the keynote address to the assembly. On 22 September 1910 he opened the conference by delivering a long, emotional plea for railroad honesty. He claimed that railroads had upped their profits hundreds of millions of dollars in the past twenty years through increased tariffs and that they could actually reduce freight charges at this time. He said that the argument of railroad officials that increased operating expenses necessitated higher rates was disproven by statistics. "The general policy of railroads," he told his predominantly rural audience, "is to favor large centers and build up great cities at the expense of the rural communities . . . [which] is little less than a crime against civilization." Such a program robbed hundreds of thousands of children of their natural right to wholesome surroundings, sunshine, pure air, and healthy social conditions. "The true policy," he concluded, "should be to so regulate transportation rates that the rural districts will be developed and the population normally distributed. The government, and not the railroads, should determine absolute policies of this character."[19]

In addition to providing Stubbs with an excellent opportunity to champion popular ideas, the rate conference fashioned a series of nine resolutions, which it presented to the Interstate Commerce Commission and President Taft. The resolutions were signed by a member of the Texas Railroad Commission, William D. Williams, who doubled as chairman of the Traffic Federation of the Middle West. The resolutions, however, were the work of Stubbs. Following the rate convention, the governor received added publicity in connection with the proposed freight increases by appearing before I.C.C. hearings in Chicago, where for one day he explained why freight rates should be lowered.[20]

His crowning achievement in the affair came after the conference and the Chicago meeting. Angered by Stubbs's exertions, the railroads denounced his arguments for lower rates in friendly newspapers and in a well-publicized exchange of letters between E. P. Ripley, president of the Santa Fe, and Stubbs. They tried to show that the governor was unfair, incorrect, and guilty of damaging the best interests of Kansas. As usual, they misconstrued the attitude of the Kansas public by failing to realize that Stubbs's position in favor of lower rates was inherently popular.[21]

The anti-Stubbs campaign began on October 1, when a long rebuttal of statements that he had made at the Topeka rate conference appeared in an open letter from Ripley to the governor. In reply Stubbs wrote that at last the gumshoes were off, and the railroads had met him in the open. The exchanges between Stubbs and Ripley continued until the first week in December. At first the letters were tedious discussions of the proper way to assign railroad rates, but towards the end they became spiced with personal accusations. The railroad position as presented by Ripley was threefold. He argued that the basis used for setting freight rates should be the value of the services rendered, rather than the value of the property owned by the railroads. He stated that increased rates were necessary in order to pay higher wages and maintain adequate pension funds for employees. His final point was that Kansas, past and present, profited immensely from the railroads in the state.

Stubbs dismissed Ripley's first argument as a railroad way of saying that they should charge all that the traffic would bear. The governor noted that the Supreme Court had held that public-service corporations should have their rates based on "a fair return upon a fair valuation of property," and railroads were public-service corporations. Ripley answered: "We are a private corporation with private capital at risk—the Government guarantees us nothing and we therefore have a right to demand fair play." Stubbs evaded Ripley's second point entirely, although he did imply that railroads failed to pay their employees as much as they deserved.

The governor completely denied the third point. Listing rates that discriminated against Kansas towns in favor of Kansas City, Missouri, he argued that railroad extortion had caused people, wealth, and industry to avoid Kansas. He concluded, "If the balance sheet could be struck,

... the Santa Fe would owe the people of Kansas one hundred dollars for each dollar the Santa Fe has given to the people."[22]

The discussion closed on a sensational note. Ripley claimed at one point that the Santa Fe was not overcapitalized, that investors in the railroad received small returns on their investments, and that Stubbs, if he wished, could check the books of the Santa Fe to verify this. The governor lost no time in sending his chief accountant to the Santa Fe offices in Topeka. At first his emissary was allowed free rein, but he was asked to leave when he supposedly overstepped Ripley's invitation. Taunted by Stubbs because of the dismissal, Ripley stated that the figures that Stubbs needed were not in Topeka but at the Chicago office and that the governor's employee "was endeavoring to build a statement which would lead to conclusions as full of errors as . . . those usually given public expression." "Your situation," Stubbs telegraphed in his final message, "is more ridiculous than ever." Why, he asked, was Ripley afraid to allow the public to know the facts about properties owned by the Santa Fe? Obviously, because Ripley knew that the Santa Fe was overcapitalized.[23]

Ripley's unwillingness to let the governor inspect the records of the Santa Fe was actually a godsend for Stubbs. From 1908 onward he had been advocating a public-utilities law that would make it possible for the state to examine railroad accounts as a means of evaluating their properties. When Ripley forced Stubbs's accountant to leave the railroad's offices, the public became convinced that things were surely amiss in the railroad's records, and they demanded that previously reluctant legislators support the governor's public-utilities bill. Although controversy over the public-utilities measure consumed much of the effort of the 1909 session, a number of other laws were enacted. At first Stubbs was reluctant to enter into an open fight for the utilities bill. He had endorsed it in his message to the legislature on 12 January 1909, but had not engaged in a serious effort until a combination of Democrats, anti-Stubbsian Republicans, and representatives of corporations demonstrated that more than a general endorsement was needed to secure passage of the bill. In February, Stubbs began to ask local politicians by letter to force legislators to pass the bill. He circulated a form letter from a progressive member of the Kansas Railroad Commission who favored the bill, and he induced the reform press to encourage the legislature to pass it.[24]

On February 25 he appeared before the two houses to deliver a special message on behalf of the bill. He discussed its provisions, its purposes, and the opposition to it. For years, he stated, one vast overshadowing problem had confronted the people—the proper regulation and control of public-service corporations. Recently, such state leaders as Charles Evans Hughes of New York, Robert La Follette of Wisconsin, and Joseph W. Folk of Missouri had developed "scientific, legal, business-like" ways to supervise these bodies. In 1908 Kansas Republicans had specifically promised to enact laws for the purpose of governing public-service businesses by indicating that these corporations should have limits placed on their issues of stocks and bonds and by asking for the physical evaluation of railroad property. The utilities bill was designed to do this.

"Under present conditions," Stubbs said, "the state through its legislature or Board of Railroad Commissioners makes orders, and the railroad companies go into federal court under a pretense of confiscation of property and secure exemption from . . . those orders." The state could not disprove their claims, and "state officers . . . [had] been humiliated and made to appear ridiculous for lack of information and evidence." No one, he concluded, should be fooled by the opposition's argument that local governments would lose control of local utilities because of the law. Many communities had never governed them anyway. Small local utilities were not the targets of regulation; rather the big corporations were the institutions that Kansas needed to control. The governor finished his address by noting that the regulation of banking by the state had helped Kansas banks and that, in the same manner, regulation by the state would help public utilities.[25]

His speech added a few supporters and reinvigorated old champions such as the reform press, Senator Bristow, and, after the speech, the famous Topeka clergyman the Reverend Charles Monroe Sheldon. Moved by Stubbs's message, Sheldon wrote that he wished to congratulate the governor for acting as a servant of the people in advocating the public-utilities law. "I for one," he noted, "want to go on record as opposed to any method in our political life which favors falsehood or greed by any person or corporation."[26] But the governor's appeal was to little avail. The bill was defeated in late February, and a measure written by Billy Morgan, which would have allowed local councils to regulate public-service corporations, was substituted. The administration, with Democratic help, defeated Morgan's version.[27]

Opposition to the public-utilities bill came from a number of sources. Democrats and anti-Stubbs factionalists opposed it in order to embarrass the governor, while certain economic interests feared that it would hurt them financially. Although railroad leaders were not its most effective opponents, they were against the bill, since it threatened to limit their profits to a fixed percentage of their Kansas holdings. Investors in electric railways, gas and light enterprises, and telephone companies were the chief enemies of the measure, since they considered the law to be an invasion of property rights and a menace to economic freedom.

The reform press claimed that Stubbs was not interested in regulating these utilities and that the argument about local utilities was a straw man created by the corporate opponents of the bill. This was untrue. Although Stubbs claimed publicly that he was not interested in local utilities, he wanted to regulate them, as well as the statewide enterprises. In letters to the opponents of the bill who objected only to the inclusion of small businesses, he said that railroads and insurance companies were not suffering from state regulation, and neither would small utilities.[28]

Aware of the sentiments of small businessmen, corporation attorney J. Willis Gleed organized an effective publicity campaign against the bill. He presented the measure as one that would allow the state to fix rates, permit competitors to use the equipment of local utilities, require elaborate reports, hear complaints against the services of small businesses, and engage in many drastic and costly enterprises that would negate the traditional meaning of private ownership of property. Gleed pointed out that in Wisconsin in one year its commission had cost $65,000, and work had just begun. "The people [of Kansas] are getting better service now," he concluded, "than they pay for."[29]

The *Topeka State Journal*, which had favored the bill, felt that the most effective arguments that had been used to defeat it were the claims that the state would have complete control over small local utilities and that the bill would halt the construction of interurban rail lines in Kansas. These arguments convinced Henry J. Allen that the bill was unwise; nevertheless, he promised Senator Bristow and White that he would work for its passage. "At the present moment," Allen wrote, "we are trying in Wichita . . . to interest capital in a system of suburban railways. A law, stating to these men, that they could not make . . . over ten per cent, would not . . . make it easier to secure this great public convenience."[30]

A whisper campaign in Topeka during the session stated that Stubbs's only interest in the bill was to make the commission appointive, which would have given him more political patronage. Some Republicans pointed out that the bill had been defeated because the platform of 1908 had not specifically committed the party to such a law. The astute Topeka correspondent Jay House decided that the bill had failed to pass because of inept administrative handlers. "High-mindedness and independence," he said, "are all right on the stump but are not of much value in legislative halls when trying to enact legislation." He later concluded: "The opposition was cunningly and boldly led and the Lord was on the side of the heaviest battalions."³¹ In a sense the fate of the public-utilities bill symbolized Stubbs's lack of success in the 1909 session. Most of the laws that he requested were either amended to diminish their effectiveness, or, like the public-utilities bill, failed to pass.

Stubbs had greeted the 1909 session of the legislature with a message that was notable for its similarities to those being delivered by governors across the reform-minded Middle West. In addition to asking for a public-utilities commission, he sought consolidation of the state eleemosynary institutions under one board of management, and he requested home rule for Kansas cities. He noted that better roads were needed in the state in order to facilitate commerce, and he suggested that the 1908 decision of the Railroad Commission to limit passenger rates to two cents per mile be made part of the Kansas statutes. He told the legislators that the power of special interests in representative assemblies needed to be reduced by the passage of an antilobbying law, and he asked them to curb the same influences in elections by requiring candidates for state and national offices to file reports explaining their campaign expenditures. To satisfy a demand voiced after the passage of the State Tax Commission Law in 1907, the governor stressed the need for an amendment that would make tax commissioners and county assessors elective officials. He also reminded the session that the people of Kansas wanted to have a law enacted that would guarantee bank deposits. He closed by emphasizing the brevity of his program and by imploring the legislators to keep economy uppermost in their minds.³²

The legislature failed to pass four of Stubbs's suggestions—the public-utilities bill, the bill providing for the reorganization of state eleemosynary institutions, the proposal for an elective tax commission, and the bill to establish a two-cent passenger rate. It did pass an antilobbying measure, the Campaign Expenditures Law, the Rock and Dirt Roads Law, a law enabling cities to have a commission form of government, and the Bank Deposit Guaranty Law. By all standards this last piece of legislation was the most important measure enacted during the session.³³ It withstood a difficult fight in the legislature, and then it faced two years of legal maneuvering in the federal courts by its opponents before the Supreme Court upheld its constitutionality.

The Bank Deposit Guaranty Law, which was passed in March of

1909, provided that incorporated banks that met surplus capital requirements could voluntarily insure specified types of deposits in a fund established and supervised by the office of the Kansas bank commissioner. The fund, which would protect all eligible deposits, was to be created by levying a rate of one-twentieth of 1 percent on the deposits of member banks until $500,000 was collected. Unlike the Oklahoma plan, which antedated it by two years, the Kansas program was voluntary.[34]

A generation that accepts the broad coverage of the Federal Deposit Insurance Corporation as normal can hardly appreciate the opposition that the state guaranty program raised. One banker denounced it as "impractical, unjust . . . populistic, socialistic and paternalistic and repugnant to the spirit of our institutions and to those qualities of individualism and of individual responsibility which our forefathers sought to preserve, encourage and establish through the Constitution."[35] J. W. Berryman, a conservative banker-stockman-legislator from Ashland, considered it "a worse fallacy than the free silver craze." He said that if it were enacted, it would "crush all industry, paralyze all business and destroy [all] confidence, leaving the state and country more prostrate than war or pestilence."[36]

But behind the bluster of these attacks on the measure lay an economic reality which any generation can understand. One of the main features of Kansas banking in the early twentieth century was a vicious competition between banking concerns that were state-chartered and those that were nationally chartered. National banks, because of higher capital requirements, because of federal deposits, and because of limited national supervision, normally held the edge in the struggle for business. State bankers, hoping to improve public confidence in their enterprises, wanted the bank-deposit guaranty law as a prop that they could exploit in their struggle for customers. They said that the law would assure depositors that accounts in state banks were as secure as accounts in competing national banks. They knew that Attorney General Charles J. Bonaparte had ruled in 1908 that national banks could not participate in state guaranty plans. They were aware that President Taft did not support the idea of insurance for bank deposits, since he had campaigned against it and its national champion, William Jennings Bryan, in 1908. The state bankers felt that national banks would not be allowed to participate under the Kansas program during Taft's administration. This would enhance the position of their banks even more.[37]

National bankers were equally aware of these facts, and they interpreted them in much the same light. Consequently, they tried to block passage of the bill; but when it became apparent that the measure would be enacted in some form, they tried to rewrite it so that the one class of customers that was apt to be influenced most by its provisions would not be covered. The depositor who received interest on his account would almost certainly place his funds in a guaranty bank. Not wanting to seem overly callous in their opposition, the national bankers, through the Kansas Banker's Association, attacked this provision by charging that it would make it possible for "incompetent, reckless and unsafe bankers . . . to exploit, buy . . . and demoralize banking business" in the state. They developed a letter-writing campaign in February, established a large lobby in Topeka, and packed the hearings on the bill with their friends. Through J. W. Berryman and the Wichita banker C. Q. Chandler they enlisted the support of the Long faction in the Kansas legislature. They were also able to secure the help of the most influential Democrat in Kansas, State Senator George Hodges of Olathe. Their effort was rewarded when a limitation was placed on the amount of interest that could be paid on savings accounts covered by the plan.[38]

Having been kept from taking part in the Kansas program by a decision in March of 1909 by Taft's attorney general, George Wickersham, the national banks organized the Bankers' Deposit Guaranty and Surety Company, which had a larger capital than the state fund. They did not limit the interest that could be paid on insured savings deposits, as did the state program. Thus, national banks were able to advertise that they would pay a rate of interest higher than the 3 percent allowed by state banks and would still provide the security of insured deposits.[39]

The creation of the privately owned guaranty company caused a sudden reversal of sentiment in many state bankers who had supported the state system. To keep this group active in the program, Governor Stubbs threatened to call a special session of the legislature in order to halt the private concern from insuring savings deposits that received more than 3 percent interest. A special session was averted when Kansas Attorney General Fred Jackson ruled that the superintendent of insurance could forbid the private guaranty company from insuring certain classes of interest-bearing savings deposits. Superintendent Charles W. Barnes used Jackson's ruling to refuse the Bankers' Deposit Guaranty and Surety Company a certificate of authority to do business in Kansas until it agreed not to insure savings deposits with interest over 3 percent. In December 1909 the Kansas Supreme Court held Jackson's opinion invalid and ordered Barnes to issue the certificate of authority.[40]

This victory did not satisfy the national bankers. They decided to test the constitutionality of the state law. In March former Senator Long had written a leader of the Kansas Banker's Association that he would like to be employed to fight the guaranty plan in the federal courts, saying: "I am intensely interested personally in defeating the Kansas guaranty law, . . . and if I am employed I assure you that I have never had a case or subject to which I will give as close attention." After meetings in July, the association hired Long, as well as J. Willis Gleed, Balie P. Waggener, and John L. Webster, all of whom were highly competent corporation lawyers. These men initiated action in the U.S. Circuit Court, Kansas District.[41]

During late 1909 an old political henchman of Long's, Judge John Pollock, heard several cases involving the Kansas law and granted a temporary injunction against the state bank commissioner, Jonathan N. Dolley, while ruling the law unconstitutional. The state attorney general appealed the decision to the Eighth Circuit Court of Appeals at St. Louis, and in May 1910 Pollock's decision was reversed. Long next filed a writ of certiorari with the United States Supreme Court, which rejected it in October. The Supreme Court did, however, accept the Kansas case on an appeal from Pollock's initial decision. In January 1911 Justice Oliver Wendell Holmes, Jr., wrote the majority opinions upholding the constitutionality of the Kansas law, as well as that of somewhat similar enactments in Oklahoma and Nebraska. Although another case relating to the Kansas law was pending in the Supreme Court at the time, the opposition had been defeated, and the subsequent action proved meaningless.[42]

Stubbs had helped himself politically during the controversy by siding with state bankers. In 1909 the Kansas State Bankers Association had been formed to offset the Kansas Banker's Association, which was controlled by the national banks. During 1910 the new group worked for Stubbs's reelection, and it sponsored candidates for the legislature that were favorable to the governor. "Stubbs and Dolley," wrote C. C. K. Scoville, president of the association, "are with us heart and soul . . . and we ought to see they are upheld by sending men who are not enemies of the state banks of Kansas to the legislature."[43]

The 1909 legislature, which ended its session on March 13, passed 269 out of 1,800 bills introduced. But of the pledges in the 1908 Republican platform and of the requests made by Stubbs, only a few had been fulfilled. A Topeka reporter wrote that the session was "remarkable for the amount of work done as compared with actual results."[44] The defeats suffered by the governor also caused a political enemy, Mort Albaugh, to gloat that the legislature had administered a thrashing to Stubbs, which "if the leading papers were half way fair . . . would make him appear . . . as the most worsted governer . . . we have ever had."[45]

But Stubbs's opponents had unwittingly contributed to his political future. They had given him an issue to take before the voters in 1910. He could demand that a progressive legislature be sent to Topeka to work effectively toward reform goals in the next session. Stubbs's political future was also being helped by events transpiring outside of Kansas. President Taft's actions during his first few months in office indicated that 1910 would be a critical year in the future of progressive Republicanism in Kansas. He had been unable to satisfy middle western reform Republicans in his stand on the Payne-Aldrich tariff and the fight against "Cannonism." His attitude had created a deep split in the Kansas congressional delegation, and as a result, controversies that began in the national capital were transferred to Kansas, to be fought out in the 1910 primaries.

On 29 January 1910 conservatives had momentarily embarrassed Stubbs by refusing to commend his administration at the meeting of the Kansas Day Club in Topeka. But a few weeks later it became apparent to everyone except the most diehard opposition and the governor's worrying friends that Stubbs and his allies would win a smashing victory in the August primaries. Thus, when victory came, few were surprised. Progressive Republicans were nominated to nearly every spot on the party ticket, and the reformers controlled the party council, where they wrote a comprehensive, progressive platform. In November, although Republican percentages were lower than usual, the state returned a Republican House and reelected Stubbs.[46]

Once again the governor was able to go before the legislature to request the fulfillment of party pledges. In his message he reiterated the demand for a public-utilities measure, the consolidation of state eleemosynary institutions under one board, and the two-cent passenger-fare law. He asked for more money for rock and dirt roads and for aid to rural school districts. The Campaign Expenditures Law of 1909 did not satisfy him, and now he asked for an enactment that would require candidates to file statements of their political expenses, revealing the sources of the funds. He requested ratification of the federal income tax amendment that was circulating throughout the United States at that time.

The portions of the governor's speech that represented the popular aspects of progressivism in 1911 were those calling for the establishment of the initiative, referendum, and recall by constitutional amendment. Stubbs also asked for two other laws designed to advance democracy in Kansas. He sought a presidential-preference primary and the direct election of senators under the Oregon plan. His address was shorter than the one of two years earlier. It lacked color and style, but it was clear and definite.[47]

As in the case of the 1909 session, by February the legislature of 1911 still had not acted on the governor's proposals. On February 8 he delivered a special message to the assembly, repeating his requests and demanding action. He pointed out that every party platform in Kansas had pledged its legislators to those laws and that they were binding personal obligations on every member of that legislature.[48]

His troubles with reluctant legislators had begun weeks before the 1911 session commenced. Although a progressive-Republican house had been elected in November, the senate had not stood for reelection and thus was nearly the same body that had met in 1909. The governor and his supporters had traced many of their failures in the first legislature to the upper house and especially to the Senate Judiciary Committee, which was headed by Francis Price of Ashland. According to one account, 245 senate bills and 50 house bills had been pigeonholed by that committee after the conservative lieutenant governor, W. J. Fitzgerald, had referred them there in 1909. The lieutenant governor elected in November, however, was a progressive Republican, Richard J. Hopkins of Garden City, and progressives indicated that he would appoint liberals to the Judiciary Committee.

In 1909 the number of standpat Republicans in the senate had constituted a bare majority, but after the fall elections in 1910 three former progressive members had switched their allegiance. Emerson Carey of Reno County had succeeded in gaining favorable rates for salt shipments from Hutchinson and had decided that "the less legislation we have the better off we are," while J. H. Stavely of Osage City and J. H. Stewart of Wichita had announced their opposition to the administration because of the proposals for the initiative, referendum, and recall. "I am not anxious," Stewart said, "for legislative experiments." In tallying their strength in the senate, conservatives estimated in late November 1910 that of forty members in the upper house, twenty-five were "standpat" against Stubbs's program.[49]

The first test between the governor and his senatorial opposition came on 10 January 1911, when both houses of the legislature were organized. Lieutenant Governor Hopkins, true to his word, announced his decision to remove antiadministration leaders from the Judiciary Committee and other important committees. His statement sparked an uprising against his power to appoint committee members. The conservatives, evoking memories of the recent cry against the dictatorial powers of Speaker Cannon in the national House of Representatives, justified an assault on Hopkins's power by announcing that they were going to do for the state what insurgents had done for the nation.[50]

Stubbs fought back in vain. He countered their argument by noting that the voters of Kansas had just recently elected the progressive Hopkins as lieutenant governor, and they wanted him to exercise the full power of that office so that reforms that had hitherto been denied could be passed. The senators, he added, had not gone before the public since 1908, and therefore they needed someone who had recently been a candidate for office as their leader. The governor had been spurred on by Senator Bristow, who provided the principal argument—that the defeat of Hopkins would violate the good faith of the people of Kansas, who had elected progressive Republicans to office because they had promised change.

The comparison between Cannon's powers and those of Hopkins, Bristow noted, was only superficial, and it was not hypocritical to oppose one and support the other. Men were elected time after time to Congress, and committees were permanent bodies that were controlled effectively by the Speaker. In Kansas, men were rarely elected more than twice, and no permanent combination could exist by virtue of this fact. Thus, the powers of the lieutenant governor were considerably less than those of the Speaker. "The Kansas legislature," Bristow concluded, "responds to the state sentiment which prevails . . . at the time of elections." This made the situation entirely different.[51]

The Kansas senate disagreed. By a vote of 21 to 18 it sheared away the lieutenant governor's appointive power and created a Committee on Committees to perform this function. Senator Price, the progressives' *bête noire*, remained chairman of the Judiciary Committee.[52]

A similar attempt to take the appointive power away from the Speaker of the Kansas house was made simultaneously by a combination of regular Republicans, Democrats, and disaffected progressives. House Speaker G. H. Buckman of Winfield was a standpat Republican who had been converted to progressivism. He was supported by the administration in the race for the speakership in 1911. This resulted in resentment among progressive-Republican friends of Representative Robert Stone of Topeka. Stone was also a candidate for the speakership, and because of his longer allegiance to reform, he seemed to have a better claim than Buckman had to Stubbs's support. Stone, however, was unpopular with the governor, because he had failed to win the confirmation of the United States Senate when Stubbs secured a presidential appointment for him to the Department of Justice in 1910.

Stone had allegedly been involved in a swindle earlier in the century, and old evidence had been used against him during the fight for confirmation. According to Arthur Capper, publisher of the *Topeka Daily Capital*, Stone was an honest person who had been kept from the Justice Department position by the then National Committeeman David Mulvane, the Republican machine, and the Topeka booze crowd. Nonetheless, Stubbs self-righteously wrote Stone out of the progressive faction after he failed to get the confirmation. Having lost the speakership to Stubbs's candidate, Stone organized the movement to remove the appointive prerogative of Speaker Buckman. But the governor's hold over recently elected representatives was too powerful for Stone, and so the movement collapsed. Stone had to wait until later to get his revenge, when he engineered the defeat of the governor's legislation concerning the Board of Control, which would have provided for the consolidation of state eleemosynary and penal institutions, and other such bodies, under one authority.[53]

The battle for Stubbs's program at the 1911 session was even more emotional than that in 1909. Two fistfights erupted on the floor of the legislature during the session. While debate over the Board of Control bill waxed hot, progressive Republican H. E. Ganse of Burlington attacked Democratic Senator George Hodges, who promptly knocked Ganse senseless. Later, Representative Stone was smashed in the eye by A. H. McCormick of Pittsburg after a heated argument. The senate, wrote one reporter, was now operating under the Queensberry Rules! "Not since the days of the legislative wars in the early nineties," he added, "has there been such clamorous demands for blood. . . . Topeka is like Paris in the time of the Fronde."[54]

More excitement was added by the campaign for Stubbs's program in the reform press. William Allen White, a constant critic of the conservative senate, was forced to appear before it to give testimony on his charges that opponents of Stubbs were trading "pork-barrel legislation" for votes against administration bills. He was asked to sustain his charges, and when he could not, he was humiliated. To use the Kansas vernacular, he had "to crawfish out of what he had written." His performance reminded one reporter of White's earlier attempt to make a prepared speech before an assembly of school teachers. He "shed great globules of perspiration," the reporter wrote, "lost his place on the manuscript repeatedly and finally fell like a pound of overheated butter."[55]

A far more acrimonious exchange of this sort occurred as a result of published charges by Governor Stubbs's private secretary, David D. Leahy. Leahy, a former Democrat and Populist, was the exact opposite of White in give and take. He had been a member of the *Wichita Eagle* staff before joining Stubbs's administration and had had a colorful career in state politics. His flashy Anglophobic speeches had earned him the title of the Irish Prince, and he knew how to befuddle enemies. On February 12 "Prince Dave," visiting in Wichita, was asked to explain why Stubbs's program was faring so poorly. His answer was a reply that was normal for a man of his temperament. "The old regime of special interests," he said, "is making its last stand, and the remnant of their willing tools . . . is determined to defeat every demand of the people." Crookedness was rampant, and political pirates were more reckless than in the palmiest days of long ago. "Pork barreling" and "lying" were the major methods being used by the enemies of the governor to defeat him in the senate.[56]

A week later Leahy was called before the senate. Unable to prove his assertions, he, too, was forced to back down; but once free of the senate floor, he attacked again with full main. "No one," he wrote to a friend, "disproved my charges of lying, no one can deny porkbarreling, and so far as the accusation of political crookedness is concerned, I stand by it unwaveringly."[57] He was answered in a speech by Senator Sim Brewster of Troy, who accused the Irish Prince of hypocrisy, demagoguery, and dishonesty. Leahy replied: "I should have written you earlier thanking you for your abuse of me. . . . To be openly denounced by a Senator in the act of betraying his constituents . . . is a compliment that I did not expect."[58]

The clamor by reformers against the senate illustrated a significant fact regarding the 1911 session. As in 1909, important parts of Stubbs's program were failing. On February 23 the senate defeated the initiative, referendum, and recall amendment by a 24 to 15 vote. Stubbs had been reluctant to recommend the measure, feeling that the public was not prepared for so "radical" a step, but White and Bristow had convinced him that the device was necessary for the future of democracy.

His reticence had been caused by the position of many so-called moral reformers toward the law. Fearing that the initiative and referendum would be used to challenge Kansas liquor laws, prohibitionists demanded that initiative and referendum petitions be required to have the signatures of a high percentage of registered voters in order to be validated. But after the figure was raised to 15 and then to 20 percent of the eligible electorate, the prohibitionists still opposed the bills. "The majority of the men and women of Kansas consider the prohibition question settled," wrote an official of the State Temperance Union, "and they WANT IT KEPT SETTLED." "Is it fair," asked the Union's superintendent, Frank M. Stahl, "that a few mining districts composed largely of foreigners, should have the power to force this, or any other question upon the state?"[59]

What was democracy coming to in Kansas? A conservative state representative from Greensburg, J. W. Davis, answered the question thus:

> Like a fire bell in the night, this movement to change our Republican form of government should startle every patriotic man, for this dangerous and revolutionary doctrine would in the end lead to the destruction of all free government. . . . Our highly specialized form of representative government . . . would be set aside, and we should go back to the clumsy methods which prevailed in the infancy of all Republics.

If legislatures could be eliminated in their usefulness, he continued, so could executives and judiciaries, and thus "you are on the highway that leads to absolute anarchy."[60] The presidential-preference primary and the direct election of senators in the form of the Oregon plan went the same way as the initiative, referendum, and recall. They were defeated late in the session by the senate.

The utilities bill that had failed in the previous legislature had been reintroduced in the house at the beginning of the session, but as was the case with the initiative and referendum, it had still not been acted upon by mid February. In order to overcome the opposition, Stubbs compromised his position on the law, allowing local utilities to be exempt from its provisions. He did not attempt to neutralize the opposition of the railroads or the Bell Telephone Company, which was engaged in unifying small communication networks in the state. Each of these interests had lobbyists who were active in the legislature, and their persistence occasioned two highly significant changes in the administration's bill before it passed on March 10. Simon Bear, lobbyist for the Bell Company, succeeded in keeping mutual telephone companies from being protected under the coverage of that law. The railroads scored an even more impressive victory by negating the meaningfulness of the term "reasonable rates" as it had been used since the time of the 1906 reform movement. The commission was allowed to determine rates, but it was not required to base them on the capitalization, the current property value, or the original cost of the property of the companies. Moreover, the exact percentage of profit that the utilities were to make on the basis of any of these three figures was not specified. Thus the grounds for considerable agitation were effectively by-passed in the law.

But the passage of the utilities bill still should be considered a victory for the governor. In a watered-down fashion it realized his major legislative program, and it did include many of the features that he had wanted. The law differed from the old railroad-commission enactment in the following respects. Rather than being an elective commission, the new board was to be appointed by the governor. In addition to the power to regulate railroads, the commission was given power over private telephone and telegraph companies as well as corporations involved in the intrastate transmission of heat, light, water, and power. When determining property values and when setting rates, the commission could demand to see all accounts, books, and records kept by various corporations; and it could limit the issue of securities by the utilities. The most significant power given to the commission was the right to review any rate increases and to give widespread publicity to them. All utilities were required to file copies of existing rate schedules with the commission. Provisions of the law were to be effective immediately, but the members of the Board of Railroad Commissioners were allowed to continue as members of the Public Utilities Commission until their terms expired in January 1913. According to students of the commission, it performed creditably until 1919, when a revised program sponsored by Governor Henry J. Allen replaced it.[61]

The 1911 legislature was severely criticized by reformers during much of the session, but at its close, the administration-oriented *Topeka Daily Capital* lauded the lawmakers for having done a "good job" and for having enacted "rightly progressive" laws. Four of the governor's measures had not passed, but seven had. Moreover, a number of platform pledges that Stubbs had not mentioned in his message became law.[62]

In addition to the reforms already discussed, the 1909 and 1911 legislatures produced a series of laws affecting education, health, economic relationships, and the tax structure of the state. For instance, a schoolbook commission was created, the governing boards of the state university and the state colleges were reorganized, and vocational agricultural classes were started in rural elementary and secondary schools. In the realm of morality legislation, a law dealing with the sale of cigarettes was passed, banning the weed from Kansas, and the Kansas pure food and drug law was amended. The legislature was reapportioned, and the state primary law was rewritten so that state legislators could pledge themselves to a specific senatorial candidate in general elections. A legislative reference library was created, the present Kansas State Historical Society Building was constructed, and a woman-suffrage amendment was to be submitted to the public in 1912. Two other laws that Stubbs and his contemporaries considered extremely important had also been passed—the so-called Blue-Sky Investment Law and the Inheritance Tax Law.[63]

The Inheritance Tax Law was first enacted in 1909, but at the governor's suggestion it was amended slightly in 1911. It resulted from recommendations made by the State Tax Commission, and it was favored by Stubbs as a means of raising revenue. He also advocated the provision that made it necessary for heirs of foreigners holding stock in Kansas railroads to pay assessments that were made when death necessitated the transfer of shares from one foreigner to another. He opposed the low exemption of $5,000 that the law granted to widows and orphans; he favored beginning the tax on such estates at $25,000.[64]

The "Blue Sky" Law resulted from the establishment of an unauthorized bureau within the office of Bank Commissioner Dolley to investigate and report on possibly fraudulent stock sales. Its success encouraged the creation of a permanent body that would collect data from companies selling securities in Kansas and then publish its findings. The most important feature of the law was a provision for high fines and jail sentences when securities were mislabeled or falsely advertised and when sales of stocks and bonds were inaccurately reported to the state. Its supporters claimed that many gullible Kansans were saved money by the bureau's actions, which kept them from buying "chunks" of the state's good "blue sky."[65]

Progressive legislation did not cease with the 1911 session, nor did honest government end when Stubbs left office. But by March of 1911 the center of progressive Republicanism in Kansas had shifted from the legislative halls of Topeka to Washington, D.C. There, the state's progressive Republicans had become involved in a continuous two-year struggle with the leadership of the national Republican party. By 1911 they had joined a movement to stop the renomination of President Taft and to replace him with a presidential nominee of their own persuasion. They had started down what they hoped would be the road to national dominance for men of their inclination. Unknowingly, they were nearing the plain of Armageddon—as Theodore Roosevelt was to describe the political arena in 1912. Once there, defeat, not victory, was to be their reward.

# 8

## TAFT AND THE KANSAS INSURGENTS, 1909-1910

Even before the Republican National Convention met in June 1908, Kansas progressives had expressed concern about William Howard Taft's qualifications to head a great reform crusade. Taft had never demonstrated political sagacity, nor did his conservative nature seem to fit him for the role of a reform president such as Kansas wanted. But Theodore Roosevelt endorsed Taft, and for the majority of Republicans this alone was adequate assurance that he would try to carry out the so-called Rooseveltian policies.[1] If Taft did not, then Senator Joseph Bristow thought that Taft would be annihilated politically.[2]

Senator Bristow, of course, did not anticipate this fate. He was nearly certain that the "big, amiable island of a man" from Cincinnati would uphold the achievements of Roosevelt's years and even advance them. But Bristow did not know about Taft's advice to Elihu Root to support the election of conservative senators during the 1908 campaign. He was not familiar with Taft's classification of Bristow, Robert M. La Follette, Albert Cummins, Jonathan Bourne, and others from the West as the "Bryan wing of the Republican party." Nor was he aware of what George Mowry later called the mental separation that Taft had made from the progressive-Republican group in Congress before his inauguration.[3] He might well have been warned by Taft's cabinet selections. But in early 1909 Bristow was not one who doubted the new president's credentials as a reformer. In fact, he agreed with Taft when the president withheld support from Kansas Congressman Victor Murdock and others during their fight to unseat the conservative Speaker of the House Joseph G. Cannon at the special session of 1909.[4]

One month after Taft was sworn into office, Bristow's attitude changed abruptly. He became disillusioned with the president and privately criticized him. Before the end of 1909, his complaints were being made publicly, and though Taft was a Republican president, Bristow openly disagreed with him on important issues. At first Bristow was almost alone among Kansans in his criticisms, but within a year most Kansas progressives joined him, and by mid 1910 Judge Nelson I. Case summed up the feelings of the progressives when he claimed that Taft was a dupe of grasping corporate greed. "Mr. Taft," Case said, "evidently believed that if he took the leaders of the representatives of the special interests into his confidence he could influence, if not control, their action. . . . The whole country saw at once, what seems to have never penetrated his mental vision, that he had completely surrendered to the privileged interest and allowed them to dictate the terms of his capitulation."[5] In an emotionally charged speech, he continued:

> Because my father helped to organize the [Republican] party and instilled into my boyish nature a feeling of party pride, because I shouted for Fremont in my boyhood, and marched in the parades and spoke for Lincoln in my early . . . manhood, and cast my first . . . vote for Grant, is no reason why I shall support aspirants for office today who are pledged to a policy absolutely at variance with my interest as an individual, are opposed to the principles of free representative government, are willing to give to rich corporations the people's heritage to natural resources.[6]

Judge Case listed the things Taft had done that he and other Kansans felt were wrong. Taft had sanctioned the Payne-Aldrich tariff, had supported Secretary of the Interior Richard A. Ballinger in his controversy with Chief Forester Gifford Pinchot, had backed the reactionary Joseph G. Cannon in his struggle against progressive Republicans who were trying to reform the House of Representatives, had upheld Attorney General George Wickersham in his prorailroad regulatory bill, and had done numerous other things that indicated that he favored conservative Republicans over their progressive brethren.[7]

Although it may have appeared that Taft was utter anathema to progressive Republicans in Kansas by 1910, such was not the case. The reformers were not yet sure that Taft would fail to redeem himself during the last two years of his administration, and they were not sure how wise it would be to oppose the man who would probably head the Republican ticket in 1912. Republican candidates existed who could be challenged in 1910. Taft's position on the issues of the day aligned him against the Kansas progressives, and he kept regular Republican congressmen with him. Kansas regulars who faced renomination in the primary could be openly opposed by their intraparty rivals. Thus, the split that Taft helped to open in Washington carried over into Kansas in 1910, where an election that would have been moderately emotional became a mammoth donnybrook between standpat and insurgent Republicans. Taft alone was not responsible for this, but his failure to unite the party aggravated an already bad situation.

The trouble in Republican ranks, which reached floodtide in 1910, began as early as the previous election. In the 1908 primary, Congressman Victor Murdock made it a point to campaign against the Republican Speaker of the House—Joe Cannon—and the Republican rules enforced there. Murdock induced some progressive newspapers to support him, and he pressured a few other reluctant Republican congressmen in the state to agree, even if half-heartedly, with his attacks. Unexpectedly, Murdock's campaign did not cease after the primary, and while Democrats were making anti-Cannonism an issue in the general election, so was Murdock.[8]

The national fight against Cannonism, as it was called, did not begin with Victor Murdock, but the fiery, red-headed editor from Wichita gave it a vocal, persistent, and clever champion. Cannonism, as the term was used by Murdock and other critics, meant a system of government in which one man exercised extraordinary powers over three hundred and ninety-one representatives. It meant that a conservative, opinionated, crude politician from Danville, Illinois, could impose his will in large measure upon the House of Representatives. The system was not of Speaker Cannon's making; he had inherited it. But under his ironfisted management it rubbed sensitive congressmen raw as they watched him appoint committees, assign bills to the calendar, and control debate through an autocratic manner of granting recognition.[9]

Murdock joined in the protests against Cannon as early as 1907, after having served two undistinguished terms in office. A member of one of the most famous families in Kansas history, he was first elected to fill the seat that was vacated by Chester I. Long in 1903. His election, according to Mort Albaugh, political manager of the Seventh Congres-

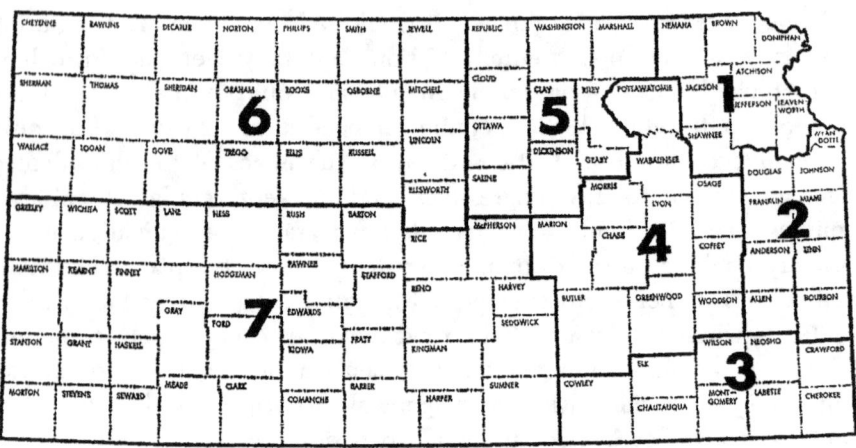

KANSAS' CONGRESSIONAL DISTRICTS, 1898–1906

sional District, was arranged in the "same old way." With the help of Long, who was a friend of Speaker Cannon's, Murdock secured an appointment to the Post Office and Post Roads Committee. In 1905 the Kansas legislature reapportioned the state, which placed Murdock in the newly created Eighth District. Freed from Long's influence, he joined the antirailroad reform movement, which was strong in Wichita and throughout his new congressional area. Against the wishes of his former Seventh District friends, he was a candidate for the Senate in 1906.[10]

Murdock became involved in the fight against Cannon as a result of an amendment that he offered to the post-office appropriations bill in 1907. During an unofficial investigation of postal practices, Murdock discovered that railroads were paid for carrying mail on the basis of the tonnage transported per day. To arrive at the daily figure, postal officials took the total weight of all mail hauled during a week and divided that number by six, since earlier the railroads had not carried mail on Sundays. This meant that the volume of mail carried in a week by the railroads was smaller than what they were being paid to carry. Murdock's amendment would have corrected this discrepancy. Railroad officials, convinced that their compensation for carrying mails was too low anyway, opposed the Murdock measure. Speaker Cannon, apparently influenced by railroad opinion, kept Murdock's amendment from the appropriations bill. When the young congressman appealed Cannon's blocking tactic to the House floor, he was soundly defeated. Undaunted, he enlisted Senator Robert La Follette's help, but La Follette, who later

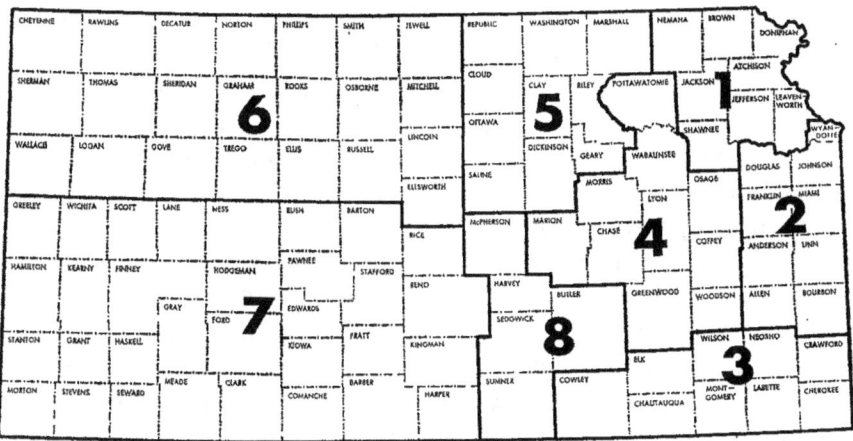

KANSAS' CONGRESSIONAL DISTRICTS, 1906-1930

introduced a similar amendment in the Senate, was likewise thwarted by its leadership. Finally, through an executive order, President Roosevelt settled the affair by making the change that Murdock had suggested. The persistence shown by the Kansas congressman in the "false divisor" episode angered Cannon and made Murdock a marked man in House affairs. Thereafter, Cannon thought of him as a Republican who, like La Follette, was a "worse Populist than Bryan himself and more dangerous."[11]

Murdock's insurgency against Cannon was the result not only of Murdock's views with regard to the Speaker's arbitrariness in the postal matter; it was in part the natural outcome of his personality. Murdock felt uncomfortable as an unnoticed member of the House. He entered the Congress hoping to be more than just another representative, but he remained unimportant. As a leader of a great popular uprising against a dictatorial Speaker, he could gain the recognition he desired. No longer would he be forced to feel as inconspicuous as he did on his third day in Congress, according to an overdramatized account that he wrote for *American Magazine*. Murdock reported that when he was going to the House chamber, he passed Speaker Cannon and rendered the usual "hello." "The Speaker," Murdock later recounted, "did not return my morning salutation. I argued that he was in a brown study over something and did not see me. But men are not blind in brown studies, except to those who are negligible. And the realization that I was negligible was a terrorizing thing which awoke me in the dead of night and would not let me sleep."[12]

There was still another facet to Murdock's anti-Cannonism. He had seen a number of moderate reforms fail in the House because of Cannon's hostility. As a champion of change and as a person interested in democratic government, Murdock wanted to eliminate what many felt was the biggest obstacle to progressive legislation in the capital. The only way to do this was to limit the powers held by Cannon or to remove him from the Speaker's chair.

By 1908 a number of reformers had grown dissatisfied with Cannon.[13] Murdock, by voicing his own complaints, expressed the sentiments of at least twenty-five other representatives. Taft had grown weary of Cannon and had indicated that, unlike Roosevelt, who had a working agreement with the Speaker, he would help opposition Republicans in Congress unseat the "Iron Duke of Danville." Taft, however, wavered, and when time came for action, he convinced himself that in order to enact the Republican platform, Cannon would have to continue as Speaker. The loss of presidential support did not swerve Murdock and his fellow representatives from their plans to rewrite House rules and ultimately to remove Cannon. Murdock, who helped to plan the strategy to be used against Cannon, was joined in the insurgency by another Kansan, Edmond H. Madison, in late 1908. Madison was also a former adherent of the Long machine; but unlike Murdock, he did not have a reputation for championing radical ideas. As a moderate, he quickly became a leader of the disgruntled Republican congressmen.

The House insurgents, as those who opposed Cannon were called, refused to take part in the Republican caucus that was held just prior to the special session in March of 1909. They knew that Cannon would easily be renominated as the party's candidate for Speaker at that meeting. If they attended the caucus, they would be bound by its decisions. Earlier, the insurgents had requested that the Rules Committee be enlarged from five to fifteen members, each representing a different geographical area of the country, that "Calendar Tuesday" be established, and that the Speaker not be allowed to appoint committees. Cannon and his house lieutenants opposed the entire program of the insurgents, but because of the popularity of the effort to establish "Calendar Tuesday," they provided for "Calendar Wednesday," late in the lame-duck session that had begun in December 1908. This proposal made every Wednesday a day when committees were to report to the House in alphabetical order, thus allowing consideration of bills that the Speaker had kept from the floor because of his scheduling.[14]

On March 15, after he had been nominated by the Republican caucus,

Cannon was easily reelected. When the motion was made to adopt the rules for governing the House, Democrats and insurgent Republicans defeated it. Then, by a prearranged design, minority leader "Champ" Clark presented a list of modified rules. These were defeated when Cannon acquired the help of Tammany Hall Democrats. The rules finally adopted at the session were essentially the same as the ones that the House had used before, but "Calendar Wednesday" was slightly revised. A unanimous-consent calendar, which allowed unimportant legislation to be passed without the Speaker's approval, was also created.[15]

Despite these accomplishments, Victor Murdock was angered by the quasi defeat of the insurgents in March of 1909. He had earlier written that five of the eight Kansas congressmen would vote with the insurgents. But when the fight developed, only Murdock and Madison voted against the established rules, while the other six representatives supported Cannon. When Cannon was elected for the fourth time as Speaker, Murdock was the only Kansan to cast a dissenting vote. He had asked Madison to join him in this vote, but the more moderate congressman from Dodge City had refused. Concerning Madison's decision, Senator Bristow felt compelled to tell critics that the vote meant nothing and that "the real hero of the Kansas delegation was Ed Madison." Bristow added that Madison had far more influence with the insurgent crowd than Murdock had, although Murdock had been given "more advertising out of the affair than anybody else."[16]

Bristow did not explain why Murdock had received more publicity, but there was an obvious reason. When he was younger, Murdock had worked as a reporter with journalists in Chicago and Washington. He had close contacts with leading members of the press in the capital. Moreover, he considered himself to be the semiofficial spokesman of insurgency, and after March 1909, he was selected as the press contact for the insurgents. He was less influential in insurgent councils than Madison, but his function as chief propagandist made him far more valuable to the anti-Cannon movement. In the long run, public scorn defeated Cannon, and Murdock played the premier role in developing a hostile public attitude.[17]

Whether Cannon could have assuaged Murdock and the insurgents by anything short of surrendering his power is a moot question, but his actions during the special session of the Sixty-first Congress were not designed to pacify them. Most insurgent leaders were relegated to last place on their respective committees or were removed from them. Murdock, of course, was demoted; but Madison, despite his actions, retained all his committee appointments and his seniority on them. During the insurgent effort to curb Cannon's power at the beginning of the special session in March, Madison was one of the three moderate insurgents who were sent to confer with President Taft when Taft complained publicly about their actions. Madison was also the only insurgent who was appointed by the House to the joint committee to investigate the Ballinger-Pinchot controversy in January 1910.[18]

From the special session of March 1909 until January 1910, Murdock continued his campaign against the Speaker. He circulated a petition at the December 1909 session of Congress, asking for Cannon's resignation. He wrote articles for magazines, deriding the Speaker, and he gave interviews in which he excoriated Cannon for his undemocratic, imperious, unfair manner. Murdock's activities gained him the title of "the Red Insurgent," while one writer compared him to Herr Joham Most, the anarchist. "His leather lungs, gift for sarcasm and drawling delivery," wrote one reporter, "rub the acid of his words into the scars left on the regulars by his performance. The old guard . . . denounce him as a more 'dangerous' man than La Follette."[19]

Murdock's campaign against the Speaker bore unexpected results in March 1910. Cannon's actions and his adverse press turned a number of important conservatives against him during 1909. Thus, when George Norris of Nebraska presented a resolution providing for revision of the rules on 17 March 1910, the insurgents were amazed to find a majority supporting it. President Taft had announced in February that he was not in favor of further attempts to change House affairs. To the disgust of the insurgents, he added that anti-Cannonism was being interpreted as a criticism of his administration. Nevertheless, Norris presented his resolution. According to Cannon's private secretary, the House in the spring of 1910 was in a "happy frame of mind," and "whenever the Speaker showed his head somebody was bound to heave a brick at him."[20] Norris's brick struck home.

For two days frenzied maneuvering by Cannon and his friends kept Norris's resolution from being considered. Then, on March 19, a vote was taken. Although minor changes were made, Norris's plan was adopted. The Speaker was not to be allowed to sit on the Rules Committee, which would be chosen by a House caucus. Immediately after the Norris resolution passed, Cannon announced that the Speaker's chair was vacant. Victor Murdock had waited for years for this moment and thought he would not be denied the opportunity of humiliating Cannon. But fainthearted supporters wavered, and the *coup de grâce* that he had planned never fell on "Uncle Joe." To Murdock's chagrin, Cannon was retained to the strains of "For He's a Jolly Good Fellow," sung by regulars, insurgents, and Democrats alike.

Joe Cannon considered the insurgents' victory the equivalent to the achievement of the King of France, who marched forty thousand men up a hill one day just to march them down again. In one sense he was correct. The Rules Committee chosen by the House under Norris's plan included many of the same men that Cannon had appointed. Despite this and despite future complaints by Murdock, the victory in March was important. Cannonism, which symbolized everything that was considered wrong in the Republican management of Congress, had suffered a defeat, and this encouraged the insurgent and progressive cause. Even though insurgents were kept from the Rules Committee in 1910, eventually Edmond H. Madison was selected to that body. Moreover, while the Democrats in 1911 tried to reintroduce most of Cannon's old prerogatives in order to increase the power of Speaker Clark, they were unable to provide him with the same dominance that Cannon had possessed.[21]

From the viewpoint of the Kansas progressive movement, the most important result of the victory over Cannon was the way that it affected the relationship between insurgent congressmen and their regular counterparts. Five of the eight Kansas representatives voted with the Speaker and were, therefore, written out of the progressive movement. Daniel R. Anthony, who represented the First District, had been absent at the time of the struggle over the Norris Amendment, but his past action was taken to indicate that he would have voted with Cannon. In Kansas, where one straw vote indicated that 1,592 voters favored Victor Murdock's activities, and only 70 opposed, any indication that a man was not progressive (anti-Cannon in this instance) could be politically fatal. Some Kansas congressmen complained bitterly about being charged with aiding Cannon. In some respects their complaints were justified. Phil Campbell of the Third Congressional District, who had left a sickbed against his physician's advice in order to vote down Norris's Resolution, conceived of the affair as a struggle between Democrats and Republicans. He claimed that he had never kowtowed to Cannon and that he had still accomplished a good deal for Kansas. Congressman William Reeder of the Fourth District also viewed the "fiasco" as a Democratic ploy to discredit Republicanism. He said: "Cannonism is an illegitimate child, conceived by an unholy union, in which Democracy seduced an unscrupulous element in the Republican party who were, and still are, attempting to wreck the party."²²

Only Charles F. Scott of the Second District spoke favorably of Cannon. Scott, who had been elevated by the Speaker to the chairmanship of the Agricultural Committee, later wrote:

> It is because I knew that in the very beginning the hue and cry against him was started through the meanest and most selfish motives, by men who could not compare with him either in personal honesty or in public service, that I would not join it. I knew perfectly well a year before the [1910] primaries, that I could have had [reform] . . . support . . . and could have been nominated without opposition if I had joined this hue and cry against Cannon. I knew that in refusing to do it I was very probably sacrificing my political life. You all harped a great deal about Murdock's "courage" in coming out against him. Don't you know that it took a lot more courage not to come out against him? Murdock followed the line of least resistance to save his political life. I lost mine rather than join in with what I knew to be an unfair and unwarranted assault upon a man who has rendered the country great service. . . . That is the trouble with all your direct government heresy . . . it makes cowards of men. It will fill Congress with a lot of moral cowards who will be for anything the people want whether it is right or not.²³

Although Scott was inaccurate about Murdock's motives, his candor was a refreshing change from the sycophancy of regulars and progressives alike who tried to appear to be favorable to both sides in the Cannon controversy.²⁴

Madison, who received applause from progressives and conservatives, was a master of middle-of-the-road tactics. He refused to vote for the removal of Cannon in March 1910, and earlier he had supported the Payne-Aldrich tariff. Under normal circumstances these votes would have branded him a regular and an opponent of reform. But Senator Bristow and Congressman Murdock kept progressives from attacking Madison. Murdock appreciated Madison's support in the rules fight when other Kansans backed out, and he believed that although Madison was no extreme progressive, he did stand for change. Bristow, likewise convinced that Madison was not an aggressive reformer, felt that the congressman's "heart was in the right place." "Madison," Bristow wrote, "is apprehensive of the power of Morgan, Lobdell, Bone and Albaugh [in his district] and you can't really blame him." Having been elected in 1906 in Long's old congressional area, Madison did have to contend with an active, powerful, conservative machine. But to assume, as Bristow later did, that Madison was taking his political life into his own hands when he stood for progressive legislation is wrong. Western Kansas had become a progressive stronghold in the state, and this made it necessary for Madison to identify himself with reform by 1910.[25]

Fortunately for Madison, in January he received an excellent opportunity to enhance his reputation as a progressive. His appointment to the joint congressional committee to investigate the Ballinger-Pinchot affair was hailed as a victory for progressive Republicanism. Although his report on the controversy was not made public until September, there was never much doubt about the conclusions that he would draw. His qualifications to be a member of a committee to investigate conservation were almost nil. His one involvement with conservation resulted from a pork-barrel project that he had inherited upon taking office. Chester I. Long, before leaving the Senate, had started an afforestation program near Garden City, Kansas. This was one of several experimental forests sponsored by Congress in arid areas. When Long failed to win reelection in 1908, Madison, as the western-Kansas member of the state's delegation in Washington, fell heir to the project. Where nature had created short-grass country, Madison, Long, and the Department of Agriculture unsuccessfully tried to create a forest. When in 1910 the program came under fire in Congress, Madison defended it on psychological grounds. He said that if anyone had ever lived in western Kansas, "he would know what tree hunger is, and he would understand of what value even a scrub is to the people upon those wind-swept plains."[26]

The Judge, as Madison was affectionately called, had been admitted to the Kansas Bar in 1888 and had immediately been elected county attorney at Dodge City. He had been an ardent prohibitionist in Ford County, and a capable foe of Populism. In 1900 Governor William E. Stanley appointed him to the Thirty-first District Court of Kansas, where he remained until his election to the House in 1906. His sonorous voice earned him the title of "Boy Orator" and made him popular as a stump speaker. Like other progressives, he supported tariff revision, regulation of the railroads, and the direct primary. There is some doubt about whether he was considered a sincere insurgent by everyone when he was appointed to the Ballinger-Pinchot investigating committee.[27]

The Ballinger-Pinchot affair, which Madison helped to investigate, was (as Elmo Richardson has pointed out) a cause célèbre over two varying opinions about conservation.[28] Technically, Secretary of the Interior Richard A. Ballinger entered into no dishonest arrangements, as was charged by the progressives, but he did oppose Gifford Pinchot's view of conservation and, thus, a "Rooseveltian policy." Ballinger, who once had lived in Kansas but had spent most of his life in Seattle, Washington, was chosen secretary of the interior in order to assuage westerners who were distrustful of conservation. During his first few months in office he returned millions of acres to the public domain and stopped large expenditures by the reclamation service. As a result he aroused the hostility of Chief Forester Pinchot, who had developed conservation programs while James R. Garfield was head of the Department of the Interior.

The controversy resulted from the Cunningham claims to coal lands in Alaska. The claims, which were in the national domain, composed approximately 15 percent of the Bering River coal field and were scheduled for exploitation by unknown investors. In 1907 Ballinger, serving as commissioner of the land office, ordered the claims validated; but an investigation by Louis Glavis, an employee of the Interior Department, indicated that the claimants had violated federal law by intending to share part of the coal lands with a Morgan-Guggenheim syndicate, which had investments in the area. Despite this information, Ballinger clearlisted the lands, only to have his decision reversed by Secretary Garfield. After leaving office in 1908, Ballinger was employed by the Cunningham claimants as a legal advisor, and when he was appointed Secretary of the Interior in 1909, Ballinger removed Glavis from the case. He then prepared to complete the validation of these lands to Cunningham.

Sensing a dishonest maneuver, Glavis asked Pinchot for help. The chief forester appealed to President Taft. After considering the complaint and talking with others, the president decided that Pinchot hoped to use the affair to embarrass the administration. Considering Pinchot's dissatisfaction with the policy of the Interior Department, Taft's assumption seems to have been correct. When Taft did nothing, Glavis, with Pinchot's help, published an article in *Collier's*, attacking Ballinger and questioning his honesty. This, plus other publicity, prompted Taft to remove Pinchot from his office as chief of the Bureau of Forestry. In turn, these developments caused a full-scale investigation of the affair by Congress in early 1910.[29] Although no votes were recorded on the resolution calling for the investigation, the entire Kansas delegation seems to have supported it. The Senate investigators were appointed by the vice-president. When the House considered how its members would be named to the joint committee, it kept the Speaker from making the appointments, choosing to elect them instead. The vote to keep Cannon from appointing the

House members saw Murdock and Madison with the majority, while the other six Kansas congressmen opposed.[30]

Senator Bristow's reaction to the Ballinger-Pinchot controversy illustrated the way that Kansas progressive Republicans responded in general. At first Bristow thought that the matter was solely a question of two men favoring different conservation policies. Not particularly concerned with this phase of conservation and disliking Pinchot's eastern mannerisms, he concluded that the inquiry would prove that Ballinger was an honest man. Early in 1910 the senator was less certain of the secretary's honesty, writing that he had been told by men who had examined evidence in the case that Ballinger in one instance had violated the law. By April, as the result of newspaper and magazine reports, Bristow was condemning Ballinger. "I don't think," he wrote, "there is any danger of Madison . . . whitewashing Ballinger. . . . In my judgment it is the rottenest condition that has existed in any Department since the whiskey scandals of the Grant administration." He continued:

> From my point of view, the criminality is on the part of the cabinet officer and his immediate subordinates who act under his direction, and the inferior officers were the ones who stood between the Government, or the people, and the plunderers. Glavis blocked the Guggenheims' game to loot Alaska, and for this invaluable service to the American people he is removed from office and stamped with official disgrace, the President denouncing him. . . . I don't say "poor Taft" any more. He is not entitled to pity. If he is so ignorant and indolent as not to know or realize what is going on in his administration—that Ballinger is the friend of crooks—it seems to me he is more an object of contempt than pity. If he does not know the characteristics of these men, then he is the worst man that has been at the head of the American Government since Martin Van Buren.[31]

Bristow was correct in assuming that Madison's report would condemn Ballinger. The majority of the joint committee, which reported in September 1910, exonerated Ballinger from fraud and corruption and lauded him as an efficient conservationist. The minority, composed of Democrats, said the opposite. But in a third opinion, which sustained Pinchot and recommended that Ballinger be removed, Madison wrote: "Mr. Ballinger's course . . . has been characterized by a lack of fidelity to the public interests."[32]

In a way perversely Kansan, Madison's report was considered by much of the Kansas press as the only accurate portrayal of the affair. The congressional investigation did nothing immediately to affect the conservation policy in Taft's administration. It did enhance Madison's reputation as a progressive, and it added to the progressives' distrust of the president. For the moment, Ballinger remained as secretary of the interior. After the sensationalism connected with the controversy had moderated, Ballinger resigned and was replaced by the proconservationist Walter Fisher. But Fisher was no more acceptable to insurgent Republicans than his predecessor, and in late 1911 Senator Bristow verbally attacked the new secretary during a public appearance with him in Kansas.[33]

Joseph Bristow became an opponent of the Taft administration as a result of tariff revision in the special session of 1909. Until that time, Bristow had been a protectionist. But because the 1908 Republican platform and the Kansas voters demanded change, he told the state legislature that elected him that among his first duties would be a downward revision of the tariff. President Taft had earlier written that he was counting on Bristow to help him secure honest tariff revision, and the senator had taken Taft's remarks to heart.[34]

Bristow was apprehensive early in the special session when the Payne bill was discussed by the House of Representatives. Before it passed on April 10 he became convinced that many of its provisions were pure and simple graft. "Between us," he wrote Harold Chase, "I haven't much faith in a tariff revision such as we want happening." Nelson Aldrich, he noted, had packed the committee that would handle the measure in the Senate with men who were opposed to revision, and Aldrich himself had indicated that he was against any fundamental change in the import tax. Bristow did not seem to be particularly agitated over these developments, and he gave no indication that he, along with La Follette and others, would engage in a spectacular fight for a lower tariff.[35]

Tariff-making was a festering sore that plagued almost every Republican administration, but it was one that Theodore Roosevelt had purposely avoided. His successor was not as fortunate. In 1908 both major parties endorsed the idea of tariff revision. Once elected, President Taft took this commitment of his party seriously, calling a special session to deal with the matter. But Aldrich and Cannon, the most powerful men in Congress, were not interested in upholding the Republican pledge. Aldrich felt that existing schedules were too high, yet he wished to leave the matter alone. His attitude was approximately the same as Cannon's. "The country," Cannon later said, "at that time was prosperous, manufacturers were satisfied with their profits and workingmen with their wages, and it did not seem to me either good business or sound politics to dislocate business and bring about hesitation and uncertainty by a tariff revision."[36]

The opinions of these men concerning the tariff were extremely important, as were the attitudes of other Republican representatives who shared Cannon's and Aldrich's views. William A. Calderhead of the Fifth Congressional District in Kansas was an excellent case in point. Calderhead, a high protectionist on the Ways and Means Committee, summed up his feeling on the 1908 tariff plank by informing a Washington contact that he planned to adhere as closely as possible to the Republican platform. But he added, "Don't announce our position until we get safe agreements for satisfactory tariffs on the products in which Kansas is especially interested."[37]

Considering that forty-six states and a number of territories sent men to Congress in 1909 with attitudes similar to Calderhead's, the tariff as finally passed would understandably not have satisfied revisionists. Bristow was not the only Kansan to become disenchanted by the tariff proceedings. Both Victor Murdock and Ed Madison complained about them while hearings were being held in the House. After the Payne bill was sent to the Senate, Madison noted that it would have been more of a revision downward if Representative Sereno Payne had actually had his way. Gloomily, he added that John Dalzell and Joseph Fordney, who were ultra protectionists, had exercised the greatest influence in shaping the measure and would probably direct House affairs when the amended bill returned from the Senate. The knowledge that Calderhead, a member of his own state's delegation, was going to be a member of the conference committee to reconsider Senate and House differences would not have cheered him.[38]

Madison was particularly surprised by Taft's inaction early in the session. Unknown to Madison, Taft was disheartened by the Payne bill and by Aldrich's intentions. The president had already considered appealing to the public in order to force Aldrich's hand. He thought about vetoing the measure if it did not meet his desires. George Mowry has suggested that Taft might have started using patronage to pressure reluctant senators to support the administration's wishes for a substantial revision. Roosevelt had done so, and Taft later used the patronage lever against progressive Republicans. In 1909, however, Taft chose a course that was far more in keeping with his personality by refusing to do anything at first.[39]

When the tariff bill arrived in the Senate, Aldrich's intentions of raising specific rates higher than those in the Payne bill became apparent. In order to dramatize Aldrich's actions, in late May a band of insurgent Republicans combined to speak on different aspects of the legislation. They realized that their effort would not affect Aldrich's schedules to any degree, but they hoped to inform the public of what was being done wrong.

In dividing the schedules to be discussed, Bristow was given those concerning sugar and lead. In order to prepare himself, he did an amazing amount of letter writing and reading. His final position on the sugar schedule, however, was substantially the same as the one that he held when he began his research. He favored a reduction of the rate on refined sugar, but he wanted raw sugar to continue to have protection. He believed that one day Kansas would produce all the raw sugar that the United States could use. "I certainly would be in favor of free sugar," he wrote," but ten years experience in beet sugar development convinces me that we will soon be producing more sugar than we consume." Like other Kansans, he opposed Cuban Reciprocity and duty-free sugar from the Philippines. His position was not that of a proponent of lower tariffs, but compared to Aldrich's, it seemed to be so.[40]

Bristow's role in the debate over the lead and zinc schedules was far less spectacular than his role in the sugar controversy, but he was more consistent in advocating a lower rate. In this respect he differed with Campbell and Scott, who represented the zinc- and lead-producing areas of Kansas. In 1908 the state produced approximately one-half of the nation's total output of spelter. These men favored the continuance of protection for their industries.[41]

Of course, Bristow's general attitude on the tariff was not totally dissimilar to the views of the other, the "regular," members of the Kansas delegation. As a moderate revisionist, Bristow's position in the topsy-turvy activity of tariff-making could be considered as one extreme. Calderhead was a protectionist, despite what he said about the party platform, and he represented the opposite extreme. The remaining members of the delegation were scattered between these men. For example, James M. Miller and Scott favored adding lumber to the "free list," although Miller, who represented the Fourth Congressional District, admitted during the debate that he would ultimately vote with the congressional leadership of his party on all schedules. His views about party discipline must have rankled the independent-minded progressives. "I am inclined, in legislative matters," he said, "to yield to the consensus of opinion of the party to which I belong, instead of adhering blindly to my own judgment upon a question of this character."[42]

Party discipline was a force that influenced Bristow, no matter how he finally reacted. In reality, Bristow feared Democratic free-trade views. He and, for that matter, other insurgents would have agreed with Congressman William Reeder of the Sixth District when he stated:

> The more nearly we permit Americans to do all the labor necessary to supply our needs and get good wages for this labor, the more prosperous all our people will be. I say this as a representative of a section which consumes a large amount of the goods manufactured by American workingmen; and we prefer to have those goods made by our own people, giving them their wages for their labor, rather than insist that our laboring people shall stand a cut in their wages to compete with pauper labor abroad.[43]

The lower-tariff posture of the insurgents was induced by the platform of 1908. If Aldrich had accepted moderate revision or if he had been less overt in fashioning higher schedules than those in the House version, most insurgents probably would not have become involved in the spectacular Senate debates.

From the point of view of the progressives, higher rates were not the worst feature of the bill. Aldrich, they believed, was using the measure to punish them by favoring the industrial East at the expense of their agricultural West. Midway through the session, Bristow wrote: "There is a combination here of New England, the Pacific Coast, and the Rocky Mountain states, West Virginia, Pennsylvania, and Louisiana that will put through the tariff bill that their people want. That is, they propose to levy tribute upon the remainder of the United States." On another occasion he added: "This tariff is being revised by a band of legislative pirates . . . taxing the rank and file of the people to increase the profits of the owners of manufacturing establishments." Here, his statement conflicted directly with Calderhead's speeches in the House. During one oratorical display, Calderhead said: "The charge is generally made that the whole tariff is levied for the protection of the manufacturer. The general answer to it is that the man who has received the most protection from the tariff has been the farmer . . . and the wage-earner."[44]

Until June, Bristow and other progressives wondered about Taft's failure to act in behalf of revision, but they said little. Taft did not intervene to help them in their fight; nor did he hinder their activities. But as the debate reached a climax, he helped to defeat an income-tax addition to the tariff bill, which was supported by the progressives and opposed by Aldrich. By this time the debate had become more than just

151

a disagreement over schedules. Aldrich and his friends had stung Bristow's pride. "When I rise," Bristow wrote, "[I am] . . . greeted with sneers and insulting remarks from the Aldrich coteries. . . . But fortunately their methods irritate me and increase my determination . . . and if they can be more disagreeable to me than I will be to them . . . they are welcome to the satisfaction they get out of it."[45]

Bristow's support of the income tax was not vindictive; he favored it because he felt that it would be a fairer way to raise the national revenues that would be needed in order to replace those lost by a lower tariff. Taft, aware of the constitutional problem involved in an income tax, wanted a corporation tax instead; but he was willing to support an income tax as a constitutional amendment. Aldrich opposed both tax plans, but he accepted the president's proposal as the lesser of evils.[46]

Taft swung Republican senators to his views through a special message to Congress. Bristow's reaction to the speech was predictable. The president had "pulled the rug" from under them. "This corporation tax," he remarked, "is an aggravating thing, aggravating because the President joined with Aldrich to defeat us upon the only occasion when Aldrich was in any danger. If Taft had been with us, in favor of revision of the tariff, so that we could have gotten a decent tariff bill, we would not have cared so much about the corporation tax." Bristow voted against the corporation-tax amendment; but his Kansas colleague, Senator Charles Curtis, and a large majority in both houses supported it. The corporation-tax amendment not only separated the junior and senior senators from Kansas, it also caused an open difference between Bristow and Madison. In extended remarks to the House, Madison said that he believed Taft was wise in rejecting an income-tax law without first having the Constitution amended. He defended the corporation tax by saying that it was just and constitutional and that it was not a dodge to avoid a personal income tax. "I confidently predict," he noted, "that the history of the future will disclose that in its enactment, the President and his party met the exigency of the hour, and placed upon the statute books a wise and beneficial law."[47]

Before the conference committee met in July to reconcile differences with regard to the tariff bills, Bristow decided to vote against their report. Taft's influence on the bill at the conference did not change Bristow's resolve, and despite considerable improvements in it, Bristow voted against the law on August 5. In the House, Murdock was the only Kansan to vote against the measure. On a motion to recommit the bill he was joined in defeat by Madison. An overwhelming majority of Senate and House Republicans supported Taft by passing the Payne-Aldrich Act.[48]

According to Taft, the 1909 tariff law was "a good bill," which could be defended "as a revision substantially downward."[49] Many progressive Republicans in and out of Congress disagreed. Influential newspapermen throughout the Middle West were particularly incensed. Colonel William Rockhill Nelson of the *Kansas City Star* ripped Taft's picture from his office wall and replaced it with a photograph of Grover Cleveland. He wrote Bristow that the people had never been as aroused as they were now "to the extortion . . . being carried on under the guise of protection." He told William Allen White that Bristow and Murdock, the two Kansans who had voted against the law, were the kind of congressmen the state liked, but the rest were unwanted baggage. The *Star's* continual assault on the Payne-Aldrich Act caused President Taft to complain that the paper would not accept the fact that he was a Republican and not a "free-trade" Democrat like Colonel Nelson.[50]

Harold Chase and Arthur Capper of the *Topeka Daily Capital* were also displeased by the bill, although not as much as Colonel Nelson. Opinion polls taken early in 1910 indicated that the people of Kansas agreed with Nelson. One group registered 1,582 negative votes on the measure, compared to 96 favorable replies. Another sampling showed that 1,063 voters disapproved of the law, while 49 felt it to be satisfactory. Despite his own opposition to the tariff, Bristow was amazed by the public's response. He wrote Senator Albert Beveridge of Indiana that the people wanted him to discuss nothing but the tariff. "There is an ominous drift against President Taft in our immediate vicinity," he added. "There is . . . abroad a spirit of intolerant hostility to the tariff. . . . I have never seen in Kansas such a unanimous sentiment of approval as I find in favor of the insurgent Senators."[51]

Insurgents profited politically from dislike of the tariff, whereas Kansas politicians who voted with Taft were hurt by it. These other politicians included Scott, Campbell, Miller, Reeder, Calderhead, and Curtis. Even Anthony and Madison, who voted regularly with the insurgents in attempts to amend the schedules downward, were criticized. They, too, had voted for the final measure. Many of the congressmen complained bitterly when Bristow continued to speak against the tariff after the session had ended. Reeder, who openly criticized Bristow, was answered by the senator in curt fashion. "If Reeder wanted to be reelected," he said, "he ought to have stood by his constituents and not by Mr. Aldrich's."[52]

Before September 1909 there had been little public criticism of President Taft, although Bristow had noted on a few occasions that the president had not upheld the 1908 Republican platform. Late in the month, however, Taft began a tour of the United States, starting in Boston, where he congratulated Aldrich as the Senate leader who worked for the welfare of the nation. Bristow dreaded Taft's tour, since he was sure that the president would say that the tariff bill was a good one, one that fulfilled the pledges made by the party. "He will make [the tariff] . . . a party measure," Bristow stated, "and put his administration behind it." If this should happen, Bristow knew that thenceforth an attack on the tariff would be tantamount to a rebuff of the president. On September 21, at Winona, Minnesota, Taft did discuss the tariff. As Bristow suspected, he defended the supporters of the measure, attacked its critics, and called the law the best tariff ever enacted by a Republican Congress, and thus the best ever passed.[53]

The reform press was stunned. The supposed leader of progressivism had switched sides on them, now choosing to uphold the reactionaries. Progressive-Republican politicians were less surprised, but no less mournful. They had come to believe that Taft had deserted them, but now he was taking a position that could only hurt them politically if they remained silent. Naturally they did not intend to allow Taft's remarks to go unchallenged. They counterattacked. The time for silence was past; they believed that if their action split the party, such an eventuality was not of their making. "It is the plan of the Aldrich and Cannon crowd," Bristow wrote, "and Taft is in accord with them, to eliminate the progressive Republican from political life. . . . The fights heretofore have been merely skirmishes—the real battles are yet to come."[54]

In Kansas, the Winona speech had a twofold effect. Regular Republicans took heart, but anti-Taft sentiment grew more bitter. In October, Bristow began to make a series of speeches against the Taft administration's tariff and against corporation congressmen. Regular Republicans began to refuse to appear on platforms with him, damning his antiadministration stand. Although the regulars were pleased with the president's position, William Allen White accurately interpreted the impact of Taft's actions on Kansas. Taft, he wrote, "has lost and the insurgents have gained, for they are now in the attitude of being persecuted by those in high authority."[55]

As a result of Taft's actions on the tariff, progressive Republicans became apprehensive about the future of reform. Bristow wrote that it looked as if Wickersham, Bowers, Nagel, and Ballinger—all trusted representatives of big business in the cabinet—were going to outline the policy of the administration regarding corporations. Bristow added that if he and his friends did nothing, the progressive revolution would be for naught. Unaided by Taft, progressives in Congress would have to enact progressive laws. Bristow recommended to Senator Moses Clapp of Minnesota that men of their views use the waterways convention in New Orleans in October to plan a program for the session of Congress that would convene in December 1909.

Although this meeting failed to materialize, sometime between September and December the progressives did manage to discuss what they would try to achieve at the coming session. Bristow later reported that Senator Cummins would manage their efforts on an interstate-commerce law; Borah would handle a proposed measure on postal savings banks; La Follette and Beveridge would concentrate on a revised tariff; and Bristow would work for the direct election of senators by constitutional amendment. Together, they were to "attack the selfish, corporation program of Aldrich and Cannon."[56]

Historians have often remarked that it was Taft's misfortune to have handled the Payne-Aldrich tariff, Cannonism, and the Ballinger-Pinchot affair badly. Thereafter, his reform accomplishments were suspect among insurgent Republicans. In the case of Senator Bristow this view offers a valid interpretation. The Mann-Elkins Act, parcel post, the postal savings bank, and numerous antitrust actions are listed as the main contributions made by Taft to progressivism. On each of these issues, Bristow opposed the president's measures or actions and disclaimed their progressive nature. As one would expect, in opposing Taft's program he often found himself at odds with other Kansas delegates in Washington, including Madison and Murdock.

Bristow, of course, was favorable to antitrust prosecutions, but he felt that Attorney General George Wickersham presented government cases ineptly, thus causing verdicts that were to the advantage of corporations. He, La Follette, and Cummins did not like the Postal Savings Bank Law, which was enacted at Taft's request. They believed that the legislation would allow deposits to be taken from western communities and placed in eastern banks. Handlers of the bill tried to persuade them that this would not be the case, but they were unconvinced and voted against the measure. That Taft made the bill a personal vote of confidence influenced them not in the least. The other members of the Kansas delegation voted with the president, except for Charles F. Scott, who failed to vote. Victor Murdock, an authority on postal affairs, was one of the warmest supporters of the law. Murdock, who seems never to have liked Bristow despite their general agreement on issues, favored postal savings because it taught the lost virtues "of simplicity, of frugality, of thrift." "It is useless," he said during debate on the bill, "to obtain inspiration [for these virtues] from the example of our rich. They answer all criticism of extravagance by a grand spectacle of continued material success. Our rich are utterly hopeless and absurd, as a rule, in their manner of expenditure."[57]

The question of improved parcel-post service also placed Taft and Bristow in antipodal positions. As evidenced by the lack of activity in the Sixty-first Congress, none of the Kansas representatives was interested in becoming involved closely with that problem. To the extent that the president and Bristow were at variance, Taft seemed to take the more equitable stance. He wanted to extend the parcel-post service so that large packages could be shipped through the mails. Postage was to be prorated according to a series of established zones. Bristow's difficulty with the proposed system was strictly political. Two powerful Kansas interests held opposite views regarding Taft's proposed revision. Farmers, who would profit from being able to purchase large-sized items by mail order from Chicago or Kansas City, generally favored the suggested change. Small-town merchants, threatened by the loss of their rural customers, opposed it.

The solution to the parcel-post problem did not come until August of 1912, thus it had no bearing on Republican politics in 1910. The system adopted at that later date was the one advanced by Taft; of the Kansans who had been involved earlier, only Victor Murdock voted against the law. For several years Murdock had advocated a plan to give the government an absolute monopoly in the carriage of mail in order to avoid a perennial deficit. He argued that as things existed, the American Express Company took lucrative short-haul carriage away from the government and expected the Post Office Department to foot the bill on unprofitable long-haul business. A monopoly would allow the government to begin operating the Post Office Department in the black by balancing the unprofitable business against the profitable.[58]

In discussing post-office finances, Murdock touched on another issue that occasioned disagreement between Taft and Bristow. In order to equalize the amount charged for carrying newspapers and magazines and the amount paid in costs by the government, and in order to eliminate a $17.5 million deficit, Taft proposed an increase of two and one-half cents per pound in rates on second-class mail. Bristow, representing magazine and newspaper sentiment, was opposed. During the debate over rates on second-class mail, Congressman Reeder supported Taft's objectives but recommended that magazines and similar matter be charged postage of one and one-half cents per pound instead of the existing one cent per pound. Reeder calculated that if periodical owners and advertisers absorbed their share of the increase, subscribers would pay about two cents more per year for subscriptions to monthly magazines. He argued that this increase would not stifle a free press, as some journal publishers claimed that it would.[59]

In a letter to a friend, Bristow had charged Taft with wanting to raise the rates in order to punish the Muckraker press. "This is," the senator wrote, "the boldest move [ever] . . . made in the history of this Government to suppress free discussion of public men and affairs." In response to a similar allegation published by the *Farmers' Mail and Breeze* of Topeka, Reeder had answered: "When an editor goes so far as to deliberately publish falsehoods to discredit a great committee of Congress or public servants [Taft and the postmaster general] individually, he becomes a menace to honesty in politics and an enemy to our form of government."[60]

Post-office affairs offered an opportunity for disagreement, but as was often the case in the progressive years, railroads drove an even deeper split between Republicans. The most divisive legislative issue to be introduced into the second session of the Sixty-first Congress was the so-called Mann-Elkins bill. In March of 1910 Bristow wrote: "This struggle is wider than a struggle over railroad rates or tariff schedules. . . . It is a conflict where representative Government, individual rights, the opportunities and liberties of the average man, are involved. The question is—Shall greed and avarice or justice and equity prevail?"[61]

A variety of factors conditioned Bristow's opinion of the way in which the Taft administration proposed to amend the Interstate Commerce Act. First of all, Bristow believed that Attorney General Wickersham, a former employee of August Belmont's, wrote the bill in cooperation with Aldrich, Cannon, and Elihu Root. In Bristow's mind this trio represented the congressional bodyguard of corporate interests. Secondly, the *Washington Post* reported that before preparing the I.C.C. legislation, Taft, at J. P. Morgan's behest, had met with William C. Brown of the New York Central and five other presidents of railroads. "Speaking to you personally," an infuriated Bristow told Fred Trigg of the *Kansas City Star*, "I believe the crisis is approaching in the controversy between corporate interests which seek to govern and dominate the commercial and industrial life of the country, and the people who are struggling for political and commercial independence."[62]

The third cause for Bristow's alarm was the administration measure itself. The bill, as presented by Wickersham, had four features that were unacceptable to Bristow. Under it, railroads could pool traffic, incorporate nationally, and create what the senator called "pure monopolies." Previously the I.C.C. had defended its judgments before the Supreme Court, but Wickersham's bill would have transferred this activity to the attorney general's office, which would thenceforth have argued the commission's cases before all federal tribunals. Worst of all, the bill would have created a commerce court. "This Commerce Court," Bristow wrote, "is for the purpose of placing Federal Judges, appointed for life, over the I.C.C. and vesting in them far more power and authority than Federal Judges now have over its rulings."[63]

To improve the bill, Bristow and other insurgent Republicans amended it over two hundred times during March and April. Of thirty-two recorded votes on amendments, Curtis and Bristow differed twenty-four times, with Bristow favoring amendment in every instance.[64] Led primarily by Senator Cummins, the insurgents forced an entirely new version to be written. They defeated national incorporation and eliminated the pooling of traffic. Their amendments made it necessary for railroads to go before the I.C.C. prior to raising rates. The insurgents were responsible for a revised commerce court. They allowed a wide latitude in appeals from it to the Supreme Court. They increased the I.C.C.'s power to regulate stock-watering, excessive rates, and other abuses. In all, by June 1910 Bristow could write: "We passed a pretty good railroad bill."[65]

At the same time Victor Murdock was claiming that the Mann-Elkins Act was the first worthwhile change in railroad regulation that Congress had passed since 1887. His enthusiasm resulted from a belief that, at last, intermediate points (small towns) on railroads would receive rates comparable to through points (large cities). He felt that the day of discrimination between rates on long hauls and short hauls was over. In voting on the bill, both Curtis and Bristow supported the amended measure. The Senate version was rejected by the House, and a conference committee was created. Madison and Murdock voted against the rejection, Anthony abstained, and the other five Kansans voted for the rejection; but the entire ten-man delegation favored the report of the conference committee.[66]

From Bristow's point of view the most unsatisfactory aspect of the controversy over the Mann-Elkins bill related to President Taft's actions. Time and again Bristow complained that the president helped the reactionaries at the expense of the reformers who were responsible for amending the measure. "We are in the humiliating position," he lamented, "of having the President and the Democrats combine to help Aldrich when we get him in a corner." Taft's interpretation of what was happening differed considerably. He explained to his brother Horace that weak-kneed senators from the West ran every time "those Populist opponents of mine [from Kansas, Wisconsin, and Iowa] . . . raise the flag of demagogy, and find some element in the legislation that I propose that savors of justice to corporate and banking interests." "They proceed," he added, "on the theory that any injustice or severity to wealth, vested interest, or corporations, must of itself bring about popular support."[67]

If he read the *Congressional Record* the day that Congressman Miller spoke regarding the president's railroad bill, he should have been pleased. "The American people," Miller said, "without regard to party, will give William Howard Taft credit for having kept the faith and the Republican party the credit for having put its platform promises into the statute books." Bristow's evaluation of Taft differed markedly. The president, Bristow had concluded, was a man of low character, low intelligence, and false sincerity. He said that he had finally sized up Taft, "that fat man with the big smile."[68]

Not surprisingly, Bristow had patronage problems in 1910. The oddity of the controversy that developed between the president and Bristow over patronage is that ultimately Bristow was allowed to select one of the four appointments allotted to Kansas senators. When Bristow first took office, he and Senator Curtis appeared to be ready to divide the appointments to the offices of district attorney, United States marshal, collector of internal revenue, and director of the pension agency in Topeka. Following the tariff struggle, Bristow publicly criticized the president's and Curtis's views. Curtis naturally decided to exploit this development.

Oddly enough, despite Bristow's opposition, Taft informed him that legislative attitudes would not affect appointments. On 27 December 1909, he called both Kansas senators to the White House to discuss patronage. Although Taft avoided the question of Bristow's failure to support administration positions, Curtis broached the subject violently. Calling Bristow a traitor to Republicanism and to the administration, Curtis demanded all four senatorial appointments. The president seemed

159

visibly embarrassed by Curtis's outburst, but he did not interrupt nor contradict him. Bristow, unprepared for the affair, was shaken. He mustered enough strength to reply that he had not forsaken the party platform and that he would not allow patronage to swerve him from supporting progressive reform. After returning to the Senate Office Building, he recovered sufficiently to write his Kansas confederates that "Curtis is the most deceitful, two-faced, hypocritical, boodling reactionary that I ever had anything to do with. I was amazed at his asininity, egotism, and gall!"[69]

After this occasion and because of his position on the administration's railroad bill and the postal savings bill, Bristow, like other insurgents, became convinced that patronage was being witheld from him. During 1910 Bristow did not receive any of the appointments made in Kansas. In February, Taft recommended Harry J. Bone for reappointment as district attorney. A little later, the names of two more Curtis nominees were sent to the Senate by the President—Freemont Leidy as collector of internal revenue and A. W. ("Farmer") Smith, an old Boss-Buster, as pension agent. The confirmations of Bone and Smith were delayed for some time because of Bristow's opposition. Bone mistakenly criticized Bristow in a letter that the senator gave to W. P. Dillingham, chairman of the Judiciary Committee. Out of courtesy, Bone's official appointment was held up for more than two years. In the case of "Farmer" Smith, Senate approval did not come until mid 1911, when members of the G.A.R. pressured Bristow to withdraw his objection.[70]

In mid 1911 Bristow was allowed to recommend his candidate for United States marshal. To the disgust of many progressives, he chose John R. Harrison, a former postal inspector who had worked with Bristow early in the decade. Presumably, the appointment of Harrison was the result of Curtis's refusal to support Taft's program of tariff reciprocity with Canada. Bristow demonstrated little interest in the selection and disregarded the advice of his friends when they told him that Harrison was a poor choice. Harrison was not a citizen of Kansas at the time. Bristow's reaction in this case was typical of his general attitude on patronage during most of 1910. He seemed to care little about who received what job, although he did oppose Bone and Smith.[71]

A minor reappointment attempt in June of 1910 did upset him. When Taft chose an anti-Bristow Republican to continue as postmaster at Salina, the senator became aroused. Not since the days of Thomas Hart Benton, he wrote, had a senator been overlooked in the selection of a postmaster for his hometown. Curtis and Taft, he charged, were drunk with power and would stop at nothing to defeat and discredit reform. Bristow believed that the president was using the Salina appointment to show party leaders that failure to support administration candidates in the forthcoming primaries would result in the loss of federal favors. Neither precedent nor tradition nor any other humane consideration, Bristow noted, would stop Taft and his reactionary friends in their effort to purge the party of its progressive element. They would not succeed, he added.[72]

During 1909 and the first half of 1910 President Taft alienated the progressive wing of his party by a series of mistakes. In the process he dragged a number of politicians who were otherwise acceptable to reformers with him. There were, of course, the old enemies of the progressive faction, who were waiting to redeem their previous defeat at the primary in 1910. Combined with the new opponents of the progressives, this group seemed to represent a formidable opposition for the reformers. In 1908 Stubbs and Bristow had led the way for new-style Republicanism, and at the 1910 primary the governor once more would stand for office. The main event now, however, centered on congressional contests as the progressives accepted the challenge offered by their opponents and, with unflagging vigor, labored to remove their "unprogressive" Kansas brethren from the House of Representatives.

# 9

## THE REPUBLICAN PRIMARY OF 1910 AND ITS AFTERMATH

President William Howard Taft's decision to withhold patronage from insurgents was only part of a program to defeat progressive Republicans in 1910. While formally reading insurgents out of the party, their archfoe, Speaker Joseph G. Cannon, predicted that the year's primaries would be used as "snake hunts" against insurgents. Early in 1910 he and other regulars began to collect campaign funds to be used against incumbent progressives. They arranged speaking tours into the Middle West, the bastion of Republican insurgency. The president himself was recruited to speak in at least one state in the upper Mississippi Valley. High cabinet officers were also to be sent into America's heartland.[1]

With these plans becoming public, a number of progressive-Republican leaders began to grow apprehensive. In February of 1910 William Allen White asked President Taft not to countenance the struggle that was being prepared against the Kansas insurgents. Progressive Republicans, he told Taft, did not oppose him. Their only interest was to "save Kansas for the Republican party." He promised that if the president would ignore the fight between conservatives and progressives that was impending in the state, the insurgents would support the Ohioan for renomination in 1912.[2]

Some regular Republicans in Kansas expected Taft to forgive the insurgents. Charles Gleed predicted that the president would gather the insurgent chicks under his wings. Politicians were made that way, he suggested. But Taft differed considerably from the typical politician, and in the primaries of 1910 he hoped to sweep insurgents out of the Republican coop. His decision thus preordained the disruption of the Republican party in Kansas—and the defeat of his hopes. Political conditions in the state destined that 1910 would be the *annus mirabilis* of progressivism; and planning by regulars, in addition to Taft's help, could do little to alter the inevitable.[3]

During 1909 and early 1910, progressive Republicans made some unusual and powerful additions to their factional alignment. Ed Madison, in the western part of the state, began to work actively with them, as did Arthur Capper in the eastern part. But more astoundingly, Cy Leland and Henry Allen enlisted in their ranks. According to White, Leland had been horned out of the old herd by younger bulls, and he was now interested in relighting friendship fires with Senator Bristow, White, and other former lieutenants. Leland, of course, claimed that the enthusiasm of the new movement sparked by Roosevelt had caused him to join the progressives. His poor showing against Governor Stubbs in 1908, however, seems to have had something to do with his switch to the ranks of the new rulers of Kansas.[4]

Allen's entry into the ranks of the progressives was more difficult. He disliked Stubbs, and as late as 1908 he had written: "[Stubbs is] a freak, and I can't get my gizzard down when I think of supporting him." But Bristow and White were persistent, and by 1910 Allen was moderately reconciled to the governor. He could, at least, support Stubbs halfheartedly while working for the election of other progressive candidates. Bristow, a former business partner of Allen's, was uncertain about the latter's progressive opinions until 1912; but Allen's amazing religious conversion by Billy Sunday seems to have convinced White much earlier that his old friend had taken a new lease on life. Allen, a powerful orator, was intensely emotional and easily moved by the moment. His conversion by Sunday has been described by Charles B. Driscoll as follows: "Henry Allen . . . stepped forward and grasped the great evangelist's hand, weeping, while the inspired community arose as one man and shouted, 'Glory to God!'" In 1906 Allen's opponents had described him as a corrupt, unreliable, dishonest grafter; and Stubbs and Hoch had removed him from the chairmanship of the Kansas Board of Charities on these grounds. Nevertheless, his dynamic personality and broad acquaintances made him an important addition to progressivism.[5]

Before an effective counteroffensive could be launched against con-

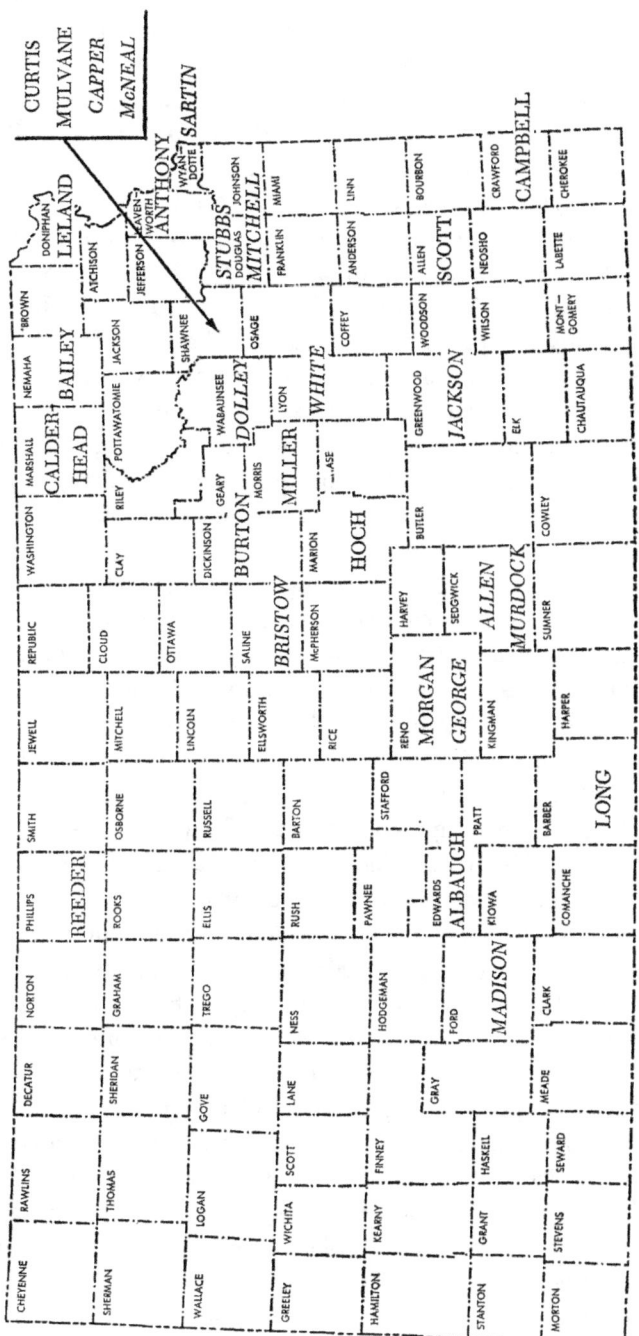

**PARTY LEADERS BY COUNTY OF RESIDENCE**

(The names of regular Republicans are printed in roman type;
those of insurgents/progressives, in italics.)

servative Republicans in 1910, the progressives had to solve an important problem that would face them two years thence. Senator Charles Curtis would stand for renomination then, and two progressives were interested in his job—Stubbs and Victor Murdock. Traditionally, either of these men would have tried to defeat the other in the 1910 primaries. But the fight developing between progressives and regulars precluded such action. In early 1910 they agreed to cooperate, but in so doing, they frightened Senator Bristow. Sensitive to all sorts of imaginary political deals, he feared that the Stubbs-Murdock arrangement meant that Stubbs would secure the senatorial candidacy in 1912 by promising that he would support Murdock instead of Bristow in 1914. Considerable effort was required to allay Bristow's suspicions; but by June he was satisfied, and he became intense in demanding progressive harmony. "We want to work as one man," he informed White, "burying any slight difference, and stand together for this great cause, because there are arrayed against us the most tremendous influences that ever were organized in American politics."[6]

By this time, White had become the engineer of insurgent politics in Kansas, and he acted as the "campaign manager" for his factional interests in the primary. Through his efforts, every incumbent conservative congressman was opposed by a candidate whom White deemed to be a progressive Republican. Neither Murdock nor Madison faced a fight for renomination, although White had to work hard to keep progressives in the Seventh District from challenging Madison. Murdock was enlisted in the primary in order to campaign nationally for insurgents, but Madison, claiming that the Ballinger-Pinchot affair was consuming most of his time, generally kept free of the intraparty struggle.[7]

The 1910 primary was a particularly difficult contest for Stubbs. He did not like President Taft, but one conservative congressman, Charles F. Scott, was an old friend whom he had helped to elect in 1906 and 1908. Scott was considered to be the worst Kansas offender against progressivism in Congress. Hoping to avoid a clash with his protégé, Stubbs quietly tried to get Scott appointed to Taft's cabinet as secretary of agriculture when it seemed that the president would remove James Wilson. His plan failed. Then, in July, the governor was forced to take a stand. On the pretext that Scott's newspapers in the Second Congressional District were opposing him, Stubbs began to include Scott among the reactionary forces to be defeated at the primaries. Scott was shocked. He wrote Stubbs that his newspapers were not unfriendly to the governor and that if some of his friends were opposing Stubbs, twice as many of

Stubbs's friends were fighting Scott. He claimed to have tried to stop Congressman Daniel R. Anthony's criticism of the governor during 1909. To a *Topeka Daily Capital* reporter he said: "I reply with the most emphatic negative at my command. I have not made a trade with the old machine politicians or with anybody else in the state or out of the state, involving my attitude in the gubernatorial contest." But Stubbs would not yield his opposition, and Scott was now the governor's foe.[8]

As a Republican governor, Stubbs at first had wished to avoid becoming involved in the national troubles caused by his progressive friends. Through 1909 he did nothing to discredit the insurgents, but he did not help them. The concerted effort to discredit Stubbs that was undertaken by regular leaders and Curtis in September consumed much of the governor's attention. The attacks in regular newspapers and in pamphlets written by Senator Curtis centered on costly reforms that Stubbs had initiated. The regulars maintained that Stubbs's programs had caused increased property taxes, allowing him to finance a political machine in the state.[9]

To counter these accusations, Stubbs demonstrated that taxes, though they had been increased in 1909, would be lowered in 1910. He argued that his programs were not responsible for the increase in 1909, although he noted that as government becomes more complex, it necessarily becomes more expensive. He added:

> The cry of high state taxes comes from the state agent of the school book trust, from the attorney of the Standard Oil Company, from the local attorneys for the railroads, and from the played out politicians of every county who find their occupations gone. It's the same old crowd that used to run Kansas under the convention system for the corporations.

In November 1909 a mysterious Republican official (probably Curtis) denounced Stubbs for being a "party wrecker" who was as detrimental to the welfare of the party as the congressional insurgents were. Despite these criticisms, Stubbs still did not want his reelection campaign to become involved with the split in Congress; but two events early in 1910 convinced him that he could not avoid being included in the larger trouble.[10]

On January 29 the annual meeting of the Kansas Day Club at Topeka was packed by anti-Stubbs, anti-insurgent Republicans. Led by Billy Morgan and David W. Mulvane, the meeting refused to endorse the Stubbs administration, and it criticized the governor and progressive legislators. Members of the Kansas Day Club lauded regular Republican congressional leaders and Curtis. They elected a conservative board of directors and chose Ralph Faxon, Chester Long's former senatorial assistant, as president of the club. Then they reported to Taft that the regular forces in Kansas had bested his opponents. By linking the governor and the insurgents in their nose-thumbing operation, the regulars increased Stubbs's appetite for revenge against them. Moreover, White and Bristow insinuated to Stubbs that a close connection existed between what had happened at the Kansas Day Club and what President Taft felt should have happened.[11]

The second development that eventually brought Stubbs into the national split occurred on March 13. Newspapers in the state reported that the Republican congressional committee on campaigns was preparing to fight not only insurgent congressmen but also such insurgent governors as Stubbs of Kansas. In a statement from Washington, regular congressional leaders were quoted as follows:

> We do not propose that a man shall be renominated for governor by Republican votes, who is going about the state inciting a rebellion against President Taft and the national administration. That is exactly what Governor Stubbs is doing. It is not in the cards for any man to be elected Governor of Kansas on the Republican ticket, whose principal campaign issue is antagonism to the national administration. Mr. Stubbs, with the insurgent candidates for Congress, will have to stand for President Taft and the new tariff law or forfeit Republican support.[12]

Stubbs thereafter began to increase the tempo of his complaints against the party's performance on tariff revision, but until May he refused to identify the president with the forces of reaction. In May he opened his bid for renomination by criticizing reactionaries, the federal courts, boodlers, and, by inference, Taft.[13]

Regular Republicans apparently had a difficult time finding an appropriate candidate to oppose Stubbs in 1910. Wanting to avoid the tried but tainted old-line leaders, they selected a political novice from southeastern Kansas, Tom Wagstaff of Coffeyville. Wagstaff was thirty-five years old at the time. A graduate of the New York University Law School, he had been a city attorney, a county attorney, and an acting district judge. As the son of Irish immigrants and the son-in-law of a leading Coffeyville banker, Wagstaff had broad appeal in southeastern Kansas. He was also a member of numerous civic clubs. He had one great shortcoming—he had been an employee of Standard Oil. Despite his earlier employment, he received the endorsement of Standard Oil's old foe, former Governor Hoch. His managers were able to induce two other former governors, Bailey and Stanley, to support him. Hoch, Stanley, and Bailey all campaigned locally for Wagstaff.[14]

But Wagstaff's debits outweighed his credits in the campaign. He was a political lightweight pitted against one of the strongest campaigners in Kansas. He lacked knowledge of state affairs and had an insufficient grasp of politics in general. His managers mistakenly allowed him to debate the governor in order to gain exposure or sympathy for the underdog. Stubbs's stinging rebuttals and cogent arguments easily demonstrated the governor's superiority. According to a biased *Topeka Daily Capital* reporter, Stubbs figuratively tore the Coffeyville novice apart in the exchange.[15]

Wagstaff had the misfortune, moreover, of being identified with those economic interests most distrusted in Kansas. Both W. J. Fitzgerald and A. C. Stich, who managed his campaign, were connected by legal and banking ties to Standard Oil. Simon Bear, another of his backers, was the recognized Bell Telephone lobbyist in Kansas, and the Republican national committeeman for Kansas, David W. Mulvane, who supported him, was considered to be a leading spokesman for railroads. Wagstaff was also designated by White as a standpat Republican, though he claimed to have Square Deal ideals.

On issues there was only one important facet to Wagstaff's campaign. He revived the charges of 1909 that Stubbs's reforms were costing Kansas taxpayers huge sums of money. A doggerel poem used by Wagstaff's supporters illustrated the profundity of much of the anti-Stubbs argument:

> Who raised the Farmer's taxes?
>   Roscoe Stubbs!
> Who's always grinding axes?
>   Roscoe Stubbs!
> Who busted up the old machine,
> Built one with patronage and long green,
> The finest you have ever seen?
>   Roscoe Stubbs!
> Don't you think it very funny,
>   Roscoe Stubbs!
> How we part with all our money,
>   Roscoe Stubbs!
> Don't you think we ever tire,
> As our taxes still mount higher?
> Don't you think it time to retire,
>   Roscoe Stubbs![16]

Once again Curtis helped to spearhead the fight against Stubbs, knowing that the governor, if he were defeated, would be eliminated as a senatorial candidate in 1912. Curtis was naïve to assume that Stubbs would lose. Many of Curtis's friends believed that by injecting his own ambitions into the campaign, he was actually helping Stubbs, while also harming his own chances two years later. Curtis's action emphasized that the gubernatorial contest was really one of regular Republican versus progressive Republican. In the process, Wagstaff naturally became a secondary figure.

Even though Senator Curtis gave a national orientation to the gubernatorial contest, Bristow complained about Stubbs's unwillingness to speak on national issues. In June, Bristow wrote White that the governor was making a "defensive campaign talking about taxes." "He should," Bristow added, "begin campaigning along national lines, discussing the tariff . . . and general progressive policies. . . . Kansas is for progress, not reaction."[17]

Actually, Stubbs had spoken about a number of progressive laws that he wanted passed, particularly the public-utilities bill that failed in the 1909 legislative session. He did, as Bristow noted, spend considerable time discussing the positive accomplishments of his previous administration and the question of higher taxes. The tenor of his campaign was summed up in the following passage from one of his many speeches in 1910: "I challenge any man to name a single state in the Union that has anything like as efficient a state government, that does not . . . [spend] more money for the administration of its public affairs than Kansas." According to Stubbs, Kansas had managed to lower railroad rates, improve food inspection, guarantee bank deposits, eliminate graft from state printing, and save hundreds of thousands of dollars on school books.[18]

The Stubbs-Wagstaff campaign was a constant source of perturbation to White. From the first he labeled the contest a smoke screen designed to hide the real culprits of 1910—the six conservative congressmen. According to White's designation, the six included: Daniel R. Anthony, Charles F. Scott, Philip P. Campbell, James Monroe Miller, William A. Calderhead, and William Reeder. White believed, as did Bristow, that Kansas regulars felt that Stubbs was politically weaker than the Washington reformers and that the regulars hoped to distract public attention from the national aspects of the primary by focusing the campaign on the governor. Although not absolutely certain that Stubbs was the weaker candidate, White was positive that the six "Cannon congressmen" should be defeated. He did not feel that they were dishonest, but that they were dispensers of patronage who traded "the economic welfare and political independence of Kansas" for mere "Indian beads." In order to eliminate the six, White engineered a gigantic primary struggle. As in the 1908 senatorial primary, he put forth a prodigious effort; and this time he was helped not only by Bristow but also by Murdock, Stubbs, Capper, and other progressive Republicans who were standing for office.[19]

White spent considerable time in late 1909 and early 1910 arranging a congressional slate. He was unable to find an acceptable opponent for the Third District, where Campbell stood for reelection, but he decided that Arthur Cranston of Pittsburg, who filed for the nomination on his own, was progressive enough to support. Diagonally across the state, in the northwesternmost Sixth District, matters were even touchier. Two men who claimed to be progressives were seeking the nomination against William Reeder. In White's opinion neither man was a progressive, but he conceded that a victory by either would be better than returning Reeder to Congress. Reeder was especially outspoken in his opposition to the "Populistic element . . . masquerading under the name of 'progressive Republicans.' " "The deportation of these men," he said in May, "is justified, as the Republican party has a right to have all of its enemies in its front." In the rest of the districts White faced no uncertainties. Madison and Murdock were tested progressives, and the four other candidates were men whom White and his factional allies had helped to induce into the race.[20]

In the First Congressional District, White joined Capper and Stubbs to encourage a willing T. A. McNeal to run against Anthony, the son of a famous pioneer family in Leavenworth and a nephew of the women's rights leader Susan B. Anthony. From White's point of view, Anthony was by far the least objectionable of the conservatives. But Stubbs, who had never done well politically in northeastern Kansas, was fiercely opposed to Anthony; and Capper, after his protégé McNeal became involved, was equally hostile to Anthony. It was Stubbs and Capper who cleared the way for McNeal by convincing Robert Stone of Topeka not to run.[21]

Accustomed to mudslinging campaigns in Cy Leland's old district, Anthony started his renomination fight early, ignoring McNeal and attacking Capper. The Topeka publisher, Anthony charged, was a friend of criminals and a man who used immoral, dirty advertisements to sell vulgarities to unwary women and children who read his columns. Capper returned Anthony's slurs kind for kind. But Anthony's greatest difficulty had nothing to do with name-calling. His trouble was party regularity. In an interview in May, he aligned himself with national Republican leaders and claimed that since these men were best qualified to solve the ills besetting America, all honest party members should support them. His district, being less reform-oriented than central and western Kansas, handily renominated him to Congress. He was subsequently reelected by a large margin.[22]

In the Fifth Congressional District, in the north central part of the state, Bristow was responsible for the entry of Judge Rollin Rees into the primary against Representative William A. Calderhead. Calderhead, who had been a member of the conference committee on the Payne-Aldrich tariff, personified the staunch, high-protectionist, old-guard Republican. Senator Bristow was particularly offended by the fact that the congressional district encompassing Salina sent a dyed-in-the-wool reactionary to Congress.[23]

The chances that Rees would defeat Calderhead were good, since the judge was a popular figure in north central Kansas, where he served on the bench of the Thirtieth District Court. He was a tariff revisionist, a proponent of an elastic currency, and a champion of the rigid regulation of railroads. The great drawback to his candidacy at first was his reluctance to run. Having failed in a prior bid, he was uncertain about whether he should seek office in a year when Republicans were badly divided. He feared losing the general election. Bristow appealed to a mutual friend, David Valentine of Clay Center, a veteran political leader and long-time clerk of the Kansas Supreme Court, asking him to convince Rees that he could win. Bristow, who had said that he would not interfere in congressional contests, promised Rees that he would work for him. In August, Rees, after he had defeated Calderhead, wrote that without Bristow's participation "the great victory in this district would not have been possible." William Allen White was also an ardent supporter of Rees, repeatedly referring to him as one of the strongest progressives in the state.[24]

White, however, was occupied more directly in two other congressional campaigns. In his own Fourth District of east central Kansas, he prevailed upon the attorney general of Kansas, Fred Jackson, to run; and he encouraged State Representative Alexander C. Mitchell of Lawrence to challenge Charles F. Scott for the Second District nomination. Scott was Cannon's closest friend in the Kansas delegation. He was popular, and he was considered the ablest, most intelligent, best informed conservative of the six who stood for reelection. Scott, a native Kansan, published the *Iola Register*. He was a proficient orator, a facile writer, and a member of many educational, fraternal, and professional organizations. He served as a member of the Kansas Board of Regents and of the Board of Trustees of the College of Emporia, and he was a past president of the Kansas State Historical Society, the state editorial association, and the Kansas Day Club. In 1905 Scott had accompanied Taft, then secretary of war, on a tour of Japan and Korea.[25]

During October 1909 White, Stubbs, Bristow, and representatives of the *Kansas City Star* and the *Topeka Daily Capital* were all needed to convince Mitchell that he could win against so formidable a foe. Though Bristow had promised Scott that he would not interfere in the Second District, he did help to induce Mitchell to run by preparing a campaign program for the potential candidate. The senator also agreed to speak in the Second District, which he did in June of 1910, when he appeared before a Mitchell rally in Kansas City, Kansas.[26]

Stubbs made similar commitments to Mitchell, but with reluctance because of his friendship for Scott. Nevertheless, after Stubbs decided to oppose Scott by supporting Mitchell, he, too, became an active factor in the congressional race. "Mr. Scott's service in Congress," Stubbs said in July 1910, "has been so satisfactory that the corporations, that the attorneys for the railroads, the packing houses, the Metropolitan Street Railway company and the big breweries are said to be solidly lined up for him in this campaign." "The old machine crowd . . . who fought him like tigers four years ago," the governor continued, "are fighting just as hard for him today."[27]

Scott claimed that although he was a regular Republican, he was also a supporter of progressive policies. "I am a 'regular' Republican," he stated, "because I believe the only way a party can keep its pledges to the people is to have harmonious cooperation of President and Congress and to do this the majority of the majority party must be able to dictate the program of the party." What was needed, he added, was "absolute, harmonious, 'team work.'"[28]

The biblical admonition about protecting one from his friends rather than his enemies was particularly apropos in Scott's case. In 1910 former Senator Long stumped the district for him, and part of a tour of Kansas by Speaker Cannon in August was in Scott's behalf. With such help, Scott needed few enemies. Nevertheless, Murdock, Mitchell, Robert M. La Follette, Bristow, and Stubbs all campaigned against him.[29]

In White's home area, the Fourth Congressional District, there were many who felt that the Emporia editor should be the candidate to unseat

James Monroe Miller. White, however, sought the backstage of politics, not its limelight. He preferred Attorney General Jackson, albeit a number of considerations kept Jackson from announcing his candidacy in 1909. Miller was a personal friend of Senator Curtis's, and Curtis was still influential in the area that had been his constituency ten years earlier. Besides, Miller was a crafty politician and a high official in the Kansas Grand Army of the Republic. Jackson was afraid that he could not beat the incumbent. Moreover, political leaders in Topeka were convinced that Jackson was the logical choice to succeed Stubbs as governor in 1912. Fortunately for the progressive movement, Jackson was not especially interested in the office of governor, although he considered the Topekans' advice.[30]

The most important deterrent to Jackson's candidacy seems to have been the lack of money. He felt that he could not afford an expensive campaign, and he also believed that he could not live on a congressman's salary in the fashion that was expected in Washington. On this count, Murdock, the spokesman of frugality, gave him no satisfaction. "Miller who boards and skimps," Murdock wrote, "saves money. The rest of the gang, incredible as it seems, have to fight to make a saving. I am ashamed of my extravagances." In December, Stubbs, White, and Bristow redoubled their efforts to make Jackson the Fourth District candidate, but not until late in January 1910 would he announce. His candidacy had the advantage, once he did enter, of having White's direct supervision. By April, White, who usually ran scared, was certain that Jackson would win. Miller's campaign was unusually quiet. The old Fourth District warhorse seemed to be tired by the political confusion that year.[31]

Despite Miller's subdued effort, the congressional campaign, which began in earnest in July, lived up to expectations. At first, Senator Bristow refused to involve himself publicly in congressional fights except for helping Rees and speaking once for Mitchell. In July, however, Kansas was overrun by regular Republicans of national stature. Speaker Cannon came into the state on a Chautauqua tour on July 15. He had come, or so he said, to set the record straight. "Kansas is the insurgent country, you know," he stated, "I understand that the mothers in that state send their sons to Congress with instructions to fight everything that comes up, just as the old Spartan mothers used to tell their boys to come back from the war a victor or a bloody corpse." The conservative Ed Howe of Atchison lamented the Speaker's arrival. "Cannon is an old man," Howe wrote, "not very good natured and very plain spoken. He will do the cause of the insurgents great good."[32]

On July 17, in a ranting diatribe against Murdock and other Kansas insurgents, Cannon, "storming like a bull," collapsed from heat prostration. Nevertheless, he made appearances in Kansas for three more days, though he finally abbreviated his schedule. Wherever Cannon had appeared, a "truth squad" organized by Murdock arrived later. As fate would have it, when Cannon could no longer meet his Kansas engagements, Murdock was hired by the Chautauqua group to replace him. Murdock continued to spread what the *Kansas City Journal* chose to call Elephadonk propaganda. An Elephadonk, the *Journal* explained, was this new Kansas political creature with the head of a donkey and the rear of an elephant. Its motto—"*In hoc signo vinces!*"[33]

When Cannon came to Kansas, Bristow decided that he should return home and take to the hustings. From mid July he spoke daily across the state, attacking Cannonism, Aldrichism, and the tariff. He was joined on the circuit by Senators Robert La Follette, Albert Cummins, and Thomas P. Gore, a Democrat from Oklahoma. La Follette came into the state armed with the voting record of each conservative congressman, and in rather hectic appearances he read their records amid rising hoots and catcalls. Cummins delivered "strong expositions of true progressive principles." "The whole campaign," wrote Bristow's father, "put me in the mind of a cyclone sweeping everything in its way."[34]

On August 5, a few days after Kansas had held its second statewide primary, Bristow wrote a Senate colleague that "the seed sown" a year earlier in Washington had just been "harvested" in Kansas. "The reactionaries here are simply stunned." William Reeder had been very wrong when, early in the campaign, he had said: "We have elected our last specimen of this new variety of Republicans, who are Republicans at home . . . and Democrats when they reach Washington." Four of the six conservative congressmen were defeated, and Stubbs easily won renomination. Kansas had given insurgency a rousing vote of confidence.[35]

As in 1908, the strength of progressivism was in the central and western parts of the state, but this time eastern Kansas responded in a limited way to reform. Although regular Republicans Anthony and Campbell were renominated in northeastern and southeastern Kansas, in the east central Second District, Mitchell defeated Scott. He won with huge majorities in Douglas and Wyandotte counties. In the other congressional areas, Jackson carried every county of the Fourth District, and Rees lost only Marshall County in the Fifth. Murdock and Madison had been unopposed. The gubernatorial race was an overwhelming victory for Stubbs. He received more than 60 percent of the vote and carried 98 of the state's 105 counties, 64 of them by more than 60 percent. He won the three largest counties—Wyandotte, Sedgwick, and Shawnee—the first two of which had voted against him in 1908. The antiprohibitionist strongholds in the southeast and northeast did not support him, nor did Reno County, where he lost by ten votes.[36]

Progressive newspapers in Kansas were ecstatic over the victory. They hailed it as a "personal tribute" to Stubbs, as a victory by the people over entrenched patronage and money, as a Republican "house-cleaning," and as a fitting rebuke to the real traitors of Republicanism. Regular Republicans were subdued. "It is only a temporary triumph," wrote the editor of the *Iola Register*, "brought about by a campaign of the most monumental misrepresentation." The *Abilene Reflector* safely predicted that the world would not come to an end because of the victory. In the *Atchison Globe*, Ed Howe wrote: "Stubbs hasn't a great deal to brag on . . . [he] defeated a college boy." In contrast, Bristow's *Salina Journal* predicted great things from the victory. Its editor noted that "the whole nation has been watching Kansas, . . . and [it] certainly saw something."[37]

If the *New York Evening Post* was any indication, the nation had seen a "political revolution." "In yesterday's primaries," a *Post* reporter stated, "[Kansas] fired a shot that will be heard 'round the country." "The prairies are literally afire with insurgency," said a *Washington Times* editorialist, while newsmen everywhere cheered or damned the election according to their own lights. There was no denying that progressive Republicanism had won a great victory. A pleased Senator Bristow wrote: "The old flapdoodle G.O.P. harangue would not count, . . . the people would not listen." U. S. Guyer, progressivism's manager in Kansas City, Kansas, gloated: "What doth it profit a Stand Pat Congressman if he saves his face in Washington and loses his hide in Kansas?"[38]

The one big lesson to be drawn from the victory, according to William Allen White, was that "the people in the long run will not be ruled by the bosses." Unorganized, discouraged, like "Injuns fighting from behind the trees, we won," he commented. President Taft was "sorely disappointed by the results," but he told Curtis that Republicans should close ranks in November. According to Senator Long, Kansas suddenly had been given two Democratic parties. "The only gratifying thing . . . is to know," he added, "that it cannot continue permanently." The leading Socialist in the state, Fred Warren, publisher of the *Appeal to Reason* at Girard, scoffed. The progressives got Stubbs, he said, and the Republicans got the courts and the rest of the state administration.[39] Warren failed to add that the progressives had retained control of the Republican party, even increasing their hold.

During August, White and Bristow collected information from progressive leaders throughout the Middle West so that the Republican platform, to be approved at the party council on August 30, would be an advanced reformist document. A few days before the council was to meet, the top progressive Republicans gathered in Topeka to discuss proposals and actually write the platform that they would later support. There was a consensus among them on most reform propositions, but the initiative, referendum and recall, as well as the short ballot, caused concern. The majority of Republican leaders and the public did not seem to favor them. Only the desire to remain ideologically pure caused progressive Republicans to include these issues in the platform. At the party council, Curtis, Campbell, and Anthony opposed the platform that had been prepared by the progressives. They were easily defeated by steam-roller tactics similar to those that had been used by the reformers two years earlier. Recalling the meeting of the Kansas Day Club in January, when regulars had brushed aside insurgent leaders and jeeringly endorsed Taft while refusing to commend Stubbs, a Topeka reporter noted: "The Kansas standpatters sowed the wind last January and reaped the whirlwind in August."[40]

In the document drawn up at Topeka the progressive Republicans endorsed those efforts by Taft "to fulfill the party platform of 1908" and sent a flowery greeting to Theodore Roosevelt, "the new world's champion of the rights of man in the world-old contest between rising humanity and . . . special privilege." They lauded Stubbs's past efforts and approved more than twenty new legislative proposals, ranging from state workmen's compensation to the election of federal judges for inferior courts. They roundly condemned Aldrich and Cannon. The council adjourned abruptly so that many of its members could attend a speech that was to be delivered the next day by Roosevelt at Osawatomie.[41]

Roosevelt played an important role in the 1910 progressive victory. The mystique of "Rooseveltian Policies" gave meaning to insurgency's reform, and his silence following claims that Aldrich, Cannon, and Taft had violated "Rooseveltian Policies" made possible the vital issues in the election. Despite appearances, Roosevelt was not trying to hurt the Taft administration, and soon after the Kansas primary he set out on a tour to try to stem the Republican party's growing polarization.

To keep a promise and to appease the town-boosters of Osawatomie, he agreed to speak at the opening of a state park commemorating John

Brown's career in Kansas. His speech was by far the most momentous delivered by a Republican during the Progressive Era. Written by Gifford Pinchot with the help of William Allen White, it placed Roosevelt squarely in the camp of the progressives, and it gave new directions to both the ideas and the events in the reform movement. Because of its radical nature, it was denounced as "Anarchistic, Socialistic, and Communistic," but it left the Kansas insurgent crowd bedazzled. The one man who might have spiked their plans had helped them. According to a *Chicago Tribune* reporter, when the former president had finished his Osawatomie address, Governor Stubbs leaped upon the stand and shouted, "My friends, we have just heard one of the greatest pronouncements for human welfare ever made. This is one of the big moments in the History of the United States." "Either Roosevelt wrote the Kansas platform," said Henry Allen, "or the insurgents wrote the speech."[42]

The progressives' exultation over the Osawatomie appearance should have been more moderate, because Roosevelt's address, whether they realized it or not, gave their intraparty rivals the materials they wanted. Hitherto, the Kansas movement had been characterized by a large amount of agrarian conservatism. The main issues had been molded into moral questions of an acceptable nature or into mild economic differences within a capitalistic framework. Now, wrote one regular journalist, F. Dumont Smith, the issue was clear. It was not a contest of men against wealth in politics; it was a pure assault on the basic tenets of capitalism. "It all really amounts to this," he added, "how much money shall a man be allowed to make out of his capital and opportunities? How much shall be allotted to labor and how much to capital?" The fact that only "big business" was under fire should not fool the small-town, agricultural entrepreneur. Capital was capital, and when men were concerned with the question of how a man might use his own investments, size was unimportant. Smith warned that the same kind of assault that the Free Silver and Populist craze had produced was beginning again, and Kansans had better beware.[43]

Many conservative Republicans decided after the primaries and after Roosevelt's radical pronunciamento that they should vote Democratic at the general election. Writing to the *Kansas City Star* in September, a Republican veteran of the Civil War, who had voted for U. S. Grant for president, noted that the Democratic gubernatorial nominee, George Hodges, would get his vote in 1910. He wrote:

> I am a "regular" as you call us. I have tried to be a good citizen.
> I have never stood for grafters and I object to being classed as

"an undesirable citizen" simply because I do not approve of the new and strange doctrines which have been incorporated into the Republican state platform and labeled Republicanism. . . . Kansas is not especially interested in the New Nationalism and "Conservation" . . . I am for George H. Hodges because if Democratic ideas must be put into operation, let us have them first hand.[44]

The most important Republican leader to desert the party's nominees was Mort Albaugh. Albaugh tried to induce Long to join him in supporting Democrats, but the former senator refused. "If I . . . should make a choice between the two Democratic candidates for Governor," Long stated, "I would vote for Governor Stubbs, not because I endorse his administration, but because I prefer him to the other Democrat who had always been his follower."[45]

In spite of ticket-splitting by Republicans and the switching of traditional allegiances, the November general election was a much quieter affair than might have been expected. The Democratic candidate for governor, Hodges, campaigned on a platform that was essentially the same as Stubbs's. From the time that he had commenced his political career in 1905 until the 1910 election, Hodges had been a close friend of Stubbsian reforms, even though he belonged to the opposition party. In 1910 he could only maintain that if elected, he would be more sincere than his opponent in presenting progressive ideals because he would not be plagued with a strong conservative element such as the one confronting Stubbs.

Hodges tried to win the *Kansas City Star* to his candidacy, and he encouraged regular Republicans to vote Democratic. He was especially perturbed by Democrats who indicated they would probably vote for Stubbs because of the governor's reactionary Republican opponents. In February a number of Democrats, arriving for their state committee meeting and party banquet in Topeka, met with Stubbs to congratulate him for the manner in which he had performed as governor.

W. H. Ryan, former chairman of the Democratic state committee, bolted the party in order to support Stubbs. Democrats also refused to oppose Murdock in his bid for reelection, and progressive Republicans everywhere were moderating complaints against their traditional opponents, hoping in this way to woo Democratic votes. Some voiced the suggestion that progressives in both parties form a new organization. After the primary, Republican reformers pointed out that in Kansas their party could function as such an alliance. To a Topeka Democrat,

Bristow wrote: "In my judgment the most practicable way to bring about reforms is to . . . control . . . the Republican party. . . . There are so many people in absolute accord with our views who by tradition are attached to the old party organization."[46]

Hodges, hopeful that he would win because of the Republican split, was angered when Stubbs defeated him with what he considered to be Democratic votes. He agreed with J. L. Caldwell, who said that the Democratic party had "saved the day for such asses as Stubbs." Caldwell added, "Honestly, . . . it's either a sad commentary on our own abilities, or a sad commentary on the wisdom of the Kansas voter, when such men as Stubbs and Mitchell can succeed with the dope they put out." During the campaign, Caldwell asked a Democratic voter if he would support Hodges. The voter answered that he thought Hodges was the best man for the job, but he would have to vote for Stubbs because Republicans planned to vote for Hodges. "The poor fool," Caldwell noted, "he was afraid to vote his ticket for fear we might elect a Governor." "You're right," Hodges replied, "the trouble with the idiots was, as you suggest, they were afraid that they would elect a Democratic Governor." "This very fact," wrote another Democratic leader, "the activity of . . . standpat Republicans for you, influenced a lot of *FOOL* Democrats to vote for Stubbs."[47]

As usual, Republicans won the general election in Kansas. This time, however, newsmen and politicians considered the victory an extremely significant accomplishment. In other states where Republicans normally won, Democratic candidates were victorious; but in the progressive-Republican Middle West the party of Lincoln temporarily survived the challenge of the opposition. White was proud that Kansas remained Republican, since the victory vindicated his view that only by becoming progressive could Republicans succeed in 1910. On the other hand, Senator Bristow was "very much disappointed" because the margins were so close. "I guess," he concluded, "we were lucky at that." The eastern United States voted Democratic wholeheartedly, and Senator Albert Beveridge, an insurgent friend, lost in Indiana.[48]

"It is too bad," wrote Mort Albaugh, "that a few more Republicans in Kansas didn't take my view . . . of which is the better Democrat—Stubbs or Hodges." Since the difference in votes had been close, Albaugh felt that "a little well directed work . . . would easily have defeated Stubbs" and would have taken "a little of the glamour from the 'tin God' business in this state."[49] Stubbs was reelected, but as a minority governor, receiving only 49.8 percent of the vote.

In congressional races other than those involving Murdock and Anthony, the change in voting percentages, comparing the nonpresidential years of 1906 and 1910, ranged from an 8 percent decrease in Campbell's Third District to a 1.4 percent gain in the Fourth by Jackson. On the average, Republican congressional votes diminished by 2.5 percent from 1906 to 1910, with losses registered in the Second, Third, Fifth, Sixth, and Seventh districts. Governor Stubbs received 1.5 percent more votes than Hoch had received in the 1906 election. Comparing Stubbs's showing in 1910 to his returns in 1908, when President Taft headed the ticket, the governor's winning margin was 2.7 percent smaller. Republicans were generally convinced that their party was losing strength because it could not bring its various elements into harmony.[50] Unstated, but obvious, was the fact that Kansas had suffered a loss as the result of the primary defeats of Scott and Calderhead, who were important members of influential House committees.

Two state races exasperated both regular and progressive Republicans. Billy Morgan, seeking reelection to the Kansas house, was defeated in Reno County, while Stubbs's right-hand man, Jonathan Dolley, lost his bid to continue as the representative from Wabaunsee County. Some party leaders lamented Morgan's defeat; almost all mourned the loss of Dolley. As Republican state chairman, Dolley had treated conservatives so fairly that both the *Topeka State Journal* and the *Kansas City Journal* felt that he should have been supported by regular Republicans.[51]

The breakdown of traditional voting patterns was of considerable concern to both wings of the Republican party, yet there was little immediate attention devoted to harmony in Kansas. The initial effort to reunite Republicans came not within the state but in Washington. In December 1910 President Taft called a harmony conference at the White House, which Bristow attended. Taft's prescription for unity did not please the senator, who left the meeting predicting a Republican disaster in the election of 1912. When Robert La Follette helped to organize the National Progressive Republican League (N.P.R.L.) in January 1911, Bristow endorsed its purpose of promoting progressive programs.[52]

Bristow was joined by Stubbs, Murdock, Capper, and other Kansas reformers in heralding the birth of the N.P.R.L. Like Bristow, however, they favored its program but not La Follette's presumed presidential candidacy. The popular prospective candidate in early 1911 was Roosevelt. Until he finally decided to seek the Republican nomination, presidential politics in the state were a confused affair. Both La Follette and Taft had influential progressive-Republican supporters up to late 1911.

Taft lost his progressive backers in part because of his advocacy of Canadian Reciprocity and in part because of his veto of the "Farmers' Free List" tariff during the special session of Congress in 1911. The Farmers' Free List favored agricultural-rural interests over those of industrial-urban areas.[53]

Taft also suffered among progressives because of his unpopularity with rank-and-file Republicans as a result of the bad press that he had received during the Sixty-first Congress. When he visited Kansas as part of a transcontinental political tour in mid 1911, he was met with unusual silence. At the state fair in Hutchinson, where the president spoke, Senator Bristow was amazed to find so gloomy an atmosphere. "There was no demonstration," Bristow wrote, "the Hutchinson parade was more like a funeral than a political rally." In an era when college youths were respectful towards national leaders, Governor Stubbs warned University of Kansas students before Taft visited Lawrence that the president should be received with the dignities befitting his office and that he should not be abused. Taft left Kansas a discouraged man, his face illustrating his deep concern.[54]

La Follette's presidential flirtation in Kansas was largely with Bristow and White. Ed Madison opposed the Wisconsin senator, while Stubbs and Capper refused to be identified with his candidacy. White privately committed himself to La Follette in January 1911. He dramatically told the senator: "Thy people shall be my people and thy God, my God." Although he claimed that Kansas progressives were trying in the autumn and early winter "to line up the state for Senator La Follette," he refused to organize an N.P.R.L. committee in Kansas. In October 1911 he wrote Roosevelt that he should get ready to run. " I think you might just as well prepare for the fireworks because it [the demand that he run] is coming [and] you can't stave it off."[55]

Bristow's attitude towards La Follette was as confusing, but not as inconsistent, as White's. He endorsed the senator in June 1911. In August he agreed with Harold Chase that La Follette did not have a chance, because he was a "John the Baptist type leader." In December, while Roosevelt's candidacy was blossoming, Bristow wrote: " La Follette is a stronger man with the American people today than Roosevelt [and] . . . would get more votes if he were the nominee." When most progressive Republicans, including White, used La Follette's physical collapse during a speech in Philadelphia on 2 February 1912 as a pretext for no longer supporting him, Bristow did not. He wrote to La Follette's friends that he was sure that after a short rest La Follette would be back in the campaign.⁵⁶ Bristow once told White: "I shall stand for La Follette to the end." On 15 March 1912 the end came, when he wrote to a friend, advising him to help nominate Roosevelt. Five days later, his newspaper, the *Salina Journal*, endorsed the former president. O. K. Davis said in *Outlook Magazine* that Bristow was "a politician of unusual sagacity . . . in close touch with the rapidly developing situation."⁵⁷

Men such as Bristow deserted La Follette in Kansas because La Follette's candidacy never took hold. Like Taft, La Follette did not seem to be capable of leading a united, successful Republican party in 1912. More than almost anything, Kansas progressive Republicans wanted to win election or reelection that year. The growing strength of their Democratic adversaries worried them, especially after two special elections late in 1911.

Midway through 1911 Congressmen Alexander Mitchell and Ed Madison died. Special elections to fill their seats were disasters for Republicans, as politicians friendly to Taft were defeated and Democrats were elected. After the second loss, when Madison's old seat was filled, the *Kansas City Star* carried a report expressing a view that was widespread among progressives: "If ever the Republican party in Kansas needed a Moses to lead it out of the wilderness it needs him now. That Moses is Roosevelt." Commenting on the Republican defeat in Madison's district, Billy Morgan touched the tender spot of Kansas Republicans when he wrote: "I think, . . . any nominee who has been supported by the Republicans will be cut by the insurgents, not by the leaders perhaps, but by many of the privates. I am of the opinion that the same result would happen if the conditions had been reversed." The losing candidate in the Seventh District, Frank Martin of Hutchinson, struck a significant chord after his loss when he noted: "Of course, Mr. Roosevelt would be very strong in this district among Republicans and Democrats." White carried this to its logical conclusion: "It is Roosevelt or Bust!"⁵⁸

Although Roosevelt's candidacy ultimately caused a bolt from the Republican party, at first it was seen as the only way to close the split. He was initially presented as the candidate of harmony. "The standpatters," White wrote in January 1912, "will all vote for him because they think he can carry the state and . . . the progressives will take him in order to beat Taft."⁵⁹

Roosevelt's correspondence for the second half of 1911 and the early months of 1912 shows how he shifted from the determination not to run to the decision to seek the presidential nomination. The Taft administration's prosecution of the United States Steel Corporation under the antitrust laws undoubtedly served as the catalyst to his candidacy by embarrassing the former president.[60] But local politicians also successfully pressured him into becoming a candidate. In these activities Kansans played important roles. For one thing, leaders such as Stubbs, Allen, Capper, and White created "grass-roots" demands for Roosevelt. They made him "the man of the hour." During 1911 they frequently wrote letters imploring him to run. Stubbs was one of the governors who signed a round-robin letter, circulated under Roosevelt's supervision, calling the Colonel into the race. In February of 1912 Roosevelt responded to this letter with his famous declaration "my hat is in the ring."[61]

The big questions of 1910 and 1911 had been answered by then. Kansas progressives were the majority group in the state's Republican party. They had easily defeated their regular adversaries, but at the cost of splitting the party. In order to repair the split, most of them were now committed to Roosevelt's presidential candidacy. What they could not know was that in endorsing Roosevelt they were creating a situation that would divide Republicans still further and would ultimately cause its progressive element to leave the party itself.

# 10

## WITH ROOSEVELT TO ARMAGEDDON, 1912

A number of Kansas progressives played important roles in Theodore Roosevelt's campaign for the Republican presidential nomination in 1912. Governor Walter R. Stubbs and Congressman Victor Murdock spoke in support of the former president in several middle western states, spending considerable time in the important Ohio primary. William Allen White wrote magazine articles extolling the Colonel's virtues, while other less significant Kansans contributed everything they could to make Roosevelt the popular candidate. But the wide public appeal of Roosevelt was to prove of no avail. National conventions are not often guided by grass-roots sentiment, and in 1912 the entrenched party leaders spurned the mandate of Republican voters, as revealed in the presidential primaries, and renominated William Howard Taft.

In 1912, as in other years, the question of contested delegates played a significant part. This time Roosevelt failed in the struggle to secure seats for his followers. Before the Republican National Convention met at Chicago in mid June, Roosevelt's managers knew that with his contested delegates voting, he could be an easy winner. Without them, he was sure to lose. It fell to the national committee, which was controlled by Taft, to decide to whom the 254 challenged delegate seats belonged. There was never much doubt about how the committee would vote. Governor Stubbs, as a proxy, was included in the national committee meeting, which convened for this purpose on June 7. In almost every instance he and other

Roosevelt managers protested the committee's decisions, but they were overruled. In all, Taft received 235 of the contested seats to Roosevelt's 19.

Despite having lost before the national committee, Roosevelt would not concede defeat. When the convention opened on June 18, he tried to get the credentials committee to reverse the previous action. But the credentials committee upheld the earlier opinions, and when the conservative Elihu Root was elected temporary chairman, Roosevelt realized that he had lost.[1] In the confusion after June 18, while Root and Taft were winning on the floor of the convention, other important developments were taking place.

The possibility that Roosevelt would lose had entered the minds of Kansas progressives at least a month earlier. Aware of the unrepresentative methods used to select convention delegates, they felt Roosevelt's chances were definitely doubtful. If he were not nominated, they wondered what they should do. The idea of bolting the Republican party had crossed their minds, but almost all of them opposed this. Senator Joseph Bristow felt that public opinion would force the national committee to rule in Roosevelt's behalf, but he also contemplated what might happen if the committee did not. He was against any suggestion of bolting, claiming that it was a device fashioned by regular Republicans to rid the party of its progressive element. Congressman Rollin Rees, who reluctantly switched to Roosevelt in June after working for Robert La Follette, was also against bolting. He said that he "preferred to stay with the old party" and "support its *duly selected* nominee." He added that he believed that if Taft were nominated, it would be possible to campaign for state Republicans and still support some candidate for president other than the one chosen by the party. White, Arthur Capper, Stubbs, and Murdock also opposed the idea of bolting.[2]

Their resolution was severely tested on June 17. During his first use of the famous Armageddon speech, Roosevelt stated that he would not be bound by the convention if certain contested delegates were to help organize it. This raised the possibility of a bolt. On June 21, when the credentials committee indicated that the Taft delegates would be seated, Roosevelt called leaders of his forces to his hotel, and there they agreed to quit the Republican convention the next day. On June 22, prior to the nomination of Taft, Henry Allen rose to explain why Roosevelt's supporters could no longer take part in the proceedings. Amidst a tumult that drowned out his booming voice, Allen said: "We do not bolt, we merely insist that you, not we, are making the record, and we refuse to be bound by it. . . . We fight no more, we plead no longer, we shall sit in silent protest and the people who sent us here shall judge." Ominously, a majority of the Roosevelt Republicans left the convention hall after Allen's speech. Afternoon newspapers carried stories about a rally, planned for that evening at Orchestra Hall in Chicago, where a new party would be formed. Roosevelt, the stories said, would be endorsed at that meeting. The bolt had taken place.[3]

It is fair to say that the majority of progressive Republicans in Kansas were sore at heart about what had happened. Pleas made by his political friends kept Stubbs from leaving Chicago on the day of the bolt. Capper and Harold Chase were beside themselves with anger, criticizing Roosevelt for not having compromised after his defeat. White, too, was against the formation of a third party, as was Senator Bristow. Among the eighteen-man Roosevelt delegation sent to Chicago by Kansas Republicans, only Allen, U. S. Sartin of Kansas City, and Harry Woods of Wellington favored the move. "Henry Allen," wrote Jay House, "cried like a baby when the delegation voted not to bolt, and announced he would bolt alone."[4]

There were other Kansas Republicans who were far from sorry about these developments. Charles Scott wrote on June 21, "Aren't things going beautifully in Chicago? I have been on a broad grin for two days. If only Stubbs and the rest of the Kansas bunch could be induced to follow T.R. off into the wilderness." David Mulvane had already stated his views on the matter. "We can't elect Taft," he said, "but we are going to hold on to this organization, and when we get back four years from now we will have it and those damned insurgents."[5]

A number of Kansas progressives attended the Orchestra Hall meeting called by Roosevelt on June 22. It was with trepidation that they heard the Colonel call men of their faith to his banner. "Go to your several homes," he said, "to find out the sentiment of the people at home, and then . . . come together . . . to nominate for the Presidency a Progressive candidate on a Progressive platform." If the future convention desired, he would be available as that candidate.[6] Kansas progressives desired, but they were not interested in a third party. Before Governor Stubbs had reached home, he was explaining that in Kansas, Roosevelt could remain in the Republican column and run as a Republican. Senator Bristow noted that leaders of the third party had promised that they would not oppose any Republican candidates who supported Roosevelt. There was one big problem. In every presidential election since 1864 the candidate chosen by the Republican National Convention had headed the Republican ticket in Kansas, and Taft was the Republican nominee in 1912.[7]

The Progressive National Convention met on August 5 in Chicago. By that time, Kansans had created the semblance of a state Progressive party, athough one had not been formally organized. William Allen White, one of the seventeen leaders who had signed the call for the national convention, controlled the Roosevelt organization in Kansas. He had been elected Republican national committeeman for Kansas, but had resigned to serve in a similar capacity for the new party. On July 7 his confederate Henry Allen had issued a call for delegates to the August meeting, and enough activity had developed to send a group headed by White and Allen to Chicago. Enthusiasm for the Progressive party was not great in Kansas, since, except for White and Allen, none of the major political leaders took part in it. The resolution to remain within the old party was firm, even though the commitment of key Republicans to Roosevelt's candidacy was complicating matters.[8]

The Kansas delegation was only moderately important at the Progressive national convention. Allen, who had been scheduled to make a seconding speech for Roosevelt at the Republican convention, did so this time; and the remainder of the group contributed to the revivallike atmosphere in Chicago's Coliseum. Their voices helped to raise the cry for "Battle Hymn, Battle Hymn." They bowed reverently while chanting the doxology at the end. A number of suggestions by White and by Bristow, who did not attend, were incorporated into the platform of the Progressive party. They encouraged the statement on the protective tariff. White also was a leader in the effort to withdraw a planned temperance plank, although he was theoretically a supporter of prohibition. Bristow sought a more moderate statement on the recall of judicial decisions than that voiced earlier by Roosevelt at Columbus, Ohio. The senator also favored a compromise position on the question of trusts. He noted that many progressives had been wanting a strong antitrust plank, but he suggested that Roosevelt and the new party endorse the idea of preserving competition where practical and that they "state that under modern conditions in many instances competition has been eliminated and cannot be successfully restored" even if it were desirable.[9]

White was intrumental in the struggle over the antitrust plank in the platform. George Perkins, the financial angel of Roosevelt's campaign in 1912, wanted a statement that would not place the Progressive party in opposition to business consolidation. Supposedly, White and other radical Progressives fought unsuccessfully, as things developed, for a strong antitrust position. It was presumed that Perkins's activity in the affair had made White his avowed enemy, but such was not the case. After the national convention White nominated Perkins as chairman of the party's executive committee, and while the Emporian did state on numerous occasions that he was dubious about Perkins as a reformer, more often than not White spoke favorably of him.[10]

The Progressive National Convention unanimously chose Roosevelt as its presidential candidate. It then named Governor Hiram Johnson of California as his running mate. Kansans left Chicago pleased with both choices and with the platform. According to White, the document included all the promises of David Lloyd George, Aristide Briand, Georges Clemenceau, the German liberals, and the Italian radicals, as well as the combined wisdom of Wisconsin, Kansas, Arizona, Oklahoma, and Massachusetts.[11] His enthusiasm would have been less had he reflected for a moment about the agrarian ideas of his native state.

The Progressives' "Contract with the People" was designed largely to appeal to the so-called subdued masses, but few Kansas voters were included in this group. Moreover, the document was urban and industrial in its emphasis, and Kansas was 66 percent rural in population. Roosevelt, to be sure, was a knight in shining armor in the minds of many voters, but his sword of righteousness was blunted because of the wrong pattern in the Sunflower state. It did not augur well for his chances that a staunch Kansas Socialist should joyously describe the new movement as a "half-baked" kind of socialism. Even in a half-baked form the doctrines of Karl Marx were unpopular with most Kansans.[12]

A month before Roosevelt was nominated by the Progressive party his presidential campaign had begun in Kansas. Like leaders of the party in other progressive-Republican states, Kansas leaders planned to place his name at the head of the Republican ticket in the November election. A number of Republican voters indicated that they agreed with this idea, since it would not necessitate the formation of a third party. Stubbs, Bristow, Murdock, and White all concurred. Roosevelt, too, approved of the plan, having wired the governor on July 3 that he was pleased with the way that Kansas Republicans were standing by progressivism. The rationale for putting Roosevelt's name in the old party slot was that Taft, through "corrupted" means, had "stolen" the nomination; thus, in states where Roosevelt had been endorsed, the only honest action was to keep his name in the Republican column.[13]

Not all Republicans agreed with this simplistic notion. Former National Committeeman Mulvane, upon returning from Chicago, was informed of the coup that was under way, and he prepared to block it. Because a number of electors chosen before the Chicago convention had publicly announced that they would vote for Roosevelt, Mulvane filed a new list of names with Secretary of State Charles Sessions. These men were bona-fide Taft supporters, and Mulvane asked that their names be printed on the Republican ballot in place of the old Roosevelt electors. Sessions, aware that the Progressives would fight any attempt by him to remove the old list, did nothing at first. He was a regular Republican, but he was standing for renomination in August, and he wanted both factions of the party to support him at the primaries.

Hoping to satisfy both sides, he figured a way out of his dilemma. County clerks, rather than the secretary of state, determined the final form of the primary ballots. He could send both lists of electors to the counties, thus letting the clerks decide. In the second week of July he carried out his plan, which favored the Progressives. Most county officers were supporters of Roosevelt, and since Roosevelt state headquarters informed them that the primary was to be used to determine who would head the Republican ticket, chances were nearly certain that the two sets of electors would be printed in most of the hundred and five counties.

But Dave Mulvane was not defeated. On July 17 his attorneys secured a temporary injunction from Judge C. E. Branine of the Harvey County District Court, restraining county clerks from putting the Roosevelt electors on the Republican ballot. Because two of the old electors had indicated that they would vote for Taft, Judge Branine's order dealt with only the eight remaining Rooseveltians. On July 18 Attorney General John Dawson, acting on an order from Governor Stubbs, filed for a writ of mandamus from the state supreme court that would compel county clerks to include the eight Roosevelt electors on the Republican primary ticket. He asked the court to assume jurisdiction over Branine's injunction.[14]

The supreme court heard arguments on the request on July 22. The Roosevelt presentation was handled by a former standpatter, Frank Martin, the recently defeated candidate of the Seventh Congressional District, while Chester Long managed the defense for the regular Republicans. United States Marshal John Harrison has left a brief account of the hearing. For once, the chambers of the Court were overrun with spectators, but they were of the sort who voted for Topeka's regular-Republican organization. Harrison wrote that Martin was magnificent in arguing for the writ, although the audience thought otherwise. Long made an impassioned plea for upholding the injunction. He compared the Republican party to the Methodist Church, likening the power of the National Convention to that of the Methodists' National Conference. His argument was popular, Harrison added, but "it convinced me the court would decide against him." The court did. The justices refused to involve themselves in a "political matter," and they suggested that the district court lift the injunction. The next day Branine removed the temporary restraining order and denied the regulars' request for a permanent injunction.[15]

Mulvane and Long quickly appealed again to the Kansas Supreme Court. On July 27 the state tribunal refused to hear the appeal.[16] Claiming that a federal question was involved, the Taft supporters sought a writ of errors from the United States Supreme Court. In a special hearing in New York City on August 1 Justices Mahlon Pitney and Willis Van Devanter, Taft appointees, upheld the writ but decided that both sets of electors should be printed on the Republican primary ballot. They indicated that a full review of the obligation of state parties to respect the proceedings of national nominating conventions would be made when the High Court reconvened in October. The Kansas cases had been given nationwide attention, and they had become intermixed with similar problems in Iowa and Pennsylvania. Before further legal action took place, however, the state primaries were held on August 6.[17]

Even in the days of populism, Kansas had not witnessed an election whose final outcome depended on a judicial decision instead of votes. In spite of statements made by regular Republicans that they were not working to nominate the Taft electors, since they deserved to be on the Republican ballot anyway, their election preparations were carried on in the usual manner. The Taft-Roosevelt question was not the only issue at stake in the primary. Arthur Capper was opposing Frank Ryan of Leavenworth for the gubernatorial nomination, and in a much more hotly contested election, Stubbs was seeking Charles Curtis's Senate seat.

There was never too much doubt about a Capper victory. The publisher was not yet the veteran campaigner who would command the Kansas vote better than anyone else, but he was a better vote-getter than his opponent, and he had a statewide reputation. His candidacy was hurt somewhat by the Republican split, but he stood by Roosevelt and seemed to be a sure winner. Ryan, who was a member of the Kansas Railroad Commission, was brought into the race by Congressman Dan Anthony in order to keep Capper from concentrating the power of his newspapers on the primary in the First Congressional District. Anthony was being opposed by a popular district judge, William I. Stuart of Troy, and he feared the effect of an all-out effort against him by the *Topeka Daily Capital* and other Capper publications. Although Ryan had little chance of being elected, his presence did keep Capper neutral in the district. Both Stuart and Anthony, who had voted and acted with the congressional progressives in 1911, claimed to be reformers, but Anthony supported Taft. Nevertheless, he won by a small number of votes.[18]

The most important race in August, other than the contest over electors, was that between Stubbs and Curtis. Since 1908 it had been apparent that they would clash in 1912. Curtis had tried to avoid the inevitable by attempting to defeat Stubbs in the 1910 gubernatorial primary. From then on, unkind words passed repeatedly between them. In 1912, however, Curtis was involved in Senate affairs until late July and thus was unable to campaign effectively. He entrusted his campaign for renomination to Albaugh and Long, as well as to federal officeholders that he had recommended. The campaign that they conducted left much to be desired. Rather than taking a positive stand, they directed their literature and speeches at Stubbs's activities. Curtis had remained loyal to the presidential choice of the National Convention; his regularity was stressed as the reason why he should win the party renomination. The brunt of his campaign centered on Stubbs's extravagances as governor and upon his role as a party wrecker. The old charges of increased taxes were renewed, and Stubbs's position on the inheritance tax and the income tax was attacked. "Governor Stubbs," one Curtis supporter stated, "says he wants to go to the Senate to work for an income tax. This will tax the income of every farmer and every property owner of Kansas. It will add to the present burden."[19]

Stubbs, while staunchly supporting Roosevelt, used the income tax in addition to his accomplishments as governor as the basis for his personal platform in the primary. He felt that he had to refute charges that he was a radical and that his reforms were costing undue amounts of money. He maintained that the changes that he had brought about were businesslike reforms, designed to secure continued prosperity. One campaign circular, reused in the general election, illustrated Stubbs's fear of losing the support of small-town merchants who had hitherto automatically voted for him. "As a large employer of labor, . . . as a man of wide business experience, as a contractor, as a banker, as a farmer," the circular read, "Governor Stubbs will approach the business of changing conditions with first hand knowledge of business conditions." He understood the "needs of business, because his life has been spent in business and not in politics." For the first time in his career, the governor was endorsed by organized labor, with Sim Bramlette, head of the Kansas Federation of Labor, and E. L. Blomberg, of the powerful railroad brotherhoods, supporting him.[20]

Despite an extensive campaign, Stubbs failed to win the popular vote in 1912, but an unusual method of counting primary returns by legislative districts gave him the election. He received 1,216 fewer votes than Curtis—48.9 percent of the total, in comparison to Curtis's 51.1 percent; but he carried 71 of the 105 counties. His greatest strength was again in mid central and western Kansas, although Wyandotte and Sedgwick counties returned slight margins for him. Curtis's victories were mostly in the northeast and southeast, where he registered majorities of from 60 to 70 percent in 12 of 25 counties; winning 14 in all. When this campaign was compared to the senatorial race in 1908, one fact became obvious. Regular Republicanism, more than ever, was located in the populous eastern areas, while the farmers in the western part were more strongly committed to progressivism. In 1908 Long had carried 22 western counties; here Curtis won only 9.

In the presidential vote, the Roosevelt electors won easily. Samuel A. Davies, a Roosevelt supporter, polled 76,610, for the highest total among the eight men committed to the former president, while John Gilmore topped the electors who were unquestionably committed to Taft with 41,565. The largest number of votes was cast for B. F. Blaker, a Taft elector who had been previously considered to be a Roosevelt supporter. Blaker was one of the original group of electors, but on July 29 he announced his intention of voting for Taft. Accidentally, White had included Blaker's name in the instructions that he had circulated concerning Republican electors, and White could not effectively change Blaker's pro-Roosevelt designation. Discounting the votes for Blaker, Roosevelt electors carried 101 of the 105 counties, losing only in Allen, Cherokee, Jefferson, and Leavenworth.[21]

Roosevelt's victory in the primary was a personal triumph for White. With the help of Earl Akers, a state employee and the Republican candidate for state treasurer, White had solicited funds, scheduled speakers, distributed campaign literature, and found time to write articles that were distributed to Kansas newspapers in July and August. His political effort, however, had just begun. Roosevelt's success caused another series of court actions, as well as an important protest about the Progressives' theft of the Republican column. It took considerable effort on White's part to organize his party's defense on these counts. White also had to prepare for the general election, in which three major presidential candidates in addition to state nominees were involved. In all, he was extremely busy from August to November.

The organizational structure that White used in the primary was the one that Henry Allen had created before the State Convention in May. By establishing local Roosevelt clubs during April, Allen had won every congressional district for Roosevelt except the First, and he had carried the State Convention for him on May 8. Allen had been aided by White and Ralph Harris of Ottawa. The Roosevelt clubs did not fall into disuse after the State Convention but were converted by Akers into the nucleus of a progressive-Republican group. Akers continued to add the names of sympathetic Republicans to the rolls of the clubs, hoping by June to have ten men in each county ready to support the Progressive cause. When the decision to bolt was made, White assumed control of Akers's work, and with the approval of Stubbs, White kept Akers on the job. The main headquarters of the movement was transferred to Emporia, but a subheadquarters was kept in Topeka.[22]

Prior to the primary, White used this organization to accomplish two tasks: he labored to increase voter support for the Roosevelt electors, and he instructed potential voters on how to mark their ballots. To accomplish the first he brought national figures such as James R. Garfield, Gifford Pinchot, Moses Clapp, and Hiram Johnson to the state. He also used Stubbs, Murdock, and Jackson to campaign for the former president. During July, he complained in pamphlets and news articles about Taft's "stolen nomination." In mid July, to insure that voters who favored Roosevelt would mark their ballots properly, he published lists of Roosevelt electors through paid advertisements in state newspapers, and he sent form letters to nearly every registered Republican. Replies to White's letters indicated that the idea of the "stolen nomination" carried the state for Roosevelt. White's argument was a rather twisted one, linking the theft to greedy corporations. By stealing the nomination, these avaricious corporations had stolen the presidency and the national party. The only way to redeem these institutions was by defeating Taft in August and then electing Roosevelt in November. After August 6 it appeared that perhaps this would be done.[23]

But regulars would not allow the decision of the voters to go unchallenged. Fred Stanley, who succeeded White as Republican national committeeman, continued to assert that the Roosevelt electors had no place on the primary ballot, and after the primary, he demanded that they be removed in favor of Taft. Regular Republicans began to charge that the real theft was being carried on by White in Kansas. Taft may have "stolen" the nomination, as Roosevelt claimed, but his theft was hidden from the voters. The taking of the Republican column and the Republican emblem by Roosevelt was obvious to everyone. More and more the question was being asked, Who is guilty of violating the slogan of the Progressive party, "Thou Shalt Not Steal"?[24]

On August 7 the regular Republicans reopened legal proceedings against the Rooseveltians by appealing to the state supreme court in regard to its earlier opinion and by initiating actions once more in the state district courts. They received an injunction restraining the printing of the November ballots, and they were involved in a suit before a federal district court when a nonjudicial decision gave them what they sought. On September 21 Secretary Sessions, with the acquiescence of White, ordered that the Taft electors be placed in the Republican column.

White's resolution to continue Roosevelt's name under the Republican emblem had diminished rapidly after late August. Only Roosevelt's desire to remain under the old party banner kept White from switching the Colonel's electors to an independent column. White became increasingly discouraged by the entire affair. He was certain that Republican charges of "party stealing" would hurt Roosevelt at the general election. He could think of no way to offset this complaint, and he believed that only by relinquishing the column could the Progressive campaign be free of this distasteful issue. He was also swayed by the possibility that the federal courts would order that the Roosevelt electors be removed from the Republican ballot. According to White, if this were to happen after mid September, it would be impossible to include Roosevelt on the ballot. The regulars seemed to be willing to have their man eliminated from the ticket if they lost in the courts; but White, believing that Roosevelt could carry Kansas, was not. He could hardly prepare for having the Roosevelt electors in a separate column while still claiming that they belonged in the Republican column.[25]

By September it was apparent that Sessions would order Taft's name placed at the head of the Republican column no matter what happened. This, then, would mean that court action would be needed in order to stop the secretary of state. It would leave things undecided until just prior to the election. Then, too, pressure from Republican candidates who were lower on the ticket became intense. That the regulars planned to oppose Stubbs was common knowledge, but they had not threatened to vote against every progressive Republican on the ticket. They began to hint that they would do so if Taft electors were not given their proper place.

An epic struggle had already occurred over the ballot question. Considerable resentment had resulted from actions in August. The state committee, for example, had met to demand that the names of the Roosevelt electors be removed from the ballot, but on the same day the party council had voted to retain them. The votes, however, indicated that many progressive Republicans were discouraged by developments. Sixteen reformers voted with regular Republicans at the committee meeting. At the party council, hitherto a progressive stronghold, 62 of the 142 members present favored removal of the Roosevelt electors. White, not relishing his uncomfortable position, tried to have Stubbs call the legislature into session to settle the matter. Stubbs refused to do so.

During the first week of September, then, White began to indicate privately that he was ready to compromise on the problem. He had previously claimed that Kansas law made it impossible for Roosevelt's name to appear safely on the ballot, since all sorts of cranks could be included along with the set of Roosevelt electors in an independent area of the ballot. Regulars, especially Sessions, were anxious to assure him that this would not happen. They promised that Roosevelt would be given a separate column in which the names of no other candidates would be placed. Roosevelt had insisted all along that he remain in the Republican column, but White, who understood the local situation better, could not do his leader's bidding.[26]

White's first meaningful step towards compromise came on September 7, when he wrote to Mort Albaugh, suggesting a number of alternatives with regard to the electors. He asked whether or not the regulars were willing to split the Republican column five and five with Roosevelt. If this were unacceptable, he wondered if they would leave the Republican column blank, running Taft and Roosevelt electors in separate columns. Taft's supporters, acting under instructions from the president, were not willing to compromise.

For another week White refrained from withdrawing the Roosevelt group. He indicated that he felt that a withdrawal was imminent and that it would be done with the assurance that Roosevelt would have a protected independent column. Then, on September 18, he yielded. He formally withdrew the Roosevelt electors, and on September 24 he replaced them with ten members of the Progressive party in a separate column. At last Roosevelt was to be the standard-bearer of the Progressive party in Kansas. Chester Long, who had helped to prepare the Republican court cases, rejoiced. His happiness was not due to an expected victory for Taft, but rather because he believed that Roosevelt would lose the state under these circumstances. "It is gratifying," he wrote, "to know that Roosevelt is out of the Republican party at last." He anticipated a Democratic victory.[27]

Predictions that the Democrats would win in 1912 had been current for two years in Kansas, but after Woodrow Wilson's nomination for president in early July, they increased. On a number of occasions White himself predicted as much, but he said at other times that Roosevelt would win. He recognized in Wilson the main opponent of the Progressive party, and for this reason he had been particularly disturbed by the struggle over electors. Having resolved this problem, he could begin to concentrate on the general-election campaign. Roosevelt, who had broken a promise to tour Kansas in July, arrived in late September, speaking in eastern Kansas for two days. Bristow also took to the hustings for the Colonel in September. He was unenthusiastic about his role, but he decided not to forsake his friends. Victor Murdock, seeking reelection, also helped out. But in the remaining congressional areas, progressive-Republican candidates were less responsive. To substitute for local talent, national Progressives, including Jane Addams of Hull House, former Senator Beveridge, and Judge Ben Lindsey of Denver, were used until October 8. After that date the Progressives' speakers bureau in Chicago refused to send other leaders to Kansas.[28]

Speaking tours were not the main things emphasized in Kansas. The only address that seems to have made any impression was Roosevelt's Milwaukee speech, when an attempt to assassinate the Colonel failed. After this incident, White wrote a letter to Roosevelt, saying that sentiment had switched wholeheartedly to him and emphasizing that there was now "a big, beautiful, generous, expansive feeling for you."[29] The major effort in support of Roosevelt came in newspaper articles, letters, and pamphlets that were mailed across the state.

Earl Akers, who did yeoman's work until the primaries, resigned in mid August to supervise his own campaign. To replace Akers, White used an employee of the *Gazette*, David Hinshaw. It was Hinshaw who amassed a list of 300,000 names before the general election and who inundated the voters with literature supporting Roosevelt and with instructions on how to split their ballots. Since Roosevelt electors were listed in one column and progressive Republicans in another, this seemed crucial. Upon entering the campaign, Hinshaw was shocked by the "horrible" condition of mailing lists, and he quickly set about requesting names from every precinct in the state. He was equally discouraged by the state that existing Roosevelt clubs were in, and he discarded them as being ineffective. He helped to organize the Negro vote, the Jewish vote, and the "college boy" vote, although he doubted their importance. He helped White solicit for money, and he also wrote form letters and newspaper copy.

Among the many pitfalls in the campaign for Roosevelt, finances were an urgent problem. White had had a difficult time raising funds for the primary, but after August his task was doubly hard. He refused to take money from national headquarters because of George Perkins's connection with the campaign treasury. He summoned large contributions from Capper, Stubbs, and other relatively well-to-do men, but his main source, as he later said, was the common man. He received letters from "hundreds enclosing dollars and fifty cents and twenty-five cents in stamps."[30]

Where finances were concerned, Roosevelt's candidacy in Kansas certainly took on the appearance of a people's crusade. "I am an old Methodist preacher and a Civil War veteran," wrote one contributor, "but I will gladly [give] . . . one dollar per month till election time for the support of the progressive cause." This performance was repeated endlessly. Nevertheless, in early October, White and Hinshaw felt that the campaign was faltering from lack of funds. They launched a "corps of solicitors" to raise money; with the help of these funds, as well as money diverted from what was owed to the national party, they broke even. White could not afford to pay for the usual poll workers on election day, but he secured enough canvassers by enrolling people in the "Kansas Corporation of Good Government" as recompense for their helping out. In all, it cost about $8,000 for Roosevelt to lose the Sunflower State in 1912, but this did not include the endless hours that White, Hinshaw, and people at the *Emporia Gazette* spent on the struggle.[31]

While Roosevelt's friends worked feverishly for him in Kansas, both Democrats and Republicans were busy trying to offset their efforts. The campaign for Taft was never impressive, since the major efforts of regular Republicans were devoted to defeating Stubbs and Capper. Some did take time to write letters to White, criticizing the Emporian and thus, indirectly, the Colonel. Midway through the race F. Dumont Smith, for example, fired off a letter to White in which he contended that Taft was responsible for the current prosperity in the country and that Roosevelt's campaign would upset it. He suggested that when White sent forth instructions to voters on splitting their ballots, he should also include a list of prices for horses, cattle, hogs, wheat, and so forth, for 1912 and 1893. In this way, voters would be able to appreciate Taft's greatness.[32]

Another Republican answered a plea from White by declaring that he "respected good Socialists and Democrats" but had no use for "traitors." "I beg to advise," he added, "there is nothing doing here for T.R. or his kind of mice." There was a crueler description of Roosevelt and the Progressives in the offing. One irate citizen described the movement as follows: "A freak party headed by a selfish and insincere egotist, a man of infinite inconsistencies, a habitual liar, a modern Jehu, backed up by rich blackmailers, manipulators, swindlers, . . . [and] cranks." Another one thought it best to attack the real culprit, "Bill Allen White, the new boss of Kansas Republicanism." "He . . . has undertaken to fix the standard," this critic wrote. "No man is a progressive Republican unless he thinks just as White does, or agrees to do as White does."[33]

But White was not the real issue in the election. A more damaging charge was raised by Charles Gleed, although it was more effectively used by Democrats and other opponents of the Progressive party. Gleed asserted that the Progressive party, with a membership that included William Rockhill Nelson, Stubbs, Perkins, Medill McCormick, and William Flinn, could hardly claim to be the party of the poor or claim to be untainted by wealthy connections. The Democrats hammered away on this count. Statements of the Progressive party about the need to curb great wealth were hollow, wrote the state's Democratic national committeeman, Colonel Bill Sapp. In a letter to White he added:

> If I am correctly informed, you have J. Pierpont Morgan who through his leading satellite, Mr. Perkins, is financing the Roosevelt campaign, and Perkins means the United States Steel crowd; the Wall Street money trust; the tobacco trust; the Standard Oil Crowd; and their kindred interests that have dominated this government for a quarter of a century. The real truth is, you, representing Mr. Roosevelt, are not fighting for the people any more than Mr. Stanley representing Mr. Taft is fighting for the people. You both represent enormous wealth.

Sapp's explanation hurt. Kansas Progressives were unable to answer him satisfactorily.[34]

Difficulties caused by Perkins's presence in the party were burdensome, but they were not nearly as important as the nomination of Woodrow Wilson. For a year, progressive-Republican newspapers had been extolling Wilson's virtues and describing his triumphs in New Jersey. As fate would have it, after a hard-fought convention in July, Wilson was nominated by the Democrats as their presidential candidate, and their choice of him did not splinter the Democratic party.[35]

After the Progressive bolt, White and his Kansas supporters had hoped to woo Democrats to Roosevelt's banner. In the past they had always asked Democrats to vote against party regulars and to vote for progressive Republicans. Now their position was complicated by the fact that the Democrats had a progressive of their own to vote for. What could Rooseveltians do? White had the answer, but it was not a very convincing one. He said that just as the nomination of Taft had not represented the true sentiment at Chicago, the nomination of Wilson had not been the result of the true feeling at Baltimore. Wilson, to be sure, was a progressive, but his party was the stronghold of reactionaries from the South and corrupt politicians from New York. Even if Wilson were elected, he would not be able to work with his party, because they were ideologically miles apart. It would be better, he concluded, to elect Roosevelt, who could function with the progressive element that dominated Republicanism. There was a monstrous flaw in his logic. If the Republican party was progressive, why was Taft its nominee? Having read earlier descriptions of Taft that White had written, Colonel Sapp decided that instead of the Democrats joining the Progressives, these former Republicans should come over to the really advanced party. "Get out of that old bunch," he told White, "and get on the side of the people!"[36]

Wilson's candidacy was disturbing not only because of his reputation, which was problem enough, but also because of his "New Freedom" platform. The Progressives' "Contract with the People" was an advanced reform document dealing with what were essentially urban problems. The Democrats, on the other hand, because of William Jennings Bryan's influence and because of Wilson's predilections, wrote a traditional, rural-oriented reform platform.

On one issue Roosevelt was particularly vulnerable in Kansas, and to make matters worse, his supporters created another for him. Roosevelt opposed broad antitrust actions, favoring rather the regulation of monopolies. During his September speaking tour he explained his position in favor of a federal commission to control business and to channel bigness into constructive lines. Bigness itself was not a crime; the crime was in how great wealth was used. If it was properly regulated, it could be made into a positive force. Two weeks after Roosevelt's visit, Bryan and Wilson came into the state and spoke exclusively about antitrust laws and the "mother-of-the-trusts," the tariff. They attacked Roosevelt's idea of regulation with an old Kansas progressive cry of "Who would regulate the regulator?" and they asked Kansas voters to support a man who would increase the power of the federal government not in order to encourage monopolies but in order to dissolve them.

Wilson spoke in favor of a lower tariff that would give farmers a fair opportunity to buy as well as sell on an international market. Everyone knew, he stated, that the tariff helped to foster trusts by making high prices possible. If trusts were to be effectively broken, this action had to be accompanied by lower tariffs or free trade. But the local Progressives mistakenly attacked his assertion. The tariff, they argued, was not related to the trust question, nor could it solve this problem. Protection benefited the working man by insuring his wages. Because of this, they could not simply be lowered; they had to be studied by experts. Only after a tariff board had made recommendations could revisions be undertaken. Statements such as these coming from Kansas Progressives seemed unusual and particularly disquieting. Two years earlier, progressive Republicans had promoted lower tariffs and better antitrust laws for exactly the same reasons that Wilson now offered. The thought that perhaps Perkins and the J. P. Morgan money trust had seduced the state leaders of the party undoubtedly crossed the minds of many Kansas voters.[37]

However, when prices were high and crops were good, issues were never exceptionally important factors in Kansas' general elections, and 1912 was not greatly different. In prosperous years, party designation was the all-powerful force. Thus, the decision in November, as in the past, turned not on Wilson's views on the tariff and Roosevelt's position on the trusts but rather on party loyalties. Roosevelt lost Kansas in 1912 because many Republicans refused to desert the party of their fathers for a new political organization. Since only a few Democrats failed to support their party's nominee, Roosevelt fell roughly 26,000 Republican votes short of what was needed to win. Many of the 75,000 Republicans who voted for Taft in the election had favored Roosevelt before the Chicago convention. The split had tested their fundamental reason for being members of the Republican party, and this "unthinking electorate," as White called it, would not leave the old party ranks. A Democratic candidate with less to offer than Wilson would probably have been unable to keep the allegiance of his party. Alton B. Parker had not done so in 1904 against the Colonel. But where Parker failed, Wilson succeeded. His totals in Kansas indicate that he lost only 3 percent of the Democratic vote that had been given to Bryan in 1908. In 1912 Wilson received 143,795 votes, approximately twice as many as Taft and about 26,000 more than Roosevelt.

Considering that Roosevelt represented a new party, his returns were not completely disheartening. In 89 of the state's 105 counties he was either first or second in total votes. He carried a number of counties in southwestern Kansas, as well as Wyandotte and Sedgwick counties. Despite his appeal in urban areas, he lost Wichita, Kansas City, and Topeka, in addition to the semi-industrial southeastern corner. He ran second to Wilson in the three cities, and he trailed the Socialist candidate, Eugene V. Debs, in the southeast. Because his name appeared at the head of the Progressives' column, Roosevelt ran well behind Stubbs and Capper, who had supported him, but whose names appeared in the Republican column. Party loyalties were the major reason for Roosevelt's defeat, but party sentiment was not strong enough for Stubbs and Capper to win.[38]

Regular-Republican opposition to Stubbs and Capper was too strong to be swayed by party feeling. At the time of the state committee and council meetings on August 27, a number of regulars formed a Taft Republican League in Topeka. It was designed to promote the candidacies of Taft Republicans and to "defeat every candidate on the Republican ticket who is lined up for Roosevelt." A week earlier the State Republican League was organized for the purpose of defeating Stubbs and Capper. Former Boss-Busters such as Patrick Henry Coney, Al Williams, David Mulvane, and Charles Curtis organized these groups.

At first only Stubbs and Capper were designated as Republicans who should be defeated, but later the names of some congressional nominees were added. The meetings of these organizations were not kept secret, and the enthusiasm of each group was comparable to the revivalistic atmosphere that accompanied the formation of the Progressive party in August at Chicago. When the State Republican League was founded, the Reverend John Bright of Topeka led the regulars in singing an 1896 campaign song, "It's the Old Time Party and It's Good Enough for Me." Resolutions were adopted unanimously at this meeting, and according to one reporter, every speech was aimed at "roasting" Roosevelt and "drawing and quartering" Stubbs. By late August the Taft League claimed that ninety-five counties were organized against the progressive Republicans.[39]

It was no surprise, then, that Stubbs was roundly beaten in 1912. For one thing, Curtis campaigned actively against him. The senator had been unable to stump Kansas prior to the primary, but he made up for his absence after he had lost that election. In typical Curtis fashion he campaigned with half-truths and exaggerations. He concentrated on

Stubbs's reluctance to support women's rights and on the traditional charge of his lack of economy. He justified his actions on the grounds that Stubbs was no Republican because he was not supporting Taft, but Curtis's real reasons were to get revenge and to prepare for the future. Stubbs had been the biggest problem within the party for a politician of Curtis's style, and Stubbs could be eliminated politically in 1912.

The Republican League circulated pamphlets describing traitors to party fidelity, and it always insisted that Stubbs was the head of this immoral conspiracy. It worked closely with Henderson Martin, the Democratic campaign chairman, supplying him with literature and information designed to damage the governor's chances for election to the Senate. But fate had an even more unexpected reversal in store for Stubbs. He had hoped that his opponent in the general election would be the conservative Democrat Hugh Farrelley, but at the August primaries the Democrats chose Judge William Thompson of Garden City. The Judge was relatively unknown over the state, but he was considered a Wilsonian progressive and a devotee of reform. Thus, much like Roosevelt, Stubbs seemed to have little or no chance of picking up desperately needed Democratic votes.[40]

Stubbs, however, made his usual strong campaign, and in spite of Thompson's reputation, he tried to win Democratic support. There were the normal complaints from White that Stubbs was concentrating too much on his past record and too little on national issues. But in his speeches the governor discussed the income tax, a federal inheritance tax, the direct election of senators, workmen's compensation, child-labor laws, and so forth. Although it was unwise of him to champion national prohibition in eastern Kansas, he courageously advocated it anyway in the "whiskey counties."

His pamphlet literature, while of a much more general nature than his speeches, indicated that he continued to worry about the support of businessmen. His reputation as a radical bothered him, and he tried to show that as a business leader himself, he would look after business interests best. Once again Stubbs was endorsed by labor organizations, with Sim Bramlette "acknowledging the many courtesies and kindly interests shown by Governor Stubbs towards labor in the past." In his bid for Democratic votes, Stubbs used the Republican split to advantage. Arguing that the old-guard Republicans were helping the Democratic candidate, he asked all loyal progressives of both parties to put their "shoulders to the wheel" in the last final charge against "corrupt rule."

"Let us not drop from the ranks," he urged, "but lead on the final victory."[41]

Stubbs got few if any Democratic votes. He received thirty thousand more votes than Roosevelt, but twenty thousand fewer than Thompson. He carried only thirty-one counties and lost a majority of the all-important legislative districts. His strength, as before, was in western Kansas, but he lost numerous votes there and in other areas because of the split. Actually, fewer Kansans voted in 1912 than in 1908. In the 1908 gubernatorial election roughly ten thousand more votes were cast than in the senatorial contest in 1912. The same was true in the presidential race. In the gubernatorial election itself, fifteen thousand fewer ballots were registered. It appears that apathy had nothing to do with the 1912 election; instead, a number of Republicans chose to stay home. Roosevelt's candidacy injured Stubbs's chance for election everywhere except in Harvey County. He carried this previously Democratic stronghold by a slight margin in 1912.[42]

Of the major political contestants in 1912, Arthur Capper made the strongest showing among Progressives and progressive Republicans. In his first attempt to become governor of Kansas he lost by just twenty-nine votes. Capper, who sacrificed his credentials as a harmony candidate by endorsing Roosevelt, faced the popular Democrat George Hodges in the race. From 1911 onward, the Democrats had shown unusual interest in the contest for governor, sensing that 1912 would be their year. A few had tried to clear the way for Hodges by keeping him free of a primary fight in August. But Democrats also had intraparty problems. Colonel Sapp and J. B. Billard of Topeka did not like Hodges's views on woman suffrage and prohibition. Hodges supported both reforms, while Sapp and Billard were wet and antisuffrage.

Knowing that their party might win the governor's chair, they shuddered to think that a Democrat could be in a position to advocate such "damn foolishness" as women voters and temperance. To avoid such a result, Billard was encouraged by Sapp and other Democrats to seek the party nomination. Billard was strong in the German beer-drinking communities of western Kansas. He was, of course, popular in the "whiskey counties," and he had large followings in Kansas City and Wichita. For some his candidacy represented Kansas' last chance to keep free of "manifold attempts . . . by a few all too ambitious women to foist electoral duties upon their sex." "If this is accepted," wrote a worried Democrat, "it will prove . . . disastrous to the entire population . . . and bring about many other evil results too numerous to mention." One thirsty Wichita citizen stated that Billard was the last hope for defeating "the whole bunch of hypocritical grafters" in this town. But the last stand of "sanity," as one voter called it, failed in August. Hodges defeated Billard by nine thousand votes, amassing a total of 57 percent of the Democratic ballots.[43]

After Billard was defeated in the primary, the Democrats closed ranks, partly because they wanted to obtain office and partly because Capper was a more determined advocate of prohibition and woman suffrage than was Hodges. Capper's campaign, however, rather than illustrating great devotion to reform, indicated why he was considered a moderate by many and a conservative by others. His speeches and his pamphlet literature did contain some amount of progressivism, and he was a resolute champion of Roosevelt, but there was much in his utterances that the next generation of Muckrakers would consider Republican conservatism. At Coffeyville, during his campaign, Capper stated, "I can only say to you that I stand pledged to a BUSINESS administration—and by that I mean an administration that will look after the business of the STATE, first, last and all the time." He continued: " I think the people of Kansas should regard their state government as a great big corporation, in which every citizen is an equal stockholder. Your chief executive is the man whom you choose to manage the business of this corporation, with fairness and justice to every stockholder." He promised economy, good roads, and a progressive-Republican party; and he stood staunchly behind the church, labor unions, and the G.A.R. His personal approach was magnificent. To voters he wrote: "I thought it best to write now to say I would like very much to count you one of my friends, and if you will speak to a few of your friends in my behalf it will be of great assistance." It is doubtful that he intended not to count anyone as his friend.[44]

Capper correctly assumed some responsibility for the progressive achievements in Kansas from 1906 onward, and he told voters that he had long led in "the great battle for clearing out the wrong and purging out the evil . . . in all departments of our state and national activity." After the formation of the Progressive party, he made it clear to voters that he intended to remain a Republican even though he supported Roosevelt. He could support the Colonel because "highway robbery" had been used by the national committee to nominate Taft, and thus it was all right to vote for Roosevelt. But the voter needed to remember that Capper had "always been a Republican, . . . always supported the Republican ticket, and . . . expected to remain a Republican." He would accept the "support of every good citizen," he said, "I will make no brassband campaign . . . [but] shall go before the people with nothing more than a plain, straight forward platform of the things I believe my business experience equips me to do."[45]

He did not make a "brass band campaign," but his friends, and perhaps he, slung mud pretty hard at Hodges. Towards the end of the struggle, the Hodges Brothers Lumber Company was excoriated for its activities as part of the lumber trust. Hodges answered in kind. He renewed the charges against Capper for printing indecent literature, and he stressed the publisher's connection with mail-order houses, the enemies of small-town businesses. Hodges's campaign was far from negative. He spoke in favor of lower tariffs, antitrust laws, economy in government, decreases in state taxes, and the entire run of progressive legislative and political reforms, such as the initiative, referendum, and recall. He emphasized his moderate wealth in contrast to Capper's riches. At Pittsburg, he said: "I don't want to be elected because of the demerits of the Republican party and its split. I want to be elected on my own merits." He accepted his victory graciously, nevertheless.[46]

After the general election on November 5 there was still considerable doubt concerning the outcome of the Capper-Hodges race. At first the *Topeka Daily Capital* announced a Capper victory, and not until November 12 did it report that the publisher had lost to Hodges. Later it again claimed a victory for Capper, but when the official returns were made available in December, Hodges had received twenty-nine more votes than the Topekan. Because improperly marked ballots were cavalierly discarded in Wabaunsee County, Capper contested the election commission's report in a state district court; but though the tribunal held in his favor, it refused to order the commission to reconvene and recount the ballots. Capper could have appealed to the Kansas Senate for a full review, but since Democrats had captured the legislature as well, he felt that it was useless to do so. If the returns reported by the secretary of state were correct, Capper received 167,408 votes and Hodges received 167,437. There was .008 of one percent separating the two candidates. Capper carried sixty-two counties, while Hodges won only forty-three, but Hodges's counties were in the populous eastern part of the state. Like other progressive-Republican candidates, Capper was strongest in western Kansas.[47]

In the congressional elections, Democrats won five of the eight seats, losing to regular Republicans Daniel Anthony and Phil Campbell in the First and Third districts, respectively, and to the popular progressive

Victor Murdock in the Eighth. The Republican split caused the defeat of five progressive-Republican candidates, three of whom were nominated for the first time at the 1910 primaries. The Democrats also won a majority of seats in the state legislature, but in contests for minor offices, Republicans were returned to offices from the secretary of state down. By comparing the county returns of the Republican candidate for secretary of state to those of Stubbs and the five defeated Republican congressional candidates, it becomes obvious that the secretary received in most instances from 5 to 8 percent more votes than these candidates. While there is no way of determining whether 5 to 8 percent of the voters who supported the secretary of state refused to vote for Stubbs and the congressmen, or whether 2 to 4 percent split their votes, it was this difference in percentages that made Democrats jubilant in 1912.[48]

While it might seem to those who know what happened to the Progressive party after 1912 that party hopefuls would have been saddened by the results, such was not the case. In fact, most Kansas Progressives were as exuberant as their Democratic counterparts. In their mind, Roosevelt had made an impressive showing. Senator Bristow called it a "magnificent success," and White, in a telegram to George Perkins, noted that, all things considered, the party had done well. Naturally, Stubbs and Capper did not feel requited by the defeats they had suffered, so they had little encouraging to say. The election had demonstrated, however, that about a hundred thousand Kansas voters were devoted to progressivism and that many of them would support a Progressive party. Since it seemed to progressive Republicans that their leaders had not received the votes of many regular Republicans, a number of them concluded that they had no need for the old party connection and should begin to work seriously at organizing a third party. These people were convinced that harmony within the old organization was useless and that now a party of their own should be formed in Kansas.[49]

The progressive movement within the Republican party had reached a crossroads in 1912. With a national Progressive party in existence, Republicans of the progressive inclination had to decide whether or not they should join the new organization. Decisions were made by many in the three-month period following the November election. By February 1913 Kansas possessed a state Progressive party.

# 11

## A NEW PARTY, A PARTING OF OLD FRIENDS, 1913

Despite the opposition of many powerful progressive-Republican leaders, a number of reformers had wanted the national committeeman of the Progressive party, William Allen White, to form a third party in Kansas during the 1912 campaign. But White had refused. He had an excuse for not responding to this demand: state law required that new parties file a declaration of intent with the secretary of state several months before an election in order to be included on the ballot. By the time the Bull Moose party became a national reality, the date for filing had passed.[1]

White, of course, knew that a more important reason for not establishing a third party was the need to secure Republican votes for Walter R. Stubbs and Arthur Capper. Both men stood a better chance of winning in November if their names appeared in the Republican column. To White's chagrin, he found that not even the Republican label was sufficient to induce many regulars to vote for them.[2] More than anything else, this realization convinced him that a new party should be organized. He was also impressed by Theodore Roosevelt's showing in the general election, and he expected a bright future for Progressives.[3]

White's personal preference was only one of the factors forcing him towards the creation of a Progressive party in Kansas. After the election he received tremendous pressure from a majority of progressive-Republican leaders to do so. Of the eight hundred Republican precinct committeemen with whom he corresponded, more than six hundred indicated a desire for a Progressive organization, as did a majority of county chairmen. They had grown tired of the old party, or so they said, and they wanted to align with men of their own beliefs. They predicted that if they had a new organization, hundreds of Democrats and Socialists whose votes had been lost in 1912 could be added to their fold. "There is a lot of fight left in us," wrote one county leader, "and I have been unable to find any [Progressive] . . . who intends to go back to either of the old parties."[4]

Local leaders were not alone in their insistence that a permanent party be formed. Roosevelt had asked White to undertake the task; and at a national Progressive conference in Chicago during the first week in December, resolutions were passed, calling for the creation of state parties throughout the country. White, accompanied by Stubbs, Henry Allen, and Cy Leland, attended this meeting and left it aware that a Kansas Progressive party was expected.[5]

Men who favored a third party were not the only Kansas progressives who were expressing opinions about the future of state politics. A number of reformers were willing to explain why they thought that a new organization was not needed. Many minor officeholders were naturally frightened by the possibility of a party that would be fashioned largely from Republican support. Having been elected as Republicans, they claimed to be honor-bound to remain so, but this was mostly a way of hiding their real reasons. They actually feared that Democratic strength would increase under a new political alignment. W. D. Ross, a reformer from Boss-Buster days, had recently been elected superintendent of public instruction, and he was a man, so he said, who still stood for progressive ideals. He could not, however, join in the recent move. "I believe," he explained, "the best results can be obtained by the existence of not more than two great parties. I do not think the Republican party is going to die. It goes without saying the Democratic party is not." Why not stay Republican and dominate things that way? he asked. "I know," he added, "you feel that it is impossible to get together with the [regulars] . . . but there are bound to be differing views and discordant elements sooner or later in all parties." Ross felt that as Republicans, Kansas reformers had done well in the past and would do well in the future.[6]

Congressman Daniel R. Anthony, who claimed to be a recent convert to progressivism, expressed somewhat the same view and asked that he not be left alone like an island in a sea of conservatism. The Republican party, he asserted, had always been the progressive party, and if White stayed on, it would continue that way. Old La Follette supporters were also insistent and seemed to be more sincere than Anthony in their opinions. "I am not sure that your plan of a separate party organization in this state is wise," wrote Rodney Elward. "It seems to me like giving up all we have fought for, for years." Elward did not intend to surrender so easily.[7]

The opinions of these men were important, since they indicated that some previous reform strength would be lost; however, if leading progressive Republicans acted together, there was hope that even wavering La Folletteites and state officeholders might eventually join the exodus from Republicanism. In any case, White believed that with a united leadership the main body of progressive voters would join the new party. What the Emporian failed to understand was that the leading progressives in Kansas were not of one mind. In fact, some were opposed to White's actions, and others were silent because they did not know what to do. Governor Stubbs attended the Chicago meeting of Progressives, but he was not the same dynamic force as in years past. In Kansas he was even more lethargic, evincing none of the old fire and planning, none of the old stratagems, that had previously characterized his design. He seemed to be neither particularly opposed to nor disposed towards the third-party movement; he was just uninterested.

Arthur Capper, on the other hand, excused himself from the delegation to Chicago in December, thereby causing speculation that he was planning to remain a Republican. Nonetheless, he indicated to Progressive leaders that if the new party were formed, he would be found in its ranks. But though avowedly ready to join the Progressive party, in January 1913 Capper began to finance publicity for a movement to promote Republican harmony. His final decision, at least the public one, was slow in coming; nearly a year elapsed before Progressives were forced to concede that the publisher of the *Daily Capital* was still just another Republican.[8]

The attitude being taken by Senator Joseph L. Bristow, however, was considered more important than that of either Capper or Stubbs. In Kansas, Bristow and progressivism were nearly synonymous, his election in 1908 having signaled the first important progressive victory. At no time did White consider that "Joe" would not join the movement; so White, without checking with Bristow, wrote Albert Beveridge in late November that Stubbs, Bristow, and he were "stripped to the waist" and ready to fight for the new organization.[9] But if the senator were stripped, as White said he was, he was exposed in a way that White did not appreciate. After four years of publicity and importance, Bristow had begun to enjoy playing the role of senator, and he was unwilling to chance losing so glamorous a station for what might be transient reasons. Reformers never say as much, however; and to the end, Bristow gave other reasons for not breaking with the Republicans.

There were many politicians who were undecided in 1912 and 1913, and Bristow belonged in that category. He felt that his best course was to remain steadily at anchor. He suggested in November that progressive clubs be created throughout the state, so that the party would not lose the thirty thousand voters who cast their ballots for Republicans regardless of the candidate. This, of course, made good sense, much more than did his other suggestion, that the clubs would give Republicans time to see that it was impossible to continue their party. Bristow also told an intimate friend in December 1912 that he was not going to declare for a third party just then. In the future he would fight for the right things and stand aggressively for progressivism.

He added that time would determine what he should do; but time would determine nothing. The senator would have to decide for himself, and the advice he was then receiving with regard to what course his supporters wished him to follow was a confused conglomeration. He should have remembered his warning to Senator Long in 1908 about sticking with one's friends; but 1912 was narcotic—it kept sound judgments at a minimum. Understandably, Bristow wrote to his sons that he was tired and sore at heart. "Politically," he added, "there is a state of chaos and no man's future is at all certain." He should have added, "Least of all mine."[10]

But if Bristow was cool towards a new party, he was equally cool towards suggestions of Republican harmony. Men's thoughts are complex things to disentangle, and Bristow's were always especially abstruse. It is hard to determine why he should throw dampers on suggestions for harmony when he admitted that such developments would help him politically. Nevertheless, he did so. To Judge J. S. West he wrote that harmony would be good politics for his candidacy, but how it could be accomplished was beyond his imagination. West's plans for a harmony dinner could not possibly help as a solution, even if the general idea was useful. Moreover, when Governor Herbert Hadley left Jefferson City, Missouri, to reorganize the Republican party nationally at a conference at Washington, Bristow was unusually critical of what he considered Hadley's naïveté.[11]

Bristow's presence in the Kansas Progressive party no doubt seemed necessary for its success, but it was possible to form the organization without his approval. On December 17 a conference that White had called in November met at Topeka to discuss the creation of a new party. Two hundred county leaders were present, the majority of whom had formerly been Republicans. Several tedious speeches were delivered, explaining the advantages of a separate organization. Sentiment favored the creation of a Progressive party, and U. S. Sartin of Kansas City was appointed provisional chairman of the new group. The official birth of the party was deferred, however, until February 1913. Before the meeting adjourned, Sartin was instructed to make preparations for a grand Progressive rally to be held on Lincoln's birthday. He was advised to continue to expand the list of voters who were known to support the Progressive cause.[12]

Although Sartin was personally disliked by many progressive Republicans, he was an effective organizer. By the end of January 1913 he boasted of provisional Progressive parties in 71 of the 105 counties in Kansas. Allen, White, Murdock, and others responded enthusiastically to developments in January, and prospects for an impressive rally at the February meeting seemed good. The annual Kansas Day Club meeting on January 29 also helped to promote the Progressive cause, since, once again, regular Republicans dominated it. Although a harmony movement was under way among moderate Republicans, the people who controlled the Kansas Day Club were not of the conciliatory type. They were primarily the ones who had voted against Stubbs and Capper in November, and they used the Kansas Day meeting "to roast" their adversaries further. A few suggestions for harmony had been voiced, but William P. Hackney of Winfield commanded the most attention by announcing that he was glad to see the progressives leave the Republican party and that he would do what he could to help them go. "Cave men," wrote one observer, would have been at home among these "noble savages."[13]

If the "rankest kind of standpatter" was present at the Kansas Day Club meeting, the Lincoln Day rally of Progressives was equally dominated by extremists—the avant-garde of that movement. Among the out-of-state speakers were Albert Nortoni of St. Louis, Mrs. Raymond Robbins of Chicago, Henry Cochems of Wisconsin, and Dr. Anna Shaw of New York. Their topics ranged from "Lincoln the Fearless Progressive" to "Woman's Obligation as a Citizen." The home talent included Allen, who rhapsodized on the future of the Progressives, and John Maddens of the M.K.T. Railroad, who talked about their past. Maddens, a Parsons lawyer, had recently retired as general attorney for the railroad, and thus carried none of its taint. Lieutenant Governor Sheffield Ingalls, son of the late John J. Ingalls, served as toastmaster of the meeting and announced that he hoped to play an important role as a Progressive officeholder in Kansas. Republicans had already recommended that he resign.[14]

Since he was unable to attend, Senator Bristow sent a letter, which was read to the assembly. His absence caused some questions concerning his loyalty to the cause. In his message Bristow called for "advanced positions" on issues, although in some cases, the most notable being the tariff, he seemed to retreat strategically back into the nineteenth century. After recommending moderate protection, he stressed the need for a tariff that would be adequate to the demands of industry and labor. He asked for the enactment of initiative, referendum, and recall laws, the direct election of senators, and a national referendum that would allow the people to reconcile differences that might arise between the president and Congress on various pieces of legislation. Bristow had come full circle to Roosevelt's position on trusts, and so he called for an industrial commission to supervise big corporations. His admonition regarding cooperation "with all who are fighting for these principles" could have meant anything, but it seemed to indicate too great a fondness for progressive Republicanism to some. Henceforth, a man was either a Progressive or he was a Republican, since the consensus now was that all true Progressives had left or were leaving the old party.[15]

The Lincoln Day banquet, wrote John Harrison to Bristow, was quite an affair. Funds were raised at the meeting to finance a permanent secretary and staff for the next six months, and Sartin was named state chairman of the Progressive party. One embarrassing incident occurred when Cy Leland hopped upon a table and, in a gauche manner, sarcastically subscribed thirty cents for a memorial honoring Chester I. Long, the father of the Kansas progressive movement. Otherwise, decorum and devotion marked the official birth of the party. The fervor that Progressives demonstrated in February was not approximated again until the 1914 campaign. When the banquet ended, many politicians who had previously been cool towards the party were fired by the meeting's enthusiasm. It took less than two months, however, for the flames to begin to diminish.[16]

Except for Sartin, who worked hard and spent much of his own money trying to perfect the organization, important state leaders did little to help the party grow. Many were involved in trying to decide what would be the wisest political move for them. By April, Sartin was depressed, and he complained to men who he knew would carry his tales to the founders of the party. Imploring Bristow to speak out in support of the Progressives, he sadly related that since the Lincoln Day meeting, he had had little assistance from anyone other than Allen. "Even our old friend, William Allen White," he wrote, "has hardly had a line in the papers for the cause." Sartin was discovering what Bristow knew—that parties were more easily born than built.[17]

By April, Sartin, Sheffield Ingalls, and other Progressives were becoming critical of Bristow and Capper because neither would commit himself to the organization. But White, Allen, and Stubbs insisted that such criticism be halted. White and Allen were sure that without Bristow the movement was doomed in Kansas, but they still believed that perhaps he and even Capper would belatedly join the party.[18]

After a trip home in March to talk with White, Stubbs, Allen, and Colonel William Rockhill Nelson, Bristow appeared to indicate to Sartin that he would announce his membership in the Progressive party in 1914. He had, however, told Sartin only that he would make public his party affiliation at that time. "I have taken the course that I did," he wrote, "because I want a large number of progressive Republicans who hesitate to leave the old party to feel that I have shown all the consideration that I could be expected to show to those who wanted to make the Republican party the real progressive party." There is no indication in Bristow's files that progressive-Republican sentiment was really as strongly in favor of the Republican party as he said it was. One factor that was making Sartin's job doubly difficult and was perhaps contributing to Bristow's reluctance to join the Progressives was the harmony movement among Republicans early in 1913.[19]

The impetus to resolve the Republican split in Kansas came from the party's legislative leaders near the end of the 1913 session. On March 8 James A. Troutman, one of the founders of the Square Deal movement of 1906, held an impromptu meeting of Republican members of the Kansas senate and house. They agreed to call a statewide harmony conference for June. Troutman sent invitations to the state's old guard and to officials of the Progressive party. His plan, so he explained, was to remove major grievances by "committing the [Republican] party, as a united organization, to Progressive policies." Since it was well known that progressive Republicans had written all the significant reform legislation in Kansas for ten years, he did not believe that this task would be difficult. "We trust," his invitations ended, "that the Republican party will go forward as a united organization and that the progressive cause may reach its fruition through the Republican party." In accompanying notes he explained that the basis of representation in the national convention might also be changed to meet the complaints that reformers had expressed regarding the party's "rotten borough" system in the South. "Rotten boroughs" had been one of the topics discussed at a national harmony conference that Troutman had attended in May in Chicago.[20]

Considering the emphasis that Troutman placed on things progressive, it is amazing that any standpatters or regulars attended the June meeting. Nevertheless, they did. Once again, Bristow refused to take part in talks about harmony, stating that such efforts were neither productive nor desirable. Capper, however, did attend the June meeting. While he was there ostensibly to report the affair for his newspapers, he stayed around after the meeting had adjourned to make peace with the regulars. According to one story, the harmonizers lacked the facilities for printing literature to promote their cause, and Capper was able to offer this service. Capper was already paying for harmony publicity in the First Congressional District, and he felt that a small investment in it after the Topeka meeting would be wise politics.[21]

Troutman's conference, of course, was a failure. None of the important Progressives attended the meeting. Capper's actions were premeditated, and he did not allow any public expression of his flirtation with the regulars. Thus, any propaganda value that Capper's acts might have had was lost. If some wavering Republicans were convinced to stay with the old party because of the harmony conference, they kept it to themselves. No doubt the attitude at Topeka did help to hold progressive Republicans who were already disposed towards remaining Republicans, but this opinion cannot be documented.

Troutman's lack of success was not the result of any unwillingness to seek harmony. The resolutions adopted at the conference were designed to meet the major complaints that had previously been raised by Progressives, and Troutman's own attitude was conciliatory. The meeting agreed to demand that the tenure of the national committee be changed so that newly elected committeemen would take office prior to a national convention. It suggested that national conventions be reapportioned so that the Republican Middle West would receive more delegates per person than the Democratic South. And it recommended that the Kansas constitutional amendment proposal for the initiative and referendum, which had recently been passed by the Democratic legislature, be approved by Kansas voters in the 1914 elections. This measure would give the Progressives the major reform that the Stubbs administration had failed to secure. In all, Troutman and others showed a lenient attitude towards their former brethren, but the reaction of Progressives was adverse.[22]

In May, White had called a meeting to condemn Troutman. The Progressive caucus counseled the party faithfuls to stay away from the harmony conference, and it announced that the Republican state chairman, Jonathan N. Dolley, had just quit the old party to join the Progressives. Sixty county chairmen attended White's special meeting, which had been initiated by David Hinshaw, now a member of the national publicity bureau of the Progressive party. Leaders at the national headquarters in the East were apparently worried by the national harmony gathering of progressive Republicans in Chicago in May and by the meeting planned for Kansas. They kept informed on events in the state, and after Troutman's conference they had Roosevelt write to Stubbs, Dolley, and White, telling them to keep active for the Bull-Moose cause. "There is not a state in the Union," the Colonel wrote, "to which we have a greater right to look to for leadership in the Progressive movement than Kansas. Kansas was founded in fact by the Progressive movement of the [eighteen] fifties." But Roosevelt's activities at mid year, as much as any other factor, were helping to hinder the growth of the Progressive party in Kansas.[23]

In July and August 1913 Kansas newspapers, as well as national journals, carried articles suggesting that if Roosevelt were tendered the Republican nomination in 1916, he would take it. Soon Murdock and White began to hear complaints from local Progressive leaders, who claimed that the rumors were causing "feelings of uncertainty," thus slowing party recruitment.[24] In September, White and Murdock wrote to the former president, asking him to refute the statement, so that members who were building county organizations could once more effectively resume their tasks. Roosevelt's answer was discouraging. Rather than denying that he would accept the 1916 Republican nomination, he said that there might be conditions under which he would take it. In his answer Roosevelt stated:

> Such a question cannot be answered by a simple Yes or No. It is a purely hypothetical question, and the terms of the answer must depend entirely upon what shape the actual fact takes. Supposing the impossible . . . that the Republican Party suffers a genuine change of heart, accepts the Progressive platform without a murmur, and agrees to accept any candidates that the Progressive Convention nominates, why in such a case it would be ridiculous for me or for anyone else to promise that I would refuse the nomination.[25]

Roosevelt's attitude had an unfavorable effect on White, and it encouraged Bristow's squeamishness. At the height of the discussion over Roosevelt's intentions, Bristow wrote to the former national chairman of the Progressive party, Joseph Dixon of Montana, that he was impressed with the fact that the Progressive organization was not growing and was therefore in danger of disintegrating. "My impression," he added, "is that if it should disintegrate, as many or more Progressives will go to the Democratic as to the Republican party." The impact on Capper was even greater. He had cast his lot with Republicans, and he was gratified to find that most progressive Republicans intended to stay with the Republican party if it put out a progressive platform and nominated progressive candidates. "I do not believe the 'Bull Moose' party is making much headway," he told Bristow in September, "the feeling seems to be . . . that President Wilson has put the 'Bull Moose' party out of business." With the state and national leaders of the Progressive party concerned more about the welfare of the old parties, it was small wonder that local Progressives were alarmed.[26]

Capper's observation about Wilson was an astute one. For quite some time, Progressives and progressive Republicans had known that the future of the new movement depended largely upon what Wilson accomplished as president. In December 1912 Bristow had written to Beveridge, saying that he was worried about the possibility that Wilson would cut the ground from under Progressives and progressive Republicans. Would the president break up his own party by advocating reform legislation, or would he manage to keep his party intact and still secure from Congress the reform legislation that he had promised? Bristow asked.[27] In April, when the Democratic-dominated Congress convened, Bristow had his answer. Wilson seemed to be intent upon getting most of the "New Freedom" platform enacted.

National Progressive leaders had intended to present alternatives to Wilson's program as often as possible. When they agreed with the president's recommendations, they planned to vote "present," instead of supporting them. There were, however, significant complications in this tactic. The Progressive politician, as George Mowry has suggested, was a highly individualistic creature, apt to stand as he wished on issues. Moreover, from the time that they had entered public life, some of these men had been advocating laws similar to those being suggested by Wilson. To refuse to support Wilson when he seemed to be advocating measures that they had championed would make them appear hypocritical. Kansas had only two men in Congress who could be expected to hew the Progressive line, and in a relative way each one did. Victor Murdock had been easily reelected from the Eighth Congressional District, and at the 1913 session he was chosen as the floor leader of the Progressive party in the House. Senator Bristow, though he was unwilling to commit himself to the new party, was willing to cooperate with the Progressives. Rather than support the Wilson-backed Clayton Antitrust Law and the Federal Trade Commission Act, Bristow and Murdock advocated Roosevelt's industrial-commission plan as a better substitute for regulating big business. They responded to the Federal Reserve Act much as old Populists might have done, claiming that it gave control of the nation's banks to Wall Street interests. They voted against the Underwood Tariff because it was not written by a scientific tariff commission.[28]

Unsure about whether their opposition to Wilson's program would be accepted, they attacked the president where he was most vulnerable—personally and through his advisors. William Jennings Bryan, Bristow wrote, was a "humbug" and "superficial." His main characteristic was the love of money. Bristow added: "He reminds me . . . of Ed Hoch. Of course, he has more sense than Hoch." Bristow raged even more about Wilson, especially about his "demigod" attitude and the "racy and lively goings-on in the White House." The president, he stated, "has become so accustomed to the fulsome flattery that he is . . . thoroughly confirmed in the belief that there is very little difference between the wisdom of himself and God, and if any difference [exists] it is in his favor anyway."[29]

Ranting and raving about Wilson could not, however, obscure the fact that the president was hurting the Progressive party. There was, of course, nothing that the Progressives could do about Wilson's actions as a reformer. They could only hope that the president would reverse himself while they tried to stifle favorable comments about him in Kansas newspapers. Although Wilson's reform pace did eventually moderate and he did earn an unfavorable press, neither of these things happened before the elections of 1914.

With Bristow and Capper hedging on their future political plans, with Wilson preempting the Progressives' raison d'être as a national party, and with Roosevelt uncertain about 1916, Kansas reformers understandably took time in September and October to reevaluate the wisdom of their third-party stand. In August the state was treated to a series of Chautauqua debates between Allen and former Congressman Charles F. Scott over the merits of progressivism in the Republican party. Although Scott was normally an uncompromising Republican, he advanced the argument that successful progressivism could result only from continuation of the Republican party. He felt that he had won his case, but that Allen had carried the debates.

"The people are confused by the double use of the word 'progressive,'" Scott wrote, "they get the impression that because the new party is called the Progressive party . . . it is the only party that stands for progress." Scott was particularly worried about Kansas women, who would vote for the first time in 1914. "When they hear a man pull out the tremolo stop," he added, "and weep over the 'seven million women working in sweat shops of greed for $3.00 a week,' they imagine nobody ever thought of those women before or tried to do anything to better their conditions." "They think we intend to do nothing," Scott continued, and even believe that we "are glad that they are in that deplorable condition."[30]

The impact of the debates was to reinvigorate a few leaders of the Progressive party and to bring the more radical elements in Kansas society to the support of the party. Eva Morley Murphy, an officer of the Women's Christian Temperance Union and the Kansas Federation of Women's Clubs, announced her presence in the new organization then. For years, she said, the women of Kansas had stood steadfastly for "uplift," and amid scorn and ridicule they had never deviated from this principle. Already they were trained in political tactics, which could now be used to their fullest to support a party that encompassed many phases of uplift. The women of Kansas, Mrs. Murphy confidently predicted, were prepared to give the Progressive party their undivided support.[31]

Support from the W.C.T.U. meant that there would be help from the prohibitionists, in addition to the women suffragettes; but still all was not well with the new party. White, who claimed to have recruited the best of the Kansas population—the middle-class professional—complained that clerks, small farmers, and unskilled laborers were pulling away from the organization. Their minds, he wrote, were moved "largely by two things—noise and tradition. Our noise has subsided and party tradition is pulling."[32]

Tradition was not only pulling the lesser-endowed in society; it was also tugging at White's heartstrings. He, too, was suggesting the possibility of a compromise with Republicans. His demands were extreme and possibly were not made in good faith, since he was asking as the price of reconciliation that the Republican party adopt the Progressive-party platform of 1912. Nevertheless, he offered a basis for conciliation, and no matter how unreasonable his demands, if Republicans had wanted harmony above all else, White would have made good on his offer. Fortunately for his bluff, if bluff it was, Republicans were not about to accept his suggestion, although there were some Kansas regulars who seemed to hope that this might happen.[33]

Though he was largely unconcerned about specific issues, White had come to believe that there was a major difference between Republicanism and the new Progressive spirit. On definite issues, he admitted that both groups stood close together, but he said that "the Republican party stands definitely for the rights of the individual as guaranteed by the constitution as it now is interpreted. The Progressive party stands definitely for an interpretation or amendment of the constitution which shall give the federal government power to interpose on behalf of society for the common good, even against the rights of the individual."[34]

In October 1913, because of the drift that events were taking, the possibility of compromise ended for White, and he decided that he must stand firmly on the deck of the Progressive ship, even if she were the *Nancy Brigg*. He was her captain, and like all good seamen, he would go down, if necessary, with his vessel. "Now," he wrote Bristow, "is the time for you to announce for our party because your continued absence is drawing the sheep from the flock in droves." Whether sailor or shepherd, White had arrived at his final position, and he demanded that Bristow do the same. His insistence became intense, and Bristow, hitherto a close friend of White's, began to wonder why he had never recognized the publisher's arrogance and his bosslike nature. The senator always had a way of finding the meaner character in men when it was necessary.[35]

The political odyssey of Joseph Bristow in 1913 is an intriguing story. Did he, as White and Progressives later charged, tell them that he would join the new party, or did he merely mislead them into holding that opinion? What he said in conversations with these men can never be known, but his correspondence indicates that he chose to dissimulate well, thus allowing the Progressives to draw their own conclusions. As early as mid 1912, when Roosevelt led his followers from the convention hall in Chicago, Bristow had written that the time should come "when all progressives can get together and work for the best interests of the people." After the November elections he stated that "there must be a progressive and a conservative party." He added, however, that many progressives felt that the day had not yet arrived. At about the same time, he told the wavering Capper that if progressives could not get together under the Republican name, the thing to do was to organize the third party quickly and well.[36]

From January to June 1913 he was reluctant to say anything about the new organization, although he had had his letter read to the Lincoln Day meeting. In April that "presumptive," "intolerant," "political boss" Sartin had raised the distasteful question of Bristow's affiliation, which made the senator feel distressed about not being able to announce his position. Bristow wrote to Capper that many Republicans who supported him were not yet ready to break with the party and that he had been seriously concerned over the need to renounce the old affiliation. For this reason, he added, "I have not flippantly and without consideration deserted . . . the party which originally elected me . . . as you well understand." Capper understood. He, too, wanted to be elected in 1914. It seemed strange, Bristow continued, that the very people who had cheered his Republican insurgency were now critical of his lack of fealty towards the new party.[37]

In June, Bristow wrote a letter to White that convinced the Emporian and Allen, who also saw it, that when the "trumpet soundeth," Bristow would deliver a "ringing farewell to the Republican party." The senator explained that with the Progressive party organized in Kansas, he could not get the Republican nomination if he wanted it. He added that he considered the nomination of no account anyway, since a majority of his friends had already left the old party. He concluded:

> I have seen no other course for me to pursue except to run as a Progressive but I have refrained from making any such an announcement because I have not been certain as to just what grave mistake the Democratic administration might make and I did not want to give Mr. Troutman and his friends . . . the opportunity to be pounding me for a year before I could get into the field.

"Sufficient unto the day is the evil thereof," he concluded. But the evil thereof really dated back to January, and this he failed to mention.[38]

Considering first things first, as Bristow wished to do, through his lone appointee, United States Marshal John Harrison, Bristow had been in touch with the old Long machine at the beginning of the year. In talks with Billy Morgan, Harrison had been told in January that at least one wing of the old organization wanted Bristow to "assume charge of party affairs in the state." No assurances of future support for Bristow in his reelection struggle in 1914 were given, but Morgan and others encouraged Harrison to advise the senator to "be noncommittal and make only general statements regarding party affiliation."[39] This suggestion was followed as closely as possible until October and November, when White and others redoubled their efforts to have Bristow announce as a Progressive. On a number of occasions, national headquarters of the Progressive party asked Bristow to speak in various areas of the country. Each time he refused, claiming that he had pressing duties in Washington.[40]

In September and October, talks commenced again between Harrison and Long's former lieutenants, and on November 2 Harrison was made privy to the Republican program for 1914. "The plan," he wrote Bristow, "is to nominate Capper for Governor without material opposition, but you will have to fight Curtis for the senatorship." Former progressive Republicans who were seeking minor state offices would not be opposed by the regulars; thus Bristow could not expect their help against Curtis. The consensus was, however, that Bristow could defeat Curtis under any circumstances and that therefore he should run as a Republican. "Capper . . . has an angle worm for a backbone," the report concluded, "and . . . would not be in a position to help."[41]

A week later, Capper wrote to Bristow, telling him that he could secure the Republican nomination and election in 1914. He inferred that the *Capital's* aid would be extended to Bristow in the cause, though he made no explicit promise. Morgan and several other members of the old Long machine now appeared to be enthusiastic about Bristow's prospects, and on November 18 Harrison informed the senator that Albaugh and his associates were reconciled to Bristow's candidacy as a Republican. Moreover, Secretary of State Charles Sessions and Congressman Anthony pledged their support to Bristow in the Republican primary.[42]

These developments removed whatever doubts Bristow had entertained about joining the Progressive party. After candidates of the Progressive party had made disastrous showings in Massachusetts and Maryland, he wrote Dixon of Montana in November of 1913 that he could win the Republican nomination "overwhelmingly" in the primary, and that both former Taft supporters and progressive Republicans wanted him to remain a Republican so that he could do so. "A fellow," he noted, "has got to have sense in advocating his reforms or he never gets anywhere with them, and while I do not intend to waver in the slightest degree in my devotion to progressive policies and principles, I would like to sustain a relation to political organizations that will enable me to be of some use in effectively promoting these policies."[43]

In mid December the senator was contributing money to the publicity bureau of Troutman's harmony group, and he was praising the results of a meeting of the Republican National Committee, which purportedly had opened the door for reconciliation. His "ringing declaration," which

White and Allen had expected in mid 1913, was near at hand; but it was to be no clarion call for the Progressive party. In Bristow's mind the Republican party was once more the most effective instrument for reform.[44]

As Bristow made his way towards the Republican party after September, Capper also continued his course in that direction, becoming increasingly open in his actions. He was involved in the talks between Long's former lieutenants and Harrison during September and October, and he helped to plan the future strategy of the Republican party. Although White and other Kansas Progressives were aware of the attitude of the Topeka publisher, they were not convinced that he was resolute in his stand. Thus, late in the year, White attempted to swing Capper to the new party by pretending that Bristow would soon join the Progressives and by threatening Capper with their power in case he defected.[45]

White's hopes that Capper might join were dashed by Capper's reply on October 11. Thereafter, White bothered him no more. Capper wrote that he had never quit the Republican party and that he had never attended Progressive affairs. "I have thought best," he continued, "to take an independent course, encouraging everything that is progressive, no matter what political party it comes from." Since he had sampled opinion by having had the usual postcards circulated to Kansas subscribers of his journals, Capper estimated that only one-fourth of the Republican voters who had supported Roosevelt had quit the old party, and he added that he did not believe that he or anyone else could be elected governor on the Bill Moose ticket. He claimed that since 1912 the Republican party had become the truly progressive party. His concluding remark undoubtedly made White shudder. Capper asserted that he did not intend to run for governor in 1914. "The thing of greatest importance . . . next year," he stated, "is the overthrow of this Hodges administration. Hodges is the smallest, the most unscrupulous, the least progressive Governor this state has had in many years."[46]

Even if, as Capper had said, he did not plan to run for governor, he felt that he had to remain a Republican to make certain that Hodges would not be reelected. Of course, he surprised no one when he decided to seek the office. On the occasion of his announcement he said: "I am a Republican because I believe that that party in this state stands for clean government and untainted politics; that it is the champion of human rights, and that it has been a power in the creation and crystallization of the progressive sentiment." He added that he was the highest type of

Republican, which meant that he practiced the highest form of party regularity.[47]

Events moved fast for the Progressives in late 1913. After having concerned themselves with Republican affairs throughout the year and after having expended time trying to convince Capper and Bristow to join the new party, they were suddenly confronted with the need to outline their own plans for the next year's elections. They had not given up on Bristow as a possible Progressive-party candidate, but there were other arrangements to discuss and other nominations to fill. In mid November, Sartin issued a call for county chairmen and top state leaders of the Progressive party to meet in Topeka on the twentieth of the month. The need for money to finance the impending campaign was uppermost in his mind, and he hoped to create enthusiasm among county leaders so that they would build at least a hundred local organizations by February.[48]

The response to Sartin's invitations for the November meeting were encouraging, as two hundred delegates arrived. The order of business, however, had a deadening thud about it. Rather than committing itself to a full ticket, the meeting was noncommittal, deciding to resolve that question in February. A move was started to wire Bristow in order to have him announce his intentions of running for the Senate on the Progressive ticket, but Harrison and former Congressman Fred Jackson stopped that move. Of the important leaders present, only White showed great concern for the third party, while Stubbs and Allen indicated that they felt that Republicans should be sounded out about whether they would accept Progressive candidates and a Progressive platform. Much depended upon the action that the Republican National Committee took at its December meeting, they said. If the committeemen proved conciliatory, they believed that there was reason to expect that a reunion with Republicans could take place.

The sentiment against harmony came from men like Cy Leland and Sheffield Ingalls, as well as from a number of county chairmen. White, though he was sincere about the Progressive party, was willing to admit that things looked bad, especially because of the chance that Bristow would not enter the organization. The only real accomplishment of the November meeting was to prepare for the Lincoln Day affair and to allow certain county politicians to announce their candidacies. The men who would represent the party, if it were represented, in the gubernatorial and senatorial races were not agreed upon. Two names had been rumored as possibilities. If Bristow defected, there was hope that Victor Murdock might run. Congressman Murdock was as firmly committed to the new party as anyone, and possibly he was the most popular person available. Allen was the favorite for governor, but Allen was unwilling as yet to seek the job.[49]

In the few weeks after the meeting was adjourned, White increased his efforts to force Bristow to run for reelection as a Progressive. Allen went to Washington to engage the senator for the party, but Allen's attitude was not clear cut. Rather than encouraging Bristow to join, as White wanted, Allen agreed that the senator might possibly do better by remaining on the Republican ticket. After his return to Kansas, Allen wrote Bristow that if the Progressive party used Ingalls or Stubbs against him in the senatorial election, he should have no worry in 1914. There was, however, a serious contender who would possibly challenge Bristow in November. Victor Murdock seemed to be prepared to run as a Progressive if Bristow announced as a Republican. "His candidacy," Allen noted, "is no bluff, he is hoping you will run on the Republican ticket."[50]

The meeting of the Republican National Committee that Allen felt would eliminate the need for a third party in Kansas was held in December. By Progressive lights it was a dismal failure. More than ever, the Progressives were ready to continue their organization and perfect its strength. Even Allen was affected by the refusal of Republican committeemen to hold a national convention in order to reconcile party differences. He believed that the national committeemen were afraid that they would lose their jobs if they took such action. So deeply was he disillusioned that a week after the committee met, he began encouraging Bristow to discontinue his plans of seeking reelection as a Republican and to join the Progressive party.[51]

Although Bristow did not publicly announce the retention of his Republican affiliation until 3 January 1914, he informed White on Christmas Day that he planned to remain within the old party. Bristow probably did not intend that his decision should arrive as an unwelcome Christmas message, but so it did. White, of course, had been expecting such a declaration. Beginning in October, Bristow's replies to White's entreaties indicated that this would happen, but White seemed to have hoped against hope that it would not. On December 26 he telegraphed the senator, asking him to wait before making his announcement public. He had been, White said, a good friend of Bristow's, but he would now have to be his political enemy. Murdock was bound to run for the Senate, and with Murdock the Progressives would defeat Bristow. Perhaps after talking the problem through, White and Bristow could arrive at acceptable alternatives.[52]

The conference that White wanted did not come before the senator made his announcement. On January 4 leading metropolitan dailies carried stories reporting that Bristow had decided to stop the speculation about his party affiliation. The rank and file of the Republican party were progressive, Bristow said, and he, too, was a progressive. It was impractical to have three parties under the American system, because American tradition supported the two-party ideal. Thus, while he sympathized with many of the ideas of the new organization, he planned to make his fight for the senatorial renomination within the Republican party. Bristow's decision was the biggest political news in Kansas in early 1914, but similar announcements by other progressive Republicans, including Capper and Fred Jackson, also made headlines.

Reaction to Bristow's statement varied among Republicans and supporters of the new party. Curtis was naturally displeased, as was Charles F. Scott, who had hoped that progressives of Bristow's sort would remain outside the party. The *Kansas City Journal*, on the other hand, was elated by the senator's decision. Bristow's reasoning was sound, it said, and his courage was great. When Scott complained to Charles Gleed, the publisher of the *Journal*, Gleed wrote him that he had had his editor speak kindly of Bristow's return "by way of encouraging other progressives to come back." The paper, Gleed added, would not support Bristow. The *Topeka Daily Capital* was effusive in its praise of the senator. "Progressivism is a cause, not a party issue," an editorial announced. Bristow was still a progressive, but not a member of the Bull Moose party. The senator could not be bossed by the new political machine that had been organized in Kansas.[53]

William Allen White waited a while before commenting on Bristow's defection, and then, in a letter to the *Kansas City Star*, he applied his regular literary roast to his one-time ally. His comments caused a minor county leader of the Progressive party to write that White had shown Bristow in his true light, as a man who "became and was a progressive for office alone." Henry Allen supplied one of the harshest judgments rendered. Privately, he told White that Bristow had worked himself "into a real John-the-Baptist sentiment" and now thought that he was "a rare sample of courage." "I think," he added, "it's the foolhardy courage of the burglar who tries to break into a house in the daylight and gets caught."[54]

Bristow's own opinion was that he had done what every progressive Republican ought to do. It was easier, he explained two days after his announcement, to use an established party to attain progressive goals than to form a new, untried instrument in order to get those results. "Thousands of us are not willing to abandon the organization which we have captured from the reactionaries and let them come back and take possession of it with all its opportunities." Progressive clubs that everyone could join should have been formed, he added; but they had not been. Thus, he had taken the position that he considered best under the circumstances.[55] After his statement had been circulated, Bristow met with White, Murdock, and Stubbs, but he failed to convince the trio to join him in his action. Their decision, which the senator blamed on White, caused him to attack White for planning the defeat of the progressive cause. "If the Republican party ceases to be progressive," Bristow declared, "it is because the progressives divided and turned the organization to the standpatters, and that's where White is making his fatal mistake." He added that if he were beaten, it would not be by standpatters but by Murdock, White, Stubbs, and Allen.[56] They would be the culprits.

# 12

## THE YEAR THEY REALLY STOOD AT ARMAGEDDON, 1914

When Joseph Bristow informed Kansas voters that he would remain a Republican, Victor Murdock countered by announcing that he would seek the Progressive-party nomination for the Senate. Murdock, rather than being disheartened by developments in late 1913, had been encouraged. He wrote that the Progressive was "distinctly a new type" politically, one that was here to stay: "He is not merely the old insurgent of a different degree—he is a different kind. The prototype is the new Roosevelt, the radical who came out of Africa, waded in at Osawatomie, and went in over his head at Columbus and emerged as out of the waters of the Jordan. The progressive Republican hasn't got it, and can't get it."[1]

Congressman Murdock was about the only Kansan of importance to assume a buoyant attitude as the New Year dawned. With Bristow and Arthur Capper defecting, William Allen White was worried that Walter R. Stubbs would soon follow. Because of his defeat in 1912, Stubbs had allowed himself to be pushed aside during the past year. His close association with Capper since 1911 caused many to speculate that he would rejoin the Republican party. He had assumed a "spoiler's" determination, some said, but he remained convinced that he was obligated to support Capper because of aid given to his senatorial candidacy by the *Topeka Daily Capital* in 1912. Since Stubbs seemed to be on the verge of joining Capper in January 1914, White worked at keeping him a Progressive. According to White, Stubbs had led him to the movement eight years earlier, and Stubbs had been a main force in organizing the new party. As long as any chance of victory remained, White wrote, Stubbs was honor-bound to continue to work for the party.[2]

The rumor that Stubbs might rejoin the Republican party worried national Progressive leaders as well, since the governor had been, as *Chicago Tribune* publisher Medill McCormick said, "a sort of Progressive Cato." McCormick asked Stubbs: "What will be . . . [the standpatters'] jubilation, . . . when a two-fisted, iron-ribbed, battered-battler like yourself supports a Republican candidate for Governor, whatever his virtues?"[3]

Despite outward appearances, Henry Allen's allegiance to the party was also doubtful in December of 1913. He quieted fears, however, when he stated on 6 January 1914 that he would stand with the Progressives to the end. He added that he did not want to run for governor, which many reformers wanted him to do. He suggested that Lieutenant Governor Sheffield Ingalls be the party's choice. In mid January he asked White how long he should wait before announcing publicly that he would not be the Bull Moose gubernatorial aspirant. White's answer never came, since he, like almost every Progressive, wanted Allen to run. Fortunately, the new party could take advantage of an emotional nature that made Allen incapable of withstanding concerted pleas for his services. Billy Sunday had converted him to Christian fundamentalism at a revival meeting in 1911. Bull Moosers had made him weep for Roosevelt and a third party at Chicago. And at the Lincoln Day rally in 1914 the Progressives induced him to run for governor.[4]

In early January, Mort Albaugh, the Republican wheel horse, predicted that an Allen boom would make the Wichita newspaperman a candidate in 1914. Albaugh explained:

> Henry isn't a candidate now and he has no idea that he is going to be . . . but he is as emotional as a prima donna. The first time they get Henry in a corner, the Bull Moosers will start a pow wow. Henry's feelings will be wrought upon and finally they will overpower him. In the end he will arise with tears in his eyes. He will choke with emotion and his voice will falter and break. After stuttering a little Henry will manage to say "I'll take it!"

It happened essentially that way! At the Lincoln Day banquet, after an emotional session, Murdock advised the delegates to go to room 270 of the National Hotel in Topeka, take Allen by the hand and by the collar, and push him into the governor's race. About half of the delegates began to push, and though Allen tried to ward them off, in the end he yielded.

On the afternoon of February 12 his hat joined Murdock's in the Bull Moose ring.[5]

The Lincoln Day meeting in 1914 was a gala affair, even though only half of the hoped for 2,400 delegates attended. Allen was the master of ceremonies, and he introduced the featured guests—Albert J. Beveridge and Raymond Robbins, who had been sent by national headquarters. Beveridge delivered the keynote speech, being joined in the oratorical lists by Robbins, Murdock, and Mrs. Eva M. Murphy, a representative of the W.C.T.U. The main order of business, in addition to subscribing funds, was to write a tentative party platform, one that could be amended in midyear, after the primaries. The goal was to present ideas that would represent some advances over previous years, but that would still retain the essential social-welfare emphasis of the new organization. The presence of large numbers of women among the delegates insured that the document would include strong welfare planks such as those asking for minimum-wage laws, widows' pensions, and child-labor laws.[6]

The most radical suggestions came from Stubbs, who was unable to attend the rally because of illness. From Lawrence he sent a message encouraging the Progressives to make national prohibition and government ownership of communications and transportation networks part of the temporary platform. He was especially concerned with the possibility of state-owned and -operated railroads, and at the time he was preparing an article for the *Saturday Evening Post* on the subject.[7]

Despite worry caused by the disappointing attendance, the meeting was a smashing success for advocates of the new party. By now, most reluctant members had been winnowed from the group, and only the devoted remained. Some concern had existed because it had not been possible to find any important Kansas Democrat who would join the party so that the bipartisan heritage of the organization could be demonstrated. This did not, however, discourage many; and some found solace in the fact that the absence of Democrats showed that their party was based on more than the traditional national political divisions. A feeble attempt was made to identify the Progressive party with European liberal parties, and a few warped comparisons of White and David Lloyd George were made. Since there were no important primary contests facing the Progressives, little activity of a popular nature was planned before August. Progressives agreed that the party council should convene then to make final preparations and write a permanent platform. The meeting adjourned without incident and apparently with the hope that the future would be brighter than had previously been predicted.[8]

The major concerns of Progressives between February and August were national party affairs and the Republican senatorial primary. If Bristow should win in August, and most Progressives assumed that he would not, the chances that Murdock would make a strong showing in November would be appreciably lessened. If Curtis won, some Bull Moose leaders felt that they might be victorious at the general elections. They assumed that, in either case, the Bristow-Curtis battle could only aid their cause if disharmony between the two continued after August 5. They believed that unity in their own ranks was now certain, but they failed to consider national party developments in this appraisal.

At the national level a struggle had been brewing since 1912 between the national chairman, George Perkins, and the so-called radical members of the party. Because Perkins had blocked the antitrust plank offered at the Chicago convention and because he had been a partner of J. Pierpont Morgan, a number of Progressives were skeptical of his commitment to reform. During 1913 and early 1914 Amos and Gifford Pinchot quietly tried to have Perkins removed as head of the party; in May, having failed previously, Amos Pinchot sent a letter to state committeemen, condemning the New York financier and calling for his resignation. In it he charged Perkins with misdirecting the true intent of the Progressive party and with making it into a tool of big-business interests. In June, the Pinchot letter was made public.

Pinchot's assault came at the least propitious time for Progressives. They did not need a public quarrel over corporation influences in their organization when the party was facing its most crucial test. In a state like Kansas, Perkins had been an important issue in 1912, and the party's local leaders preferred that the presence of the Wall Street banker be felt financially rather than that he be seen or heard. When Progressives revived the distasteful Perkins issue in mid 1914, the Kansans were not merely displeased; they were utterly dismayed.

Moreover, some important Kansas Progressives, particularly White, were friendly towards Perkins, who had worked hard for the movement during the past two years. They had chafed under the attacks in 1912, but they were politicians who were capable of understanding the importance of the capitalist to the party. While White did not think that Perkins was an able politician, he understood that it would be disastrous if the multi-millionaire's pocketbook were closed in the future. In addition, White believed that the attack on Perkins had resulted not from the New Yorker's stultifying effect on reform, but from his unwillingness to compromise with progressive Republicans. Apparently Perkins had decided that the greatest malefactors in America were those political leaders who refused to join the new party, remaining instead with their old associations. Pinchot supposedly wanted to carry forth the crusade by supporting progressive Republicans wherever possible. Because of the Kansas situation, White and most local leaders were violently opposed to this position.[9]

In April, Gifford Pinchot contacted White to ask him if he would join in a call requesting Perkins to resign. Pinchot had heard that White was dissatisfied with the national chairman's domination and that White felt that the time had arrived to push the financier aside. White, who may have criticized Perkins to Pinchot in private, was not in favor of such a move; he answered that Pinchot should stop complaining, since such activity damaged the party and did no one any good. He added, however, that if Perkins were removed, Stubbs would make an excellent national chairman. In June, following the publication of Amos Pinchot's letter, White wrote Beveridge that it had been a "stupid" move made by a jealous politician. White predicted that Pinchot's message would soon be used with full force against Progressivism.[10]

Considering that White and the Kansas Progressives believed that the Perkins-Pinchot feud had developed from Perkins's desire to withhold aid from progressive Republicans, the Kansans must have been aghast when another blow to their hopes was delivered in June. They had been critical of Roosevelt's silence regarding what attitude to take towards progressive Republicans who were seeking election on the old ticket. But because they thought that Perkins was opposed to helping these reformers, they assumed that Roosevelt intended to withhold his aid as well. In July, Roosevelt and Perkins both endorsed the Republican candidate for Governor of New York, Harvey D. Hinman.

Their action brought instantaneous complaints from Progressives across the country, and particularly from those in Kansas. State chairman U. S. Sartin predicted that the end had come for at least 75 percent of the Progressive parties in other areas, and he wondered whether Kansans should bother to go on. Charging that Roosevelt had turned the November elections into personality contests, Sartin questioned the wisdom of having Allen and Murdock continue in the race, since Capper and Bristow were also reformers. White, too, was angered by Roosevelt's endorsement of Hinman, as were a number of minor leaders in the state organization. The woes of the Progressives, however, were meat to their hungry opponents, who hoped that the final disintegration of the new party had now begun. But by July there was no turning back; Bristow might chortle about Roosevelt's actions, but he would still have to face his contest the next month without Progressive aid.[11]

Political campaigns normally have an identifying characteristic about them, and the 1914 primary race between Curtis and Bristow was no different in this respect. Six years earlier, Bristow's victory over Long had been characterized by Bristow's whirlwind tour of the state and by White's trenchant pen, which cut the ground from under the old senator. This year the fire of 1908 was gone, and in its stead Billy Morgan, Long's former manager, stepped forth. Bristow, who stayed out of Kansas during the preprimary period, allowed Morgan and Harrison to handle his affairs; and true to form, the result was a well-planned, dull, traditional campaign. Railroad henchmen were sent along the major lines to whip up support, and the lieutenants of the old Long faction went to work in their home areas. From Washington, Bristow and his staff franked several major speeches and other campaign literature to at least ninety thousand voters, and they solicited funds from some of the least progressive sources in the state.[12]

Back-room deals, too, had a place in the campaign, with Morgan executing a meaningful maneuver early. In January the Curtis faction seemed to control the Kansas Day Club meeting. Hoping to embarrass Bristow, the faction tried to have the state committee hold the 1914 Kansas Republican convention in May. According to tradition the party platform could be written then. Curtis's supporters assumed that a conservative document, which would illustrate that Bristow was out of line with the mainstream of the party, would be agreed upon. Morgan, with the aid of Harrison, blocked the move by a 37 to 34 vote. A compromise arrangement to write a preprimary declaration of general principles was fashioned, but the failure to provide for a meeting to do so kept this from coming to pass. It was finally agreed that the party council, as usual, would convene in August, after the primaries, to write the platform.[13]

The Curtis forces probably would have written a preprimary platform that would have illustrated the lack of Republican rejuvenation; but the assumption that, as such, it would have disagreed with the issues of Bristow's campaign was incorrect. Bristow, who for the most part had run out of steam as a reformer, discussed only the things that he had helped to accomplish in the past and a few long-established reform demands such as woman suffrage. Unlike the Progressives, he lacked new suggestions and avoided social-welfare ideas, which the Progressives stressed. The fact that he was less interested in new reforms was illustrated by a plea that he made in early 1914 to the old-guard boss of Crawford County, publisher J. T. ("Doc") Moore of the *Pittsburg* (Kansas) *Headlight*. To Moore, who had been anathema to the progressive Republicans after 1909, Bristow wrote that he did not think "Doc" and he "materially disagreed on public questions," and he noted that they certainly agreed on the importance of the party. Wouldn't "Doc" support him because of these facts?[14]

Until June, Bristow appeared confident about the election, despite Curtis's ability as a campaigner. He received reports from his managers indicating that he would assuredly win, and he even spent time considering how Murdock's antiprohibition, anti-woman-suffrage views would help his candidacy in November. Numerous Taft Republicans favored Bristow; and La Follette's old supporters, such as Rodney Elward, also endorsed him after the Wisconsin senator recommended that he be renominated. Strangely enough, White and the Progressives did not try to defeat Bristow, and they privately indicated that they felt little anger over what he had done. They did, White noted, think that Bristow had been dishonest in remaining a Republican only for the sake of keeping the office, but they planned no anti-Bristow campaign before the primaries. Old friendships died slowly with White, and it was Bristow, in the final analysis, who demonstrated a bitter attitude over the events of 1914.[15]

But while the Progressives held back, Curtis and other regular Republicans felt no limitations on what they could say about Bristow. Scott had been particularly incensed when Bristow's friends had stopped the movement for a preprimary convention, and he charged them with being afraid of a platform that said something. He added that Bristow wanted to go out "and fool the voters by pretending to be one thing to one man and another to another." Scott hoped that the senator's opportunism would convince "true Republicans" not to vote for him. Scott admitted that since 1912 Bristow had been a good party member, working hand in glove with Elihu Root, Henry Cabot Lodge, and the rest; but in his first two years as a senator he had been an assistant Democrat and probably would have been a Chinaman if it would have helped him politically to be one. Curtis, he added, had been a great congressional leader, was industrious and influential, and had broad experience. If Kansas wanted a real senator, they had better send Curtis back to Washington and bring Bristow home.[16]

On June 10 Capper informed Bristow that Curtis, through an active personal campaign, was making inroads into Bristow's strength. He suggested that Bristow return to Kansas to counterbalance the trend. Curtis's advocacy of tariff protection for agricultural products was convincing Republican farmers of all persuasions to support him, and his handshaking walks through city streets were even more effective in lining up urban areas solidly behind him. Equally important, Curtis was spreading the word that Capper was in favor of his nomination, and Capper's magnetic appeal was a significant factor in Republican politics. In July, Bristow appealed to Capper to stop these rumors by endorsing him, but Capper remained noncommittal. He offered Bristow full use of his newspaper columns, but he would not publicly intervene in the senatorial race.[17]

The primary campaign closed in August with an unfavorable turn of events for Bristow. Since Curtis had bolted Stubbs in 1912, there was considerable speculation that neither of the two current candidates would support the other after losing the primary. Curtis had publicly denied that he had such intentions, claiming that circumstances were different now. Bristow would not publicly make a similar admission. He told Harrison confidentially that he would not bolt, but he refused to state his position to newsmen. Bristow argued that if he were to say that he would support Curtis, he would lose progressive votes; if he stated that he would bolt, he would lose the support of regular Republicans. He decided, therefore, to say nothing. This attitude naturally gave Curtis's backers an opportunity to assign to Bristow whatever position they wished to on the question of bolting. As a consequence, Bristow was bound to lose some support because of this issue.[18]

Progressive Republicans feared that there would be a smaller-than-usual turnout of voters in 1914. They assumed that this would hurt the incumbent, Bristow. The fact that Murdock was running on the Progressive ticket almost assured that fewer Republican votes would be cast in the primary. As expected, a light Republican vote was cast. The result was a victory for Curtis. He defeated Bristow by 1,890 votes, even though his vote in eastern Kansas was reduced somewhat by the candidacy of H. H. Tucker of Kansas City. The votes for the three leading Republican candidates for the Senate were: Curtis—44,612; Bristow—42,722; and Tucker—20,374.[19]

In comparing Curtis's and Bristow's returns, it becomes apparent that Curtis, as always, was strong in the eastern part of Kansas, while Bristow received his main support from west of the Flint Hills. This time, however, the Flint Hills district voted for Curtis. In previous years White had swung the area for progressive Republicans. This year he was working in the Progressive primary. The support of the former Long machine had helped Bristow to increase his vote over his 1908 vote in the west, where he lost only nine of sixty-three counties. In comparison to Stubbs's senatorial returns in 1912, however, Bristow polled fewer votes in thirty-seven of these same counties. The Progressive candidate, Murdock, running unopposed, was particularly successful in half of the thirty-seven. Murdock was popular in his home Eighth Congressional District and in the Seventh District, which he had earlier represented in Congress.

When the 1914 support for Tucker is compared to the votes for Curtis in the 1912 and 1914 primaries, it appears that Tucker, a Kansas City oilman, hurt Curtis in twelve eastern counties, especially in the traditionally regular-Republican strongholds of Atchison, Leavenworth, Bourbon, Crawford, and Wyandotte counties.[20]

In evaluating his defeat, Bristow ignored Tucker's role, but he bitterly assailed Capper and the Progressive party. He said that Capper, after having enticed him into the race, had double-crossed him. On election night, just before the tallies for Shawnee County were reported, Bristow led Curtis by 500 votes; but when Bristow lost Shawnee by roughly 2,200 votes, he never again regained the lead. In Bristow's view, as well as in the view of his main supporters, the loss of Shawnee County indicated that Capper wanted Curtis on the Republican ticket in November and that he therefore had opposed Bristow in the county. If he had been objective, Bristow might have noted that Stubbs had lost the county to Curtis in 1912, polling fewer votes than Bristow received in 1914, and he might have considered that Topeka was Curtis's hometown. But Bristow was in no mood to be analytical, so he agreed with the observation that Capper had "sold him out."[21]

Despite having lost the popular vote, Bristow would have won in 1914 had the primary law of 1908 still been in effect. In 1913, however, Democrats had rewritten it so that popular majorities rather than legislative districts would determine the nomination. Bristow had carried a majority of the districts, but he had lost the popular vote, so he understandably complained about the new departure. The one-time champion of the "average voter," the man who had authored the amendment to the United States Constitution that provided for the direct election of senators, now felt that the change to increased democracy had been a mistake. He lamented the fact that in order to be a senator a man had to "shake hands and palaver over his constituents" like a common sycophant. There was no reason, he added, why populous Shawnee County in eastern Kansas should have more say in a primary election than Barton County in western Kansas. The people, he hoped, would see the lack of wisdom in this change and would demand a new, proper system of representation. In a long letter reviewing his defeat, Bristow wrote that he was grateful to Morgan for his work. "I have," he added, "more resentment towards Will White than anybody else, though Henry Allen could have nominated me." He held similar views towards Stubbs, whose real interest, he said, was in Congressman George Neeley, who was the Democratic candidate for the Senate and was Stubbs's brother-in-law.[22]

On August 11 Bristow announced that he would not bolt the party by opposing Curtis. It might be the expedient thing to do, he stated, since Curtis had won under similar conditions two years after he had deserted Stubbs. "Don't worry," he said, "I have never done the expedient." Bristow later canvassed the state for Republican candidates, and in October he spoke in behalf of Curtis's election. He was permanently ensconced in the Republican party again, seemingly having lost his concern for the reform movement. He had paid politics' highest price because of his reunion, having been defeated in his struggle to be renominated. In the long run, of course, he would undoubtedly have been finished as a senator anyway. There is no reason to assume that, as the Progressive party candidate, he would have secured many more votes than Murdock received in November.[23]

The Progressive party's showing at the primary was poor, with Murdock, their most popular candidate, receiving twelve thousand votes. Their low tallies caused the Republican press to conclude that the results indicated that Progressivism as a separate organism was dead or, at least, dying. Party leaders denied these statements, claiming that the absence of contests caused most Progressive voters to stay home. They had hoped to make a strong showing in the primaries, but apparently they were sincere when they claimed that the results mattered little. Their greatest joy was that Bristow was defeated. They viewed his losing as proof positive that the Republican party was as reactionary as ever. Some said that his defeat illustrated what happened to authentic progressive politicians who remained Republicans. They failed to say what Capper's overwhelming victory in the gubernatorial primary represented, but they were sure that it did not demonstrate that Republicanism had been regenerated or that conservatives had been forced to relinquish their grip on the party.[24]

In late August the councils of both the Republican party and the

Progressive party met in Topeka to write their platforms. Although the Progressives charged that conservatives still dominated the Republican party, some old-guard leaders were not so certain, fearing that a "milk and water platform" would be adopted. They believed that it would be lacking in good, fundamental conservative doctrine. "Of course," wrote Albaugh, "this will be Capper's desire and realizing the precariousness of his situation . . . Curtis will not in my opinion want to stand up and make a fight for a real platform." The only hope for conservatism, Albaugh predicted, would be James A. Troutman, who might be able to influence Capper to accept "a reasonably conservative" document.[25]

Had Albaugh understood the recent developments in Capper's thinking, he would have known that the future governor would undoubtedly support moderately conservative measures. Capper sensed a new attitude among Kansas voters, and of late he had decided that the wisest policy was to deemphasize reform. "I look upon the affairs of Kansas as a *business* proposition," he wrote in March, "and I stand pledged to give you a *business* administration, which will look after the *business* of the state, first, last and all the time." When announcing his candidacy, Capper had stated that he was becoming "more progressive by the minute," but his primary campaign consisted largely of promises to lower taxes, provide governmental economy, and build better roads.[26]

Still, Albaugh's assertion that Capper would not want what Albaugh considered a "real platform" was a wise one. Despite Capper's recognition of the new trend in Kansas, he was, unlike Albaugh, favorable to specific reforms, and he was interested in securing the remaining progressive-Republican votes. Progressives, who were more fully aware of Capper's methods, speculated that no matter what type of document was written, Capper would call it progressive, since he had insisted that the progressive movement could survive only by rejoining the Republicans. True to form, the Topeka publisher did what was expected of him. His influence at the council forced some reform planks into the Republican platform, thereby giving more credence to his position than Progressives would admit. He maintained that little difference existed between the platforms of the Republican and Progressive parties in 1914, and he suggested a reconciliation between them on the basis of these documents.[27]

If Capper's assertions were to remain unchallenged, they might affect the attitudes of independent or undecided voters. The honor of giving the lie to Capper's statements fell to White. According to the Emporian, the Republican platform was entirely different in spirit from that of the new party. The Republicans included the same old political "bilge" in theirs, and they used a vague terminology that was capable of allowing any candidate to take any position he liked. The two documents, White argued, were also dissimilar in that the Progressives went further than the Republicans in support of "advanced reform."[28] To a degree, White was correct in his position. He had worried early in 1914 that the Progressive party would not develop a position that was sufficiently radical to justify its independence, but his fears had proved to be largely unfounded. His party brethren were not lax in bringing forth new ideas. Their platform was as comprehensive in its support of reform as any document written in Kansas from the 1890s to the depression years of the 1930s.

The ability of Kansas Progressives to conjure up new programs was not their biggest problem or their greatest worry in 1914. Interest in the new party and its finances were by far the major concerns. Despite White's boasts that Progressives had been organized in ninety-seven to a hundred counties and that a full ticket had been arranged in seventy-three, state chairman Sartin reported in late July that he could not even afford to call a party council meeting for August. Progressivism was bankrupt, and Sartin could no longer afford to meet expenses by advancing personal loans to the organization. He could not even buy stamps and stationery to make the call, and he suggested that unless White would assume the responsibility, the Progressive party of Kansas should be disbanded. But political parties rarely die from want of money alone, least of all because of a lack of funds to buy a few hundred stamps and some paper; so in mid August, White issued the necessary invitations.[29]

On August 25, in response to White's instructions, representatives from forty-seven counties were present at Topeka for the first and last Progressive-party council. There they wrote their only state platform and discussed plans to establish a state headquarters. Sartin was reelected as state chairman. The council meeting was controlled by White, Murdock, and Allen. Although these men wanted to have "advanced ideas" incorporated in the platform, they kept a proposal providing for a special tax on unused land from being included in it. They also managed to keep Stubbs's demand for government ownership of the railroads and communications systems out of the document. Stubbs had become an adamant champion of nationalization, and he insisted that it be embodied in the platform. The Kansas Progressives agreed at first. But Stubbs's *Saturday Evening Post* article about the proposal aroused Theodore

Roosevelt, who told White that he did not favor it. Roosevelt's opposition was enough to keep the one-time Populist doctrine out of the platform.[30]

Roosevelt's equally strong complaint against national prohibition did not stop the Kansans from declaring in favor of that measure. Their attitude in part was controlled by a desire to secure W.C.T.U. votes. In all, White, Allen, Murdock, and the council wrote a platform that was fully consistent with their wish to take extreme positions. As such, it was essentially different in spirit from the Republican and Democratic documents in 1914. In specifics, however, it agreed with the Republican platform on a number of issues, giving some validity to Capper's claim that there were no differences between them. What happened was that the Progressives included every reform that the Republicans demanded, and then some.

Among the significant issues that the Progressives and Republicans both supported were a protective tariff to be written by a nonpartisan commission of experts, national prohibition, woman suffrage, presidential primaries, child-labor laws, and legislation regulating the condition of women in Kansas industry. In addition, the Progressives favored legislative and congressional caucuses that would be open to the public. They demanded minimum-wage laws, pensions for mothers, reorganization of county government to eliminate all elective offices, farm-credit measures, and a short-ballot law.

They requested a permanent board of arbitration to hear and settle disputes between labor and management, as well as a poll tax on individuals who were eligible to vote but did not do so, and a state-owned life-insurance system. In many ways they anticipated the next twenty years, since some of their suggestions, in different terminology, would become the so-called social-security laws and the Kansas Industrial Court Law. Their candidates, they said, were bound to uphold promises of the party, but otherwise they were free "to act conscientiously" as they saw "the right" on measures.[31]

They did not say, but it was understood, that the candidates would advocate those portions of the document that they approved or favored most of all. Despite the presence of a full slate of congressional hopefuls and of many candidates for minor state offices, there were two contests that obscured all others in 1914. The candidates for governor and senator were not only top leaders in Kansas; they represented the national elite of the Progressive party. On their shoulders rested its future as a distinct party. Should Murdock or Allen make a strong showing or perhaps win, there was reason to believe that the party might continue. On the other hand, should they lose badly, there were few who would want to go on.

The haunting problem was how elections in other states would go, for although the Kansans were uncertain of their own chances, they were even more worried about those of other areas. A single state party could not hope to survive without a national affiliation, and the Kansas Progressives were doomed without a significant national party or without Roosevelt on hand to command the "Teddy vote." Roosevelt had shown a particular pessimism in endorsing Hinman of New York, but Hinman had not accepted the Colonel's terms and was not supported by him after all. By late 1914 Roosevelt was resigned to his own party and to the role that he would have to play in it. Late in the year he stumped the country for various candidates, paying his old political debts. The Kansas Progressives were enlivened by his activities. They were wise enough to know that eventually Roosevelt would determine what course they should follow, and his joining them on the stump seemed to augur well for their future.[32]

Although there was nothing spectacular about the Progressive party's campaign in 1914, a moderate effort was made to elect Murdock and Allen. In September, campaign headquarters were opened, speaking tours were planned, and literature was disseminated to hundreds of voters. White was largely responsible for this activity, but the individual candidates also did their share. A certain optimism began to infect both Allen and Murdock; they began to predict victory. They said that their main opponents were the Democratic candidates on the ticket. Both Capper and Curtis, the Republican nominees, had similar feelings; that is, they felt that the Democrats constituted their major opposition. The Progressive party, the *Topeka Daily Capital* predicted, was as finished as last year's romance. "There is," it happily explained, "a revival of Republican spirit and interest in Kansas." On election eve the *Kansas City Journal*, while predicting a Democratic victory, thought that both Capper and Curtis might possibly win.[33]

Curtis's campaign had been helped in October by Bristow, who spoke in his behalf; and as usual, Curtis made strong, personal, handshaking, backslapping tours of the state. Capper's candidacy had been attacked by some Republican newspapers after the primaries, the most notable being Frank McLennan's *Topeka State Journal*. McLennan was neither progressive nor conservative to any marked degree, but he was anti-Capper. In an effort to keep the record straight, the *State Journal* published a speech that Capper had made at Independence in December of 1912. In it Capper seemed to support the Progressive party. The speech, the *State Journal* editor argued, placed Capper "in the light of a true progressive and an enemy of the Republican principles." Capper answered that his party fidelity was unmoved and that he had never been out of the Republican organization. He claimed that the *State Journal* had misquoted him, and he demanded an immediate retraction. No retraction came. Instead, the Progressives helped out by indicating that McLennan was substantially correct.[34]

This and other unfavorable comments by White and his cohorts caused a factotum of Capper's, Marco Morrow, to charge that the *Emporia Gazette* and the Progressives were playing "peanut politics." Capper made the George Hodges administration the main issue in 1914, attacking the governor for dishonesty and corruption. Here again, White and the Progressives contradicted Capper, claiming that his exaggerations were not designed to reveal alleged wrongs but to put an ambitious Republican into office. In a letter to White, Morrow wrote: "Don't stultify yourself . . . by excusing and minimizing the rottenness of Hodges and his unspeakable helpers."[35]

In 1914 Hodges, whose administration seems to have been honest, despite Morrow's asseverations, had his bid for reelection complicated by the presence of J. B. Billard, who had contested him in the 1912 Democratic primary and who was back now as an independent candidate for governor. Anti-Capper Republicans speculated that Capper had brought Billard into the race in order to limit Hodges's appeal in eastern Kansas. This may have been what happened. Billard certainly took "wet" votes from Hodges, since both the Progressive and the Republican candidate had the reputation of being "drier" than Hodges.

Capper's hopes for election were given a slight boost by the fact that Stubbs, though a Progressive, did not actively campaign against him; indeed, Stubbs allowed his former followers to endorse Capper. During the campaign, Stubbs remained silent on all races, seeming to be unconcerned about the fate of the Progressive party's nominees. It appears that his lack of effort was due to the desire of White, Murdock, and Allen to keep him unimportant in the new party, and Stubbs was a man who wanted to lead a political organization if he were to be involved in it at all.[36]

The main issues raised by Allen and Murdock during their speaking tours and in their campaign pamphlets were the reorganization of county government and the reorganization by Congress of its methods of conducting its own business. Early in 1914 Allen had been converted to a new plan for county government. He liked the idea because, to his knowledge, no other politician had developed the issue. What he wanted was a nonpartisan county ballot and later, if possible, a civil-service system to replace elective officers at that level. Presumably, the ballot reform would be unnecessary after the classified service list was implemented, but Allen did not specifically note whether all county offices were to be on a merit basis in the future. When speaking in urban areas, he was particularly insistent in his arguments for this innovation. His campaign in metropolitan centers was helped by the fact that the Kansas Federation of Labor endorsed him in 1914. During the campaign, however, he was challenged by a printers' local, on the grounds that he operated a nonunion newspaper. He countered this by mailing his journal, which carried a union label, to labor leaders across the state. Possibly some local labor officials were reluctant to support Allen because he advocated compulsory arbitration, which the Progressive platform recommended.[37]

Murdock's campaign centered largely on his work as a congressional leader, thus constituting what White called a "defensive contest," that is, a contest where few positive proposals were advanced. The most important aspects of Murdock's program was directed towards Senate rules regarding caucuses and unlimited debate. He favored open caucuses, opposed unlimited debate, and was against senatorial courtesy whenever it interfered with legislative procedures. His campaign, like those of other Progressives, was criticized for being too ideological and impractical. David Leahy, a Democrat-turned-Republican who was an employee of Murdock's, felt that established issues such as tax reform and governmental economy would win more votes.[38]

By September, both Murdock and Allen were avoiding the most meaningful reforms offered by the platform of the state party. Their change in tempo undoubtedly reflected the impact of criticisms akin to that of Leahy. Presumably, they discovered what Capper had found out earlier—Kansas was not reform-minded in 1914. Why reform sentiment was diminishing is hard to tell, since the campaign was singularly free of foreign-policy issues and the war question. Nonetheless, a revision in sentiment regarding governmental change did take place. War news occupied a large place in Kansas newspapers after August; and it, in addition to the declining economy, was considered by White to be a cause for the new attitude towards reform.[39]

On November 5, Kansans went to the polls, and by the weight of their marks in the Republican and Democratic columns indicated that they did not favor a third party. In all, half a million votes were cast in each major election, and only 100,000, or roughly 20 percent of them, went to Progressive candidates. Because the Progressive party made such a poor showing, a statistical analysis is not particularly revealing. Murdock, who polled 116,755 votes in leading the ticket, carried only three counties, all in his former congressional district. He was second to Curtis or to George Neeley, the Democratic candidate, in fourteen others, mostly in the southwest. He did fairly well in a number of western counties, where he registered his highest percentages, but he gained most of his numerical total in the populous east.

The fact that Murdock's name was on the ballot limited traditional Republican strength in the western districts, where Neeley carried the majority of counties. Neeley, congressman from the Seventh District, won all but two counties in that area. Murdock may have taken some Democratic votes from Neeley in the east, for there Neeley fared poorly in Democratic strongholds. It is more than likely, however, that regular Republicans who had been voting against their progressive-Republican brethren in the past returned to the Curtis fold. This seems particularly true of Allen, Atchison, Crawford, Doniphan, Jefferson, Leavenworth, Miami, Shawnee, Wabaunsee, and Washington counties, where Curtis's vote jumped 5 to 10 percent over Republican returns in previous elections. Curtis's victory, as was to have been expected, was far from a stunning sweep. He defeated Neeley by 3,897 votes—seven-tenths of 1 percent of the ballots cast.[40]

Capper's victory was significantly larger, with the Topekan defeating Hodges by approximately 48,000 votes, or a 9.1 percent difference. As was normally the case, more votes were cast in the gubernatorial race than in the senatorial contest. Despite this fact, it seems obvious that many people who voted for Capper did not support Curtis. Capper received about 30,000 more votes than Curtis, while Murdock received 32,000 more votes than Allen. The relationship of these figures indicates that after voting for Murdock, about 30,000 people switched over to vote for the Republican gubernatorial nominee.[41] Allen polled 84,000 votes, or 15.9 percent of the total, carrying only Wyandotte and Sedgwick counties. Much of his deficit relative to Murdock's vote was in the Eighth Congressional District, which surrounded Wichita.

Compared to Roosevelt's showing in 1912, the election proved that even with the addition of women voters the Progressive party had lost strength everywhere except in counties where the candidates or powerful party leaders lived. Statistically, Kansas Progressives were a third party of minor strength in 1914, not the second-ranking party that White envisioned. But while statistics tell a uniform story, men do not always read results in the same manner, and those who worked hardest for the cause in 1914 came out of the campaign with varying opinions about the future.[42]

Nationally, the showing of the Progressive party was worse than it was in Kansas. East of the Mississippi River, Progressives received less than 20 percent of the vote. Only in the Far West were a few Progressives elected to office. Before the sobering fact of what had happened nationally had dawned upon White, he was ready to "take up the fight" with full force, as were Allen and Murdock. Even former pessimists like Sartin felt that they had done "fairly well"; and a long-time champion of unpopular causes, Mrs. Eva Morley Murphy, wrote: "I cannot bring myself to believe that a party born of such a passion for justice, a party of such lofty purposes and ideals . . . can perish."[43]

By mid November, however, the meaning of the national disaster had impressed itself on White. He had become particularly critical of eastern Progressives and of the middle-class orientation of the movement, which had failed to inspire the working class. Editorially, he suggested that all seemed undone and that perhaps the party should be disbanded. But nothing could be gained by such actions, and even a party in its death throes was worth something. The first serious decision to be made came later in the month, when, on the advice of Roosevelt, leaders of the state party agreed to wait a year to eighteen months to see what would happen to Republicanism. Temporarily, then, the party was to be preserved, but in a state of "unanimated suspension."[44]

Progressive Republicans had viewed the election both with chagrin and with satisfaction. It had confirmed their belief that a third party was impractical and that progressivism could not survive in this form, but it had brought Curtis back to the Senate. Regular Republicans were naturally elated by what happened, but the man most comforted by developments was not a native of Kansas. From his home in Danville, Illinois, Joseph G. Cannon wrote: "I am satisfied that he [Murdock] failed. His career reminds me of Lincoln's saying . . . 'You cannot fool all the people all the time.' Mr. Murdock has my permission, and I believe the people's permission, to devote the remainder of his life to Chautauqua addresses and other private callings as he may desire." Once again Cannon was to be disappointed by Murdock. Rather than retiring from public life, the Wichita editor, supported by almost all Progressive leaders, was elected to the national chairmanship of the party, and after the party had collapsed, he was appointed by President Woodrow Wilson to the Federal Trade Commission in 1917.[45]

# 13

## EPILOGUE: HOW THINGS CAN END

The three years that followed the defeat in 1914 saw most Kansas Progressives work their way back into the confidence of Republicans and then into the old party itself. Their return did not occur suddenly, since Theodore Roosevelt prevented the reentry of many Progressive leaders until mid 1916. Yet during the twelve months after November 1914 the trip back was made by numerous members of the lower echelons.[1] The enlisted men of Progressivism had good reason for deserting the party during 1915.

According to Roosevelt's instructions, the Progressive organization continued in Kansas until 1916, but in fact it discontinued operations after the 1914 elections. When the state legislature convened in January 1915, for example, ten recently elected Progressives were seated. They did not organize independently, as they had done in the previous session, but chose to caucus with the Republicans.[2] In February there was no Lincoln Day rally, and except for a state convention prior to the national nominating convention of the Progressives in 1916, not one of the usual committee or council meetings was held. Party leaders accepted Colonel William Rockhill Nelson's suggestion that they do nothing, "and darn little of that." The nation, Nelson wrote, was in a reactionary mood and wanted "civility," and there was no sense in hoping that time would improve things appreciably.[3]

Kansas leaders were disheartened by word that they received from David Hinshaw at national headquarters. According to Hinshaw, the bottom had fallen out of things there and had somehow gotten lost. "My own opinion," he noted, "is that we are doomed as a party." Moreover, Roosevelt was not encouraging. He told William Allen White that east of Indiana the party did not need to continue, but that it might well go on in the West. Roosevelt's advice was that White should keep the Progressive party of Kansas intact but that he should do nothing until 1916, when the Republicans would nominate a presidential candidate. He was not bold enough to say that he hoped to be that candidate, but White undoubtedly knew that it was possible that Roosevelt would be running again as a Republican when the time came.[4]

On 2 December 1914 the leaders of the Progressive party met in Chicago. Except for providing that the national committee convene to call a national convention before January 1916, they did nothing to indicate that the organization was going to go on in the same old way. As a matter of note, a statement written by William Allen White and Chester Rowell of California indicated that despite much talk by radical Progressives, who wished to stress more advanced portions of the 1912 "Contract with the People," the entrenched, moderate leadership controlled affairs. In the White-Rowell announcement the social-justice ideas of 1912 received no special mention. Rather than emphasizing reform, White and Rowell explained that the defeat of the Progressives in 1914 had resulted from declining prosperity, which had been caused by the Underwood tariff. So far as reform activism was concerned, White expressed his own opinion that party members were tired and needed a spiritual rest, after which they might again rejoin the battle. Actually, the Emporia publisher was terribly uncertain of any future action, and in late 1914 he wanted to be left alone politically.[5]

Progressivism as an ideological force was nearly spent in Kansas, although it remained for two more years in the fashion in which it had been strongest all along, as an intraparty question. The progressive-Republican faction had disintegrated after the 1912 bolt. Although Joseph Bristow and Arthur Capper continued the fiction of its survival, they had become the wariest of friends and the most moderate of statesmen. Bristow, after leaving the Senate, was appointed public utilities commissioner by Capper, but instead of appreciating the largess, he called it a bribe to keep him out of the senatorial race in 1918. By late 1914 he was sure that the tempo of the progressive movement had slowed and that progressives would have to yield their extreme position. He agreed with John Harrison's Burkean statement that "the way to being [was] . . . by remembering that the civilization of the present is an evolution of centuries and . . . can not be made perfect in a day by getting a lot of the truly good in politics together and adopting a high sounding set of resolutions." He was sure that conservatives would be willing to give a little if the progressives would come part of the way.[6]

Although Capper was able to secure some laws from the 1915 legislature that should properly be considered to be progressive, he, too, was moderate in his political expressions. Rather than describing his administration as one devoted to reform and social uplift, he wrote Charles Gleed that in essence it was "nothing more than a big business corporation." "The same principles which operate successfully in private business," he said, "can and must be applied to the public business." This meant that Capper was not going to be overly concerned about the failure of progressivism's ideals.[7]

Capper and Bristow were reacting to developments that were taking place in Kansas at the time. Prior to the convening of the state legislature in 1915, a series of inquiries was sent to state legislators, asking them to express their views on what laws needed to be enacted at the coming session. Fully two-thirds answered that no new laws were needed and that any legislation considered by them ought to be sound, sane, and conservative. When they met, one of their first orders of business was an expansion of the initiative and referendum, which every party had endorsed in 1914. In February 1915 they defeated this measure by a large majority, causing widespread joy among regular Republicans who saw its rejection as symbolic of the death of reform.[8]

In May, journalist Frederick M. Davenport, on the "trail of progress" in the Middle West, found that in Kansas it had slowed down. He said that "a flabby state of public muscle" had developed as a result of the previous election. Capper, he added, was the kind of leader that Kansans wanted because he was a moderate. Kansas, he concluded, "does not want to do anything, but wants to be left alone."[9]

The dose of moderation or conservatism that was being swallowed by progressive Republicans during 1915 was also being taken by Progressives. Attuned to the times, these leaders made repeated concessions in their letters and published articles, explaining why the movement was not successful in its goals. Since there were no party meetings, nothing like a consensus of party opinion is available, but there is reason to believe that William Allen White and Henry J. Allen, in their ruminations, represented the general attitude of many leaders in the state. During 1915 the *Emporia Gazette* repeatedly carried stories stressing that issues were no longer important in politics. The real thing, so far as its famed editor could tell, was the purely strategic question of getting ready for affairs in 1916. But White's new attitude was never better expressed than in November of 1915, when he wrote Charles Gleed that Ed Ripley, president of the Santa Fe, represented what was best in the nation's business world. "I am not . . . sure," said the one-time railroad critic, "whether it was the Santa Fe spirit that made Mr. Ripley or Mr. Ripley who made the Santa Fe spirit. But the Santa Fe spirit as he incarnates it is one of the fine things America has developed."[10]

The kind of change that was taking place in White's attitude was also occurring in Allen's mind. On a number of occasions the *Wichita Beacon* carried articles that were favorable to the business interests of Kansas; and when it slipped in late 1915 and mistakenly printed inaccurate criticisms of the Southwestern Bell Telephone Company, Allen hastily apologized to Gleed, Bell's manager in Kansas City. "I think," Allen noted, "it is a good thing that public service corporations take the trouble to call down uninformed editors who ought to be just as anxious to be square with corporations as with anybody else." Allen did not overlook the opportunity of applying the "public-service corporation" label to Bell, but, as he said, he was anxious to be "square with corporations."[11]

Lest the change in their opinions become too obvious, White and Allen had to moderate their growing conservative attitudes. As part of a plan to force the nomination of a reformer as the Republican presidential candidate in 1916, they had to make Republicans believe that they were still committed to the Progressive party and its ideals. Otherwise they would have lost their major bargaining position.

In January 1916 Progressives launched a campaign to persuade Republicans to nominate a reformer as the G.O.P. presidential candidate. Pretending to support the continuation of the third party, White and Allen began to advance reform ideas that they claimed were crucial to Progressives in 1916. Their ideological program, however, was flat; even tactical reasons were not enough to make their statements appear to be sincere. During 1915 White and Allen had followed Roosevelt's advice to do nothing publicly with the Kansas party. Midway through the "watch and wait" period, Allen wrote to his Emporia confederate that Roosevelt's suggestion was good politics. "I don't seem to have any plans or convictions or movements of any kind in my head," he noted. "I'm sitting around about as stale and helpless and useless as the Kansas legislature." A little later he reported that Democrats had asked him to join their party and to run as their gubernatorial candidate in 1916. Republicans, he added, "don't give a damn if Progressives come back into their party."[12]

Allen, of course, was incorrect. Standpat Republicans were not overly concerned about the return of White and Allen, but progressive Republicans wanted the Progressives to come back. White, for example, received numerous entreaties to rejoin the Republican fold. By coming back, his friends insisted, he and Allen could make the party progressive again. "Get back into the old party," one progressive Republican wrote, "and hammer away there for uplift measures." There, he added, his energy would work and would not be waste. "The Republican party is pretty keen," another said, "consider what they did to the candidates for Congress [in 1914] who were labeled standpat and also that Curtis got by with less than 4,000 [votes]." This same correspondent told White to reenter the party, where, with Bristow, Capper, Walter R. Stubbs, and Allen, they could "lick the platter clean" before the regulars ate the whole meal. During most of 1915 White and Allen did not show their hand. Late in the year, however, they began to act.[13]

The principal aim of White and Allen in 1916 was to accomplish a return to the national Republican party without losing stature and power as political leaders in the process. In order to do this they hoped to secure the nomination of an acceptable candidate for president on the Republican ticket. In this fashion they believed that they could rejoin the party and that they would be given recognition within the organization for their support in the presidential election. They hoped that the Republican candidate would be Roosevelt, but at first they indicated that they would favor any man of progressive convictions. At no moment when they were being rational did they seem interested in continuing the Progressive party, although their actions after March could have been construed as leaving ample room for doubt.

In January 1916, White's and Allen's desire for a reunion among Republicans was advanced in two ways. The Progressive national meeting in Chicago issued a call for a nominating convention to be held at the same time as the Republican convention, and the Progressives indicated that they would support the Republican nominee in 1916 if he were a genuine reformer. Just after the Chicago meeting, Henry J. Allen began to hold discussions with Billy Morgan and Mort Albaugh concerning a possible amalgamation of Progressives and Republicans in Kansas. Morgan suggested that, under the existing circumstances, Charles Evans Hughes would make an ideal compromise candidate for the presidency, and Allen noted that he had given "a rip-snorting sort of approval" to the idea. The discussions between Allen and the regular Republicans were hurt somewhat by Allen's insistence that a progressive Republican replace Fred Stanley as the state Republican committeeman in 1916. Allen's attitude caused Albaugh to complain that Allen was unable to "reconcile himself to coming back into the party without immediately assuming leadership of it." Nevertheless, until March it seemed as if the Kansas Progressives would rejoin the Republican party in 1916 without a serious hitch.[14]

In March, however, White and Allen, possibly because of advice from other national leaders, began to raise the price for reunion. There is no evidence to show what made the Kansans change from moderate demands as the cost of a reunified Republican party to the stipulation that Roosevelt be nominated by the Republicans in 1916. Probably George Perkins or Roosevelt asked them to take this line, since, as George Mowry has pointed out, Roosevelt was becoming anxious over his prospects of securing the Republican nomination. John Garraty has stated that Perkins was becoming aware that a strong line was needed if Roosevelt were to be chosen in 1916. Whatever the reason, in late February, White began to hint that Roosevelt should be nominated by the Republicans, and in early March he warned that this should be done if Republicans expected peace in 1916. When the Kansas Republican convention was controlled by politicians hostile to Roosevelt and when a delegation opposed to the former president was sent to the national convention in Chicago, White realized that if the Progressives were to have any impact on the Republicans, they would have to make a forthright threat of continuing their party.[15]

At the Progressive State Convention on May 23, both Allen and White, in emotional speeches, specified that compromise with the Republicans would be possible only if Roosevelt were the candidate of the national party. Newspapermen, who were apparently not well informed about the changing tactics of White and Allen, were amazed by the turn of events. They seemed to believe that "harmonizers" and "political pacifists" would control the state convention of the Progressives. Moreover, the Progressive's national executive committee had already announced that state conventions should send uninstructed delegates to Chicago in June. Only the *Topeka Daily Capital* seemed to be well-enough informed to report what happened. Kansas Progressives, the *Capital* headlined, are "FOR TR FIRST, LAST AND ALWAYS!" Since a militant "Roosevelt-or-nothing" sentiment carried the day, the delegation that Allen led to the Progressive National Convention was instructed to help nominate

Roosevelt and then to adjourn so that Republicans could endorse this action.[16]

By June, only two men, White and Allen, were influencing Kansas Progressivism to any extent. Publicly they had taken a "Roosevelt-or-nothing" position, but apparently they were aware all along that Roosevelt would spurn the Progressive nomination if Republicans refused to select him as their candidate in 1916. At least they discussed a list of progressive Republicans whom they considered to be eligible for the presidential nomination, and they expressed the belief that if the Colonel were not nominated by the Republicans, he would endorse any man whose name appeared on the list.[17]

Victor Murdock was the only other important Kansan who was involved nationally in the Progressive party. He did not seem to be aware that Roosevelt would compromise with Republicans on another candidate. After leaving the House of Representatives, Murdock had been named as national chairman of the Progressive party, and following the tradition of the first chairman, Joseph Dixon of Montana, he had been a party leader in name only. He attended the Progressive National Convention under the assumption that Roosevelt would be quickly nominated, thus forcing the Republicans either to tender the Colonel their nomination or to face a continued split. When the plan failed, Murdock became one of the vocal critics of George Perkins.[18]

The Republican and the Progressive national conventions were held simultaneously in 1916 in order to allow the two parties to agree on the same candidate. When the Republicans were unwilling to accept Roosevelt as their party's nominee, George Perkins, following Roosevelt's instructions, kept the Progressive convention from nominating the Colonel. Roosevelt and Perkins hoped that when the Republicans made their selection, the Progressives would choose the same man as their nominee. Because Perkins's delaying actions did not fit in with Victor Murdock's plan to nominate Roosevelt before the Republicans had selected a candidate, Murdock raised a number of protests against Perkins and finally joined with Hiram Johnson, John Parker of Louisiana, White, and others in nominating Roosevelt.

White, who had been privy to Perkins's intentions and Roosevelt's wishes, supported Murdock; in later years he insisted that he had been in full accord with Murdock's desire to select Roosevelt over Perkins's protest. Writing in 1924, White claimed that Perkins had betrayed the Progressive party by his actions at the convention in 1916. He later agreed with a similar condemnation of Roosevelt by Harold Ickes in

1941. In his book *Right-hand Man: The Life of George Perkins,* John Garraty has done an excellent job of impeaching White's statements on these counts. It need only be said that White did work with Murdock and recalcitrant Progressives on the day that Roosevelt was nominated.

When Roosevelt refused the Progressive nomination in a letter read to the Progressive National Convention on the afternoon of 10 June 1916, Murdock felt that he had been misled. However, Roosevelt had never stated that he would accept the dubious honor of leading the Progressive ticket again, and his activities after May had indicated that he was really interested in the Republican nomination. Murdock was aware of Roosevelt's flirtations with the Republicans. Nevertheless, Roosevelt had led the Progressives to Armageddon, and to men of Murdock's views this meant that the Colonel was obligated to run for the presidency in 1916 if the Progressives wanted him to do so. Roosevelt's letter of refusal was conditional, suggesting that the national committee, at a meeting that would be held later, be allowed to determine the course of action that Progressives should pursue. This suggestion was approved by the national convention before it adjourned. "I am not sore or sad," Murdock reportedly said, "but I am impressed with the tremendous force against us; power [and] money."[19]

On June 26 the Progressive National Committee met to consider whether it would endorse the Republican candidate, Charles Evans Hughes. Roosevelt had endorsed Hughes by this time. A heated debate developed at the June 26 meeting, and for a while it appeared that Murdock might be the presidential nominee of "radical" elements within the Progressive organization. To his relief, this move failed. Murdock, however, was dissatisfied by the National Committee's final decision to endorse Hughes. He refused to join the majority of Progressives in this move. He allowed his newspaper, the *Wichita Eagle,* to support President Woodrow Wilson, although he personally did not work for Wilson. Reviewing what had happened, he wrote in August 1916:

> It wasn't so much the collapse of things at Chicago as it was the manner of collapse which galled me and galled me more deeply than I supposed I could be hurt. For, as you know, I have a rather effective barrier against injury in my humor. It didn't serve this time. If I could have figured anything gained by surrender, I could have smiled. But the setback was sordid and without qualifying hope. I seemed to see, for the first time vividly, that futile battles are worse than no battle at all, because the defeat fortifies the opposition against even the efficacy of threat which is the only thing which keeps those in power in anything

like good behavior. I do not identify in myself anything like personal disappointment and I try to boil out of my feelings anything that is mean or cheaply pessimistic. We did stand for advance, which neither of the old parties divine, and our failure spells, to my mind, future disaster for the country.[20]

When a group of former Progressives met in July to endorse Wilson, Murdock did not attend the meeting, but he did allow them to report that he sympathized with their plans.[21]

On June 20 William Allen White announced that the Kansas Progressive party supported Hughes. At the same time, he withdrew the party's list of presidential electors, which had been filed previously with the secretary of state. He said that he had consulted the Progressives' state chairman, U. S. Sartin, who concurred in the action. His decision to have the party support the Republican candidate resulted from his foreknowledge of what would happen a week later at the meeting of the Progressive National Committee. White's decision, wrote the editor of the *Topeka State Journal*, means "that all the big league men in the Progressive party in Kansas—with the exception of Victor Murdock—will be back under the Republican banner in November." It also meant the end of the Progressive party in Kansas.[22]

"Who are the pussy-footers now," asked an angry Progressive, "those who returned to Republicans two years ago or those who return now?" White claimed that the party's support of Hughes was only a temporary measure, but his Progressive followers understood that this was not true. "Are you not aware," asked A. M. Breese, "that we cannot get on the ballot two years from now if we wished?" Breese, like a number of other party members, indicated that he did not intend to vote for Hughes, and he added that ten thousand other former Progressives would join him in supporting Wilson.[23]

Despite his having used the Kansas Progressive party to endorse Hughes, White's private opinion of the Republican candidate differed very little from Murdock's or Breese's. In October he told Norman Hapgood that although he could not help Wilson in any positive fashion, he cared not a whit who won the election. White planned to support Republican candidates in Kansas and to avoid the national campaign whenever possible.[24]

White's disposition indicated the general attitude of Kansans toward Hughes in 1916. The Republican nominee lacked voter appeal. He took what was essentially the wrong position on the war that was raging in Europe. He failed to handle reform issues as adroitly as Wilson did.

Thus, in November he lost not only the nation but Kansas as well. His defeat, while not totally unexpected, was worse than many thought it would be. In assessing the results, many regular Republicans believed that Hughes's poor campaign, plus Arthur Capper's unwillingness to help Hughes, caused the party's defeat in Kansas. Murdock's *Wichita Eagle,* however, argued that Hughes's campaign had not cost him the election; the public had simply preferred the better candidate, Wilson. Kansans realized, *Eagle* writers continued, that the president was abler and more sincere than Hughes. Capper's *Topeka Daily Capital* attributed the results to America's war prosperity and to the catchy Democratic slogan "He Kept Us out of War!" Henry J. Allen and William Allen White agreed with Capper's opinion, and in a manner that hinted of satisfaction, they suggested that Kansas Progressives had also done their bit to "Keep Republicans out of the White House."[25]

Progressive voters helped to defeat Hughes in 1916. Refusing to honor the endorsement of their party, about one-third of the former supporters of Progressivism voted for Wilson in Kansas. Returns for the president increased by 10.7 percent over his 1912 figure, but in the thirty counties that Roosevelt had carried in 1912, Wilson's increase was 13.7 percent. Although Hughes received 44.1 percent of the popular vote in Kansas, his percentage in the thirty counties that had formerly gone to Roosevelt was only 42.3 percent. It appears that of the thirty-seven thousand votes that separated Wilson and Hughes in the state, Progressives supplied the lion's share.[26]

Lost elections rarely revive interest in defunct political organizations, but the 1916 general election did cause this to happen in the case of William Allen White. In December he continued his political wooing of Kansas Republicans by telling them that his ideas were fully compatible with Republican beliefs. To Roosevelt he wrote that he planned to rejoin the old party, since he could not be a Democrat. On December 4 he met with five other Progressives in Chicago to announce his abandonment of the Bull Moose party. But early in 1917, because regular Republicans had begun to prepare for complete conservative control of the national party, he helped to plan for a possible revival of the Progressive party. He suggested to his "radical" allies that George Perkins, who was conducting a bluff similar to White's, be removed from any position in the Bull Moose organization. He also noted that issues that would relate to the European War should be developed for the party.

Until February 1917 White continued to correspond with Progressives, but after February his interest flagged, and by March all trace of any concern for a revived Progressivism disappeared from his letters. In April 1917 Murdock, who had had little to do with the birth of the Progressive organization, presided over its final meeting. At St. Louis, where he chaired the last convention, this champion of the unrestricted sale of liquor ironically helped to adopt a resolution that joined the Progressive party with the Prohibition party. Like its Kansas offspring, the national Progressive party was at last dead.[27]

The passing of Progressivism did not end the political careers of many of its key leaders. Of the top six men in Kansas who were involved in either the progressive-Republican faction or the Progressive party, only Murdock immediately ceased to be important in state politics. He did serve, however, as a Wilson appointee on the Federal Trade Commission until 1924. He joined the Democratic party, but in the late twenties and thirties he devoted much of his time to journalism only.[28]

White, Allen, and Capper survived the storm at the end of the movement and assumed leading roles in the Republican party almost as soon as they deserted the Progressives, either in 1914 or in 1916. Stubbs and Bristow tried to win the seat that was open in the United States Senate in 1918; but after their failures in that election they faded as significant figures in the party. In 1922 Stubbs, backed by White, made an unsuccessful attempt to gain the Republican gubernatorial nomination. Bristow left Kansas, moving to a farm outside of Washington, D.C., and eventually he became wealthy as a result of earlier investments in real estate in the vicinity of the national capital. According to John Harrison, who was still a close friend of the senator's in the twenties, Bristow remained hostile towards White and other Kansans because of their role in his 1918 senatorial defeat. "Why he [Bristow] should have been embittered at his defeat in 1918," White noted, "is beyond me."[29]

In 1918 Kansans were presented with the interesting spectacle of a four-way struggle for the United States Senate, in which three former progressive friends—Stubbs, Capper, and Bristow—were involved. The fourth candidate was their old enemy Charles F. Scott. In 1918 White tried to revive the progressive-Republican faction in order to clear the way for the nomination of Arthur Capper. When he failed, he washed his hands of the election, writing Henry Allen that he was opposed to Bristow, Stubbs, and Capper because they were anticonscription pacifists and that he was opposed to Scott because he was pro-German. "If you know a good, honest, two-legged man who believed in the Star-Spangled Banner and the Bull-Moose platform," he wrote, "who would run for the Senate as an American citizen . . . trot him off."[30]

Although each one developed a spirited campaign, Scott, Bristow, and Stubbs did not have much chance against the popular Governor Capper in 1918. Taking a moderate position on the war, somewhere between Bristow's pacifism and Stubbs's belligerency, Capper won easily. Capper's moderation, however, was not the deciding factor. Capper was always exceedingly popular with Kansas voters, to whom he always catered. He was normally able to leave the impression that he stood foremost for righteousness and goodness, tempered with wisdom. Most political leaders did not like Capper, since they considered him at best a spineless wonder and at worst a well-practiced demagogue. But the real masters of political fortunes, the people, heartedly endorsed him, and in 1918, for the first time, they elected a two-term Kansas governor to the Senate. There Capper served continuously and honorably for thirty years, until 1949, when, nearly incapacitated, he relinquished his seat to a new, more conservative Republican leader.[31]

The major interest of William Allen White, even before mid 1917, when he realized the hopelessness of re-creating the progressive-Republican faction, was the contest involving his friend Allen. Allen had stuck to the Kansas Progressive party to the bitter end, and to White's way of thinking, he deserved a fate other than political failure.[32] Early in 1917 White became convinced that Allen was an unbeatable candidate for governor and an ideal choice for regular Republicans to support if they wanted to demonstrate their willingness to compromise with their wayward brothers. With this in mind, he set about seeking support for the Wichita publisher, and luckily he secured the aid of Mort Albaugh. Albaugh was interested in Republican harmony, and he was appreciative of the work that Allen and his *Wichita Beacon* had done for Hughes in 1916. Albaugh was also aware that the senatorial primary in 1918 could conceivably upset things so badly that Republicans might be split at the polls in November. Albaugh had only one problem confronting him in 1918: Billy Morgan, his confederate of bygone days, was a candidate for governor. From 1914 onward, however, Albaugh and Morgan had moved farther and farther apart. Thus, in 1917 Albaugh did not find it exceptionally hard to support Allen while deserting Morgan.[33]

Together, White and Albaugh were able to secure additional help from former Senator Chester I. Long, former Governors Willis J. Bailey and Edward W. Hoch, David W. Mulvane, Charles Gleed, and Standard Oil attorney Sam Fitzpatrick. "It looks good," wrote a regular to White, "to see your name and that of Mort Albaugh signed to the same document and with that sort of harmony we ought to be able to make it a parade for Henry." Others, such as the third candidate for the gubernatorial nomination, S. M. Brewster, who was an old Lelandite and now attorney general of Kansas, did not agree. "I have just a little curiosity," he wrote White, "to know how it is possible for Henry Allen to represent your views on public questions and also represent the views of Fitzpatrick and a few others I could name?"[34]

For the first time in years a progressive Republican, or at least a former member of that group, received favorable attention at the Kansas Day Club. What was true in January 1918 was also true in August, when Republican voters in Kansas nominated Allen, who was then in Europe with the Red Cross. Albaugh had encouraged Allen to volunteer for duty in Europe so that the aging *Beacon* editor could appear to be a war hero. Unfortunately, Albaugh did not live to see the fruits of his planning mature, since he died suddenly in February 1918.[35]

Allen was elected in 1918 and again in 1920. He served two hectic terms as governor, during which he was involved in the great Kansas coal strike of 1919 and in problems caused by his pet project, the Kansas Industrial Court. It has been said that Allen barely missed being nominated as Harding's vice-presidential running mate in 1920. Had he been nominated, he, rather than Coolidge, would have become president. In 1929 he was appointed to fill the unexpired senatorial term of Charles Curtis when Curtis became vice-president of the United States. Although he failed to secure the Senate seat on a permanent basis in 1930, he continued to be an important politician until the Great Depression. Thereafter, his influence declined.[36]

Allen's election to the governor's office in 1918 made White a reconfirmed member of the Republican party, and there he stayed until his death in 1944. He was never a good Republican, although he associated often enough with the party to be considered an acceptable one. In 1924 he ran for governor on an anti–Ku Klux Klan, independent ticket, but he was neither seriously interested in being elected nor was he considered as having left the national Republican party.

Allen's first campaign helped White make his peace in the state, but Emporia's most famous citizen also used his own personal charm to win the confidence of other Kansas regulars. The best example of White's making peace on his own was his reconciliation with Senator Curtis. In December 1916, after twenty years during which the two men had not exchanged letters, White wrote to the senator, congratulating him for his stand in favor of a bill that would require federal licensing in order to sell liquor. Curtis answered that he was pleased to hear from a constituent on issues, and he recalled that midway through the progressive movement, when the two men were barely on speaking terms, the senator had secured an appointment for one of White's friends. From then on, they continued to have frequent exchanges, and in early 1918 White was admitting that the war had softened his views to the point that he could now understand many things that four to six years earlier had caused him to disagree with Curtis. "Things," he added, "which justify you in your viewpoint and I presume which allow . . . you to see that many of us who disagreed with you were neither crazy nor selfish in our activities." The important goal now, said White, was to blast Democrats, so that in 1920 the nation might return a Republican president to lead the country.[37]

After 1917 the entry of the United States into the World War and the end of the Progressive party further advanced the conservative reaction that had begun three years earlier in Kansas. From 1917 until 1920 what was once a progressive citadel became a bastion of conservatism, and at the end of that period, one man who was intent on keeping some ideals of the old movement alive, Governor Henry Allen, gloomily admitted that progressivism was dead in his state, even if reactionaries had not completely reclaimed it. White had come to a similar conclusion. The war and a general pattern of cyclical revulsion against reform, he wrote, had placed a check on progressivism. "No one," he lamented, "pays attention to us anymore."[38]

Before April 1917 there were those who were sanguine enough to believe that after the war, progressivism would flourish once again; but this hope was shattered by the election of Warren G. Harding in 1920 and by the return to power of such Kansas conservatives as Curtis and Mulvane. After Allen left office, a former progressive was not reinstalled in power until Clyde Reed was elected governor in 1928, and he lost his bid for renomination in 1930. A new brand of reformer became governor in 1933, when a former county chairman of the Progressive party, Alfred M. Landon, assumed the office of chief executive. By then, issues and ideas had changed somewhat as a result of the Great Depression.[39]

Progressivism had become the dynamic element in Kansas Republicanism beginning with the elections of Senator Bristow and Governor Stubbs in 1908. Its roots had been in the state's tradition of factionalism, which had caused the creation of the Boss-Busters in 1899 and of the Kansas Republican League in 1904. An equally important origin of the progressive Republicans had been grounded in the protest of the Kansas Civic League and the Square Deal Club of 1906, two organizations that were devoted largely to the redress of abuses on the part of the railroads. Other factors had contributed to the rise of progressivism in Kansas, including Theodore Roosevelt's inspiration, the work of Muckraking journalists, the motives of small businessmen who were on the make, the ambitions of western-Kansas town boosters, and the lingering influence of populism.

After 1909 Kansas progressive Republicans had their future enmeshed in the party's insurgency movement in Congress. Unable to extricate themselves from national involvement, they had bolted the Republican party with Roosevelt. Although many had been reluctant, they had gone, giving up control of their G.O.P. and the state government. Ironically, their places had been taken in the leadership of the party by the people whom they had initially deposed.

But Kansas politics had been changed forever. Charles Curtis was re-elected to the Senate in 1914, but in a manner far different from his first selection. The sordid practice that gave railroad counsels in Topeka and in places east of the Mississippi an important part in Kansas senatorial caucuses no longer existed. The party primary and the Bristow Amendment to the U.S. Constitution had altered affairs permanently. These artifices had not created the perfect political arrangement, as progressives had believed that they would, but they had solved some problems. Unfortunately, money, biased newsmen, political sycophancy, and modern demagoguery were all elements of power in government that made the new system distasteful. The reformers had been wrong in believing that "perfect" election machinery could be devised to solve the political puzzle. Like many who would do good, they failed to reckon with man's capacity to do wrong. They forgot the human predicament—imperfectability.

In order to create genuinely democratic government they granted home rule to cities, they required lobbyists to register, and they made candidates in statewide elections report their campaign expenditures. Because they supported efficiency, they compromised their commitment to popular government, replacing the old elective railroad commission with a new appointive public-utilities commission. They extended the vote to women, and then advocated electing fewer officials through short-ballot reform. They spoke enthusiastically about the initiative and the referendum, and then failed to act energetically for them.

While many favored the concept of greater human liberty, they improved the enforcement of the state's prohibition statutes and banned the sale of cigarettes for two years. Whether they were serious in this latter action is doubtful, but many were solemn advocates of Sabbatarian legislation. Only the popularity of baseball and other entertainment saved Kansas from stringent blue laws. The progressive Republicans contributed significantly to the betterment of public education; they reorganized the state eleemosynary system so as to help the helpless more effectively; and they aided workingmen with an employer's liability law and a workmen's compensation act.

Economic legislation was their greatest passion. They tried to restructure the tax laws more equitably with an inheritance tax and a state tax commission. The paucity of complaints about these measures can be used to argue about the justice and wisdom of them or to argue about their inadequacy. Among their railroad regulations, they considered the Maximum Freight Rate Law, the two-cent passenger-fare decision, and the Public Utilities Act the most important. In fact, like so much of their legislation, these acts were not nearly as significant as they believed them to be.

The progressives in Kansas and elsewhere were contributing more than they realized to a new day, one that would make their activities far less momentous than they assumed them to be. Kansas might establish a plan for guaranteeing bank deposits, and it might write a Blue Sky Investment Law, but the statutes that would be most influential and that would endure were not being written in Topeka. Much as was the case with populism before it, the ultimate effect of progressivism was to be felt on a reform movement that came after it. The New Deal laws establishing the Federal Deposit Insurance Corporation and Securities Exchange Commission were the banking and investment legislation that would last. Increasingly, progressives looked to the national government for solutions to their great passion—economics. Thus, there is a degree of irony and pathos in ending this study by suggesting that their greatest reform was unintentional. Without fully realizing it, these state politicians, these progressive Republicans, helped to create the modern national regulatory state.

# NOTES

The following abbreviations are used in the notes:

AHR   *American Historical Review*
BP    Joseph L. Bristow Papers, KSHS
HGP   Edward W. Hoch Gubernatorial Papers, KSHS
KHQ   *Kansas Historical Quarterly*
KSHS  Kansas State Historical Society
LP    Chester I. Long Papers, KSHS
MVHR  *Mississippi Valley Historical Review*
SGP   Walter R. Stubbs Gubernatorial Papers, KSHS
TDC   *Topeka Daily Capital*
TSJ   *Topeka State Journal*
WAW   William Allen White Manuscripts, Library of Congress

## Chapter 1

1. William Allen White, *The Autobiography of William Allen White* (New York, 1946), p. 297.

2. William Allen White, "Why I Am a Progressive," *Saturday Evening Post*, 23 April 1921, pp. 3–4.

3. Richard M. Abrams, *Conservatism in a Progressive Era: Massachusetts Politics, 1900–1912* (Cambridge, Mass., 1964), p. 20.

4. Homer E. Socolofsky, *Arthur Capper: Publisher, Politician, and Philanthropist* (Lawrence, Kans., 1962), p. 68, quoting Albert T. Reid in the Leavenworth *Post*.

5. George E. Mowry, *The California Progressives* (Berkeley, Calif., 1951).

6. Hoyt L. Warner, *Progressivism in Ohio, 1897–1917* (Columbus, Ohio, 1964).

7. In addition to Mowry and Warner, see Ransom E. Noble, Jr., *New Jersey Progressivism before Wilson* (Princeton, N.J., 1946), and William D. Miller, *Memphis during the Progressive Era, 1900–1917* (Memphis, Tenn., 1957). For a listing of other local studies see: Arthur S. Link and William M. Leary, Jr., eds., *The Progressive Era and the Great War, 1896–1920*, Goldentree Bibliographies in American History (New York, 1969), pp. 9–12.

8. Russell B. Nye, *Midwestern Progressive Politics: A Historical Study of Its Origins and Development, 1870–1950* (East Lansing, Mich., 1951), and Theodore Saloutos and John D. Hicks, *Agricultural Discontent in the Middle West, 1900–1939* (Madison, Wis., 1951).

9. Robert H. Wiebe, *The Search For Order, 1877–1920* (New York, 1967).

10. D. P. Thelen, "Progressivism as a Radical Movement," in *Main Problems in American History*, ed. Howard H. Quint, Milton Cantor, and Dean Albertson, 2 vols., 3d ed. (Homewood, Ill., 1972), 2:149–58.

11. William Agnew Johnston Collec-

tion, KSHS, "Speech before Grange," 1916.

12. Walter R. Stubbs, "Opening Address Delivered in University Hall, Sept. 8, 1905," *Graduate Magazine of the University of Kansas* 4 (October 1905):6.

13. G. Kolko, *The Triumph of Conservatism: A Reinterpretation of American History, 1900–1916* (New York, 1963).

14. Raymond H. Pulley, *Old Virginia Restored: An Interpretation of the Progressive Impulse, 1870–1930* (Charlottesville, Va., 1968).

15. O. Gene Clanton, *Kansas Populism: Ideas and Men* (Lawrence, Kans., 1969).

16. Richard Hofstadter, *Age of Reform* (New York, 1955).

17. This was the view made famous by John Hicks in *The Populist Revolt* (Minneapolis, Minn., 1931).

18. *Kansas City Journal*, 10 September 1910.

19. James C. Malin, *A Concern about Humanity* (Lawrence, Kans., 1964), p. 9.

20. Raymond C. Miller, "The Background of Populism in Kansas," *MVHR* 11 (March 1925):469–70.

21. *Thirteenth Census of the United States, 1910*, 11 vols. (Washington, D.C., 1913), 1:24, 27, 30; 5:78–79, 531, 539, 545; 8:445; 11:26, 83.

22. Edward W. Hoch, "Advancement and Prosperity of Kansas," *Earth* 3 (January 1906):3.

23. Charles M. Harger, "The Middle West and Wall Street," *American Monthly Review of Reviews*, July 1907, p. 84.

24. John K. Mumford, "This Land of Opportunity: How Kansas Has Enriched Her Farmers," *Harper's Weekly*, 26 September 1908, pp. 24–25, 30.

25. *TSJ*, 31 January 1905.

## Chapter 2

1. The best discussions of nineteenth-century factionalism can be derived from the following studies by Malin: *The Contriving Brain and the Skillful Hand in the United States* (Lawrence, Kans., 1955), *Confounded Rot about Napoleon* (Lawrence, Kans., 1961), and *A Concern about Humanity*. See also Marvin A. Harder, "Some Aspects of Republican and Democratic Party Factionalism in Kansas" (Ph.D. diss., Columbia University, 1959). For Bryan's influence in Kansas and other western states see: Paolo E. Coletta, *William Jennings Bryan*, 3 vols. (Lincoln, Nebr., 1964–1969), vol. 1, chaps. 11, 12, and 15. For Kansas politics see Clanton, *Kansas Populism*, chap. 12.

2. Patrick Henry Coney MSS., KSHS, A. W. Smith to Coney, 20 September 1899.

3. White, *Autobiography*, pp. 222–23.

4. Johnston Collection, "Outline of Remarks for Leland Dinner, June 15, 1901, by W. A. Johnston."

5. Cyrus Leland, "My Recollections," *Kansas City Star*, series in Sunday editions 26 January to 23 March 1913 (hereafter cited as "Leland Recollections").

6. Coney MSS., E. N. Morrill to J. G. Wood, 18 January 1900.

7. LP, W. P. Hackney to Long, 2 December 1907.

8. While there has never been a detailed study of Leland, numerous references to him appear in Kansas studies. The works that provided the foregoing information were: Malin, *A Concern about Humanity*, p. 49; Walter T. K. Nugent, *The Tolerant Populists: Kansas Populism and Nativism* (Chicago, 1963), pp. 180–82; John M. Blum, *The Republican Roosevelt* (Cambridge, Mass., 1954), p. 41; White, *Autobiography*, pp. 191–93, 273–74, 291–95, 303; Bliss Isely, "The Big Boss and the Boss Busters," *Kansas Teacher* 66 (February 1958):20–21; Raymond L. Flory, "The Political Career of Chester I. Long" (Ph.D. diss., University of Kansas, 1955), p. 57; "Leland Recollections."

9. Joseph Kennedy Hudson Scrapbook, KSHS, A. W. Horton to Hudson, 21 January 1899; Mulvane Scrapbook, KSHS, D. W. Mulvane Obituaries; Corabelle Tolin, "The Political Career of J. R. Burton" (Master's thesis, University of Kan-

sas, 1940), pp. 16–17; BP, J. M. Simpson to Bristow, 17 January 1900, J. R. Harrison to Bristow, 25 February 1900, A. A. Graham to Bristow, 21 October 1912; letter from A. W. Smith to Leland, reprinted in *TDC*, February 1900, in Republican Party Clippings, vol. 6, pt. 1, KSHS library; Coney MSS., Smith to Coney, 4 December 1899, R. W. Blue to Coney, 26 September 1899 and 8 April 1900, J. Seaton to Coney, 21 April 1900; "Leland Recollections."

10. Coney MSS., Smith to Coney, 20 September 1899, Smith to V. H. Grinstead, 26 October 1899.

11. Marvin Ewy, *Charles Curtis of Kansas: Vice-President of the United States, 1929–1933* (Emporia, Kans., 1961), pp. 21–22; Flory, "Long," passim. Curtis had the most devoted following in Kansas. Illustrative of his adherents was Thomas J. Faxon, the father of a minor Kansas political leader and journalist, Ralph Faxon. According to the elder Faxon, many had wavered when Curtis failed to answer the charges of Leland concerning the Horton Agreement, but when Curtis repudiated the bargain, he restored the faith of the faithful in him. LP, Faxon Correspondence, T. J. Faxon to R. Faxon, 18 January 1900.

12. BP, Leland to Bristow, 19 January 1900, F. L. Brown to Bristow, 16 and 30 January 1900, Harrison to Bristow, 28 and 30 January and 25 February 1900.

13. John S. Dawson MSS., KSHS, "Politicians of Yesteryear," a speech, ca. 1940.

14. Ibid.; Tolin, "Burton," pp. 7, 9, 11–16; William E. Connelley, ed., *A Standard History of Kansas and Kansans*, 5 vols. (Chicago and New York, 1918), 2:1334–35.

15. *TDC*, 13 and 16 May 1900.

16. The best source for Boss-Busters affairs is the Coney MSS., especially letters dated September 1899 to May 1900. See also *TDC*, 13–16 May 1900; *TSJ*, 16 May 1900; *Farmers Mail and Breeze* (Topeka), 19 May 1900, Republican Party Clippings, vol. 6, pt. 1, KSHS.

17. *TSJ*, 16 May 1900; *TDC*, 16 and 17 May 1900.

18. Coney MSS., Smith to Coney, 9 June 1900.

19. Coney MSS., Smith to Coney, 24 May 1900.

20. WAW, T. Roosevelt to White, 6 and 14 November 1901, White to Roosevelt, 18 November 1901, Leland to White, 16 November 1901, White to Leland, 15 and 25 November 1901.

21. Blum, *Republican Roosevelt*, p. 42.

22. WAW, Roosevelt to White, 27 August 1901.

23. LP, Long to White, 26 November 1901.

24. LP, Leland to Long, 6 January 1902, Long to M. Albaugh, 7 February 1902; Coney MSS., L. P. Burwell to Coney, 26 March 1902; *TDC*, 19 and 20 February, 23 March, and 15 April 1902.

25. C. S. Jobes was a Kansas City, Missouri, banker who was active in Kansas politics. Long, while a member of the House, had succeeded in having Jobes's bank designated as a depository for Oklahoma's territorial funds. He had also tried to secure postal deposits for Jobes's interests. LP, Long to Jobes, 16 December 1901.

26. LP, Long to Jobes, 7 February 1902, Long to Albaugh, 7 February 1902.

27. Alexander G. Cochrane is called "Judge Blub Blub" in White's autobiography. Of Cochrane's activities in 1902 White wrote: "I knew Judge Blub Blub. He was a man to whom the Long forces appealed when they took the Union Pacific from Curtis. Judge Blub Blub always came to our state conventions in a private car and participated in Republican and Democratic politics with equal keenness and perspicacity. He was Jay Gould's political fixer for the upper Mississippi Valley—the very type of man who represented . . . 'predatory wealth'" (White, *Autobiography*, pp. 353–54).

28. LP, Jobes to Long, 12 April 1902, Albaugh to Long, 4 April 1902, Long to Simpson, 4 April 1902.

29. LP, Albaugh to Long, 6 February

1902; *TDC*, 8 November 1901 and 3 April 1902.

30. *TDC*, 26–28 May 1902.

31. LP, Long to Simpson, 4 April 1902, Albaugh to Long, 6 February 1902, Jobes to Long, 12 April 1902; Coney MSS., Coney to Curtis, 10 February 1902.

32. *TDC*, 26–30 May 1902; *Wichita Eagle*, 28 and 29 May 1902.

33. *TDC*, 29 May 1902.

34. *TDC*, 29 and 30 May 1902.

35. LP, J. A. Burnette to Long, 29 May 1902, W. D. Greason to Long, 30 May 1902, T. J. Womack to Long, 30 May 1902.

36. LP, Long to Jobes, 13 June 1902, Jobes to Long, 20 June 1902.

37. Flory, "Long," passim.

38. LP, Jobes to Long, 12 and 30 April 1902, Long to Jobes, 16 April 1902, Long to Albaugh, 16 April 1902, Jobes to Cochrane, 30 April 1902.

39. LP, Cochrane to Long, 20 December 1902.

40. LP, Cochrane to Long, 20 and 22 December 1902.

41. Kolko, *Triumph of Conservatism*, pp. 70, 91; John A. Garraty, *Right-hand Man: The Life of George W. Perkins* (New York, 1960), pp. 188, 232. On 27 January, 1903, following his selection by the Kansas legislature, Long wrote Beer the following: "I thank you for the interest that you have taken in my candidacy and for the assistance that you have rendered me. I also want you to inform Mr. Perkins of my appreciation of what he did in this contest." Beer Family Collection, Yale University Library, Long to W. C. Beer, 27 January 1903.

42. Long was probably familiar with Perkins's use of a lobbyist in Topeka in 1897. See Garraty, *Perkins*, p. 181.

43. LP, Long to Jobes, 13 June 1902.

44. LP, Bristow to Long, 18 December 1902.

45. LP, Bristow to Long, undated telegram, ca. 16 September 1902. This telegram included code words that I could not decipher. The main part, however, is quoted above.

46. LP, Bristow to Long, 17 September 1902.

47. LP, W. S. Pierce to Long, 15 December 1902.

48. "Leland Recollections"; *TDC*, 2 May 1906.

49. Joseph R. Burton, *My Case and the Political Community of Interests* (Abilene, Kans., 1908), pp. 60–61.

50. William Allen White, "Free Kansas: Where the People Rule the People," *Outlook*, 24 February 1912, p. 408.

51. LP, A. A. Richards to Long, 3 April 1904, with newspaper clipping attached, Albaugh to Long, 12 February 1903, Long to Cochrane, 28 December 1903, Cochrane to Long, 12 January 1904, E. D. Kenna to Long, 12 February 1904; *Congressional Record*, 58th Cong., 2d sess., 1904, 38:2850; White, *Autobiography*, p. 354.

52. LP, W. Y. Morgan to Long, 29 November and 1 December 1902, Leland to Long, 3 December 1902; *Ottawa Evening Herald*, 13 January 1903.

53. LP, Bristow to Long, 12 January 1903; *TDC*, 22 January 1903; *Wichita Eagle*, 22 January 1903; *Topeka Daily Herald*, 30 January 1903; Harder, "Kansas Factionalism," pp. 60–70. According to Governor Alfred M. Landon, Henry J. Allen was able to buy the *Wichita Beacon* with the spoils he received from the office of state printer. Landon interview, 13 July 1958, as cited in Harder, "Kansas Factionalism," p. 70. In 1914 Allen had the following to say about the bargain: "I am probably somewhat atrophied in my vision on the . . . transaction. I never thought there was any moral wrong involved. It did not make any difference to the state whether the state printing plant was owned by one man or two men. I hated the thing at the time because I thought it was hard on Hoch, but after watching Hoch . . . I even quit being sorry about him." WAW, Allen to White, 5 February 1914.

54. LP, Long to Jobes, n.d., ca. Feb-

ruary 1902, Long to Jobes, 13 June 1902, Jobes to Long, 20 June 1902, Long to Bristow, 29 August 1902.

55. *TDC*, 21 and 23 January 1903.

56. LP, W. J. Bailey to Long, 9 February 1903, Johnston to Long, 9 February 1903, Long to Albaugh, 17 February 1903, Long to W. E. Stanley, 17 February 1903.

Chapter 3

1. *TDC*, 14 January 1904.
2. LP, Albaugh to Long, 18 January 1904.
3. *Kansas City Star*, 15 March 1903; *TDC*, 15 March 1903; William F. Zornow, *Kansas: A History of the Jayhawk State* (Norman, Okla., 1957), p. 210; John D. Bright, ed., *Kansas: The First Century*, 4 vols. (New York, 1956), 2: 22–23.
4. *TDC*, 15 March 1903.
5. Ibid.; *Kansas City Star*, 15 March 1903.
6. LP, Albaugh to Long, 13 March 1903.
7. *Kansas City Journal*, 15 November 1903; *TDC*, 16 November 1903.
8. *TDC*, 14 July 1903.
9. *Ottawa Evening Herald*, 28 April 1903; *Emporia Gazette*, 11 May 1903. On 7 March 1904, White wrote in the *Emporia Gazette*: "The crusaders in the New Movement in Kansas, will end the same way [as the Populists]. . . . To expect much from the Hoch movement . . . will be to cherish a false hope. To expect a new era, is absurd."
10. LP, Bailey to Long, 18 January 1904.
11. Nelson I. Case MSS., Kansas Methodist Historical Society, Baker University, Baldwin, Kans., Manuscript Book 4, p. 52; Michael J. Brodhead, "The Early Career of E. W. Hoch, 1870–1904" (Master's thesis, University of Kansas, 1962), pp. 77–78.
12. *TSJ*, 16 and 26 November 1903; LP, Long to J. Pollock, 4 December 1903; "Leland Recollections"; WAW, White to Roosevelt, 31 October 1903.
13. LP, Richards to Long, 23 January 1904.
14. *TDC*, 24 January 1904.
15. Brodhead, "Hoch," pp. 21–22; *The National Cyclopaedia of American Biography*, 1st suppl., s.v. "E. W. Hoch"; Bright, *Kansas*, 2:22–25; Connelley, *Kansas*, 2:853, 857.
16. Edward W. Hoch, "The Success of Prohibition in Kansas," *Annals of the American Academy of Political and Social Science* 32 (November 1908):104–5; James H. Timberlake, *Prohibition and the Progressive Movement, 1900–1920* (Cambridge, Mass., 1963), pp. 1–3.
17. *Dictionary of American Biography*, 1st suppl., s.v. "Walter Roscoe Stubbs"; Connelley, *Kansas*, 4:2380; Samuel G. Blythe, "A Red-headed Quaker: Being an Account of Some of the Activities of Walter Roscoe Stubbs," *Saturday Evening Post*, 19 November 1910, p. 3.
18. *Kansas City Star*, 15 March 1903; *TSJ*, 7 March 1903; *TDC*, 11 March 1903.
19. *Dictionary of American Biography*, "Stubbs"; "The Revolt against the Machine in Kansas," *Outlook*, 9 April 1904, pp. 858–59; Robert Clark, Jr., "Breaking Up a State Machine," *Cosmopolitan*, October 1904, p. 670; WAW, "W. R. Stubbs' Notes," Box 292.
20. Historical Collection, Republican Party, KSHS, G. P. Morehouse to G. W. Martin, 5 February 1904. At the 1903 session, in action that was unrelated to the political maneuvering, Morehouse was responsible for having the sunflower adopted as the Kansas state flower.
21. LP, Albaugh to Long, 8 January and 6 February 1904, Jobes to Long, 5 and 6 February 1904; Burton, *My Case*, pp. 258–59; Bright, *Kansas*, 2:23; Brodhead, "Hoch," pp. 95–97; *El Dorado Republican*, 28 September 1903; *TDC*, 6 January 1904.
22. LP, Morgan to Long, 26 January 1904; Biographies Compiled by the Library, KSHS library, s.v. "W. Y. Morgan."
23. LP, Richards to Long, 26 January

Notes to Pages 29–38

1904; Clark, "Breaking Up a State Machine," pp. 665–70.

24. LP, Albaugh to Long, 26 January 1904.

25. *Wichita Eagle*, 31 January 1904.

26. LP, Albaugh to Long, 26 February 1904.

27. "A Senator Convicted," *Outlook*, 9 April 1904, p. 858; *United States* v. *Burton*, 131 F.R. 552 (D.C., Mo., 1904).

28. WAW, White to J. Folk, 16 April 1904, Folk to White, 26 April 1904.

29. LP, Albaugh to Long, 1 April 1904, Richards to Long, 3 April 1904, Long to Albaugh, 6 April 1904; WAW, White to Bristow, 1 April 1904; *Emporia Gazette*, 31 March 1904; Tolin, "Burton," pp. 42, 55–58.

30. David Graham Phillips, "The Treason of the Senate," *Cosmopolitan*, March 1906, pp. 487–89; LP, Faxon to Long, 26 January 1904; Tolin, "Burton," p. 95.

31. *Burton* v. *United States*, 196 U.S. 283 (1905); *Burton* v. *United States*, 202 U.S. 344 (1906); Tolin, "Burton," pp. 93, 98.

32. LP, B. P. Waggener to Long, 9 February 1904, S. R. Peters to Long, 8 February 1904.

33. LP, Morgan to Long, 31 January 1904, D. R. Anthony to Long, 16 February 1904.

34. LP, Morgan to Long, 31 January 1904, Albaugh to Long, 26 January and 6 February 1904, Richards to Long, 18 March 1904, Jobes to Long, 24 March 1904.

35. There are no letterpress books in the Long collection for this period. His incoming mail indicates that his position was the one discussed above. LP, Peters to Long, 8 February 1904, Morgan to Long, 6 February 1904, Albaugh to Long, 6 February 1904.

36. *TDC*, 9 and 10 March, 1904; LP, Morgan to Long, 13 March 1904, Jobes to Long, 17 March 1904.

37. *TDC*, 9 and 10 March 1904. The *Topeka Daily Capital* claimed that J. C. Morse, who was nominated as a candidate for the railroad commission, represented a concession to the federation. This was inaccurate, since Morse was an associate of railroad officers and one of their nominees. See LP, Long to Jobes, 13 March 1901, Long to Morse, 13 March 1901, Low to Long, 25 March 1901.

38. *TDC*, 9 and 10 March 1904.

39. LP, Richards to Long, 18 March 1904, Albaugh to Long, 19 March 1904, Jobes to Long, 24 March 1904.

40. *Senate Journal, State of Kansas*, 1905, pp. 10–13.

41. *Addresses Delivered at the Fourteenth Annual Banquet of the Kansas Day Club, 1905* (Clay Center, Kans., 1905), p. 71.

42. LP, Morgan to Long, 16 February 1905, Albaugh to Long, 19 February 1905. For an extensive discussion see: Francis W. Schruben, "The Kansas State Refinery Law of 1905," *KHQ* 34 (Autumn 1968):299–324.

43. *Kansas City Star*, 8 March 1905.

44. "Speech by E. W. Hoch, Marion, Kans., Sept. 1, 1904," Republican Campaign Literature, 1904, KSHS library.

45. *Addresses Kansas Day Club, 1905*, p. 71.

46. Allan Nevins, *John D. Rockefeller: The Heroic Age of American Enterprise*, 2 vols. (New York, 1940), 2:582.

47. Edward W. Hoch, "Kansas and the Standard Oil Company," *Independent*, 2 March 1905, p. 461.

48. Ralph W. and Muriel E. Hidy, *Pioneering in Big Business, 1882–1911*, vol. 1 of *History of Standard Oil Company* (New York, 1955), pp. 395–97.

49. John Ise, *The United States Oil Policy* (New Haven, Conn., 1926), pp. 242–43; Hidy, *Pioneering*, pp. 395–99.

50. HGP, W. T. Higgins to Hoch, 2 February 1905.

51. Ise, *Oil Policy*, p. 242; Charles S. Gleed Papers, KSHS, Gleed to B. P. Cheney, 29 December 1906, Gleed to H. H. Rogers, 29 December 1906 and 10 February 1907; HGP, C. D. Webster to Hoch, 7 February 1905; Charles M. Harger, "Kansas' Battle for Its Oil In-

terests," *American Monthly Review of Reviews*, April 1905, p. 473; Isaac F. Marcosson, "The Kansas Oil Fight," *World's Work*, May 1905, p. 6160. An investigation by the Bureau of Corporations in 1906 concluded that railroad companies had not treated independent oil refineries and Standard equally. See Bureau of Corporations, Department of Commerce and Labor, *Transportation and Freight Rates in Connection with the Oil Industry*, 59th Cong., 1st sess., 1906, Senate Documents, no. 428, serial set 4915, pp. 42–45.

52. Connelley, *Kansas*, 2:1005–6.

53. *TSJ*, 7 February and 15 March 1905; *Kansas City Star*, 2 February 1905.

54. William L. Connelly, *The Oil Business As I Saw It* (Norman, Okla., 1954), p. 22; Marcosson, "Kansas Oil Fight," p. 6161; *TSJ*, 3 February 1905; *Senate Journal, State of Kansas*, 1905, pp. 159, 226.

55. Hoch, "Kansas and Standard Oil," pp. 461–63; *Senate Journal, State of Kansas*, 1905, p. 368; George W. Ogden, "How Kansas Was 'Rolled,'" *Appleton's Book Lovers Magazine*, September 1905, p. 339; *TSJ*, 26 January and 7 February 1905.

56. *State, ex rel., Coleman v. Kelly*, 81 P.R. 450 (Kan. S.C., 1905); *Fifteenth Biennial Report of the Attorney-General of Kansas, 1905–'06* (Topeka, 1906), pp. 7–8; Connelly, *Oil Business*, p. 23; Ise, *Oil Policy*, p. 244; Ogden, "Kansas Rolled," p. 338.

57. Hidy, *Pioneering*, pp. 675–718; Nevins, *Rockefeller*, 2:503; Bureau of Corporations, *Transportation*, passim.

58. *TDC*, 21 February 1890, as cited by Karl A. Svenson in "The Effect of Popular Discontent on Political Parties in Kansas" (Ph.D. diss., State University of Iowa, 1948), pp. 54–55; HGP, Hoch to E. W. Evans, 2 January 1907.

59. Harger, "Kansas' Battle," p. 474.

Chapter 4

1. WAW, H. W. Young to White, 25 December 1909.

2. Coletta, *Bryan*, vol. 1, chaps. 11, 12, and 15.

3. *Fifty Years of the Star*, pamphlet dated 18 September 1930, KSHS library, pp. 4–6.

4. A Kansas Progressive Republican, "How I Was Converted—Politically," *Outlook*, 17 December 1910, pp. 857–59. The general causes of dissidence given here are the same as those presented by Charles M. Harger in 1911, except that he did not stress railroads sufficiently. Harger, "Lessons in Nation-Building: Kansas Progressive, but Prudent," *World To-Day*, October 1911, pp. 1206–9. Although some historians have recently questioned the validity of the fight for the Hepburn bill, Kansans in 1905 viewed it as the major issue of the time. The I.C.C. had steadily declined as a regulatory agency during the 1890s, and Kansans wanted to resuscitate it. Theoretically, the act of 1906 allowed the commission to enforce "reasonable rates," but as Robert La Follette expected, railroads began to secure injunctions against I.C.C. rulings, occasioning long, drawn-out litigation. La Follette's experience with rate-making in Wisconsin made him a logical spokesman for the Middle West on this issue. See *La Follette's Autobiography: A Personal Narrative of Political Experience* (Madison, Wis., 1913), chaps. 7–9.

5. Walter S. Lyerla, "The History and Development of Public Utility Regulation in Kansas" (Ph.D. diss., State University of Iowa, 1936), pp. 11–12, 18, 33, 40–42; Zornow, *Kansas*, pp. 143–45.

6. Edwin O. Stene, *Railroad Commission to Corporation Commission: A Study in Kansas Administrative History* (Lawrence, Kans., 1945), pp. 38–42; Lyerla, "Public Utility Regulation," pp. 33–39.

7. Lyerla, "Public Utility Regulation," pp. 33–39. William Z. Ripley, commenting on the widespread efforts by states to regulate railroads, wrote in 1912: "No less than fifteen new or remodeled commissions were created in the two years

1905–1907, bringing the total number to thirty-nine" (*Railroads: Rates and Regulations* [New York, 1912], p. 603).

8. Legislative Documents, Miscellaneous File 5, KSHS library, "A Bill for the Control of Railroads, Suggested and Authorized by the Kansas Federation of Commercial Interests, Jan. 29, 1904"; LP, C. L. Davidson to Long, 30 January 1905; *Kansas City Journal,* 9 March 1905.

9. *TSJ,* 18 January and 31 August 1906; *TDC,* 5 January and 29 July 1906; *Kansas City Journal,* 4 January 1907.

10. *TDC,* 4–9 January 1907.

11. Legislature, 1905, 1906, 1907, History Files, KSHS, "Legislative Demands of 17th Annual Meeting of Kansas Improved Stock Breeders' Association, Jan. 7–9, 1907"; Legislative Documents, Miscellaneous File 6, U.C.T.A., Kansas Division to ——, n.d., ca. 1906; J. N. Forbes, *The Railroad Situation, 1908,* pamphlet in Arthur Capper Papers, KSHS; *TDC,* 18 July and 1 October 1903; *TSJ,* 30 October 1907.

12. SGP, E. P. Ripley to Stubbs, 25 October 1910.

13. SGP, J. S. George to Stubbs, 3 January and 25 May 1909; J. S. George, "As a Wholesale Point," in *History of the City of Hutchinson and Reno County, Kansas* (n.p., ca. 1895), KSHS library.

14. SGP, George to Stubbs, 17 December 1910.

15. Republican Campaign Literature, 1906, KSHS library, Bristow to J. A. Troutman, 31 July 1906, *Square Deal Handbook* (ca. August 1906). For three contemporary discussions of freight rates see O. P. Byers, "Kansas Jobber Rates," *Kansas Magazine* 2 (December 1909): 34–36, "Kansas Intrastate Freight Rates," *Kansas Magazine* 3 (January 1910):16–18, and "Kansas Interstate Freight Rates," *Kansas Magazine* 3 (February 1910): 31–32.

16. Charles M. Harger, "A New Business Alliance," *North American Review,* September 1897, pp. 380–83; John L. Powell, "The Freight Rate Problem," *Kansas Magazine* 2 (July 1909):14–17.

17. LP, E. B. Cowgill to Long, 8 March 1907.

18. SGP, George to Stubbs, 17 November 1910; LP, H. L. Resing to C. E. Potts, 2 January 1903, Davidson to Long, 30 January 1905; BP, Bristow to C. W. Bleuhe, 16 May 1910; HGP, copy of an article by Hoch appearing in *The Railway Age,* 27 December 1907; "Gives Both Sides," Railway Clippings 2, KSHS library.

19. LP, Resing to Long, 4 January 1907.

20. SGP, W. S. Cochrane to Stubbs, 18 October 1912.

21. WAW, White to G. Nicholson, 5 April 1906, White to T. J. Norton, 27 January 1908.

22. "Some Taps," *Kansas Knocker* 2 (July 1900): unnumbered page, KSHS library.

23. Case MSS., 4:224.

24. LP, Jobes to A. G. Cochrane, 30 April 1902; *Topeka Daily Herald,* 31 January 1903; "Leland Recollections."

25. WAW, White to Stubbs, 9 November 1904.

26. Charles N. Glaab, *Kansas City and the Railroads: Community Policy in the Growth of a Regional Metropolis* (Madison, Wis., 1962), p. 216. Glaab notes that by the 1890s "Santa Fe railroad interest bought up the *Journal*'s mortgage and began to dictate its policies." In 1909 Gleed wrote the following to the publisher of the *Lyons Republican:* "I notice you have adopted the Kansas City Star's favorite lies about the railroad ownership of the Kansas City Journal. Since my connection with it no person, partnership, or corporation has ever had a penny in the Journal except my partner and myself." Gleed Papers, Gleed to C. Conkling, 24 February 1909.

27. Gleed Papers, Gleed to E. Zumwalt, 8, 14, and 26 June 1910, Zumwalt to Gleed, 21 June 1910.

28. BP, Bristow to Capper, 4 January 1910, Capper to Bristow, 7 January 1910.

29. Capper Papers, E. E. Critchfield to Capper, 11 January 1907; Gleed Pa-

pers, Gleed to G. T. N., 3 March 1910, Capper to E. L. Jones, 18 April 1914, [Jones] to Capper, 4 April 1914 and 23 August 1916.

30. Gleed Papers, Ripley to Gleed, 4 December 1912.

31. *TSJ,* 18 January 1907; *TDC,* 2 May 1906.

32. Gleed Papers, Gleed to E. L. Copeland, 20 May 1911, Gleed to B. F. McLean, 23 May 1911.

33. LP, Faxon to Long, 2 July 1905.

34. WAW, Waggener to White, 13 February [1910]; Gleed Papers, Gleed to J. R. Koontz, 23 June 1911, Koontz to Gleed, 5 July 1911; "The 'Harmony' Campaign," *Santa Fe Employes' Magazine* 4 (November 1910):73–75; *TDC,* 25 May 1911.

35. Thomas B. Lillard MSS., KSHS, N. H. Loomis to G. Lathrop, F. C. Dillard, M. L. Clardy, and J. M. Bryson, 1 October 1912.

36. Lillard MSS., J. O. Brinkerhoff to C. Ware, 14 November 1912, P. Walker to W. T. Tyler and E. Stenger, 13 November 1912, W. R. Smith to R. W. Blair, 15 December 1912, M. Frey to J. McMahon, 23 January 1913, Loomis to Blair, 28 January, 6 February, and 10 April 1913, Blair to N. K. Candee, 21 February 1913, Blair to Loomis, 25 January and 12 April 1913; Legislature, 1909, 1910, 1911, History Files, L. E. Goodrich, J. A. Duree, R. V. Snider, and J. A. Bostic to Members of the Legislature, 25 February 1913, Loomis to Blair, 28 February 1913.

37. Lillard MSS., Blair to Loomis, 13 and 14 March 1913; *TDC,* 27 January 1913.

## Chapter 5

1. Kansas reformers lacked the insights into the motivation for railroad reform, which Gabriel Kolko discusses in his provocative *Railroads and Regulation, 1877–1916* (Princeton, N.J., 1965), chaps. 6–8. For Kansas opinion on the Hepburn Act see the next chapter of this study.

2. *TSJ,* 6 January 1906.

3. *TSJ,* 10 January 1906; *Kansas City Journal,* 11 and 12 January 1906; *Kansas City Star,* 11 January 1906.

4. *TDC,* 11 January 1906.

5. **Ibid.**

6. *Emporia Gazette,* 11 January 1906.

7. *TSJ,* 12 January 1906.

8. *Kansas City Journal,* 10–12 January 1906.

9. *TSJ,* 10 January 1906.

10. LP, Morgan to Long, 4 December 1905 and 24 November 1906.

11. Although this realignment is abundantly clear in the correspondence of Long and other political leaders, the state's leading political analyst, Jay House, discussed it extensively in the *Topeka Daily Capital,* 2 May 1906.

12. LP, Albaugh to Long, 10 January 1906, C. E. Denton to Long, 15 January 1906, W. J. Fitzgerald to Long, 9 and 28 February 1906.

13. LP, Bristow to Long, 10 May 1905; *Emporia Gazette,* 30 March 1905; *Kansas City Star,* 4 February 1905; *Kansas City Journal,* 7 February 1905; *TDC,* 23 April and 24 September 1905; Schruben, "Refinery Law," pp. 311–12.

14. *TDC,* 24 September 1905 and 12 March 1922.

15. Case MSS., 4:53; WAW, White to Hoch, 6 May 1906; HGP, State Dept. Files, 1905–1908, Governor, Special Investigation of the Treasury.

16. *TDC,* 1–3 May 1906; *TSJ,* 28 May 1906. U.S. Marshal J. R. Harrison referred to the allegation years later as if the affair were commonly accepted as true. BP, Harrison to Bristow, 8 March 1913. At the time, Mort Albaugh dismissed it as a "most outrageous trick." LP, Albaugh to Long, 5 May 1906.

17. WAW, White to Stubbs, 6 January 1914; William Allen White, "Political Signs of Promise," *Outlook,* 15 July 1905, pp. 667–70; *Emporia Gazette,* 7 March, 15 April, 9 November, and 20 December 1904 and 13 January and 11 November 1905; Bright, *Kansas,* 2:27; Ewy, *Curtis,* pp. 26–27; LP, T. B. Murdock to Long, 1

February 1904, Peters to Long, 10 December 1906, Waggener to Long, 21 November 1906, Hackney to Long, 2 December 1907; *Kansas City Journal,* 3 May 1906; "Leland Recollections."

18. LP, Bristow to Morgan, 1 February 1906, Morgan to Long, 2 February 1906, Long to Denton, 12 March 1906, Denton to Long, 8 March 1906, Albaugh to Long, 17 March 1906, Long to Mulvane, 23 April 1906, J. Schilling to Long, 29 December 1905. There are also a number of letters in the Long Papers from Bristow to Long, further documenting this view, that were sent either in late 1905 or early 1906, but they are undated.

19. LP, Albaugh to Long, 17 January 1906, Morgan to Long, 2 February 1906, Fitzgerald to Long, 13 April 1906; WAW, White to Roosevelt, 16 August 1906; *Kansas City Journal,* 3 May 1906; *TDC,* 2 May 1906.

20. LP, Fitzgerald to Long, 9 and 28 February 1906, George to [Kansas Newspapers], 15 January 1906; *Kansas City Journal,* 3 May 1906.

21. Bristow seemed to be convinced that any hope of working with Long's faction in the future was futile. He, therefore, supported Stubbs, but later tried to secure Long's support for his senatorial candidacy. Leland's reasons for helping Stubbs are unclear. Later he was working with the Albaugh group at the convention.

22. *TDC,* 3 May 1906; *Kansas City Journal,* 3 May 1906; LP, Albaugh to Long, 5 May 1906, Faxon to Long, 11 May 1906.

23. *TDC,* 3 May and 24 October 1906; *Kansas City Journal,* 3 May 1906; Zornow, *Kansas,* p. 212.

24. *Kansas City Journal,* 3 May 1906.
25. *Topeka Daily Herald,* 3 May 1906.
26. *TSJ,* 14, 18, and 19 July 1906.
27. *TSJ,* 19, 23, and 27 July 1906.
28. *TSJ,* 19 July 1906.
29. Republican Campaign Literature, 1906, *Square Deal Handbook; TSJ,* 6, 14, and 19 July 1906; *TDC,* 24 October 1906.

30. Republican Campaign Literature, 1906, "Statement made by George A. Root, 5 October 1934, concerning the Square Deal Hand Book of 1906"; *Kansas City Journal,* 5 August and 29 October 1906.

31. *TSJ,* 14 July 1906.

32. *Kansas City Journal,* 5 August 1906; *Topeka Daily Herald,* 6 August 1906; *Wichita Eagle,* 16 February 1906; *TDC,* 10 October 1906.

33. WAW, White to La Follette, 6 July 1906; Harder, "Factionalism," p. 80; *TSJ,* 18 July 1906; *TDC,* 27 September 1906.

34. *Fifteenth Biennial Report of the Secretary of State of Kansas, 1905–'06,* pp. 157–74, 177–79.

35. WAW, White to W. A. Harris, 22 November 1906; HGP, H. L. Anderson to Hoch, 11 July 1906. Hoch contributed to his poor showing by stating at the 1906 state convention that Kansas "was in more danger . . . from the demagogues than from the railroads" (HGP, Hoch to F. L. Vandegrift, 28 August 1907).

36. *Wichita Eagle,* 7 and 8 November 1906; *TDC,* 8 and 9 November 1906; *Emporia Gazette,* 16 November 1906; *Kansas City Journal,* 7 and 9 November 1906.

37. *TDC,* 12 March 1922; LP, Long to Albaugh, 11 June 1906.

38. LP, Long to L. M. Axline, 22 December 1906, Long to T. F. Noftzger, 22 December 1906.

39. WAW, White to Bailey, 6 December 1906; LP, Long to Gesner, 11 December 1906, Long to E. H. Madison, 22 December 1906, Morgan to Long, 24 November 1906.

40. LP, Albaugh to Long, 13 January 1907; *Kansas City Journal,* 8 January 1907; *TDC,* 5, 8, and 11 January 1907; *TSJ,* 6, 7, and 11 January 1907.

41. *TSJ,* 11 January 1907; LP, Albaugh to Long, 13 January 1907, F. D. Smith to Long, 13 January 1907.

42. *TSJ,* 17 January 1903.

43. *Read Curtis' Record in Congress,* pamphlet, Kansas Biographical Pamphlets

9, KSHS library; White, *Autobiography*, p. 366. In 1907 White expressed his attitude toward Curtis as follows: "I have no personal malice against Mr. Curtis. I don't think that he would steal, I don't think he would lie . . . and I don't believe that he would *knowingly* violate a trust. Yet, I do believe that he is dominated by the wrong influence in public life." WAW, White to Judge Slonecker, n.d., ca. January 1907. Curtis received the type of railroad support that had been given Long in 1903. See Beer Family Collection, Curtis to Beer, 3 September 1906.

44. Gleed Papers, Gleed to H. Blythe, 27 March 1907. According to the *Emporia Gazette* (16 February 1907), since most senators had not signed the handbook, the Kansas Senate was the stronghold of corporate influence.

45. *Senate Journal, State of Kansas*, 1907, pp. 26–52.

46. HGP, "Special Message by Gov. E. W. Hoch to Senate and House of Representatives, Feb. 25, 1907," "Address by Gov. Hoch to the House of Representatives, 9 March 1907."

47. Case MSS., 4:224.

48. "Some Taps," *Kansas Knocker* 2 (July 1900): unnumbered page, KSHS library.

49. *TDC*, 2 and 6 March 1907 and 1 January 1908; *TSJ*, 24 January 1907; *Wichita Eagle*, 7 March 1907.

50. *Nineteenth Annual Meeting of the Bar Association of the State of Kansas, Topeka, Jan. 30–31* (Clay Center, Kans., 1902), p. 89; Harley L. Lutz, *The State Tax Commission: A Study of the Development and Results of State Control over the Assessment of Property for Taxation* (Cambridge, Mass., 1918), pp. 425–26, 429–32.

51. *First Report of the Tax Commission, State of Kansas, for the Period between July 1, 1907, and October 15, 1908* (Topeka, Kans., 1908), p. 6.

52. *Sixteenth Biennial Report of the Attorney-General of Kansas, 1907–'08* (Topeka, 1908), pp. 19–21, 24, 26, 40; J. K. Codding and E. W. Hoch, "Prohibition in Kansas," *Annals of the American Academy of Political and Social Sciences* 32 (November 1908):97–103.

53. HGP, Hoch to the Board of Railroad Commissioners, 22 August 1907, J. S. Silvey to Hoch, 23 August 1907, J. G. Maxwell to Hoch, 23 August 1907, G. Hanna to Hoch, 23 August 1907, T. Sawyer to Hoch, 23 August 1907, C. W. Coffin to Hoch, 24 August 1907, E. A. MacFarland to Hoch, 12 September 1907, W. J. Conner to Hoch, n.d., ca. September 1907, Hoch to Conner, 17 September 1907, G. F. Grattan to Hoch, 20 September 1907, W. S. Thompson to H. Hoch, 17 August 1907, R. Lake to H. Hoch, 17 August 1907; Legislative Documents, Miscellaneous File 5, "Resolution by the United Commercial Travelers of America, Kansas and Oklahoma Council"; *Emporia Gazette*, 16 February and 23 August 1907; *TDC*, 4 March, 27 July, and 23 August 1907; *Wichita Eagle*, 13 and 15 March 1907; *Wichita Beacon*, 25 February 1907.

54. *TSJ*, 4, 11, and 25 September and 4 and 5 October 1907; *TDC*, 11, 12, 17, and 24 September and 4 and 5 October 1907; *Eighteenth Biennial Report of the Attorney General of Kansas, 1911–12* (Topeka, 1912), pp. 5–6; *Nineteenth Biennial Report of the Attorney General of Kansas, 1913–1914* (Topeka, 1914), p. 5.

55. LP, Albaugh to Long, 18 March 1907; Long to Curtis, 1 April 1907; *TSJ*, 12 and 24 April 1907; *TDC*, 24 March and 24 and 25 April 1907.

CHAPTER 6

1. WAW, White to H. Chase, 7 February 1908.

2. WAW, White to Bristow, 16 April 1907, White to My Dear Henry, 29 April 1907, White to S. Ingalls, 22 May 1907, White to Stubbs, 31 May 1907, White to Long, 3 February 1908; *Emporia Gazette*, 27 and 29 January 1908.

3. William B. Shaw, "The Direct Pri-

mary on Trial," *Outlook*, 24 October 1908, p. 384.

4. LP, Noftzger to Long, 13 March 1905, Long to Albaugh, 21 April 1906, Long to Morgan, 21 April 1906, Long to Mulvane, 23 April 1906, Albaugh to Long, 5, 6, and 14 March 1907, Morgan to Long, 10 March 1907, Long to Morgan, 14 March 1907. In 1904 a city and county primary could be held if party leaders desired. This primary was not regulated by state law and was relatively insignificant. See: HGP, White to Hoch, 19 December 1907.

5. LP, Long to H. J. Bone, 17 January 1907.

6. Gleed Papers, Gleed to A. E. Riling, 4 February and 24 March 1909.

7. Hodges MSS., Hackney, *The Primary Election Law*, pamphlet dated 8 March 1910.

8. SGP, J. N. Dolley to A. Ludington, 6 February 1909.

9. SGP, Stubbs to Ludington, 23 February 1909, Stubbs to C. E. Hughes, 15 February 1909; BP, Bristow to J. E. Benton, 5 December 1908; White, *Autobiography*, pp. 394–95.

10. HGP, Hoch to White, 20 December 1907; *TSJ*, 18 and 20 October 1907.

11. *TSJ*, 28 December 1907.

12. LP, Albaugh to Long, 9 November 1907, Long to Albaugh, 1 and 11 November 1907, Long to J. Mulvane, 1 November 1907, Long to Noftzger, 7 November 1907. John G. Blocker, *The Guaranty of State Bank Deposits*, Kansas Studies in Business, no. 11 (Lawrence, Kans., 1929), pp. 8–10. For the Kansas law see the next chapter of this study.

13. HGP, M. C. Polley to Hoch, 4 January 1908. For examples, see HGP, F. M. Johnson to Hoch, 27 December 1907, T. Cox et al. to Hoch, 27 December 1907, F. C. Wood to Hoch, 2 and 21 January 1908, Businessmen of Scammon, Kans., to Hoch, 2 January 1908.

14. *TDC*, 31 January and 3 and 4 February 1908.

15. BP, Bristow to Stubbs, 19 January 1908, Bristow to Allen, 11 January 1908; *Emporia Gazette*, 3 and 21 February 1908.

16. LP, Long to Albaugh, 11 January 1908.

17. LP, Long to Albaugh, 10 January 1908.

18. LP, Long to Albaugh, 10 January 1908; *TDC*, 31 January and 1 and 4 February 1908; Charles E. Merriam and Louise Overacker, *Primary Elections* (Chicago, 1928), chap. 5.

19. HGP, Hoch to Benton, 3 December 1908; *Seventeenth Biennial Report of the Attorney General of Kansas, 1909–1910* (Topeka, 1910), pp. 58–59, 65.

20. LP, Albaugh to Long, 31 January and 7 February 1908, Bristow to Long, 3 February 1908, Jobes to Long, 18 February 1908, Long to Bone, 18 February 1908; White, *Autobiography*, p. 394.

21. LP, Fitzgerald to Long, 13 April, 1906, Long to Bone, 18 February 1908.

22. BP, Bristow to Long, 1 February 1906.

23. LP, Denton to Long, 8 March 1906.

24. Walt Mason, "Senator Bristow, of Kansas," *American Magazine*, October 1909, p. 557. For a sympathetic study of Bristow see A. Bower Sageser, *Joseph L. Bristow: Kansas Progressive* (Lawrence, Kans., 1968).

25. BP, Biography File, "Joseph L. Bristow," Bristow to Stanley, 1 October 1908; Joseph L. Bristow, *Fraud and Politics at the Turn of the Century: McKinley and His Administration As Seen by His Principal Patronage Dispenser and Investigator*, ed. Joseph Q. and Frank B. Bristow (New York, 1952), pp. 29–30; Flory, "Long," pp. 122–24.

26. Sageser, *Bristow*, pp. 38–41.

27. Theodore Roosevelt, *The Letters of Theodore Roosevelt*, ed. Elting E. Morison, 8 vols. (Cambridge, Mass., 1951–1954), 3:444–45, Roosevelt to J. H. Woodward, 10 March 1903; ibid., 3:472–73 and 543, Roosevelt to H. C. Payne, 27 April and 6 August 1903 (hereafter cited as *Roosevelt Letters*).

28. *Roosevelt Letters*, 4:1266–67, Roosevelt to E. A. Hitchcock, 8 July

1905. See also ibid., 4:741–42, Roosevelt to Payne, 27 February 1904, and 4:1301–2, Roosevelt to Hitchcock, 14 August 1905.

29. Eugene Fitch Ware Papers, KSHS, E. F. Ware to My Dear Nettie, 31 July 1904. See also White, *Autobiography*, p. 405; C. G. Dawes, *A Journal of the McKinley Years* (Chicago, 1950), pp. 405–6; Clarence H. Matson, "Joseph L. Bristow: The Argus of the Post-Office Department," *American Monthly Review of Reviews*, January 1904, pp. 45–48.

30. LP, Roosevelt to Long, 18 May 1905.

31. BP, Biography File, "Joseph L. Bristow"; Frank C. Lockwood, "Senator Bristow, of Kansas," *Outlook*, 21 November 1908, pp. 617–21.

32. LP, J. E. Howard to Long, 10 November 1905, Maxwell to Long, 4 November 1905, E. D. Strafford to Long, 15 November 1905, W. D. Atkinson to Long, 1 December 1905, G. W. Hackney to Long, 1 December 1905, I. F. Collins to Long, 4 December 1905, T. M. Deal to Long, 20 December 1905; Gleed Papers, Gleed to M. A. Low, 13 November 1905, Gleed to J. H. Elward, 20 November 1905; *TDC*, 15 November 1905.

33. LP, Hackney to Long, 28 November 1905.

34. LP, Low to Long, 3 November 1905, Loomis to Long, 3 November 1905; *TDC*, 10 and 19 November 1905.

35. LP, Schilling to Long, 29 December 1905, E. G. Jacobs to Long, 22 December 1905, Bristow to Long, 23 December 1905, Madison to Long, 24 December 1905, Long to Roosevelt, 3 February 1906; Kolko, *Railroads*, pp. 128–29; Nathaniel W. Stephenson, *Nelson W. Aldrich: A Leader in American Politics* (New York, 1930), pp. 274–75; George E. Mowry, *The Era of Theodore Roosevelt and the Birth of Modern America, 1900–1912* (New York, 1958), pp. 203–4; Flory, "Long," pp. 143–44; *TDC*, 15 November 1905.

36. LP, Long to Albaugh, 9 April 1906.

37. *Roosevelt Letters*, 5:3803–4, Roosevelt to Long, 31 January 1906.

38. LP, Richards to Long, 9 January 1907; Flory, "Long," pp. 144–46; Anna M. Edwards, "The Congressional Career of Victor Murdock, 1903–1909" (Master's thesis, University of Kansas, 1947), pp. 24–25, 48.

39. LP, Albaugh to Long, 18 March 1907, Fitzgerald to Long, 13 April 1906, Long to Howard, 17 and 28 July 1906, Howard to Long, 20 July 1906, G. W. Smith to Long, 20 July 1906; *TDC*, 24 February 1907.

40. LP, Long to Curtis, 1 April 1907. In 1906 Roosevelt, convinced that he should pick his successor, wrote: "I am sure Kansas will like [Taft]. . . . He would be an ideal President. He is the kind of broad-gauged American that Kansas ought to like. . . . I think he and Kansas speak the same language—the American language—the language which perhaps is spoken best in some districts of the West." This endorsement assured Taft of Kansas support in 1908. WAW, Roosevelt to White, 11 August 1906.

41. *Roosevelt Letters*, 5:735–37, Roosevelt to White, 30 July 1907; ibid., 6:936–37, Roosevelt to A. P. Gardner, 10 February 1908; *TSJ*, 28 December 1907.

42. LP, Hackney to Long, 14 November 1907, Bone to Long, 15 February 1908, Faxon to Long, 12 May 1908; WAW, Bristow to White, 22 February 1908; White, *Autobiography*, p. 395.

43. LP, Bone to Long, 15 February 1908, Long to C. Q. Chandler, 20 April 1908, Long to P. G. Walton, 20 April 1908, Long to Jobes, 21 April 1908, Faxon to Long, 12 May 1908, F. E. Grimes to Long, 16 May 1908, Low to Long, 16 May 1908, Long to Grimes, 30 May 1908, Norton to Long, 13 July 1908, Long to Bone, 7 September 1908, Long to W. J. Buchan, 7 September 1908, Long to Loomis, 7 September 1908, Long to Pollock, 7 September 1908.

44. LP, Grimes to Long, 6 and 13

May 1908, Albaugh to Long, 10 and 13 May 1908, Faxon to Long, 12 May 1908.
45. LP, Morgan to Long, 5 May 1908, Low to Long, 16 May 1908; Gleed Papers, Gleed to Long, 29 April 1908.
46. White, *Autobiography*, pp. 395–96.
47. LP, Faxon to Long, 21 May 1908, Albaugh to Long, 22 May 1908.
48. Gleed Papers, Gleed to Long, 19 May 1908.
49. LP, Long to Albaugh, 23 and 28 May 1908.
50. WAW, White to Long, 19 December 1901 and 14 April 1903.
51. *Emporia Gazette*, 25 May 1907.
52. WAW, White to Chase, 7 February 1908; *Emporia Gazette*, 27 January 1908.
53. WAW, White to O. G. Villard, 14 April 1908, White to Morrill, 13, 25, and 26 May 1908; White, *Autobiography*, pp. 396–97; William H. Mitchell, "Joseph L. Bristow: Kansas Insurgent in the U.S. Senate, 1909–1915" (Master's thesis, University of Kansas, 1952), p. 51.
54. WAW, White to W. F. Allen, 13 July 1908; *Emporia Gazette*, 10 and 11 June 1908; Flory, "Long," pp. 174–77.
55. WAW, White to Bristow, 9 May 1908, Bristow to White, 10 and 26 May 1908.
56. LP, Long to Axline, 6 October 1910, Long to W. W. Smith, 14 February 1911; Democratic Campaign Literature, 1860–1928, KSHS library, Facsimile Letter, Bristow to Long; *TSJ*, 3 August 1908.
57. LP, Long to Grimes, 14 May 1908; WAW, White to V. Murdock, 29 June 1908, White to A. B. Kimball, 30 June 1908, White to Bristow, 13 July 1908; Kansas Collected Speeches and Pamphlets, vol. 22, pt. 1, KSHS library, "Speech of J. L. Bristow, Wichita, July 10, 1908."
58. LP, Long to My Dear Friend, 20 April 1908; Republican Campaign Literature, 1908, "Senator Long's Platform."
59. LP, Long to Grimes, 14 May 1908.
60. WAW, White to Roosevelt, 5 August 1908; LP, Blair to Long, 9 December 1914, Long to Blair, 21 December 1914; White, *Autobiography*, p. 397; *TSJ*, 3 August 1908.
61. J. M. Oakison, "Long of Kansas: The Third in a Series of Studies of Senate Undesirables, Showing Why 'Joe' Bristow Should Be Sent to the Senate to Replace Chester I. Long," *Colliers*, 11 July 1908, pp. 8–9; Walter Johnson, *William Allen White's America* (New York, 1947), p. 167; WAW, White to Bristow, 18 May 1908.
62. Republican Campaign Literature, 1908, "The Line-up of Long: For Delegate and Dollar vs. People and Popular Government."
63. "The Careers of Long and Bristow: A Review of Their Work As Seen by James A. Troutman," Collected Biography Clippings 2, KSHS library, p. 163.
64. WAW, Bristow to White, 10 May 1908, White to Bristow, 4, 9, and 14 May 1908, White to Dolley, 29 May 1908, White to D. A. Valentine, 23 June 1908, White to Allen, 27 June 1908; LP, Albaugh to Long, 13 May 1908; Kansas Collected Speeches, vol. 22, pt. 1, "Speech of J. L. Bristow, Wichita, July 10, 1908."
65. BP, Bristow to R. P. Bass, 4 June 1910, Bristow to C. C. Garland, 20 August 1908, Bristow to Dolley, 20 August 1908; LP, Albaugh to Long, 13 May 1908; Mitchell, "Bristow," pp. 25–26.
66. Republican Campaign Literature, 1908, "Comments on the Candidacy of J. L. Bristow for the United States Senate"; Kansas Collected Speeches, vol. 22, pt. 1, "Speech of J. L. Bristow, Wichita, July 10, 1908"; BP, Bristow to E. R. Daniels, 20 July 1908, Bristow to W. H. Taft, 15 August 1908.
67. BP, Bristow to Harrison, 8 August 1908.
68. BP, Bristow to Long, 20 June 1908, Bristow to Dolley, 23 July 1908; WAW, White to Bristow, 14 May and 13 July 1908; *TSJ*, 3 August 1908; *Emporia Gazette*, 3 and 4 August 1908.
69. BP, Bristow to P. P. Campbell, 19 August 1908; Kansas Election Returns,

1908, Office of the Secretary of State, Records, microfilm reel no. 11, KSHS.

70. *TDC*, 23 July 1908.

71. Capper Papers, Stubbs to Capper, 18 May 1908; WAW, White to Leland, ca. August 1908; *TSJ*, 22 July and 4 August 1908; Kansas Election Returns, microfilm reel no. 11.

72. BP, Bristow to P. H. Cahill, 14 August 1908, Bristow to B. Lindsey, 11 August 1908; *TDC*, 5 August 1908; *Wichita Beacon*, 5 August 1908; *Emporia Gazette*, 5 August 1908; *Wichita Eagle*, 23 October 1908.

73. LP, Long to Madison, 11 August 1908, Long to Albaugh, 11 August 1908, Long to A. D. Crotts, 12 September 1908.

74. BP, Bristow to R. A. Elward, 27 August 1908.

75. *TDC*, 25 and 26 August 1908; WAW, White to Bristow, 10 August 1908.

76. BP, Bristow to Jobes, 7 August 1908, Bristow to C. F. Scott, 11 August 1908, Bristow to S. S. Reynolds, 11 August 1908, Bristow to G. W. Marble, 11 August 1908, Bristow to Dolley, 21 and 27 August 1908, Bristow to Elward, 27 August 1908, Bristow to J. G. Cannon, 2 October 1908; WAW, White to Allen, 11 August 1908; LP, Long to Richards, 29 August 1908; *TSJ*, 22 and 25 August 1908; *TDC*, 25 and 26 August 1908.

77. *TDC*, 2–5 November 1908; *Sixteenth Biennial Report of the Secretary of State of Kansas, 1907–'08* (Topeka, 1908), pp. 78–93, 108–10, 114–24.

CHAPTER 7

1. WAW, White to Hanna, 18 November 1913.

2. BP, White to Bristow, 23 February 1911.

3. WAW, White to Capper, 25 July 1908; *TDC*, 9 and 13 January 1909.

4. SGP, Stubbs to T. F. Gregg, 23 June 1909.

5. SGP, Stubbs to E. Akers, 18 September 1909; WAW, Valentine to White, 20 November 1909, E. S. McCormick to White, 25 January 1910; *TSJ*, 6 October 1909.

6. SGP, White to Stubbs, 21 December 1908, Murdock to Stubbs, 22 January 1909; White, *Autobiography*, pp. 431–32.

7. WAW, White to Bristow, 18 December 1908, J. M. Nation to White, 2 February 1910.

8. SGP, J. K. Codding to W. L. Dexter, 30 August 1905.

9. A special file on the enforcement of liquor laws in Cherokee and Crawford counties is located in the Stubbs Gubernatorial Papers. For letters illustrative of the above, see Stubbs to G. Steussi, 12 January 1910, Stubbs to E. Merriweather, 7 January 1910, Stubbs to S. H. Smith, 1 February 1910, W. L. Scott to Stubbs, 18 January 1910, Stubbs to S. S. Oylear, 1 March 1910, D. D. Leahy to A. Burril, 3 June 1911, Stubbs to C. S. Huffman, 28 June 1911; WAW, Dolley to White, 7 September 1911; Kansas Prohibition Pamphlets, vol. 3, KSHS library, *What Prohibition Has Done for Kansas* by J. Dawson; *Eighteenth Biennial Report of the Attorney-General of Kansas, 1911–1912* (Topeka, 1912), pp. 4–5. In their elementary-school textbook on Kansas history, two ardent prohibitionists of the 1930s cite several temperance-union tracts that support the above (Bliss Isely and W. M. Richards, *Four Centuries in Kansas* [Wichita, Kans., 1936], pp. 301–2).

10. SGP, V. R. to Stubbs, 12 January 1910; Walter R. Stubbs, "'Mob Rule' in Kansas," *Saturday Evening Post*, 11 May 1912, p. 54.

11. SGP, M. Wood-Simons to Stubbs, 3 November 1911, Stubbs to Dawson, 4 November 1911, Dawson to W. P. Montgomery, 6 November 1911, E. Haworth to Stubbs, 29 January and 9 March 1912.

12. SGP, J. R. Crowe to Stubbs, 6 May 1910, C. S. Keith to Stubbs, 14 May 1910, Stubbs to Keith, 15 May 1910.

13. SGP, Stubbs to Keith, 15 May 1910, E. L. Blomberg to Stubbs, 19 May 1910.

14. *TDC*, 2, 7, and 24 February 1911;

Domenico Gagliardo, "Development of Common and Employers' Liability Law in Kansas," *KHQ* 10 (May 1941):165–66.

15. Legislature, 1909, 1911, 1913, Joint Legislative Committee, State Society of Labor, State Federation of Labor and Brotherhood of Railway Trainmen to Members of the Legislature, 2 March 1911; S. A. Bramlette, W. A. Morse, and J. Ramey to Members of the Senate, 7 March 1911; *TDC*, 13–15 March 1911; Domenico Gagliardo, "The First Kansas Workmen's Compensation Law," *KHQ* 9 (November 1940):384–90, 394.

16. *TDC*, 8 November 1909; W. L. Hamilton, "The Stag at Eve," *Shawnee County Historical Society Bulletin*, no. 40 (December 1963), pp. 49–52.

17. SGP, Stubbs to G. Gould, 19 November 1909, Gould to Stubbs, 22 November 1909, Stubbs to F. S. Adams, 29 November 1909, D. E. Ballard to Stubbs, 26 November 1909, Stubbs to E. M. Clift, 8 December 1909, C. S. Clarke to Stubbs, 9 December 1909, McFarland to Stubbs, 9 December 1909, Citizens of Barnard, Kansas, to Stubbs, 14 December 1909, L. A. Palmer to Mayor of City, 18 December 1909, Bristow to Stubbs, 23 December 1909, H. R. Wayne to Stubbs, 28 December 1909, Citizens on Salina-Oakley Branch of U.P. to Stubbs, 28 December 1909; C. F. Griffin to Stubbs, 29 December 1909; Gleed Papers, Gleed to H. U. Mudge, 11 March 1910.

18. SGP, White to Stubbs, 16 January 1912, E. Peterson to Stubbs, 16 January and 3 February 1912, Stubbs to Peterson, 13 February 1912, T. B. Armstrong to Stubbs, 15 and 16 February 1912, "Report of Armstrong," ca. March 1912; WAW, White to Stubbs, 25 and 27 November and 15 December 1911, 5 January 1912.

19. Kansas Governors' Miscellaneous Pamphlets, KSHS library, *Railroad Freight Rates*, ca. 1910.

20. Ibid.; *TDC*, 22 and 23 September 1910; SGP, W. D. Williams to Stubbs, 21 March 1911, Secretary-to-the-Governor to Williams, 13 April 1911.

21. SGP, A. C. Jobes to Stubbs, 21 October 1910, Blomberg to Stubbs, 29 October 1910; "Open Letter to Governor Stubbs, A. J. Ewing to Stubbs," *Santa Fe Employes' Magazine* 4 (November, 1910):59–60; "Kansas, President Ripley, Governor Stubbs and Hobo Employees," *Santa Fe Employes' Magazine* 4 (November 1910):65–72; *Kansas City Journal*, 22–24 September and 1–4, 11–13, and 28–29 October 1910.

22. SGP, Ripley to Stubbs, 1 and 25 October and 13 December 1910, Stubbs to Ripley, 10 October and 3 and 20 December 1910.

23. SGP, Ripley to Stubbs, 25 October and 27 and 29 December 1910, C. W. Kouns to Stubbs, 24 and 28 December 1910, Stubbs to Ripley, 24, 28, and 30 December 1910, Stubbs to Kouns, 26 December 1910.

24. SGP, Stubbs to T. Blodgett, 20 February 1909, Stubbs to W. M. Gray, 23 February 1909, G. W. Kanavel to ———, ca. February 1909; BP, Bristow to Allen, 20 February 1909; *Kansas City Star*, 16 and 17 February 1909; *TSJ*, 16 and 24 February 1909.

25. *TSJ*, 25 February 1909.

26. SGP, C. M. Sheldon to Stubbs, 25 February 1909.

27. SGP, B. F. McMillan to Stubbs, 25 February 1909; BP, Bristow to Allen, 12 and 22 March 1910; *Kansas City Journal*, 15 March 1909; *TSJ*, 15 March 1909.

28. SGP, Stubbs to W. M. Gray, 23 February 1909, Legislative Committee of Kansas Gas, Water, Electric Light and Street Railway Association to Berryman, 20 February 1909, Gray to Stubbs, 4 February 1909, Jobes to Stubbs, 25 January 1909, Ripley to Stubbs, 15 May 1909; BP, Allen to Bristow, 16 March 1909; Legislature, 1909, 1911, History Files, J. D. Joseph to W. W. Caldwell, 26 January 1911.

29. SGP, J. W. Gleed to Dear Sir, 5 February 1909.

30. BP, Allen to Bristow, 16 March 1909; *TSJ*, 15 March 1909.
31. *TSJ*, 16, 19, and 24 February and 1 March 1909.
32. *Senate Journal, State of Kansas*, 1909, pp. 5–13.
33. *TDC*, 14 March 1909.
34. *Session Laws, State of Kansas, 1909*, pp. 96–103.
35. HGP, J. B. Adams to Hoch, 21 December 1906.
36. LP, Berryman to Hoch, 30 December 1907.
37. SGP, C. C. K. Scoville to The State or Private Bank Addressed, 2 May 1910, W. MacFerran to Stubbs, 29 September 1909, F. L. Travis to Stubbs, 10 July 1909; Wayne D. Angell, "A Century of Commercial Banking in Kansas, 1856 to 1956" (Ph.D. diss., University of Kansas, 1957), pp. 366–67; *Official Opinions of the Attorneys-General of the United States*, vol. 27 (Washington, D.C., 1909), p. 37.
38. SGP, Berryman to The Bank Addressed, 5 February 1909; LP, Long to Chandler, 5 September 1908, Long to Taft, 5 September 1908; George W. Hodges MSS., KSHS, C. M. Sawyer to Hodges, 7 February 1909, Hodges to Sawyer, 8 February 1909.
39. *Official Opinions of the Attorneys-General*, 27:272–73, 278; SGP, "The Federal Bank Guarantee Company," copy of proposed charter, ca. March 1909; *Kansas City Star*, 27 June 1909.
40. *TDC*, 14–16 July and 11–13 December 1909; SGP, Stubbs to ——, 10 July 1909, and sundry replies; *Bankers' Deposit Guaranty and Surety Co. v. Barnes*, 105 P.R. 697 (Kan. S.C., 1909).
41. LP, Long to Chandler, 19 March and 16 August 1909, Chandler to Long, 21 July 1909, Long to F. R. Zacharia, 23 September 1909.
42. *Larabee v. Dolley, Assaria State Bank v. Same, Abilene Nat. Bank v. Same*, 175 F.R. 365 (C.C. Kan., 1 D., 1909); *Dolley v. Abilene Nat. Bank*, 179 F.R. 461 (8 Cir. 1910); *Abilene Nat. Bank v. Dolley*, 218 U.S. 673 (1910); *Assaria State Bank v. Dolley*, 219 U.S. 121 (1911); *Abilene Nat. Bank v. Dolley*, 228 U.S. 1 (1913).
43. SGP, Scoville to The State or Private Bank Addressed, 2 May 1910.
44. *TDC*, 14 March 1909.
45. LP, Albaugh to Long, 5 March 1909.
46. See above, pp. 180–81.
47. *Senate Journal, State of Kansas*, 1911, pp. 5–11.
48. *Kansas City Star*, 8 February 1911.
49. *TDC*, 4 March 1909; *Kansas City Journal*, 26 November 1910; LP, Faxon to Long, 22 November 1910; BP, Chase to Bristow, 5 January 1911, Leland to Bristow, 21 January 1911.
50. *TDC*, 12 January 1911; BP, Bristow to White, 30 December 1910.
51. BP, Bristow to Stubbs, 2 January 1911.
52. *TDC*, 12 January 1911; *TSJ*, 12 January 1911.
53. *TSJ*, 10 and 12 January 1911; *TDC*, 10–12 January 1911; WAW, Capper to White, 12 January 1911, R. Stone to White, 12 January 1911.
54. *TDC*, 24 January 1911; *TSJ*, 26 January and 2 March 1911.
55. *TSJ*, 17 February 1911; *TDC*, 17 February 1911.
56. *Wichita Eagle*, 12 February 1911.
57. SGP, Leahy to R. Hopkins, 18 February 1911; *TSJ*, 15 and 17 February 1911; *Kansas City Star*, 17 and 19 February 1911.
58. *Kansas City Star*, 23 February 1911.
59. Legislative Documents, File 7, State Temperance Union to Members of the Legislature, ca. 1911; SGP, H. G. James to Stubbs, 29 December 1910, Secretary-to-the-Governor to A. E. Bell, 6 April 1911; BP, Valentine to Bristow, 23 February 1911; *TDC*, 20 February 1911.
60. *TSJ*, 17 February 1911.
61. Lyerla, "Public Utility Regulation," pp. 52–76; Stene, *Railroad to Corporation Commission*, pp. 42–43; *TDC*, 3, 12, and 15 February and 5, 10, 15,

and 16 March 1911; WAW, White to Nelson, 15 February 1911; SGP, Joseph to Stubbs, 10 March 1911.

62. *TDC,* 14 March 1909.

63. *TDC,* 14 March 1909; *TSJ,* 10 March 1911; *Summary of Kansas Primary Laws* (Topeka, Kans., 1913), pp. 8–9; Stubbs, "Mob Rule," pp. 7, 54; Dana Gatlin, " 'What I Am Trying to Do': An Interview with Hon. W. R. Stubbs," *World's Work,* May 1912, p. 62.

64. SGP, Private Secretary to C. Harvey, 4 November 1910, Stubbs to H. Dick, 11 December 1911.

65. Isaac F. Marcosson, "Barring Out the Stock Thieves," *Munsey's Magazine,* February 1912, pp. 677–80; Will Payne, "How Kansas Drove Out a Set of Thieves," *Saturday Evening Post,* 2 December 1911, pp. 3–5, 71–72.

### Chapter 8

1. *TDC,* 20 August 1907 and 18, 19, and 24 June 1908; *Emporia Gazette,* 4 March 1908; *Wichita Beacon,* 4 March 1908; *Wichita Eagle,* 19 June 1908.

2. BP, Bristow to Harrison, 4 February 1909.

3. Mowry, *Era of Roosevelt,* p. 237.

4. BP, Bristow to Taft, 9 December 1908, Bristow to F. Trigg, 20 March 1909. The term "insurgent" was used by regular Republicans, by the press, and by many to whom it was applied to describe Republicans who opposed party leadership, including President Taft, during 1909 and 1910. A good many "insurgents" were later referred to as "progressive Republicans," and some became members of the Progressive party in 1912.

5. Case MSS., 4:229.

6. Ibid., 4:221.

7. Ibid., 4:221–23, 228–30.

8. WAW, Anthony to White, 18 April 1908; *TDC,* 5 April 1908 and 8 November 1909; Victor Murdock, "A Congressman's First Speech," *American Magazine,* August 1908, pp. 406–11; Murdock, "A Congressman's First Bill," *American Magazine,* October 1908, pp. 545–50; Blair Bolles, *Tyrant from Illinois: Uncle Joe Cannon's Experiment with Personal Power* (New York, 1951), p. 149; William R. Gwinn, *Uncle Joe Cannon: Archfoe of Insurgency* (New York, 1957), p. 148; Edwards, "Murdock," pp. 73–74; Jack B. Pringle, "The Congressional Career of Edmond H. Madison, 1907–1911" (Master's thesis, University of Kansas, 1955), p. 19.

9. Gwinn, *Cannon,* pp. 6–7, 97, 118, 131, 169; Joseph G. Cannon, *Uncle Joe Cannon: The Story of a Pioneer American, As Told to L. White Busbey* (New York, 1927), p. 244.

10. LP, Cannon to Long, 14 November 1902, Albaugh to Long, 4 and 14 February, 2 March, and 3 June 1903, 28 March 1906, M. M. Murdock to Long, 4 and 14 February 1903, V. Murdock to Long, 8 June 1903, Madison to Long, 29 March 1906.

11. WAW, Roosevelt to White, 6 March 1907; Victor Murdock, "The False Divisor," *Kansas Magazine* 1 (January 1909):9–12; Hastings MacAdam, "The Insurgents: The Story of the Leaders Who Fought and Won against the Machine Control of Congress," *Everybody's Magazine,* June 1912, p. 773; Gwinn, *Cannon,* p. 143; Edwards, "Murdock," pp. 31–37.

12. Murdock, "Congressman's First Speech," p. 407; Edwards, "Murdock," p. 17.

13. The best discussions of Cannon and his opposition may be found in the biographies by Gwinn and Bolles and in Richard Lowitt, *George W. Norris: The Making of a Progressive, 1861–1912* (Syracuse, N.Y., 1963).

14. Kenneth W. Hechler, *Insurgency: Personalities and Politics of the Taft Era* (New York, 1940), p. 47.

15. LP, Long to Morgan, 19 March 1909; *TDC,* 10–12 March 1909; *Congressional Record,* 61st Cong., 1st sess., 1909, 44:18, 20–22, 33–34.

16. BP, Bristow to F. B. Bristow, 18 March 1909, Bristow to Chase, 14 March 1909; SGP, Murdock to Stubbs, 22 January 1909.

17. WAW, White to Mrs. V. Murdock, 25 March 1909; F. Dumont Smith, "The Real Victor Murdock," *Kansas Magazine* 4 (November 1910):33–36; Lillian Tuttle, "The Congressional Career of Victor Murdock, 1909–1911" (Master's thesis, University of Kansas, 1948), p. 61.

18. Mowry, *Era of Roosevelt*, pp. 240–41; Hechler, *Insurgency*, p. 48; Pringle, "Madison," p. 23; Tuttle, "Murdock," p. 61; *Wichita Eagle*, 10 March 1909; WAW, White to Elward, 19 January 1910.

19. A Washington Journalist, "Men We Are Watching: Victor Murdock, Member of Congress," *Independent*, 3 March 1910, pp. 474–75; Smith, "Real Murdock," pp. 33–36; Victor Murdock, "Cannon and Cannonism," *Kansas Magazine* 2 (November 1909):14–17; "Murdock: 'The Red Insurgent,'" *Current Literature*, February 1910, pp. 149–50; WAW, Murdock to White, 9 December 1909; *Wichita Eagle*, 12 January 1910.

20. Cannon, *Cannon*, p. 252.

21. Lowitt, *Norris*, pp. 171–77; Cannon, *Cannon*, pp. 268–69; *Wichita Eagle*, 16–19 March 1910; Victor Murdock, "The Insurgent Movement in Congress," *North American Review*, April 1910, pp. 510–16; Murdock, "After Cannonism—What?" *Independent*, 22 September 1910, pp. 622–25; Lenis Boswell, "The Political Career of Victor Murdock, 1911–1917" (Master's thesis, University of Kansas, 1949), pp. 19–20; *Congressional Record*, 61st Cong., 2d sess., 1910, 45:3436–39.

22. *Congressional Record*, 61st Cong., 2d sess., 1910, 45:3408–10, 6542.

23. WAW, Scott to White, 21 January 1912.

24. Capper Papers, Anthony to Capper, 14 May 1909; WAW, White to Scott, 11 March 1910; *TDC*, 16 January 1910; *Emporia Gazette*, 10 March 1909; Gwinn, *Cannon*, p. 168; Mowry, *Era of Roosevelt*, p. 242.

25. WAW, Murdock to White, 27 December 1909; BP, Bristow to Chase, 14 March 1909, Bristow to Elward, 17 December 1909; Capper Papers, Madison to Capper, 3 July 1911.

26. The Madison quote is from *Congressional Record*, 61st Cong., 2d sess., 1910, 45:1347.

27. BP, "Eulogy on Edmond H. Madison," ca. 1911; Pringle, "Madison," pp. 2–4, 6–8, 19, 57; Connelley, *Kansas*, 3:1240; *Iola Register*, 10 October 1910; Willis C. Sorensen, "The Kansas National Forest, 1905–1915," *KHQ* 35 (Winter 1969):386–95.

28. Elmo R. Richardson, *The Politics of Conservation: Crusades and Controversies, 1897–1913* (Berkeley, Calif., 1962), pp. 67–69.

29. Henry F. Pringle, *The Life and Times of William Howard Taft: A Biography*, 2 vols. (New York, 1939), 1:470–514. Ballinger, as well as Pinchot, sought exoneration by the congressional inquiry.

30. *Congressional Record*, 61st Cong., 2d sess., 1910, 45:404, 406, 467, 683, 749, 841.

31. Ibid., 360–70, 383–406, 466–67; BP, Bristow to Chase, 11 April 1910.

32. *Investigation of the Department of the Interior and the Bureau of Forestry*, 13 vols., 61st Cong., 3d sess., 1910–1911, *Senate Documents*, no. 719, serial set 5892–5903, 1:192.

33. BP, Bristow to P. Lovewell, 27 December 1909, Bristow to E. M. Randall, 2 January 1910, Bristow to F. S. Jackson, 11 January 1910, Bristow to F. Hageman, 15 January 1910, Bristow to C. Wesley, 21 March 1910, Bristow to J. Bourne, 2 October 1911; WAW, White to Elward, 19 January 1910, Madison to Capper, 18 July 1910; Richardson, *Politics of Conservation*, pp. 67–69; Mowry, *Era of Roosevelt*, pp. 253–56; *TDC*, 10 and 11 September 1910; *Emporia Gazette*, 11 September 1910; *Wichita Eagle*, 10 and 11 September 1910.

34. Legislative Documents, file no. 6, KSHS library, "Address of Joseph L. Bristow, before the Joint Session of the Kansas Legislature upon Being Notified of His Election as United States Senator"; WAW, Taft to White, 2 March 1909.

35. BP, Bristow to Chase, 14 and 26 March 1909, Bristow to F. Bristow, 18 March 1909, Bristow to Stubbs, 24 March 1909, Bristow to M. M. Beck, 3 April 1909, Bristow to J. H. Stavely, 31 May 1909, Bristow to Trigg, 21 June 1909.
36. Cannon, *Cannon*, p. 211; Stephenson, *Aldrich*, pp. 142, 334, 347.
37. LP, W. A. Calderhead to Long, 27 January 1909.
38. SGP, Madison to Stubbs, 8 June 1909; Edwards, "Murdock," p. 57.
39. Mowry, *Era of Roosevelt*, p. 243.
40. BP, Bristow to Beck, 23 March and 3 April 1909, Bristow to G. Guernsey, 14 April 1909, Bristow to A. Mitchell, 13 May 1909, Bristow to F. A. Gillespie, 22 May and 3 and 14 June 1909, Bristow to Chase, 23 May 1909, Bristow to A. Miller, 1 June 1909, Bristow to Trigg, 21 June 1909; Mowry, *Era of Roosevelt*, p. 245.
41. *Congressional Record*, 61st Cong., 1st sess., 1909, 44:146, 527.
42. Ibid., p. 592. Although Bristow championed moderate revision during the debate on the wool schedule, he tried to explain his general tariff views by saying: "Being a Republican, believing in the principles of protection, and believing that the duty should cover the difference between the cost of production here and abroad, I cannot vote for these amendments." The amendments would have put woolens on the free list. Ibid., p. 3132.
43. Ibid., p. 404.
44. BP, Bristow to Leland, 7 June 1909, Bristow to White, 9 June 1909; *Congressional Record*, 61st Cong., 1st sess., 1909, 44:1087.
45. BP, Bristow to Hull, 15 May 1909, Bristow to Chase, 22 May 1909.
46. BP, Bristow to Bryant, 2 July 1909, Bristow to Trigg, 21 June 1909. On the question of submitting the Income Tax Amendment to the states, only Calderhead of the Kansas delegation voted no. *Congressional Record*, 61st Cong., 1st sess., 1909, 44:4120, 4440.
47. BP, Bristow to Trigg, 2 July 1909, Bristow to Chase, 19 June 1909, Bristow to Allen, 3 July 1909; *Congressional Record*, 61st Cong., 1st sess., 1909, 44:4066 and app., p. 140.
48. BP, Bristow to Harris, 9 August 1909, Bristow to Chase, 23 May 1909; *Congressional Record*, 61st Cong., 1st sess., 1909, 44:4754–55, 4949.
49. Mowry, *Era of Roosevelt*, p. 246.
50. WAW, Nelson to White, 17 August 1909; BP, Nelson to Bristow, 26 August 1909, Bristow to Nelson, 30 August 1909; William Howard Taft Papers, Library of Congress, Taft to Long, 12 December 1909; "Who's Who—And Why: Serious and Frivolous Facts about the Great and the Near Great, the Baron of Kansas City," *Saturday Evening Post*, 26 November 1910, p. 21.
51. BP, Bristow to A. J. Beveridge, 28 August 1909; *TDC*, 16 January 1910; Mitchell, "Bristow," p. 83.
52. BP, Bristow to Chase, 7 April and 22 May 1909, Bristow to Hull, 22 June 1909, Bristow to F. Lockard, 4 September 1909; Capper Papers, Anthony to Capper, 14 May 1909, Curtis to Capper, 17 May 1909, Capper to Curtis, 13 May 1909; *TDC*, 11 August, 8 and 31 October 1909; Pringle, "Madison," p. 75; Morgan R. Ewing, "Charles F. Scott: His Decade in Congress" (Master's thesis, University of Kansas, 1951), p. 56. In May 1910, from the floor of the House, Reeder said, in response to a widely publicized interview in which Bristow blamed the tariff for high prices, the following: "The junior Senator from Kansas [Bristow], through the press, deplored the high prices of beef and other farm products. Of course he did this to further arouse an adverse sentiment toward Republicanism and did not credit the farmer with having brains enough to detect that this was an attack on the farmers' market" (*Congressional Record*, 61st Cong., 2d sess., 1910, 45:6540).
53. BP, Bristow to A. Cummins, 7 September 1909; Mowry, *Era of Roosevelt*, p. 249.
54. BP, Bristow to Cummins, 20 Sep-

tember 1909, Bristow to C. W. Fairbanks, 20 September 1909, Bristow to F. P. Flint, 20 September 1909, Bristow to La Follette, 20 September 1909, Bristow to Allen, 20 September 1909; *TDC*, 20 and 21 September 1909; *Kansas City Star*, 20 September 1909; *Iola Register*, 21 and 23 September 1909; *Kansas City Journal*, 20 September 1909.

55. BP, Bristow to My dear Senator, 27 September 1909, Bristow to Beveridge, 4 October 1909, Bristow to Cummins, 4 October 1909, Bristow to O. K. Davis, 20 October 1909; Taft Papers, Taft to Long, 27 September 1909; Sageser, *Bristow*, pp. 98–99; White to W. R. Nelson, 23 September 1909.

56. WAW, Bristow to White, 24 August 1909; BP, Bristow to M. Clapp, 7 September 1909, Bristow to Cummins, 7 September 1909, Bristow to Jackson, 15 December 1909, Bristow to Lovewell, 20 December 1909, Bristow to White, 24 December 1909.

57. BP, Bristow to Allen, 16 December 1909, Bristow to E. Munday, 8 February 1910, Bristow to F. W. Clark, 14 February 1910, Bristow to H. J. Hoover, 7 March 1910, Bristow to Jackson, 12 March 1910, Bristow to White, 22 June 1910; *Congressional Record*, 61st Cong., 2d sess., 1910, 45:2780, 7670, 7768, 8741.

58. Numerous letters concerning parcels post are in Bristow's correspondence for the period 1909–1912. The following are representative: BP, Bristow to C. E. Rummell, 18 December 1909, Bristow to R. J. Morrison, 2 March 1909, Bristow to J. B. Pitts, 17 January 1912; *Congressional Record*, 62d Cong., 2d sess., 1912, 48:4678, 11677, 11761, 11819.

59. *Congressional Record*, 61st Cong., 2d sess., 1910, 45:2332, 2350–53; Pringle, *Taft*, 2:566–67.

60. BP, Bristow to Allen, 23 February 1911, Allen to Bristow, 26 February 1911, Bristow to Capper, 13 February 1911 and 26 March 1912, Bristow to My dear Mr. Graham, 16 February 1911; Taft Papers, Taft to W. M. Crane, 3 August 1912; *Congressional Record*, 61st Cong., 2d sess., 1910, 45:2355.

61. BP, Bristow to Jackson, 12 March 1910.

62. WAW, Bristow to White, 5 January 1910, Bristow to Trigg, 5 January 1910.

63. BP, Bristow to Chase, 12 February 1910.

64. *Congressional Record*, 61st Cong., 2d sess., 1910, 45:4507–8, 4659, 5567, 6213, 6342, 6346, 6462, 6914–15, 6920–21, 6923, 6972, 6975, 7135, 7196, 7199, 7203, 7218, 7257–58, 7264, 7266, 7271, 7341, 7347, 7351, 7355, 7365, 7369.

65. BP, Bristow to Allen, 25 June 1910.

66. *Congressional Record*, 61st Cong., 2d sess., 1910, 45:5736, 6032, 7375, 7577, 8391, 8485.

67. Taft Papers, Taft to H. Taft, 5 March 1910; BP, Bristow to F. Quincy, 27 May 1910.

68. *Congressional Record*, 61st Cong., 2d sess., 1910, vol. 45, app., p. 124; BP, Bristow to Allen, 16 December 1909, Bristow to Chase, 11 April 1910, Bristow to George, 1 April 1910, Bristow to Hoover, 7 March 1910; Hechler, *Insurgency*, pp. 163–66.

69. SGP, Murdock to Stubbs, 22 January 1909; BP, Bristow to F. Bristow, 18 March 1909, Bristow to W. L. Huggins, 26 July 1909, Bristow to Leland, 30 October 1909, Bristow to Allen, 16 and 30 December 1909, Bristow to White, 16 December 1909, Bristow to Burnette, 30 December 1909; Capper Papers, Bristow to Capper, 28 and 31 December 1909; WAW, Bristow to White, 30 December 1909. Bristow had trouble in August 1909 over the appointment of census supervisors. He did not understand that these were strictly presidential patronage. Moreover, he probably did not appreciate reports that Taft was using them against insurgents. Taft Papers, Taft to Bristow, 18 and 23 August 1909, Taft to Curtis, 23 and 30 August 1909, BP, Bristow to Taft, 23 August 1909; *Congressional Record*, 61st Cong., 2d sess., 1910, 45:1395.

70. BP, Bristow to Allen, 15 January 1910, Bristow to Burnette, 7 January 1910, Bristow to W. P. Dillingham, 21 May 1910; WAW, Bristow to White, 29 January 1910, J. C. Laughlin to White, 24 January 1910; Taft Papers, Taft to Stubbs, 17 February 1910; LP, Curtis to Long, 8 January 1912; *TDC*, 1 September 1910.

71. BP, Bristow to White, 22 December 1910, Bristow to Harrison, 4 January and 24 July 1911; WAW, Allen to White, 9 December 1910; Taft Papers, Taft to Bristow, 2 January 1911; Gleed Papers, Gleed to C. S. Page, 26 July 1911.

72. BP, Bristow to Hull, 27 June 1910, Bristow to E. C. Manning, 3 December 1910; WAW, White to Nelson, 29 June 1910. As Sageser points out in his interesting biography of Bristow, Taft did not succeed. A Bristow politician was finally appointed. Sageser, *Bristow*, p. 108.

CHAPTER 9

1. BP, Bristow to Leland, 14 April 1910; Mowry, *Era of Roosevelt*, pp. 266–67; Gwinn, *Cannon*, pp. 192, 195–98; Pringle, "Madison," p. 33.

2. WAW, White to Taft, 3 February 1910.

3. Gleed Papers, Gleed to Hackney, 19 January 1910.

4. WAW, White to Leland, 21 December 1909, White to Bristow, 21 December 1909; "Leland Recollections."

5. WAW, White to Stubbs, 4 February 1908, Allen to White, 27 July 1908 and 16 February 1911; BP, Bristow to Allen, 4 and 20 February and 12 March 1909, Allen to Bristow, 16 March 1909; SGP, Allen to Dear John, 18 January 1909; *TSJ*, 9 February 1905; Political Pamphlets, portfolio size, KSHS library, *To The Republicans of the Second Congressional District*; Biographies Compiled by the Library, s.v. "Henry Justin Allen"; Charles B. Driscoll, "Kansas in Labor," *American Mercury*, March 1929, p. 345.

6. WAW, Murdock to White, 13 December 1909, Bristow to White, 13 June 1910; BP, Bristow to Trigg, 13 June 1910, Trigg to Bristow, 17 June 1910, Bristow to White, 23 June 1910; Tuttle, "Murdock," p. 32.

7. WAW, T. A. McNeal to White, 13 November 1909 and 6 April 1910, Madison to Capper, 18 July 1910; BP, Bristow to Elward, 17 December 1909.

8. SGP, Stubbs to the President, 22 April 1909, Stubbs to Scott, 28 April 1909, Scott to Stubbs, 16 July 1910; *TDC*, 11 July 1910.

9. WAW, W. W. Payne to Stubbs, 30 December 1909; *TSJ*, 27 and 29 September and 5 and 12 October 1909; *TDC*, 19 and 23 August, 8, 13, 21 and 30 September, 4 and 8 October 1909; *Wichita Eagle*, 29 September 1909.

10. WAW, Stubbs to White, 5 October 1909; SGP, "Counting the Cost," article, taxation file, 1909–1912; *TSJ*, 8 November 1909.

11. BP, Bristow to Jackson, 3 February 1910, Bristow to Allen, 7 February 1910; WAW, Bristow to White, 3 February 1910, Allen to White, 14 February 1910; Capper Papers, Bristow to Capper, 2 February 1910; Taft Papers, Taft to Long, 15 and 26 February 1910; Kansas Day Club Clippings, KSHS library, pp. 178–288.

12. *St. Louis Republican*, 13 March 1910, in Republican Party Clippings, vol. 7, KSHS library.

13. *TSJ*, 5, 6, and 10 May 1910; *TDC*, 10–12 May 1910.

14. Connelley, *Kansas*, 3:1253–54; *Kansas City Journal*, 10 May and 31 July 1910; *Wichita Beacon*, 19 and 20 May 1910; *TDC*, 2 June 1910.

15. *TDC*, 19 May 1910.

16. Republican Campaign Literature, 1910, "Roscoe Stubbs, A Poem."

17. Ibid., pamphlets, *A Brilliant Record—Tom Wagstaff's*, *The Governorship by W. P. Hackney*, *Senator Curtis Answers Governor Stubbs*; WAW, Bristow to White, 10 June 1910; *Kansas City Journal*, 10 and 17 May 1910; *Kansas City Star*, 9 July 1910; *TDC*, 29 May 1910.

18. SGP, "The Governor on State Tax-

ation," "An Additional Statement," "Counting the Cost," articles, taxation file, 1909–1912; Hodges MSS., D. O. McCray to Hodges, 1 March 1910.

19. BP, Bristow to Lovewell, 4 June 1910; *Kansas City Star,* 22 June 1910.

20. WAW, White to H. J. Haskell, 14 November 1909, White to Capper, 29 December 1909, White to Murdock, 13 January 1910, Madison to White, 21 February 1910; BP, Bristow to G. I. Idzorek, 20 July 1910; *Congressional Record,* 61st Cong., 2d sess., 1910, 45:6541, 6544.

21. Charles Curtis Collection, KSHS, Curtis to G. Huron, 21 May 1909; SGP, Stubbs to R. Stone, 28 April 1909, Stubbs to Taft, 14 May 1909; WAW, McNeal to White, 26 and 28 October 1909.

22. Capper Papers, Anthony to Capper, 30 August and 4 September 1909, Capper to Anthony, 1 September 1909; *TDC,* 21 May 1909.

23. BP, Bristow to Valentine, 22 November 1909, E. R. Fulton to My dear Sir, 29 July 1910.

24. WAW, Valentine to White, 19 and 27 October and 20 November 1910; BP, R. R. Rees to Bristow, 8 August 1910; Kansas Biographical Pamphlets, vol. 7, KSHS library, *A Sketch of the Life and Works of Judge R. R. Rees.*

25. C. F. Scott Correspondence, KSHS, O. Zoppone to Scott, 5 August 1910, J. Wilson to Scott, 14 February 1911; WAW, White to Scott, 9 January 1912, Marble to White, 30 September 1909; Connelley, *Kansas,* 3:1360; *Proceedings of the Bar Association of Kansas, 1912* (Topeka, 1912), unnumbered page, s.v. "Alexander C. Mitchell."

26. Gleed Papers, W. W. Finney to Gleed, 26 October 1909; BP, Bristow to Scott, 6 October 1909, Bristow to Mitchell, 18 October 1909; WAW, Bristow to White, 28 June 1910.

27. *TDC,* 9 July 1910.

28. *TDC,* 21 May 1910; *TSJ,* 23 April 1910.

29. Scott Correspondence, Long to Scott, 6 August 1910; Ewing, "Scott," pp. 57–58.

30. WAW, White to Taft, ca. December 1908, McNeal to White, 28 October 1909, Dawson to White, 6 and 9 December 1909, White to Madison, 18 April 1911.

31. BP, White to Bristow, 14 December 1909, Bristow to White, 16 December 1909, Bristow to Leland, 14 April 1909; WAW, Murdock to White, 22 November 1909, White to Murdock, 13 January 1909, Bristow to White, 15 and 18 April 1910.

32. BP, Bristow to J. A. Kimball, 3 June 1910, Bristow to White, 28 June 1910, Bristow to Beveridge, 20 July 1910; *TDC,* 16 and 17 July 1910; *Kansas City Journal,* 28 July 1910; Case MSS., 4: 215–18.

33. BP, Bristow to J. P. Dolliver, 20 July 1910; *Kansas City Journal,* 15 July 1910; *Osawatomie Graphic,* 28 July 1910; Tuttle, "Murdock," pp. 35–36.

34. BP, Bristow to Dolliver, 20 July 1910, Bristow to T. P. Gore, 2 August 1910, Bristow to Cummins, 3 August 1910, W. Bristow to Bristow, 6 August 1910; *Kansas City Star,* 15 July 1910; Ewing, "Scott," pp. 57–58.

35. BP, Bristow to Beveridge, 5 August 1910; *Congressional Record,* 61st Cong., 2d sess., 1910, 45:6543.

36. *Seventeenth Biennial Report of the Secretary of State of the State of Kansas, 1909–'10* (Topeka, 1910), pp. 80–89, 110–13.

37. *Atchison Globe, Abilene Reflector, Fort Scott Tribune, Hiawatha World, Hutchinson News, Iola Register, Lawrence Journal, Manhattan Mercury, Wellington News*—all cited in *Kansas City Star,* 5 August 1910; *Emporia Gazette,* 5 August 1910; *Wichita Beacon,* 5 August 1910.

38. BP, Bristow to Beveridge, 18 August 1910, U. S. Guyer to Bristow, 3 August 1910; *Baltimore News, Chicago Tribune, New York Evening Post, Chicago Record-Herald, Washington Times*—all cited in *TDC,* 5 August 1910.

39. Taft Papers, Taft to Curtis, 23 August 1910; LP, Long to Gould, 6 August 1910, Long to J. M. Miller, 6 August 1910; WAW, F. D. Warren to White, 2 September 1910, White to Roosevelt, ca. August 1910; BP, Guyer to Bristow, 3 August 1910, Bristow to Beveridge, 18 August 1910; Gwinn, *Cannon*, p. 227.

40. WAW, White to W. T. Bell, 9 August 1910, White to W. C. Jones, 9 August 1910, White to Dolliver, 9 August 1910, White to K. Hubbard, 9 August 1910, White to R. Stout, 20 August 1910; BP, Bristow to Bourne, 8 August 1910, Bristow to Cummins, 18 August 1910; LP, Albaugh to Long, 5 September 1910, John H. Todd, "Insurgency in Kansas: An Analysis of the Political Situation in the Sunflower State," *Voter* 89 (September 1910):46–47; *TDC*, 31 August and 1 September 1910.

41. *TDC*, 31 August and 1 September 1910.

42. George E. Mowry, "Theodore Roosevelt and the Election of 1910," *MVHR* 25 (March 1939):523–34; Robert S. La Forte, "Theodore Roosevelt's Osawatomie Speech," *KHQ* 32 (Summer 1966):187–200.

43. Nemo, "Men and Things," *Kansas Magazine* 4 (August 1910):18–19; ibid., 4 (September 1910):49–51.

44. Hodges MSS., Letter to the Editor of the *Kansas City Star* from a Member of Franklin Post No. 68, G.A.R., and Late Sergeant, F Company, 7th Indiana Cavalry, ca. October 1910.

45. LP, Long to Albaugh, 31 October 1910.

46. WAW, White to D. Barton, June 1910, Barton to White, 22 June 1910, Murdock to White, 9 August 1910; BP, Bristow to Lovewell, 23 February 1910, Bristow to M. V. Rork, 19 September 1910, Bristow to Nelson, 30 September 1910; LP, Albaugh to Long, 8 and 25 October 1910, Axline to Long, 11 and 19 October 1910; Hodges MSS., H. W. Young to McCray, 28 March 1910, McNeal to Hodges, 4 May 1910, Hodges to McNeal, 12 May 1910, McCray to Hodges, 4 and 19 June 1910, Hodges to McCray, 18 June 1910; *The Legislative Record of George H. Hodges*, pamphlet, 1910; *Kansas City Journal*, 22 February 1910; *TSJ*, 24 February 1910; Tuttle, "Murdock," pp. 37–38.

47. Hodges MSS., J. L. Caldwell to Hodges, 26 November 1910, J. D. Botkin to Hodges, 28 November 1910, Hodges to Caldwell, 9 December 1910.

48. WAW, White to Taft, 22 November 1910; BP, Bristow to J. Myers, 9 November 1910, Bristow to Clapp, 10 November 1910, Bristow to Bass, 10 November 1910, Bristow to Jackson, 10 November 1910, Bristow to Davis, 11 November 1910.

49. LP, Albaugh to Long, 9 November 1910.

50. Voting returns are taken from the appropriate reports of the secretaries of state. For 1910 see *Seventeenth Biennial Report of the Secretary of State*, pp. 125–26, 140–42, 146–49.

51. *TSJ*, 12 November 1910; *Kansas City Journal*, 30 December 1910.

52. BP, Bristow to F. Bristow, 10 December 1910; Archibald W. Butt, *Taft and Roosevelt: The Intimate Letters of Archie Butt*, 2 vols. (New York, 1930), 1:279; Mowry, *Era of Roosevelt*, p. 291.

53. In voting on the "Farmers' Free List," which would have allowed agricultural implements, leather goods, fence wire, lumber, and other items to enter duty free, Anthony, Jackson, Madison, Murdock, and Bristow favored it, while Campbell, Rees, Young, and Curtis opposed. On the House's effort to override Taft's veto, Jackson, Madison, and Murdock voted "yea," Anthony, Campbell, Rees, and Young, "noe." On Canadian Reciprocity the vote was mixed between regulars and progressives as follows: For—Anthony, Madison, Mitchell, and Murdock; against—Campbell, Jackson, Rees, Young, Bristow, and Curtis. *Congressional Record*, 62d Cong., 1st sess., 1911, 47:11, 559–60, 3175, 3435, 4061, 4083–84, 4174.

54. WAW, White to La Follette, 3 January 1911, Bristow to White, 16 January 1911; BP, Bristow to Chase, 30 January and 20 February 1911, Bristow to Trigg, 26 June 1911, Bristow to Allen, 8 July 1911, Bristow to White, 30 September 1911; Capper Papers, White to Capper, 14 July 1911, Madison to Capper, 3 July 1911; *TDC*, 26–28 September 1911; Mowry, *Era of Roosevelt*, p. 291; Bright, *Kansas*, 2:39–42; Tuttle, "Murdock," p. 53.

55. WAW, White to La Follette, 3 January 1911, White to Roosevelt, 18 October 1911, W. L. Houser to White, 9 and 16 January 1912; Capper Papers, Madison to Capper, 3 July 1911; White, *Autobiography*, p. 448.

56. BP, Bristow to Allen, 8 June, 8 July, and 29 December 1911, Bristow to Harrison, 19 June 1911, Bristow to Chase, 9 August 1911, Bristow to F. K. Beam, 9 February 1912; *Salina Journal*, 5 February 1912; "The Presidential Campaign: Mr. La Follette's Withdrawal," *Outlook*, 17 February 1912, p. 337.

57. BP, Bristow to White, 31 December 1911, Bristow to Kimball, 15 March 1912; Oscar King Davis, "Senator Bristow's Views on Present Political Conditions," *Outlook*, 30 March 1912, p. 725; Mitchell, "Bristow," p. 170; Albert Dimmitt, "The Progressive Party in Kansas, 1911–1917" (Master's thesis, University of Kansas, 1958), passim.

58. BP, Bristow to White, 12 November 1911; LP, Morgan to Long, 12 January 1912, F. L. Martin to Long, 13 January 1912; *Emporia Gazette*, 10 January 1912; *Kansas City Star*, 10 January 1912; Kansas Election Returns, Special Elections, 1911, 1912, Office of the Secretary of State, Records, microfilm reels nos. 11a and 12, KSHS.

59. BP, Allen to Bristow, 26 December 1911, White to Bristow, 28 December 1911, Bristow to White, 31 December 1911 and 11 January 1912; WAW, White to Bristow, 8 January 1912.

60. *Roosevelt Letters*, 7:286–508.

61. BP, Chase to Bristow, 6 August 1911, Leland to Bristow, 25 December 1911, Capper to Bristow, 23 December 1911; WAW, White to Roosevelt, 17 January and 18 October 1911; *Emporia Gazette*, 7 and 15 January 1912.

## Chapter 10

1. Philip C. Jessup, *Elihu Root*, 2 vols. (New York, 1938), 2:196–98; George E. Mowry, *Theodore Roosevelt and the Progressive Movement* (Madison, Wis., 1946), chap. 9.

2. WAW, Rees to White, 16 May 1912; BP, Bristow to W. A. Smith, 30 March 1912, Bristow to Borah, 8 June 1912; *Emporia Gazette*, 16 May and 6 June 1912.

3. Progressive Party Pamphlets, 1912, vol. 1, KSHS library, *Henry J. Allen's Statement to the Republican National Convention*; Mowry, *Roosevelt and Progressive Movement*, pp. 244, 248–49.

4. *TDC*, 21–25 June 1912; *Atchison Globe*, 26 June 1912.

5. LP, Scott to Long, 21 June 1912; *Kansas City Star*, 10 June 1912.

6. "The Orchestra Hall Speech: Theodore Roosevelt's Address Accepting the Nomination of the New Party," *Outlook*, 29 June 1912, p. 479.

7. BP, Bristow to G. Hull, 22 June 1912; *TDC*, 25 June 1912.

8. *Emporia Gazette*, 22 June 1912; *TDC*, 8 July 1912.

9. BP, Bristow to Roosevelt, 15 July 1912; Ernest H. Abbot, "The Progressive Convention," *Outlook*, 17 August 1912, pp. 858, 864; Johnson, *White*, p. 250.

10. Johnson, *White*, p. 205.

11. "Following the Campaign," *Outlook*, 24 August 1912, p. 915.

12. WAW, A. M. Kinney to White, 30 October 1912; Bright, *Kansas*, 2:43.

13. WAW, J. E. Ingham to White, 25 June 1912, White to Roosevelt, 8 July 1912, White to B. F. Blaker, 13 July 1912, White to W. L. Cunningham, 23 July 1912; BP, Bristow to E. M. Adams, 1 July 1912, Bristow to Harrison, 6 July 1912; *TDC*, 1, 4, 5, 11, and 12 July 1912.

14. *TDC*, 18 and 20 July 1912.

15. WAW, White to Roosevelt, 24 July 1912; BP, Harrison to Bristow, 24 July 1912; *State ex rel. Dawson v. Branine*, 125 P.R. 343 (Kan. S.C., 1912): *TDC*, July 24–25 1912; "The Case of the Kansas Electors," *Outlook*, 10 August 1912, p. 795.

16. *Marks v. Davis*, 125 P.R. 344 (Kan. S.C., 1912).

17. *TDC*, 28 July and 2 August 1912; *New York Times*, 2 August 1912; "The Case of the Kansas Electors," p. 795.

18. WAW, Capper to White, 18 April 1912, M. Applegate to White, 18 July 1912; George A. Huron MSS., KSHS, W. I. Stuart to Huron, 2 March 1912; Gleed Papers, Anthony to Gleed, 22 August 1911; *TSJ*, 3 July and 3 August 1912; Socolofsky, *Capper*, p. 77.

19. LP, Curtis to Long, 8 July 1912; WAW, Applegate to White, 18 July 1912; Gleed Papers, Gleed to Page, 15 July 1911; Hodges Papers, "Some Plain Facts by Dickinson County Taxpayers Union"; *Emporia Gazette*, 11 July 1912; *TSJ*, 13 July 1912.

20. WAW, Blomberg to Stubbs, 22 July 1912, Miscellaneous Campaign Literature, Stubbs Senate Contest, 1912, box 292; Republican Campaign Literature, portfolio size, "W. R. Stubbs to the Voters of Kansas, 1912."

21. WAW, Blaker to F. Dunkelberger, 29 July 1912; *Eighteenth Biennial Report of the Secretary of State of the State of Kansas, 1911–12* (Topeka, 1912), pp. 18–21, 26–27, 30–46.

22. WAW, White to Murdock, 29 April 1912, Harris to White, 18 May 1912, Akers to White, 24 May 1912, A. M. Strong to Allen, 8 July 1912, White to Roosevelt, 24 July 1912, Akers to E. J. Guilbert, 31 July 1912; BP, Bristow to White, 20 March 1912, Bristow to Allen, 13 April and 8 and 13 May 1912; *Kansas City Star*, 15 March 1912.

23. WAW, White to ———, 12 July 1912, White to Roosevelt, 12 and 24 July 1912, White to F. Wade, 13 July 1912; White, *Autobiography*, p. 492.

24. WAW, F. B. Stanley to E. S. Rule, 8 July 1912, Blaker to Dunkelberger, 29 July 1912, J. R. Wilkie to White, 2 September 1912; "Following the Campaign," *Outlook*, 27 July 1912, p. 665; *TDC*, 2 and 7 July and 11 and 13 August 1912.

25. Taft Papers, C. D. Hilles to Taft, 15 August 1912; WAW, White to C. A. Kimball, 26 August 1912, White to W. H. Irwin, 4 September 1912, White to Bob, 5 September 1912, D. H. to Blomberg, 21 September 1912; *TDC*, 7 and 21 August 1912.

26. BP, Bristow to Cummins, 2 September 1912; WAW, White to Roosevelt, 24 and 27 July 1912, White to R. S. Baer, 24 September 1912; *Roosevelt Letters*, 7: 599–600, Roosevelt to P. B. Stewart, 15 August 1912; *TDC*, 28 August 1912.

27. WAW, Albaugh to White, 5 September 1912, White to Albaugh, 7 September 1912, White to the Old Electors, 18 and 25 September 1912, White to C. Brandt, 17 October 1912; Taft Papers, Taft to Anthony, 26 August 1912; Long Papers, Long to Marshall, 7 October 1912; *Roosevelt Letters*, 7:582 n2; *TDC*, 14 and 18 September 1912.

28. WAW, White to C. C. Isley, 8 July 1912, J. A. Darnall to White, 15 July 1912, White to Murdock, 8 October 1912; BP, Harrison to Bristow, 24 July 1912, Bristow to White, 25 July 1912, Bristow to Harrison, 29 July 1912; *TDC*, 6 July and 21 and 22 September 1912.

29. WAW, White to Roosevelt, 24 October 1912.

30. WAW, D. Hinshaw to White, 17 August 1912, Hinshaw to Editor, *Washburn Review*, 19 September 1912, Hinshaw to S. Ingalls, 20 September 1912, Hinshaw to G. W. Ellis, 26 and 30 September 1912, White to G. P. Butt, 5 October 1912, White to Western Newspaper Union, 17 October 1912, White to Roosevelt, 24 October 1912, C. S. Roseberry to White, 7 November 1912, Perkins to White, 13 November 1912. These are only a few of thousands of letters in the White MSS. that are germane to the generalities expressed above.

31. WAW, Hinshaw to G. Adams, 30

September 1912, A. Howard to White, 16 August 1912, White to H. Parker, 1 October 1912, White to Murdock, 8 October 1912, Hinshaw to J. A. Burge, 9 October 1912, White to Perkins, 6 November 1912, Progressive National Committee to White, 28 October 1912.

32. WAW, F. D. Smith to White, 26 October 1912.

33. WAW, D. Freemeyer to White, 3 August 1912, and "The Political Boss Revived in Kansas by J. H. Crider, 1912"; Gleed Papers, Gleed to J. H. Fletcher, 15 October 1912.

34. WAW, W. F. Sapp to White, 26 July 1912; Gleed Papers, Gleed to Fletcher, 15 October 1912; Johnson, *White*, p. 207.

35. Arthur S. Link, *Wilson: The Road to the White House* (Princeton, N.J., 1947), chap. 13.

36. WAW, Sapp to White, 26 July 1912; *Emporia Gazette*, 3 July 1912; *TDC*, 3 and 6 July 1912.

37. *Emporia Gazette*, 28 August and 8 October 1912; *Salina Journal*, 21 and 22 September and 7 and 8 October 1912; *TDC*, 5, 7, 15, and 23 October and 4 November 1912; *Topeka Daily Herald*, 7–9 October 1912; Johnson, *White*, pp. 206–7.

38. Kansas Election Returns, 1912, Office of the Secretary of State, Records, microfilm reel no. 13.

39. Socolofsky, *Capper*, pp. 78–79; *TSJ*, 19 and 28 August, 4 September, and 26 October 1912; *Atchison Globe*, 21 August 1912; *TDC*, 28 August 1912; *Kansas City Journal*, 22 and 24 September 1912.

40. WAW, C. A. Bender to White, 21 September 1912, W. B. Parker to White, 23 September 1912, White to O. K. Miller, 27 September 1912, S. D. Frazier to White, 26 October 1912; SGP, Marble to Leahy, 16 October 1912, Leahy to Marble, 17 October 1912; Hodges MSS., "Some Plain Facts by Dickinson County Taxpayers Union"; Taft Papers, Hilles to Taft, 15 August 1912; Republican Campaign Literature, portfolio size, "Senator Curtis Replies to Mr. Dolley" and "Fourteen to Remember"; *Kansas City Journal*, 17 October 1912.

41. Republican Campaign Literature, 1912, "W. R. Stubbs to the Voters of Kansas"; WAW, Leahy to White, 12 September 1912, White to Sheldon, 18 September 1912, Miscellaneous Campaign Literature, Stubbs Senate Contest, 1912, box 292; *TDC*, 14 September, 15 and 23 October, 1, 2, and 5 November 1912.

42. *Eighteenth Biennial Report of the Secretary of State of the State of Kansas*, pp. 74–75.

43. Hodges MSS., Hodges to H. Martin, 6 July 1911; Billard Family Papers, KSHS, C. T. Etzold to J. B. Billard, 3 October 1911, V. E. Preston to Billard, 3 November 1911, P. E. Laughlin to H. Albach, 27 June 1912, I. Gibbs to Albach, 29 June 1912, R. E. Achterberg to Albach, 22 July 1912; WAW, E. W. Andrich to White, 21 October 1912.

44. Capper Papers, "Speech in Wyandotte County, 1911," "Speech at Coffeyville, 1912," "Speech at Hiawatha, 1912," and "Political Sheets—'J. F. Codding Says Capper Hope of Prohibition,' 'Friend of the G.A.R. Veteran,' 'Economy in Government,' 'Good Roads,' 'Friend to Labor Unions,' 'The Church,' 'Progressive Republican Policies,' 1912"; BP, Capper to Bristow, 14 October 1912, as well as a number of undated postcards from Capper mailed in October and November 1912.

45. Capper Papers, political sheet dated 21 October 1912, "Speech at Wyandotte County, 1911," and "Speech at Coffeyville, 1912"; BP, "The Capper Platform," ca. October 1912.

46. Capper Papers, "Hodges Member of the Lumber Trust," ca. October 1912; Hodges MSS., Hodges to Trigg, 29 June 1911, "Clipping, *Labor Herald*, Pittsburg, Kans., 4 October 1912," and Hodges to Dear Sir, 25 October 1912; BP, a number of undated postcards and form letters from Hodges mailed in October and November 1912; *TDC*, 1–5 November 1912; Socolofsky, *Capper*, pp. 78–79.

47. *Eighteenth Biennial Report of the*

*Secretary of State of the State of Kansas,* p. 31.

48. Ibid., pp. 78–79.

49. BP, Bristow to Roosevelt, 6 November 1912; WAW, White to Perkins, 6 November 1912; Personal Interview with Victor Murdock cited in George Callis, "A History of the Progressive Party in Kansas" (Master's thesis, Kansas State Teachers College, Pittsburg, 1933), p. 91; Landon interview cited in Harder, "Factionalism," p. 65.

CHAPTER 11

1. WAW, Ingham to White, 25 June 1912, Isley to White, 5 July 1912, Cunningham to White, 20 July 1912, Baer to White, 21 September 1912, White to Roosevelt, 6 July 1912, White to Isley, 8 July 1912, White to Cunningham, 23 July 1912, White to Perkins, 6 and 8 November 1912.

2. WAW, White to B. Bristow, 7 November 1912, White to Roosevelt, 14 November 1912.

3. WAW, White to H. C. Sticher, ca. November 1912; Johnson, *White,* p. 210; *Kansas City Times,* 18 December 1912.

4. WAW, J. H. Mitchell to White, 8 November 1912, A. Graff to White, 12 November 1912, Gray to White, 13 November 1912, L. G. Grobety to White, 18 November 1912, W. H. Hollenshead to White, 10 December 1912, S. B. Farwell to White, 12 December 1912, Gregg to White, 13 December 1912; *Kansas City Star,* 8 November 1912; *Emporia Gazette,* 29 November 1912.

5. WAW, Roosevelt to White, 15 November 1912; BP, Roosevelt to Bristow, 19 November 1912; *Roosevelt Letters,* 7:633–34, Roosevelt to A. H. Lee, 5 November 1912, and 7:640, Roosevelt to Pinchot, 13 November 1912, 645 n6; *Kansas City Star,* 10 and 11 December 1912; "Mr. Roosevelt on the Future of the Progressive Party," *Outlook,* 23 November 1912, p. 598.

6. WAW, W. D. Ross to White, 22 January 1914.

7. WAW, Anthony to White, 13 November 1912, Elward to White, 11 December 1912, White to Scott, 27 September 1913.

8. BP, Capper to Bristow, 5 December 1912; Capper Papers, E. C. Pulliam to Capper, 9 January 1913.

9. Albert J. Beveridge Papers, Library of Congress, Beveridge to Clapp, 22 November 1912.

10. BP, Bristow to B. Bristow, 7 November 1912, Bristow to F. Bristow, 29 November 1912, Bristow to White, 2 December 1912, Bristow to H. I. Maxwell, 13 December 1912, Bristow to Harrison, 21 December 1912, Bristow to C. C. Handy, 27 December 1912, Bristow to Dolley, 31 December 1912.

11. BP, Bristow to J. S. West, 5 December 1912; Capper Papers, Bristow to Capper, 7 December 1912.

12. *Kansas City Star,* 18 December 1912; *TDC,* 18 and 19 December 1912.

13. BP, Harrison to Bristow, 21, 28, and 30 January 1913; *TDC,* 30 January 1913; *TSJ,* 29 and 30 January 1913.

14. BP, Harrison to Bristow, 17 February 1913; Progressive Party Pamphlets, 1914, vol. 5, *First Annual Progressive Party Banquet; Kansas City Star,* 23 December 1912; *TDC,* 13 February 1913.

15. BP, Bristow to U. S. Sartin, 7 February 1913.

16. BP, Leahy to Bristow, 16 February 1913, Harrison to Bristow, 17 February 1913; *TDC,* 13 February 1913; *Kansas City Star,* 13 February 1913; *Emporia Gazette,* 13 and 14 February 1913.

17. BP, Sartin to Bristow, 3 April 1913.

18. BP, Sartin to Bristow, 3 April 1913, Harrison to Bristow, 9 April 1913, Bristow to Capper, 5 April 1913; WAW, Allen to White, 9 June 1913; *Kansas City Journal,* 30 March 1913.

19. BP, Bristow to Sartin, 10 April 1913, Bristow to F. Bristow, 5 April 1913, Bristow to J. Madden, 7 April 1913.

20. BP, Harrison to Bristow, 8 March 1913; LP, Troutman to ——, 6 March 1913, Troutman to Long, 23 May 1913; Capper Papers, "Article by A. L. Shultz,

*TSJ*, 29 November 1956"; *TSJ*, 12 and 24 May 1913.

21. BP, Bristow to Troutman, 10 April 1913; interview, Robert La Forte with Homer Socolofsky, 5 November 1963.

22. LP, Troutman to Long, 23 May 1913; *TDC*, 3 June 1913.

23. *Emporia Gazette*, 13 May 1913; WAW, Roosevelt to White, Stubbs, and Dolley, 1 July 1913.

24. WAW, O. W. Dawson to White, 18 October 1913. This letter is typical of many in White's correspondence which question Roosevelt's intentions in 1916.

25. *Roosevelt Letters*, 7:750–52, Roosevelt to Murdock, 30 September 1913.

26. BP, Bristow to J. Dixon, 25 August 1913, Capper to Bristow, 30 September 1913.

27. BP, Bristow to Beveridge, 21 December 1912, Harrison to Bristow, 31 December 1912.

28. *Roosevelt Letters*, 7:685–86, Roosevelt to Bristow, 31 December 1912, and 7:717, Roosevelt to Perkins, 1 April 1913, p. 715 n2; BP, Bristow to Roosevelt, 7 April 1913, Bristow to R. E. Stout, 22 April 1913, Bristow to White, 22 May 1913, Bristow to Allen, 12 June 1913, Bristow to Capper, 13 November 1913; WAW, White to Roosevelt, 9 June 1913, Murdock to White, 16 December 1913; Mitchell, "Bristow," pp. 154, 199–205; Boswell, "Murdock," pp. 14–16, 47–48 52–54; Sageser, *Bristow*, pp. 127–41, has an excellent discussion of Bristow's relations with the Wilson administration.

29. BP, Bristow to Troutman, 28 July 1913, Bristow to Allen, 5 September 1913.

30. LP, Scott to Long, 15 September 1913; *TDC*, 12, 23, and 30 August 1913.

31. WAW, E. M. Murphy to White, 13 November 1913.

32. WAW, White to Roosevelt, 24 September 1913.

33. WAW, White to Harrison, 28 October 1913; *TDC*, 1 and 2 September 1913.

34. *Emporia Gazette*, 22 September 1913.

35. WAW, White to Bristow, 29 October 1913, Bristow to White, 12 November 1913, White to Harrison, 28 October 1913.

36. BP, Bristow to Elward, 20 June 1912, Bristow to Dolley, 31 December 1912, Bristow to Capper, 7 December 1912.

37. BP, Bristow to Harrison, 1 February 1913, Sartin to Bristow, 3 April 1913, Bristow to Capper, 5 April 1913.

38. BP, Bristow to White, 19 June 1913; WAW, Allen to White, 9 June 1913.

39. BP, Harrison to Bristow, 28 January 1913.

40. BP, Bristow to Hinshaw, 30 September and 15 October 1913; WAW, White to Bristow, 29 October and 1 November 1913, White to Harrison, 28 October 1913, Hinshaw to White, 4 November 1913.

41. BP, Harrison to Bristow, 2, 18, and 22 November 1913, Bristow to Harrison, 19 September 1913, Bristow to Capper, 6 October 1913.

42. BP, Harrison to Bristow, 18 and 22 November 1913, Bristow to Harrison, 19 September 1913, Capper to Bristow, 11 November 1913, Allen to Bristow, 19 November 1913.

43. BP, Bristow to Dixon, 29 November 1913.

44. BP, Troutman to Bristow, 17 December 1913.

45. BP, Bristow to Harrison, 19 September 1913, Bristow to Capper, 6 October 1913; WAW, White to Capper, 30 September 1913, Ingalls to White, 7 October 1913.

46. WAW, Capper to White, 11 October 1913.

47. Capper Papers, "Speech at Eureka, Kans., April 24, 1914."

48. WAW, Sartin to Dear Sir, 18 November 1913, Sartin to White, 24 November 1913.

49. WAW, Leahy to White, 9 November 1913, Scott to White, 16 Novem-

ber 1913, Trigg to Bristow, 27 November 1913, White to Murdock, 4 December 1913; BP, Harrison to Bristow, 18 and 22 November 1913, Allen to Bristow, 2 December 1913, Isley to Bristow, 31 December 1913; *Emporia Gazette,* 13 October and 31 December 1913; *TDC,* 21 November 1913.

50. WAW, Bristow to White, 25 October 1913, Hinshaw to White, 4 November 1913, White to Leland, 10 December 1913, White to Bristow, 12 December 1913; BP, Bristow to Dixon, 29 November 1913, Allen to Bristow, 2, 24, and 30 December 1913, White to Bristow, 1 November 1913.

51. BP, Allen to Bristow, 24 and 30 December 1913.

52. BP, White to Bristow, 26 December 1913.

53. Gleed Papers, Scott to Gleed, 2 February 1914; *Kansas City Journal,* 4 and 5 January 1914; *Kansas City Star,* 4 January 1914; *TSJ,* 5 January 1914; *Emporia Gazette,* 5 January 1914; *TDC,* 5, 17, and 19 January and 12 and 26 February 1914.

54. *Kansas City Star,* 18 January 1914; WAW, Allen to White, 6 January 1914, H. L. Anderson to White, 19 January 1914.

55. BP, Bristow to O. W. Dawson, 5 January 1914, Bristow to Marble, 5 January 1914.

56. BP, Bristow to C. F. Lebow, 9 January 1914; WAW, Allen to White, 6 January 1914; LP, Scott to Long, 14 January 1914.

CHAPTER 12

1. WAW, Murdock to White, 16 December 1913; BP, Jackson to Bristow, 12 January 1914; *TSJ,* 4 and 5 January 1914.

2. WAW, White to Stubbs, 6 January 1914.

3. WAW, M. McCormick to White, 23 February 1914, McCormick to Stubbs, 23 February 1914.

4. WAW, Allen to White, 6, 9, and 13 January and 5 February 1914, Allen to Sartin, 9 January 1914, Allen to Stubbs, 13 January 1914.

5. *TSJ,* 19 January and 13 February 1914; *Atchison Globe,* 20 February 1914.

6. *TSJ,* 12 and 13 February 1914; Progressive Party Pamphlets, 1914, vol. 5, *Second Annual Progressive Party Banquet.*

7. *TSJ,* 13 February 1914.

8. WAW, L. T. Snediker to White, 25 January 1914, Murdock to White, 15 February 1914; *Second Annual Progressive Party Banquet; TDC,* 13 February 1914.

9. BP, Bristow to Bailey, 10 June 1914; Mowry, *Roosevelt and Progressive Movement,* pp. 301–2; Garraty, *Perkins,* pp. 303–5, 307.

10. WAW, Pinchot to White, 15 April 1914, White to Pinchot, 20 April 1914, Beveridge to White, 22 June 1914, White to Beveridge, 31 June 1914.

11. WAW, Sartin to White, 21 May and 28 July 1914, White to Roosevelt, 17 June 1914; BP, Bristow to Bailey, 10 June 1914; *TDC,* 27–29 July 1914; Mowry, *Roosevelt and Progressive Movement,* pp. 301–2.

12. BP, Burnette to Bristow, 12 April 1914, Bristow to Harrison, 4 April and 12 August 1914, Morgan to Bristow, 15 June 1914, Bristow to J. S. Simmons, 18 June 1914, W. N. Breen to Bristow, 13 July 1914, Bristow to Breen, 13 July 1914, Bristow to Chandler, 18 August 1914; Sageser, *Bristow,* p. 150.

13. BP, Harrison to Bristow, 1 April 1914; LP, Curtis to Long, 30 January 1914; *TDC,* 1 February 1914.

14. BP, Bristow to J. T. Moore, 7 February 1914; Republican Campaign Literature, 1914, "Senator Bristow's Work in the Senate"; Sageser, *Bristow,* p. 150. Ironically, John Harrison, Bristow's main political contact in Kansas at the time, attributed the senator's defeat in 1914 to too much idealism, "more than the present condition of public opinion in Kansas warranted." BP, Harrison to Bristow, 9 August 1914.

15. BP, Bristow to Morgan, 21 Feb-

ruary 1914, Burnette to Bristow, 12 April 1914, Bristow to Valentine, 19 June 1914; WAW, White to Burnette, 7 March 1914; Mitchell, "Bristow," p. 228. For a view of White's actions that is contrary to this presentation see Sageser, *Bristow*, p. 149.

16. LP, Scott to Long, 14 January 1914; Gleed Papers, Scott to Gleed, 2 February 1914; *Iola Register*, 3 August 1914.

17. BP, Capper to Bristow, 10 June and 3 and 13 July 1914, Bristow to Burnette, 3 July 1914, Bristow to C. E. Friend, 3 July 1914, Bristow to Harrison, 9 July 1914.

18. BP, Bristow to Harrison, 1 August 1914, Bristow to J. H. Stewart, 3 August 1914, Bristow to C. E. Ingalls, 11 August 1914.

19. BP, Bristow to Bailey, 22 July 1914, Harrison to Bristow, 9 August 1914; *Nineteenth Biennial Report of the Secretary of State of the State of Kansas, 1913–14* (Topeka, 1914), pp. 17–18. A fourth candidate, A. M. Harvey, received 6,060 votes.

20. *Nineteenth Biennial Report of the Secretary of State of the State of Kansas*, pp. 17–18.

21. BP, Bailey to Bristow, 9 August 1914, Harrison to Bristow, 9 August 1914, Bristow to C. E. Hathaway, 10 August 1914, Bristow to Harrison, 12 August 1914, Burnette to Bristow, 12 August 1914; WAW, Burnette to White, 29 August 1914.

22. BP, Bristow to Capper, 6 August 1914, Bristow to Harrison, 12 August 1914, Bristow to Simmons, 14 August 1914, Bristow to L. W. Bloom, 14 August 1914, Bristow to Burnette, 19 August 1914.

23. BP, Bristow to E. C. Manning, 11 August 1914; Mitchell, "Bristow," p. 238; Sageser, *Bristow*, p. 152.

24. WAW, O. P. Shelley to White, 7 August 1914; *Emporia Gazette*, 9 May, 18 June, and 5–7 August 1914; *Wichita Eagle*, 5 August 1914; *TDC*, 5 August 1914; *TSJ*, 5 August 1914; *Iola Register*, 12 August 1914.

25. LP, Albaugh to Long, 18 August 1914.

26. WAW, Capper to W. H. Buckmaster, 18 March 1914; *Wichita Eagle*, 26 February 1914; Socolofsky, *Capper*, p. 84.

27. *Emporia Gazette*, 17, 19, and 26 August 1914; *TDC*, 26 August 1914.

28. *Emporia Gazette*, 26 August 1914.

29. WAW, White to Murdock, 8 March 1914, Allen to White, 16 June 1914, White to C. D. Lamme, 24 July 1914, Stubbs to White, 28 July 1914, Sartin to White, 28 July 1914; *Emporia Gazette*, 18 June and 17 August 1914.

30. WAW, Allen to White, 16 June 1914, Stubbs to White, 28 July 1914; *Roosevelt Letters*, 7:773, Roosevelt to White, 6 July 1914; Walter R. Stubbs, "Public Ownership of Railroads, Waterways, and Water Power," *Saturday Evening Post*, 6 June 1914, pp. 3–5, 28–33; *TDC*, 26 August 1914; *Emporia Gazette*, 26 August 1914.

31. *Roosevelt Letters*, 7:773, Roosevelt to White, 6 July 1914; William Allen White, "How Kansas Boarded the Water Wagon," *Saturday Evening Post*, 11 July 1914, pp. 3–5, 44–45; Henry J. Allen, "Destruction of Kansas," *FRA: A Magazine of Business Inspiration*, April 1915, p. 32; *TDC*, 26 August 1914; *Emporia Gazette*, 26 August 1914.

32. Mowry, *Roosevelt and Progressive Movement*, pp. 300–301.

33. WAW, Sartin to White, 30 August 1914, White to Sartin, 2 September 1914, White to Burnette, 7 March 1914, Allen to White, 31 August 1914, Murdock to White, 29 August 1914; LP, Long to C. G. Marshall, 18 September 1914; *TDC*, 26 August and 1 November 1914; *Kansas City Journal*, 3 November 1914.

34. *TSJ*, 18 and 19 September 1914; *Emporia Gazette*, 20 September and 26 and 27 October 1914; Socolofsky, *Capper*, pp. 82, 84–85.

35. WAW, M. Morrow to White, 29 October 1914.

36. WAW, Sartin to White, 5 March 1914, White to Burnette, 7 March 1914;

LP, Long to Marshall, 18 September 1914; *TDC*, 1–3 November 1914; *Kansas City Journal*, 2 and 3 November 1914.

37. WAW, Bramlette to White, 23 December 1913, White to Allen, 11 January 1914, Allen to White, 14 April 1914, F. W. Ives to Allen, 26 October 1914, Secretary-to-Allen to Ives, 27 October 1914; *Kansas City Star*, 19 August 1914.

38. WAW, Leahy to White, ca. October 1914, *Why We Are for Vic*, pamphlet, *Why I Am a Candidate*, pamphlet, 1914.

39. WAW, White to Roosevelt, 15 December 1914; Dimmitt, "Progressive Party," pp. 162–64.

40. *Nineteenth Biennial Report of the Secretary of State of the State of Kansas*, pp. 45–46.

41. This assumes that the first vote cast was in the Senate race, the office listed first on the ballot.

42. *Nineteenth Biennial Report of the Secretary of State of the State of Kansas*, pp. 49–50.

43. WAW, White to Murdock, 5 November 1914, White to Capper, 6 November 1914, Sartin to White, 6 November 1914, O. W. Dawson to White, 7 November 1914, Davidson to White, 10 November 1914, E. M. Murphy to White, 24 November 1914.

44. WAW, White to Beveridge, 11 and 18 November 1914, Allen to C. P. Dodge, 25 November 1914, Allen to White, 19 November 1914.

45. LP, Cannon to Long, 9 November 1914; BP, Harrison to Trigg, 6 November 1914, Bristow to Harrison, 7 November 1914; WAW, Bailey to White, 26 November 1914; Garraty, *Perkins*, pp. 317–18; *Dictionary of American Biography*, 3d suppl., s.v. "Victor Murdock."

## Chapter 13

1. For example, see LP, Long to J. H. Weeks, 13 October 1915, Long to Waggener, 23 October 1915.

2. *TDC*, 11–14 January 1915.

3. WAW, Haskell to White, 24 November 1914.

4. WAW, Hinshaw to White, 7 November 1914, Roosevelt to White, 7 November 1914.

5. WAW, G. Pinchot to White, 9 November 1914, Allen to White, 19 November 1914, White to Roosevelt, 15 December 1914; Mowry, *Roosevelt and Progressive Movement*, p. 306; *New York Times*, 3 December 1914.

6. BP, Bristow to Harrison, 7 November 1914, Bristow to Weeks, 10 November 1914, Bristow to Allen, 23 December 1914, Bristow to White, 27 May 1918, Harrison to Bristow, 6 November 1914.

7. Socolofsky, *Capper*, pp. 89–90; Gleed Papers, Capper to Gleed, 11 February 1916.

8. Gleed Papers, Charles Session File, no. 85, contains replies from state legislators dated January 1915; LP, Long to F. Martin, 11 February 1915.

9. Frederick M. Davenport, "On the Trail of Progress and Reaction in the West: Slowing Up and Slowing Down—Nebraska and Kansas," *Outlook*, 12 May 1915, pp. 94–99.

10. *Emporia Gazette*, 17 February, 15 May, and 7 July 1915; WAW, White to Harrison, 17 June 1915, White to Gleed, 1 November 1915.

11. Gleed Papers, Allen to Gleed, 20 December 1915; WAW, Allen to Dodge, 25 November 1914; *Wichita Beacon*, 23 June, 16 August, and 16 December 1915.

12. WAW, Allen to White, 1 March and 19 August 1915. Regarding White's interest in reform and its hollow ring, see William Allen White, "Government of the People, by the People, for the People," *Independent*, 7 February 1916, pp. 188–89.

13. WAW, J. Mickey to White, 8 November 1914, Bailey to White, 26 November 1914.

14. WAW, White to Perkins, 4 December 1915 and 25 January 1916, Allen to White, 31 December 1915, White to A. R. Kinkel, 3 February 1916; LP, Albaugh to Long, 18 February 1916; Henry J. Allen, "An Interview with Senator Borah," *Colliers*, 11 December 1915,

p. 12; *Emporia Gazette,* 12 January 1916; *TSJ,* 29 January 1916; Garraty, *Perkins,* p. 331.

15. WAW, White to Kimball, 17 February 1916, White to Roosevelt, 6 April 1916; Mowry, *Roosevelt and Progressive Movement,* p. 342; Garraty, *Perkins,* pp. 331–33; *Emporia Gazette,* 9 March 1916; *TSJ,* 20–22 May 1916.

16. *TSJ,* 20–24 May 1916; *TDC,* 23 and 24 May 1916.

17. LP, Long to Albaugh, 13 April 1916.

18. WAW, Roosevelt to M. Lissner, 11 December 1914, Perkins to White, 8 February 1915, Murdock to White, 31 March 1916.

19. WAW, White to J. Kingsburg, 28 January 1924; *Kansas City Star,* 6, 10, and 11 June 1916; Harold L. Ickes, "Who Killed the Progressive Party," *AHR* 46 (January 1941):318–20, 324–32; Mowry, *Roosevelt and Progressive Movement,* pp. 347–54; Garraty, *Perkins,* pp. 339–41, 349–50, 353.

20. WAW, Murdock to White, 19 August 1916. For other information, see WAW, White to Pinchot, 23 June 1916; "Speech of Raymond Robbins at the Meeting of the Progressive National Committee, June 26, 1916," *The Progressive Party—Its Record from January to July [1916],* pamphlet, KSHS library; *Wichita Beacon,* 12 June 1916; Mowry, *Roosevelt and Progressive Movement,* p. 359.

21. For a more complete statement on Murdock's action in 1916 see Meyer Nathan, "The Election of 1916 in Kansas," *KHQ* 35 (Spring 1969):57, 59.

22. *TSJ,* 20 June 1916.

23. WAW, Elward to White, 4 October 1916, A. M. Breese to White, 20 October 1916.

24. WAW, White to N. Hapgood, 10 October 1916.

25. Gleed Papers, J. W. Gleed to Gleed, 10 November 1916; LP, Long to Albaugh, 11 November 1916; WAW, White to Roosevelt, 27 December 1916, Allen to White, 14 January 1917; *TSJ,* 8 November 1916; *Wichita Beacon,* 9 November 1916; *Wichita Eagle,* 10 November 1916; *Emporia Gazette,* 10 November 1916; *Kansas City Star,* 12 November 1916; *TDC,* 12 November 1916; cf. Nathan, "Election of 1916," pp. 50–63.

26. June G. Cabe and Charles A. Sullivant, *Kansas Votes: National Elections, 1859–1956* (Lawrence, Kans., 1957), pp. 30–33. Because women voted for the first time in a presidential election in Kansas in 1916, 263,905 more ballots were cast than in 1912, when the total presidential vote was 365,908. No one could seriously argue that voter interest was greater in 1916 than in 1912. The increased returns, however, make a numerical comparison of Wilson's additional strength in the thirty Roosevelt counties less meaningful, since in sheer numbers Hughes polled more votes in 1916 than Roosevelt had in these same counties. Percentages thus seem a better indicator. In estimating how many Progressives voted for Wilson in 1916, the fact that Roosevelt had carried the two most populous counties in 1912, Wyandotte and Sedgwick, is worth noting. As indicated, Wilson carried them in 1916.

27. WAW, White to Scott, 27 November 1916, Roosevelt to White, 2 December 1916, White to Murdock, 24 January 1917, White to Ickes, 5 February 1917, White to Perkins, 5, 9, and 13 February 1917, White to Lord Bryce, 19 February 1917; Mowry, *Roosevelt and Progressive Movement,* p. 367; Garraty, *Perkins,* pp. 357–61.

28. Boswell, "Murdock," p. 80; Leland P. Moore, "A Critical Study of the Progressive Movement in Kansas Politics from 1905 to 1936 (Master's thesis, University of Southern California, 1937), p. 27.

29. WAW, White to Morgan, 2 February 1922, White to Allen, 3 February 1922, Harrison to White, 16 February 1922, White to Harrison, 17 February 1922.

30. WAW, White to Capper, 6 November 1916, Scott to White, 24 Novem-

ber 1916, Bristow to White, 16 January 1917 and 27 May 1918, White to Harrison, ca. January 1918, White to Bristow, 20 January 1917, White to Allen, 10 May 1917, Capper to White, 25 January 1918, Dolley to White, 23 July 1918.

31. LP, Hackney to Long, 29 June 1915, Albaugh to Long, ca. December 1916; Gleed Papers, Scott to Taft, 29 September 1917, Scott to Gleed, 10 November 1917; WAW, F. D. Smith to White, 11 November 1916, Roosevelt to White, 18 December 1916 and 1 January 1917, Bristow to White, 27 May 1918.

32. In early 1917 White told Bristow that in future political battles he would help those twelve to twenty Kansas politicians who had "stuck" to the Progressive party in 1914. WAW, White to Bristow, 20 January 1917.

33. WAW, White to Allen, 10 May 1917, Albaugh to White, 2 February 1918; Jay House, "On Politicians," *Saturday Evening Post*, 30 January 1926, p. 121; *Wichita Beacon*, 13 January 1916; Harder, "Factionalism," p. 103.

34. WAW, Brewster to White, 23 January 1918, Berryman to White, 28 January 1918, Albaugh to White, 2 February 1918, J. E. Brooks to White, 2 and 14 February 1918, White to Stanley, 14 February 1918, "List of Contributors to Allen's Campaign Fund, 1918"; House, "On Politicians," pp. 25, 117–21.

35. WAW, White to Stanley, 14 February 1918, Albaugh to White, 2 February 1918; William G. Clugston, *Rascals in Democracy* (New York, 1940), p. 124; *TDC*, 29 and 30 January 1918.

36. Domenico Gagliardo, *The Kansas Industrial Court* (Lawrence, Kans., 1941), pp. 28–33. Most of the general information regarding the political activities of Allen and other Kansas political leaders who had been Progressives or progressive Republicans comes from Donald R. McCoy, *Landon of Kansas* (Lincoln, Nebr., 1966).

37. WAW, White to Curtis, 27 December 1916, 2 January 1917, and 24 May 1918, Curtis to White, 30 December 1916, 5 June 1918, and 17 August 1918.

38. William MacDonald, "The United States: Kansas in Reaction," *Nation*, 15 March 1919, p. 393; WAW, White to Murdock, 20 December 1920.

39. WAW, White to Harrison, 17 June 1915, White to R. M. McClintock, 23 February 1918, Chase to White, 7 August 1918; White, "Government of the People," pp. 188–89.

# BIBLIOGRAPHY

### Manuscript Collections

Beer Family Collection. Yale University Library, New Haven, Conn.
Albert J. Beveridge Papers. Manuscript Division, Library of Congress, Washington, D.C. (hereafter cited as MSS Div., LC).
Billard Family Papers. Manuscript Division, Kansas State Historical Society, Topeka, Kans. (hereafter cited as MSS Div., KSHS).
Joseph L. Bristow Papers. MSS Div., KSHS.
Arthur Capper Papers. MSS Div., KSHS.
Nelson I. Case Manuscripts. Library, Kansas Methodist Historical Society, Baker University, Baldwin, Kans.
Patrick Henry Coney Manuscripts. MSS Div., KSHS.
Charles Curtis Collection. MSS Div., KSHS.
John S. Dawson Manuscripts. MSS Div., KSHS.
Charles S. Gleed Papers. MSS Div., KSHS.
Edward W. Hoch Gubernatorial Papers. State Archives, KSHS.
George Hodges Manuscripts. MSS Div., KSHS.
George A. Huron Manuscripts. MSS Div., KSHS.
William Agnew Johnston Collection. MSS Div., KSHS.
Thomas B. Lillard Manuscripts. MSS Div., KSHS.
Chester I. Long Papers. MSS Div., KSHS.
Charles F. Scott Correspondence. MSS Div., KSHS.
Walter R. Stubbs Gubernatorial Papers. State Archives, KSHS.
William Howard Taft Papers. MSS Div., LC.
Eugene Fitch Ware Papers. MSS Div., KSHS.
William Allen White Manuscripts. MSS Div., LC.

### Pamphlets, Scrapbooks, and Miscellaneous Documents

Biographies Compiled by the Library. Library, KSHS.
Collected Biographical Clippings. Library, KSHS.
Democratic Campaign Literature, 1860–1928. Library, KSHS.
*Fifty Years of the Star*, pamphlet dated 18 September 1930. Library, KSHS.
*History of the City of Hutchinson and Reno County, Kansas*, pamphlet, n.d. Library, KSHS.
Joseph Kennedy Hudson Scrapbook. MSS Div., KSHS.
Kansas Biographical Pamphlets. Library, KSHS.
Kansas Collected Speeches and Pamphlets. Library, KSHS.
Kansas Day Club Clippings. Library, KSHS.
Kansas Election Returns, Elections 1908 and 1912, Special Elections 1911 and 1912, Office of the Secretary of State, Microfilm Records. State Archives, KSHS.
Kansas Governors' Miscellaneous Pamphlets. Library, KSHS.
Kansas Prohibition Pamphlets. Library, KSHS.

Legislative Documents, Miscellaneous File. Library, KSHS.
Legislature, 1905–1913, History Files. MSS Div., KSHS.
Mulvane Scrapbook. Library, KSHS.
Political Pamphlets, Portfolio. Library, KSHS.
Progressive Party Pamphlets, Campaign Literature, 1912–1914. Library, KSHS.
Railway Clippings. Library, KSHS.
Republican Campaign Literature, 1904–1912. Library, KSHS.
Republican Party, Historical Collection. MSS Div., KSHS.
Republican Party Clippings. Library, KSHS.

## Government Documents

A. United States (all printed by the Government Printing Office, Washington, D.C.).

Bureau of Corporations, Department of Commerce and Labor. *Transportation and Freight Rates in Connection with the Oil Industry*. 59th Cong., 1st sess., Senate Documents, no. 428, serial set 4915. 1906.
*Congressional Record*. 58th Cong., 2d sess. Vol. 38. 1904.
*Congressional Record*. 61st Cong., 1st and 2d sess. Vols. 44 and 45. 1909–1910.
*Congressional Record*. 62d Cong., 2d sess. Vol. 48. 1912.
*Investigation of the Department of the Interior and the Bureau of Forestry*. 13 vols. 61st Cong., 3d sess., Senate Documents, no. 719, serial set 5892–5903. 1910–1911.
*Official Opinions of the Attorneys-General of the United States*. Vol. 27. 1909.
*Thirteenth Census of the United States, 1910*. 11 vols. 1913.

B. Kansas (all printed by the State Printing Office, Topeka, Kans.).

*Fifteenth Biennial Report of the Attorney-General of Kansas, 1905–'06*. 1906.
*Sixteenth Biennial Report of the Attorney-General of Kansas, 1907–'08*. 1908.
*Seventeenth Biennial Report of the Attorney-General of Kansas, 1909–1910*. 1910.
*Eighteenth Biennial Report of the Attorney-General of Kansas, 1911–1912*. 1912.
*Nineteenth Biennial Report of the Attorney-General of Kansas, 1913–1914*. 1914.
*Fifteenth Biennial Report of the Secretary of State of the State of Kansas, 1905–'06*. 1906.
*Sixteenth Biennial Report of the Secretary of State of the State of Kansas, 1907–'08*. 1908.
*Seventeenth Biennial Report of the Secretary of State of the State of Kansas, 1909–'10*. 1910.
*Eighteenth Biennial Report of the Secretary of State of the State of Kansas, 1911–'12*. 1912.
*Nineteenth Biennial Report of the Secretary of State of the State of Kansas, 1913–'14*. 1914.
*Senate Journal: Proceedings of the Senate of the State of Kansas, 1905*. 1905.
*Senate Journal: Proceedings of the Senate of the State of Kansas, 1907*. 1907.
*Senate Journal: Proceedings of the Senate of the State of Kansas, 1909*. 1909.
*Senate Journal: Proceedings of the Senate of the State of Kansas, 1911*. 1911.
*Session Laws, State of Kansas, 1909*. 1909.
*Summary of Kansas Primary Laws, Including Non-partisan Judiciary Act*. 1913.
*First Report of the Tax Commission, State of Kansas, for the Period between July 1, 1907, and October 15, 1908*. 1908.

C. Court Reports.

*The Federal Reporter* 131. September and October 1904. St. Paul, Minn.: West Publishing Co., 1904.
*The Federal Reporter* 175. March and April 1910. St. Paul, Minn.: West Publishing Co., 1910.
*The Federal Reporter* 179. August and September 1910. St. Paul, Minn.: West Publishing Co., 1910.

The Pacific Reporter 81. 26 June through 23 October 1905. St. Paul, Minn.: West Publishing Co., 1905.

The Pacific Reporter 105. 20 December 1909 through 24 January 1910. St. Paul, Minn.: West Publishing Co., 1910.

The Pacific Reporter 125. 26 August through 23 September 1912. St. Paul, Minn.: West Publishing Co., 1912.

United States Reports 196. October Term, 1904. New York: Banks Law Publishing Co., 1905.

United States Reports 202. October Term, 1905. New York: Banks Law Publishing Co., 1906.

United States Reports 218. October Term, 1909, and October Term, 1910. New York: Banks Law Publishing Co., 1911.

United States Reports 219. October Term, 1910. New York: Banks Law Publishing Co., 1911.

United States Reports 228. October Term, 1912. New York: Banks Law Publishing Co., 1913.

### NEWSPAPERS

Of the following, only the *Topeka Daily Capital* was consulted for the entire period; the others were checked during periods when their editors or publishers would have been especially concerned with a specific event that was transpiring in their locale or within the ken of their main interests. Some newspapers used in other phases of my research are cited in the notes, but not here.

*Emporia Gazette*, 1903–1916.
*Kansas City Journal*, 1903–1910.
*Kansas City Star*, 1903–1915.
*Topeka Daily Capital*, 1900–1916.
*Topeka State Journal*, 1900–1912, 1916.
*Wichita Beacon*, 1906–1915.
*Wichita Eagle*, 1902–1913.

### PUBLISHED PAPERS, AUTOBIOGRAPHIES, AND REMINISCENCES

Bristow, Joseph L. *Fraud and Politics at the Turn of the Century: McKinley and His Administration as Seen by His Principal Patronage Dispenser and Investigator.* Edited by Joseph Q. and Frank B. Bristow. New York: Exposition Press, 1952.

Burton, Joseph R. *My Case and the Political Community of Interests.* Abilene, Kans.: Burton Publishing Co., 1908.

Butt, Archibald W. *Taft and Roosevelt: The Intimate Letters of Archie Butt.* 2 vols. New York: Doubleday, Doran & Co., 1930.

Cannon, Joseph G. *Uncle Joe Cannon: The Story of a Pioneer American, As Told to L. White Busbey.* New York: Henry Holt & Co., 1927.

Connelly, William L. *The Oil Business As I Saw It.* Norman, Okla.: University of Oklahoma Press, 1954.

Dawes, Charles G. *A Journal of the McKinley Years.* Chicago: Lakeside Press, 1950.

La Follette, Robert M. *La Follette's Autobiography: A Personal Narrative of Political Experiences.* Madison, Wis.: The Robert M. La Follette Co., 1913.

Leland, Cyrus. "My Recollections," *Kansas City Star*, 26 January, 2, 9, 16, and 23 February, 2, 9, 16, and 23 March 1913.

Roosevelt, Theodore. *The Letters of Theodore Roosevelt.* Selected and edited by Elting E. Morison. 8 vols. Cambridge, Mass.: Harvard University Press, 1951–1954.

White, William Allen. *The Autobiography of William Allen White.* New York: The Macmillan Co., 1946.

### BOOKS

Abrams, Richard M. *Conservatism in a Progressive Era: Massachusetts Politics, 1900–1912.* Cambridge, Mass.: Harvard University Press, 1964.

*Addresses Delivered at the Fourteenth Annual Banquet of the Kansas Day Club, 1905.* Clay Center, Kans.: Press of the Times, 1905.

Bar Association of the State of Kansas.

Nineteenth Annual Meeting of the Bar Association of the State of Kansas, Topeka, Jan. 30–31. Clay Center, Kans.: Press of the Times, 1902.

———. Proceedings of the Bar Association, 1912, Twenty-ninth Annual Meeting, Topeka, Jan. 30–31, 1912. Topeka: n.p., 1912.

Blocker, John G. The Guaranty of State Bank Deposits. Kansas Studies in Business, no. 11. Lawrence, Kans.: Bureau of Business Research, School of Business, University of Kansas, 1929.

Blum, John M. The Republican Roosevelt. Cambridge, Mass.: Harvard University Press, 1954.

Bolles, Blair. Tyrant from Illinois: Uncle Joe Cannon's Experiment with Personal Power. New York: W. W. Norton & Co., 1951.

Bright, John D., ed. Kansas: The First Century. 4 vols. New York: Lewis Historical Publishing Co., 1956.

Cabe, June G., and Sullivant, Charles A. Kansas Votes: National Elections, 1859–1956. Lawrence: Governmental Research Center, University of Kansas, 1957.

Clanton, O. Gene. Kansas Populism: Ideas and Men. Lawrence, Kans.: University Press of Kansas, 1969.

Clugston, William G. Rascals in Democracy. New York: Richard R. Smith, 1940.

Coletta, Paolo E. William Jennings Bryan. 3 vols. Lincoln, Nebr.: University of Nebraska Press, 1964–1969.

Connelley, William E., ed. A Standard History of Kansas and Kansans. 5 vols. Chicago and New York: Lewis Publishing Co., 1918.

Ewy, Marvin. Charles Curtis of Kansas: Vice President of the United States, 1929–1933. Emporia State Research Studies, vol. 10, no. 2. Emporia, Kans.: Graduate Division of the Kansas State Teachers College, 1961.

Gagliardo, Domenico. The Kansas Industrial Court. Lawrence, Kans.: University of Kansas Press, 1941.

Garraty, John A. Right-hand Man: The Life of George W. Perkins. New York: Harper & Brothers, 1960.

Glaab, Charles N. Kansas City and the Railroads: Community Policy in the Growth of a Regional Metropolis. Madison, Wis.: State Historical Society of Wisconsin, 1962.

Gwinn, William Rea. Uncle Joe Cannon: Archfoe of Insurgency. New York: Bookman Associates, 1957.

Hechler, Kenneth W. Insurgency: Personalities and Politics of the Taft Era. New York: Columbia University Press, 1940.

Hicks, John D. The Populist Revolt: A History of the Farmers' Alliance and the People's Party. Minneapolis, Minn.: University of Minnesota Press, 1931.

Hidy, Ralph W., and Hidy, Muriel E. History of Standard Oil Company. Vol. 1. Pioneering in Big Business, 1882–1911. New York: Harper & Brothers, 1955.

Hofstadter, Richard. The Age of Reform. New York: Random House, 1955.

Ise, John. The United States Oil Policy. New Haven, Conn.: Yale University Press, 1926.

Isely, Bliss, and Richards, W. M. Four Centuries in Kansas. Wichita, Kans.: McCormick-Mathers Co., 1936.

Jessup, Philip C. Elihu Root. 2 vols. New York: Dodd, Mead & Co., 1938.

Johnson, Walter. William Allen White's America. New York: Henry Holt & Co., 1947.

Kansas Editorial Association. Proceedings of the Kansas Editorial Association, Fifteenth Annual Session. Topeka: Tribune Printing Co., 1907.

Kolko, Gabriel. Railroads and Regulations, 1877–1916. Princeton, N.J.: Princeton University Press, 1965.

———. The Triumph of Conservatism: A Reinterpretation of American History, 1900–1916. New York: Free Press of Glencoe, 1963.

Link, Arthur S. Wilson: The Road to the White House. Princeton, N.J.: Princeton University Press, 1947.

Lowitt, Richard. George W. Norris: The

*Making of a Progressive, 1861–1912.* Syracuse, N.Y.: Syracuse University Press, 1963.

Lutz, Harley L. *The State Tax Commission: A Study of the Development and Results of State Control over the Assessment of Property for Taxation.* Cambridge, Mass.: Harvard University Press, 1918.

McCoy, Donald R. *Landon of Kansas.* Lincoln, Nebr.: University of Nebraska Press, 1966.

Malin, James C. *A Concern about Humanity.* Lawrence, Kans.: James C. Malin, 1964.

———. *Confounded Rot about Napoleon.* Lawrence, Kans.: James C. Malin, 1961.

———. *The Contriving Brain and the Skillful Hand in the United States.* Lawrence, Kans.: James C. Malin, 1955.

Maxwell, Robert S. *La Follette and the Rise of the Progressives in Wisconsin.* Madison, Wis.: State Historical Society of Wisconsin, 1956.

Merriam, Charles E., and Overacker, Louise. *Primary Elections.* Chicago: University of Chicago Press, 1928.

Miller, William D. *Memphis during the Progressive Era, 1900–1917.* Memphis, Tenn.: Memphis State University Press, 1957.

Mowry, George E. *The California Progressives.* Berkeley, Calif.: University of California Press, 1951.

———. *The Era of Theodore Roosevelt and the Birth of Modern America, 1900–1912.* New York: Harper Brothers, 1958.

———. *Theodore Roosevelt and the Progressive Movement.* Madison, Wis.: University of Wisconsin Press, 1946.

*The National Cyclopaedia of American Biography.* New York: J. T. White & Co., 1910.

Nevins, Allan. *John D. Rockefeller: The Heroic Age of American Enterprise.* 2 vols. New York: Charles Scribner's Sons, 1940.

Noble, Ransom E., Jr. *New Jersey Progressivism before Wilson.* Princeton, N.J.: Princeton University Press, 1946.

Nugent, Walter T. K. *The Tolerant Populists: Kansas Populism and Nativism.* Chicago: University of Chicago Press, 1963.

Nye, Russell B. *Midwestern Progressive Politics: A Historical Study of Its Origins and Development, 1870–1950.* East Lansing, Mich.: Michigan State College Press, 1951.

Pringle, Henry F. *The Life and Times of William Howard Taft: A Biography.* 2 vols. New York: Farrar & Rinehart, 1939.

Pulley, Raymond H. *Old Virginia Restored: An Interpretation of the Progressive Impulse, 1870–1930.* Charlottesville, Va.: University Press of Virginia, 1968.

Quint, Howard H.; Cantor, Milton; and Albertson, Dean. *Main Problems in American History.* 3d ed. 2 vols. Homewood, Ill.: Dorsey Press, 1972.

Richardson, Elmo R. *The Politics of Conservation: Crusades and Controversies, 1897–1913.* Berkeley, Calif.: University of California Press, 1962.

Ripley, William Z. *Railroads: Rates and Regulation.* New York: Longmans, Green, & Co., 1912.

Sageser, A. Bower. *Joseph L. Bristow: Kansas Progressive.* Lawrence, Kans.: University Press of Kansas, 1968.

Saloutos, Theodore, and Hicks, John D. *Agricultural Discontent in the Middle West, 1900–1939.* Madison, Wis.: University of Wisconsin Press, 1951.

Socolofsky, Homer E. *Arthur Capper: Publisher, Politician, and Philanthropist.* Lawrence, Kans.: University of Kansas Press, 1962.

Stene, Edwin O. *Railroad Commission to Corporation Commission: A Study in Kansas Administrative History.* Lawrence, Kans.: Bureau of Government Research, University of Kansas, 1945.

Stephenson, Nathaniel W. *Nelson W. Aldrich: A Leader in American Politics.* New York: Charles Scribner's Sons, 1930.

Timberlake, James H. *Prohibition and the Progressive Movement, 1900-1920.* Cambridge, Mass.: Harvard University Press, 1963.

Warner, Hoyt L. *Progressivism in Ohio, 1897-1917.* Columbus, Ohio: Ohio State University Press, 1964.

Wiebe, Robert H. *The Search for Order, 1877-1920.* New York: Hill and Wang, 1967.

Zornow, William F. *Kansas: A History of the Jayhawk State.* Norman, Okla.: University of Oklahoma Press, 1957.

ARTICLES

Abbot, Ernest H. "The Progressive Convention." *Outlook,* 17 August 1912, pp. 857-64.

Allen, Henry J. "Destruction of Kansas." *FRA: A Magazine of Business Inspiration,* April 1915, p. 32.

―――. "An Interview with Senator Borah." *Collier's,* 11 December 1915, pp. 11-12, 21-23.

Blythe, Samuel G. "A Red-headed Quaker: Being an Account of Some of the Activities of Walter Roscoe Stubbs." *Saturday Evening Post,* 19 November 1910, pp. 7-8, 52-53.

Byers, O. P. "Kansas Interstate Freight Rates." *Kansas Magazine* 3 (February 1910):31-32.

―――. "Kansas Intrastate Freight Rates." *Kansas Magazine* 3 (January 1910):16-18.

―――. "Kansas Jobber Rates." *Kansas Magazine* 2 (December 1909):34-36.

"The Case of the Kansas Electors." *Outlook,* 10 August 1912, p. 795.

Clark, Robert, Jr. "Breaking Up a State Machine." *Cosmopolitan,* October 1904, pp. 665-70.

Codding, J. K., and Hoch, E. W. "Prohibition in Kansas." *Annals of the American Academy of Political and Social Science* 32 (November 1908): 97-103.

Davenport, Frederick M. "On the Trail of Progress and Reaction in the West: Slowing Up and Slowing Down—Nebraska and Kansas." *Outlook,* 12 May 1915, pp. 94-99.

Davis, Oscar King. "Senator Bristow's Views on Present Political Conditions." *Outlook,* 30 March 1912, pp. 725-29.

Driscoll, Charles B. "Kansas in Labor." *American Mercury,* March 1929, pp. 339-46.

"Following the Campaign." *Outlook,* 27 July 1912, pp. 663-68, and 24 August 1912, pp. 912-16.

Gagliardo, Domenico. "Development of Common and Employers' Liability Law in Kansas." *Kansas Historical Quarterly* 10 (May 1941):155-74.

―――. "The First Kansas Workmen's Compensation Law." *Kansas Historical Quarterly* 9 (November 1940):384-97.

Gatlin, Dana. "'What I Am Trying to Do': An Interview with Hon. W. R. Stubbs." *World's Work,* May 1912, pp. 59-67.

Hamilton, W. L. "The Stag at Eve." *Bulletin of the Shawnee County Historical Society,* no. 40 (December 1963), pp. 49-52.

Harger, Charles M. "Kansas' Battle for Its Oil Interests." *American Monthly Review of Reviews,* April 1905, pp. 471-74.

―――. "Lessons in Nation-Building: Kansas Progressive, but Prudent." *World To-Day,* October 1911, pp. 1206-10.

―――. "The Middle West and Wall Street." *American Monthly Review of Reviews,* July 1907, pp. 83-86.

―――. "A New Business Alliance." *North American Review,* September 1897, pp. 380-83.

"The 'Harmony' Campaign." *Santa Fe Employes' Magazine* 4 (November 1910):73-75.

Hoch, Edward W. "Advancement and Prosperity of Kansas." *Earth* 3 (January 1906):3.

―――. "Kansas and the Standard Oil Company." *Independent,* 2 March 1905, pp. 461-63.

―――. "The Success of Prohibition in

Kansas." *Annals of the American Academy of Political and Social Science* 32 (November 1908):104–5.

House, Jay. "On Politicians." *Saturday Evening Post*, 30 January 1926, pp. 25, 117–21.

Ickes, Harold L. "Who Killed the Progressive Party." *American Historical Review* 46 (January 1941):306–37.

Isely, Bliss. "The Big Boss and the Boss Busters." *Kansas Teacher* 66 (February 1958):20–22, 47.

"Kansas, President Ripley, Governor Stubbs and Hobo Employees." *Santa Fe Employes' Magazine* 4 (November 1910):65–72.

A Kansas Progressive Republican. "How I Was Converted—Politically." *Outlook*, 17 December 1910, pp. 857–59.

La Forte, Robert S. "Theodore Roosevelt's Osawatomie Speech." *Kansas Historical Quarterly* 32 (Summer 1966):187–200.

Lockwood, Frank C. "Senator Bristow, of Kansas." *Outlook*, 21 November 1908, pp. 617–21.

MacAdam, Hastings. "The Insurgents: The Story of the Leaders Who Fought and Won against the Machine Control of Congress." *Everybody's Magazine*, June 1912, pp. 770–81.

MacDonald, William. "The New United States: Kansas in Reaction." *Nation*, 15 March 1919, pp. 393–94.

Marcosson, Isaac F. "Barring Out the Stock Thieves." *Munsey's Magazine*, February 1912, pp. 674–81.

———. "The Kansas Oil Fight." *World's Work*, May 1905, pp. 6155–66.

Mason, Walt. "Senator Bristow, of Kansas." *American Magazine*, October 1909, pp. 556–58.

Matson, Clarence H. "Joseph L. Bristow: The Argus of the Post-Office Department." *American Monthly Review of Reviews*, January 1904, pp. 45–48.

Miller, Raymond C. "The Background of Populism in Kansas." *Missouri Valley Historical Review* 11 (March 1925):469–89.

"Mr. Roosevelt on the Future of the Progressive Party." *Outlook*, 23 November 1912, pp. 597–98.

Mowry, George E. "Theodore Roosevelt and the Election of 1910." *Missouri Valley Historical Review* 25 (March 1939):523–34.

Mumford, John K. "The Land of Opportunity: How Kansas Has Enriched Her Farmers." *Harpers Weekly*, 26 September 1908, pp. 24–25, 30.

Murdock, Victor. "After Cannonism—What?" *Independent*, 22 September 1910, pp. 622–25.

———. "Cannon and Cannonism." *Kansas Magazine* 2 (November 1909):14–17.

———. "A Congressman's First Bill." *American Magazine*, October 1908, pp. 545–50.

———. "A Congressman's First Speech." *American Magazine*, August 1908, pp. 406–11.

———. "The False Divisor." *Kansas Magazine* 1 (January 1909):9–12.

———. "The Insurgent Movement in Congress." *North American Review*, April 1910, pp. 510–16.

"Murdock: 'The Red Insurgent.'" *Current Literature*, February 1910, pp. 149–50.

Nathan, Meyer. "The Election of 1916 in Kansas." *Kansas Historical Quarterly* 35 (Spring 1969):50–63.

Nemo. "Men and Things." *Kansas Magazine* 4 (August 1910):18–19 and 4 (September and October 1910):49–51.

Oakison, J. M. "Long of Kansas: The Third in a Series of Studies of Senate Undesirables, Showing Why 'Joe' Bristow Should Be Sent to the United States Senate to Replace Chester I. Long." *Collier's*, 11 July 1908, pp. 8–9, 22.

Ogden, George W. "How Kansas Was 'Rolled.'" *Appleton's Book Lovers Magazine*, September 1905, pp. 337–44.

"Open Letter to Governor Stubbs, A. J. Ewing to Stubbs." *Santa Fe Employes' Magazine* 4 (November 1910):59–60.

Payne, Will. "How Kansas Drove Out a

Set of Thieves." *Saturday Evening Post,* 2 December 1911, pp. 3–5, 71–72.

Phillips, David Graham. "The Treason of the Senate." *Cosmopolitan,* March 1906, pp. 487–502; April 1906, pp. 628–38.

Powell, John L. "The Freight Rate Problem." *Kansas Magazine* 2 (July 1909): 14–17.

"The Presidential Campaign: Mr. La Follette's Withdrawal." *Outlook,* 17 February 1912, p. 337.

"The Revolt against the Machine in Kansas." *Outlook,* 9 April 1904, pp. 858–59.

Roosevelt, Theodore. "The Orchestra Hall Speech: Theodore Roosevelt's Address Accepting the Nomination of the New Party." *Outlook,* 29 June 1912, pp. 479–80.

Schruben, Francis W. "The Kansas State Refinery Law of 1905." *Kansas Historical Quarterly* 34 (Autumn 1968):299–324.

"A Senator Convicted." *Outlook,* 9 April 1904, p. 858.

Shaw, William B. "The Direct Primary on Trial." *Outlook,* 24 October 1908, pp. 383–89.

Smith, F. Dumont. "The Real Victor Murdock." *Kansas Magazine* 4 (November 1910):33–36.

"Some Taps." *Kansas Knocker: A Journal for Cranks* 1 (July 1900): unnumbered page, KSHS library.

Sorensen, Willis C. "The Kansas National Forest, 1905–1915." *Kansas Historical Quarterly* 35 (Winter 1969):386–95.

Stubbs, Walter R. " 'Mob Rule' in Kansas." *Saturday Evening Post,* 11 May 1912, pp. 6–7, 54–56.

———. "Opening Address, Delivered in University Hall, September 8, 1905." *Graduate Magazine of the University of Kansas* 4 (October 1905):1–8.

———. "Public Ownership of Railroads, Waterways, and Water Power." *Saturday Evening Post,* 6 June 1914, pp. 3–5, 28–33.

Todd, John H. "Insurgency in Kansas: An Analysis of the Political Situation in the Sunflower State." *Voter* 89 (September 1910):43–47.

A Washington Journalist. "Men We Are Watching." *Independent,* 3 March 1910, pp. 473–76.

White, William Allen. "Free Kansas: Where the People Rule the People." *Outlook,* 24 February 1912, pp. 407–14.

———. "Government of the People, by the People, for the People." *Independent,* 7 February 1916, pp. 187–90.

———. "How Kansas Boarded the Water Wagon." *Saturday Evening Post,* 11 July 1914, pp. 3–5, 44–45.

———. "Political Signs of Promise." *Outlook,* 15 July 1905, pp. 667–70.

———. "Why I Am a Progressive." *Saturday Evening Post,* 23 April 1921, pp. 3–4, 52–54.

"Who's Who—And Why: Serious and Frivolous Facts about the Great and the Near Great, the Baron of Kansas City." *Saturday Evening Post,* 26 November 1910, pp. 21–22.

DISSERTATIONS AND THESES

Angell, Wayne D. "A Century of Commercial Banking in Kansas, 1856 to 1956." Ph.D. dissertation, University of Kansas, 1957.

Boswell, Lenis. "The Political Career of Victor Murdock, 1911–1917." Master's thesis, University of Kansas, 1949.

Brodhead, Michael J. "The Early Career of E. W. Hoch, 1870–1904." Master's thesis, University of Kansas, 1962.

Callis, George. "A History of the Progressive Party in Kansas." Master's thesis, Kansas State Teachers College, Pittsburg, 1933.

Dimmitt, Albert. "The Progressive Party in Kansas, 1911–1917." Master's thesis, University of Kansas, 1958.

Edwards, Anna M. "The Congressional Career of Victor Murdock, 1903–1909." Master's thesis, University of Kansas, 1947.

Ewing, Morgan R. "Charles F. Scott: His Decade in Congress." Master's thesis, University of Kansas, 1951.

Flory, Raymond L. "The Political Career of Chester I. Long." Ph.D. dissertation, University of Kansas, 1955.

Harder, Marvin A. "Some Aspects of Republican and Democratic Party Factionalism in Kansas." Ph.D. dissertation, Columbia University, 1959.

Lyerla, Walter S. "The History and Development of Public Utility Regulation in Kansas." Ph.D. dissertation, State University of Iowa, 1936.

Mitchell, William H. "Joseph L. Bristow: Kansas Insurgent in the U.S. Senate, 1909–1915." Master's thesis, University of Kansas, 1952.

Moore, Leland P. "A Critical Study of the Progressive Movement in Kansas Politics from 1908 to 1936." Master's thesis, University of Southern California, 1937.

Pringle, Jack B. "The Congressional Career of Edmond H. Madison, 1907–1911." Master's thesis, University of Kansas, 1955.

Svenson, Karl A. "The Effect of Popular Discontent on Political Parties in Kansas." Ph.D. dissertation, State University of Iowa, 1948.

Tolin, Corabelle. "The Political Career of J. R. Burton." Master's thesis, University of Kansas, 1940.

Tuttle, Lillian. "The Congressional Career of Victor Murdock, 1909–1911." Master's thesis, University of Kansas, 1948.

# INDEX

Adams, Franklin S. (Waterville mayor), 117
Addams, Jane, and Kansas Progressives, 1912, 197
agriculture in Kansas, 10-11
Akers, Earl (candidate for state treasurer), 193, 194, 197
Albaugh, Mort: associate of Leland, 20; manages Long's 1902 campaign, 22-23, 26; prepares 1902 state slate, 24; reports to Long, 31; objects to newspaper criticism, 33; backs Pollock, 34; and 1904 election, 38; advisor to Long, 42; and 1904 state convention, 43-44; leads Long's forces, 74; and 1906 convention, 74-75; and 1907 Kansas Speakership, 82; opposes party primary, 92; and Long's 1908 campaign, 100, 101, 106; on Stubbs's 1909 record, 126-27; deserts party's 1910 nominees, 179, 180; and Curtis's 1912 campaign, 192; and 1912 electors, 196; on 1914 platform, 239; and reuniting of Progressive and Republican parties, 251-52; supports Allen, 258-59; dies, 1918, 259; mentioned, 41, 93, 94, 137, 144, 223
Aldrich, Nelson (Rhode Island senator): Bristow opposes, 106, 175; and tariff, 148-52, 154; and Mann-Elkins bill, 157; 1910 Kansas platform condemns, 177; mentioned, 155, 159
Allen, Henry J.: supports Long, 28; 1903 candidate for state printer, 28-29; attacks Republican League, 33-34; removed from Board of Charities, 73, 164; and public-utilities bill, 122, 133; and progressive Republicans, 164; converted by Billy Sunday, 164, 230; at 1912 Republican convention, 186-87; and 1912 Progressive National Convention, 188; and Roosevelt's 1912 campaign, 194; at Roosevelt's December 1912 conference, 210; and Kansas Progressive party, 213, 215, 224, 225, 228, 230, 249-50; and Chautauqua debates with Scott, 219-20; his 1914 gubernatorial campaign, 226, 230-31, 233, 238, 241-44, 246; on Bristow, 227; at Progressive council, 240; loses in 1914, 244; asked to join Democrats, 250-51; asked to rejoin Republican party, 251; supports Roosevelt's candidacy, 251-53; on 1916 election, 256; Republican leader, 257; supported by White, 258; wins 1918 Republican gubernatorial nomination, 259; elected governor, 1918 and 1920, 259; fills Curtis's unexpired Senate term, 1929, 259; loses 1930 Senate election, 259; admits Progressivism dead, 260; mentioned, 4, 184
Anthony, Daniel R., Jr. (congressman): favors primary, 92; pro-Cannon, 143; on tariff, 153; and Mann-Elkins bill, 158; his 1910 campaign, 167, 171, 175, 181; opposes 1910 platform, 177; his 1912 campaign, 191-92, 206; as a progressive, 210-11; supports Bristow, 223; mentioned, 170
antitrust legislation: progressives support, 8; in Taft administration, 155; in 1912 Progressive platform, 188-89, 232; Roosevelt's position on, 200, 201; Bryan's position on, 200; Wilson's position on, 200; Hodges favors, 206; Clayton Antitrust Law, 219

307

"Armageddon," Theodore Roosevelt and, 134, 186, 229–46, 254
Armstrong, T. B. (investigator), on dairy trust, 117–18

Bailey, Joseph W. (Texas senator), 28
Bailey, Willis J.: Leland protégé, 17, 21–22; and Horton Agreement, 17–18; elected governor, 1902, 21–25; congressman-at-large, 1899–1901, 22; and 1903 state printership deal, 29; scandals in his administration, 32–34; railroads oppose, 35; Kansas Republican League opposes, 37, 72; withdraws from 1904 campaign, 38; railroad lawyers support, 61; 1902 nominee, 72; 1906 senatorial candidate, 82; in 1908 primary, 99; supports Allen, 1918, 258; mentioned, 41
Baker, Lucien (senator), 18, 19
Baker, Ray Stannard, 68
Ballinger, Richard A. (U.S. secretary of interior): Taft supports, 136; his controversy with Pinchot, 142, 145; committee to investigate, 142; mentioned, 154, 155, 166
Bank Deposit Guaranty Law: repealed, 3; issue of, 92; in 1908 platform, 109; Stubbs supports, 123, 170; passed, 1909, 123–24; Supreme Court upholds, 123–24, 125–26; mentioned, 262
bankers, state and national compared, 124
Bankers' Deposit Guaranty and Surety Co., 125
Barnes, Charles W. (superintendent of insurance), 125
Bear, Simon (telephone lobbyist), 132, 169
Beer, William C. (railroad, insurance lobbyist), 26–27
Benson, A. W. (senator), 80, 81
Bering River coal field, 146
Berryman, J. W. (banker), 124, 125
Beveridge, Albert J. (Indiana senator): tariff revisionist, 155; his 1910 defeat, 180; 1912 Kansas appearance, 197; and Progressive party founding, 211, 218; speaker at 1914 Lincoln Day meeting, 231; mentioned, 153
Billard, J. B. (gubernatorial candidate), 204, 205, 243
Bishop, J. L. (of Square Deal Club), 77

Blair, R. W. (railroad lobbyist), 65, 66
Blaker, B. F. (Taft elector), 193
Blomberg, E. L. (labor leader), 193
Blonecker, J. G. (Republican League president), 50
Blue-Sky Investment Law, 109, 134, 262
Bonaparte, Charles J. (U.S. attorney general), 124
Bone, Harry J. (district attorney), 144, 160
Borah, William E. (Idaho senator), 102, 155
Boss Busters League: tries to dethrone Leland, 13, 14, 21, 31; organizes, Topeka, 1899, 17, 260; inactive, 1900, 20–21; revived, 1901, 21; dies, 30; mentioned, 35, 202
Botkin, Jeremiah (gubernatorial candidate), 109
Bourne, Jonathan (Iowa senator), 135
Bowers, Lloyd Wheaton (U.S. solicitor general), 154
Bramlette, Sim (labor leader), 193, 203
Branine, C. E. (judge), 190–91
Breese, A. M. (Progressive), 255
Breidenthal, John (banker), 11, 13
Brewster, S. M. (state senator), 131, 259
Bristow, Joseph L.: and 1902 senatorial election, 27; and Burton case, 39; and discriminatory railroad rates, 57–58, 104; and Kansas Civic Voters League, 68–69; splits with Long faction, 74; and Square Deal Club, 77; his 1906 senatorial campaign, 80, 81; asks special session, 88; and progressive Republican faction, 89; and 1908 compromise with Stubbs, 90; opposes convention system, 92; supports primary law, 93, 95; his 1908 senatorial campaign, 95, 99, 100, 106, 110, 260; his personality, 96; his Post Office service, 96–97; his investigations, 97; his opportunism, 103; debates Long, 106–7; wins 1908 primary, 108; and 1908 platform, 109; and Taft's patronage, 113, 159–61, 283 n69; on Speaker's powers, 129; and initiative, 131; on Taft, 135, 136, 148; and insurgency, 141; protects Madison, 144; and tariff, 148–53, 214, 282 n42; supports income tax, 152; favors antitrust prosecutions,

155; on postal services, 155–56, 283 n58; and Mann-Elkins bill, 157–58; and Allen, 164; and 1910 election, 166, 170–77, 180, 182; attacks Cannonism, Aldrichism, 175; attends Taft's 1910 harmony meeting, 181; endorses National Progressive Republican League, 181; on La Follette's candidacy, 182–83; and 1912 Republican National Convention, 186; opposes bolt, third party, 186, 187, 189; and 1912 Progressive National Convention, 188; speaks for Roosevelt, 197; on 1912 vote, 207; and Progressive party, 211–12, 215, 216, 218, 219, 221–26; his positions on tariff, etc., 214; remains a Republican, 226–29; his 1914 campaign, 232–38; loses 1914 primary, 236, 238, 292 n14, then supports Curtis, 238, 242; on Kansas public utilities commission, 248–49; loses 1918 senatorial election, 257–58; moves to D.C. area, 257; his amendment to U.S. Constitution, 261; and Wilson, 291 n28; mentioned, 4, 18, 75, 121, 251

Broderick, Case (congressman), 17

Brown, John: Roosevelt's Osawatomie speech about, 177–78

Brown, William C. (of New York Central), 157

Bryan, William Jennings: speeches of, 2; his influence in Kansas, 52; supports bank deposit insurance, 124; and 1912 Democratic platform, 200; and 1908 election, 201; Bristow on, 219; mentioned, 13, 19, 139

Buckman, G. H. (Kansas Speaker), 129, 130

Bull Moose party. See Progressive party; Theodore Roosevelt

Bureau of Corporations Act, 26

Burrows, J. R. (state treasurer), 43

Burton, Joseph R.: Leland opposes, 16; and Boss Busters League, 18; accused of accepting bribe, 1889, 19; loses 1892 congressional election, 19; loses 1894, 1896 senatorial elections, 19; chairman 1898 Republican state convention, 19; wins 1900 senatorial election, 20; opposes Leland, 21; supports Troutman, 23; and 1902 senatorial election, 24, 27; convicted of bribery, resigns from Senate, 28, 40, 74, 80; as party conciliator, 30; and railroads, 34; and Hoch, 37–38; indicted, 39; imprisoned, 40, 73, 80; Curtis replaces, 83; mentioned, 31, 72

Calderhead, William A. (congressman), 149–51, 153, 170, 172, 181

Caldwell, J. L. (Democrat), 180

Campaign Expenditures Law, 109, 123, 127, 261

Campbell, Philip P. (congressman): requests investigation of Standard Oil, 50; his 1906 senatorial candidacy, 80; opposes Norris's resolution, 143; on tariff, 150, 153; his 1910 renomination, 170–71, 175, 181; opposes 1910 platform, 177; wins 1912 election, 206

Canadian Reciprocity, 182, 286 n52

Cannon, Joseph G. (U.S. Speaker): struggle to unseat, 136–42; reelected Speaker, 141, 143; and tariff revision, 148–49; and insurgents, 154, 163; and Mann-Elkins bill, 157; his 1910 Kansas tour, 173; on Chautauqua circuit, 174–75; 1910 Kansas platform condemns, 177; on Murdock, 246; mentioned, 9, 62, 129, 155, 170, 172

"Cannonism," 127, 155, 175

Capper, Arthur: and Santa Fe advertising, 63; and Square Deal Club, 77; and Stone, 130; dislikes Payne-Aldrich Act, 153; and progressive Republicans, 164; heralds National Progressive Republican League, 181; won't support La Follette, 182; and Roosevelt's candidacy, 184; opposes 1912 bolt, 186, 187; his 1912 gubernatorial campaign, 191–92, 207, 209, 213; supports Roosevelt, 198, 205; defeated, 1912, 202, 204, 206; favors prohibition, woman suffrage, 205; and Progressive party, 215–16, 218–19, 221–24; remains a Republican, 224–25, 227, 229, 243; his 1914 gubernatorial campaign, 233, 235–37, 241–43; wins, 238, 245; and 1914 platform, 239, 241, 244; and Bristow appointment, 248; his progressive legislation, 249; won't help Hughes, 256; his 1918 senatorial candi-

dacy, 257; wins, 258; mentioned, 4, 251
Carey, Emerson (state senator), 128
Case, Nelson I. (judge), 34, 61, 85, 136
Chandler, C. Q. (banker), 125
Chase, Harold (editor), 77, 89, 90, 153, 182, 187
Chautauqua tours, 174, 175, 219–20
child-labor laws, 203, 231, 241
cigarettes, sales banned, 133, 261
Clapp, Moses (Minnesota senator), 155, 194
Clark, George (state printer), 4, 28, 29, 34, 38
Clark, James Beauchamp ("Champ") (U.S. Speaker), 9, 141
Clarke, C. S. (of Missouri Pacific), 117
Clayton Antitrust Law, 219
coal: Kansas production of, 11; producers oppose tariff revision, 107; strikes, 115, 259
Coburn, F. D. (Kansas secretary of agriculture), 81
Cochems, Henry (Wisconsin Progressive), 213
Cochrane, Alexander G. (Missouri Pacific general solicitor), 23, 26, 28, 105, 265 n27
Cochrane, W. S. (of Midland Brick Co.), 60
Codding, J. K. (of Kansas State Temperance Union), 86
Cole, George (gubernatorial candidate), 23–24
Coleman, C. C. (Kansas attorney general), 23, 33, 50
Coney, Patrick Henry (Kansas G.A.R. official), 17, 202
congressional districts, Kansas: maps of, 138 (1898–1906), 139 (1906–1930); reapportioned, 1905, 138
congressional rules, 9, 243, 244
"Contract with the People," Progressives', 189, 200, 248
corporation tax, 152, 153
county government, progressives' stand on reorganization of, 241, 243–44
Court of Visitation Law, 53
Cowgill, E. G. (professor of economics), 65
Craddock, W. H. (gubernatorial candidate), 21

Cranston, Arthur (congressional candidate), 171
Creech, J. W. (state representative), 82
Crummer, S. C. (Republican state chairman), 77
Cuban Reciprocity, 150
Cummins, Albert (Iowa senator), 135, 155, 158, 175
Cunningham coal claims, 146
Curtis, Charles: elected to Congress, 17 (1898), 18 (1900); his 1902 senatorial campaign, 24; railroads support, 25, 64, 84; defeated, 28, 29; Mulvane supports, 73; and 1906 state convention, 74, 75; wins 1907 senatorial election, 80–83, 90; described, 83; Long supports, 99, 102; and Bristow, over federal appointments, 113; supports corporation tax, 152, 153; and Mann-Elkins bill, 158; and Taft's patronage, 159–61; in 1910 campaign, 166–68, 170–71, 174, 176, 177; opposes platform, 177; his unsuccessful 1912 campaign, 191–92, 193, 202; his successful 1914 campaign, 223, 227, 232, 234–37, 239, 241, 242, 244, 246, 251, 261; advocates protective farm tariff, 236; Bristow supports, 238; becomes vice-president, 1929, 259; reconciled with White, 259–60; mentioned, 91

dairy trust, 117–18
Dale, David M. (gubernatorial candidate), 44
Dalzell, John (Pennsylvania congressman), 149
Davenport, Frederick M. (journalist), 249
Davidson, C. L. (of Wichita Chamber of Commerce), 69, 77
Davies, Samuel A. (Roosevelt elector), 193
Davis, J. W. (state representative), 132
Davis, O. K. (writer), 183
Dawes Commission of the Five Civilized Tribes, 29
Dawson, John R. (Kansas attorney general), 113–15, 190
Debs, Eugene V., 202
Democratic party: coalition with Populists, Silver Republicans, 13; in 1894 election, 16; its 1914 platform, 241

Dillingham, W. P. (Senate Judiciary Committee chairman), 160
Dingley tariff, 106
Dixon, Joseph (senator), 223, 253
Dolley, Jonathan N.: state representative, 43; state senator, 77; Troutman replaces in Square Deal Club, 87; opposes convention system, 91–92; Republican state chairman, 112; Kansas Speaker, 112; and Bank Deposit Guaranty Law, 126; defeated, 1910, 181; joins Progressives, 217; mentioned, 134
Doster, Frank (judge), 8

economy in government, 8, 239, 244
eleemosynary institutions, Kansas, 46, 123, 127, 130, 262
"Elephadonks," 175
Elward, Rodney (La Folletteite), 211, 235
employer's liability legislation, 115–16, 262
Esch-Townshend bill, 67, 98

factionalism in Kansas Republican party, 1904–1906, 30–51
Farmers' Alliance, 70
Farmers' Free List, 182, 286 n52
Farrelley, Hugh (senatorial candidate), 203
Faxon, Ralph (Long's aide), 64, 100, 168, 265 n11
Federal Deposit Insurance Corporation, 4, 124, 262
Federal Reserve Act, 219
Federal Trade Commission Act, 219
female suffrage. See woman suffrage
Fisher, Walter (U.S. secretary of interior), 148
Fitzgerald, W. J. (lieutenant governor), 75, 128, 169
Fitzpatrick, Sam (Standard Oil attorney), 258–59
Folk, Joseph W. (U.S. district attorney), 39, 121
Fordney, Joseph (Michigan congressman), 149
free silver, 25, 178
Fusionists, 13, 16, 17, 19

Ganse, H. E. (state senator), 130
Garfield, James R. (Bureau of Corporations chief), 50, 146, 194

George, J. S. (Kansas Federation of Commercial Interests president), 42, 56–57, 59, 68
Getty, James F. (state senator), 80
Gilmore, John (Roosevelt elector), 193
Glavis, Louis (Interior Department employee), 146
Gleed, Charles S.: in 1902 senatorial election, 27; and Standard Oil, 48; and railroad influence on his *Kansas City Journal*, 62–65, 270 n26; defends 1907 legislature, 84; fears primary law, 91; and Long's 1908 campaign, 100–101; as Santa Fe spokesman, 116; on Taft, 163; and 1912 election, 199; his 1914 stand on Bristow, 227; supports Allen, 1918, 258; mentioned, 249, 250
Gleed, J. Willis (lobbyist), 122, 126
Gore, Thomas P. (Oklahoma senator), 175
Gould, George (of Missouri Pacific), 116, 117
Guggenheims, 147
Guyer, U. S. (Kansas City, Kansas, progressive), 176

Hackney, William P. (attorney), 15, 91, 213
Hadley, Herbert (Missouri governor), 212
Hanna, Mark (senator), 15–16, 21, 96
Harding, Warren G., 259, 260
Harger, Charles (editor), 58
Harris, Ralph (journalist), 194
Harris, William A. (senator), 19, 79
Harrison, Benjamin, 16
Harrison, John R. (U.S. marshal): appointed, 160; and 1912 election case, 190–91, 196; and Progressive party, 222–25, 248–49; and Bristow's 1914 campaign, 234, 236, 292 n14; and Bristow, 257; on Hoch-Stanley affair, 271 n16
Haworth, Erasmus (University of Kansas professor), 115
Hepburn, William Peters (Iowa congressman), 98
Hepburn bill, 52, 67, 76, 97, 98, 99, 104, 269 n4
Hinman, Harvey D. (New York gubernatorial candidate), 233, 242

Hinshaw, David (Kansas Progressive), 197–98, 217, 247–48
Hitchcock, Ethan Allen (postmaster general), 97
Hoch, Edward W.: on Kansas growth, 11; and state printership, 28–29, 34; opposes Bailey, 35; his 1904 gubernatorial campaign, 37; and Kansas Republican League, 40; on railroad issues, 41, 42, 43, 86–87; his 1905 reform program, 45; opposes Standard Oil, supports state oil refinery, 46–50, 81; prohibitionist, 72, 86; and Mrs. Stanley, 73; renominated, reelected, 1906, 75–76, 79; his 1907 legislative program, 84; and 1908 special session, 86–88, 92; supports primary law, 93–95; and 1908 primary, 99; and 1904, 1906 elections, 109; removes Allen from Board of Charities, 164; endorses Wagstaff, 1910, 169; Bristow on, 219; supports Allen, 1918, 258; mentioned, 181
Hodges, George: and Bank Deposit Guaranty Law, 125; fights with Ganse, 130; his unsuccessful 1910 gubernatorial campaign, 178–80; elected governor, 1912, 204–6; Capper on, 224; Capper's campaign against, 243; defeated, 1914, 245
Holmes, Oliver Wendell, Jr., 126
home rule for Kansas cities, 123, 261
Hook, William C. (U.S. district judge), 34
Hopkins, Richard J. (lieutenant governor), 128, 129
Horton, Albert (judge), 16
Horton Agreement, 17–18, 265 n11
House, Jay (Topeka reporter), 32, 122–23, 187
House Rules Committee, 140–43
Howe, Ed (Atchison publisher), 174, 175
Howe, Samuel T. (state treasurer), 85, 86
Hudson, General Joseph K. (Topeka publisher), 17
Hughes, Charles Evans, 121, 251, 254, 255, 256, 258
Hurd, A. A. (Santa Fe general attorney), 40–41, 64

Ickes, Harold, 253–54
imperialism, 25

income tax: progressive Republicans support graduated tax, 8; amendment, 127, 282 n46; Bristow supports, 152; Stubbs's position on, 192, 203
industrial goods produced in Kansas, 11
Ingalls, Sheffield (lieutenant governor), 214, 225, 226, 230
inheritance tax, 134, 192, 203, 262
initiative, referendum, and recall: progressive Republicans support, 8, 261; Stubbs requests, 1911, 127; opposition to, 128; defeated, 131; on 1910 Kansas platform, 177; Hodges favors, 206; Bristow's position on, 214; Progressives' position on, 216; defeated, 1915, 249
"insurgents," 4, 135–62, 280 n4
Interstate Commerce Commission (I.C.C.): and Kansas Board of Railroad Commissioners, 54; handles rate cases, 56–57; Kansas Civic Voters League endorses powers for, 69; Act, amendment of, 97, 157, 158; and Esch-Townshend bill, 98; Long opposes expanded powers for, 103; Bristow favors, 106, 155; hearings in Chicago, 118, 119; Kansans support, 269 n4; mentioned, 60
irrigation projects, 8

Jackson, Fred S.: his 1906 campaign for attorney general, 75; on liquor-law enforcement, 86; and primary law, 94–95; and bank deposit guaranty, 125; his 1910 congressional campaign, 172, 174, 175, 181; and Roosevelt's 1912 campaign, 194; at 1913 Progressive meeting, 225; remains Republican, 227
Jarrell, J. F. (Topeka reporter), 65
Jewish vote in 1912, 198
Jobes, C. S. (banker), 22–23, 26, 62, 100, 265 n25
Johnson, Hiram (California governor), 194, 253
Johnston, William A. (Kansas chief justice), 6, 15
Jones, L. M. (Santa Fe official), 63
judges of inferior federal courts, election of, 177
juvenile courts, Hoch requests, 45

Kanavel, George W. (railroad commission candidate), 75

Kansas Banker's Association, 125, 126
Kansas Board of Charities, 73, 164
Kansas Board of Regents, 173
Kansas Chamber of Commerce, 55
Kansas City, Missouri, 56–58
*Kansas City Journal*, 70
Kansas Civic Voters League, 67–70, 72, 78, 259
Kansas Corporation Commission, 3
"Kansas Corporation of Good Government," 198
Kansas Day Club: 1905 meeting, 46; 1910 meeting, 127, 167, 173, 177; 1913 meeting, 213; 1914 meeting, 234; 1918 meeting, 259
Kansas Federation of Commercial Interests, 42, 54, 55, 67, 68
Kansas Federation of Labor, 193, 244
Kansas Improved Stock Breeder's Association, 55
Kansas Industrial Court, 241, 259
Kansas Oil Producers Association, 48
Kansas Railroad Commission: made elective, 1903, 32; decrees two-cent passenger fare, 86–87; railroads bring successful suit against, 87; mentioned, 120, 191
Kansas Republican League: founded, 31–32, 34, 36–37, 260; in 1904 election, 35; splits, 44; upsets Long's stratagems, 74; mentioned, 51. *See also* Square Deal Republican Club
Kansas State Bankers Association, 126
Kansas State Historical Society, 134, 173
Kansas State Tax Commission: as 1906 campaign issue, 77; Hoch requests, 84; created, 85, 262; move to make elective, 109
Kansas State Temperance Union, 86, 132
Kelley, T. T. (state treasurer), 72, 73
Kenna, E. D. (Santa Fe general attorney), 26
Knox, Philander (U.S. attorney general), 39
Koontz, J. R. (of Santa Fe), 65

labor, 5–6, 8, 241
La Follette, Robert: his speeches, 2; and railroads, 53, 269 n4; in Kansas, 79 (1906), 102 (1908), 108; for Square Deal, 87; for regulating public-service corporations, 121; anti-Cannon, 138–39; and tariff revision, 148, 155; dislikes Postal Savings Bank Law, 155; and 1910 Kansas election, 173, 175, 182; helps organize National Progressive Republican League, 181; as presidential hopeful, 182–83, 186; mentioned, 68, 135, 142, 211, 235
Landon, Alfred M., 260, 266 n53
lead: mining in Kansas, 11; producers not tariff revisionists, 107; tariff schedules, 150
Leahy, David D. (Stubbs's secretary), 131, 244
Lease, Mary "Yellin," 106
legislative reapportionment, 133
Leidy, Freemont (internal revenue collector), 160
Leland, Cyrus K.: national committeeman, 13; his "machine" and Kansas politics, 14, 17–21, 33–34, 36, 39, 73–74; described, 15; "My Recollections," 15, 27; Missouri Valley pension agent and internal revenue collector, 16, 21; Boss Busters League opposes, 21; supports Stanley, 25; uses railroad passes, 61–62; his 1907 candidacy for Kansas Speaker, 82; and Bristow, 96; loses 1908 gubernatorial election, 107–8; and progressive Republicans, 164; attends December 1912 Roosevelt conference, 210; at 1913 Lincoln Day meeting, 214; opposes Republican-Progressive harmony, 225; mentioned, 4, 32, 41, 75
Lenroot, Irving (Wisconsin congressman), 68
life insurance system, state-owned, 241
Lincoln Day: 1913 rally, 213–15, 222; 1914 rally, 225, 230–31; no 1915 rally, 247
Lindsey, Ben (Denver judge), 197
lobbying, regulation of, 109, 123, 261
Lodge, Henry Cabot, 235
Long, Chester: wins 1903 senatorial election, 21, 25, 26, 29, 36; state senator, 25; and railroads, 28, 61, 64, 69, 70, 74, 97, 103–5; dethroned by Boss Busters, 31; opposes Hoch, 38; and Burton case, 39, 41; heads "machine," 42; splinters Kansas Republican League, 43; and Kansas Civic Voters

313

League, 70–71; supports Curtis, 1906–1907, 81, 99; opposes special session, 87, 93; opposes primary, 90–91, 99, then endorses, 93–94; his 1908 senatorial campaign, 95, 234; and Roosevelt, 97; favors Hepburn bill, 98; debates his voting record with White, 101–3; debates Bristow, 106–7; and Bank Deposit Guaranty Law, 126; and afforestation program, 145; and 1910 election, 176, 179; and 1912 election, 190–92; supports Allen, 1918, 258; mentioned, 4, 137, 212, 214, 222, 237

Loomis, N. H. (of Union Pacific), 23, 26–27, 64, 65, 98

Low, Marcus A. (Rock Island general attorney): Leland angers, 16; and Horton Agreement, 18; meets with Roosevelt, 21; and 1902 election, 22, 26–28; opposes Hoch, 37, 40–41; and Long, 98, 100

McCormick, A. H. (state representative), 130

McCormick, Medill (of Chicago), 199, 230

McKinley, William, 15–16, 21, 96

McLean, B. F. (Wichita banker), 64

McLennan, Frank (Topeka publisher), 242, 243

McNeal, Thomas A. (Topeka newspaperman), 43, 171

McPherson, Logan Grant (railroad economist), 64–65

Maddens, John (of Missouri, Kansas, Texas Railway), 213–14

Madison, Edmond H. (congressman): and Long, 108; opposes Cannon, 140–41, 144; and Ballinger-Pinchot affair, 142, 145, 147–48; and Rules Committee, 143; and tariff, 144, 149, 153; prohibitionist, 145, defends corporation tax, 152; and Mann-Elkins bill, 158; and progressive Republicans, 164; in 1910 election, 166, 171, 175; opposes La Follette's candidacy, 182; dies, 1911, 183; mentioned, 155

Mann-Elkins Act, 118, 155, 157–59

Marshall, John (of Kansas State Temperance Union), 86

Martin, Frank (congressional candidate), 183, 190

Martin, Henderson (1912 Democratic campaign chairman), 203

Martin, John A. (Kansas governor), 72

Metcalfe, Wilder (Missouri Valley pension agent), 21

Miller, James Monroe (congressman), 150, 153, 159, 170, 174

minimum-wage laws, 231, 241

Missouri, Kansas and Texas Railway Co. (M.K.T.), 48, 72

Missouri Pacific Railroad, 55, 116–17

Mitchell, Alexander C. (congressman), 62–63, 172–75, 180, 183

monopolies, 8

Moore, J. T. ("Doc") (local politician), 235

Morehouse, George P. (a founder of Kansas Republican League), 36–37

Morgan, Billy: and 1902 district convention, 22; state printer, 38; and Long, 41, 71, 100, 234; opposes state primary, 92; writes public-service bill, 121; and 1910 Kansas Day Club meeting, 167; defeated, 1910, 181; on insurgents, 183; and Progressive party, 222, 223; Bristow's manager, 234, 238; and Progressive-Republican reunion, 251; his 1918 gubernatorial campaign, 258; mentioned, 144

Morgan, J. Pierpont, 146, 157, 199, 201, 232

Morrill, E. N. (Kansas governor), 15, 16, 96

Morrow, Marco (Capper factotum), 243

Morse, J. C. (railroad commission candidate), 268 n37

Muckrakers, 51, 157, 205, 261

Mudge, H. W. (of Santa Fe), 58

Mulvane, David W.: Leland blocks for national committeeman, 16; elected national committeeman, 20; Burtonite, 37; his 1904 senatorial ambitions, 41–42; and 1904 state convention, 43–44; and Long, 71; leads Burton faction, 73; and 1906 campaign, 74, 75; opposes state primary, 92; and Stone, 130; and 1910 Kansas Day Club meeting, 167; backs Wagstaff, 169; and 1912 national convention, 187, 189; and 1912 electors case, 190–91; sup-

ports Allen, 1918, 258; returns to power, 260; mentioned, 72, 82, 202
Murdock, Thomas Bent (state fish and game commissioner), 37–38, 76, 113
Murdock, Victor (congressman): and Square Deal Club, 77, 78; his 1906 senatorial campaign, 80–82; and Taft, 136; opposes Cannon, 137–40, 142–43; and railroad postal rates, 138–39; insurgents' spokesman, 141; and Ballinger-Pinchot affair, 147; and tariff revision, 149; supports Postal Savings Bank Law, 155–56; and Mann-Elkins Act, 158; and 1910 election, 166, 171, 173–75, 179; heralds National Progressive Republican League, 181; presidential hopeful, 182; and Roosevelt's 1912 campaign, 185, 189, 194, 197; opposes bolt, 186; reelected, 1912, 207; and Kansas Progressive party, 213, 217, 225, 226, 228; Progressives' floor leader, 219; his 1914 senatorial campaign, 229, 232–33, 235–38, 241–46; at 1914 Lincoln Day banquet, 230–31; national Progressive chairman, 246, 253–55, 257; member FTC, 246, 257; his paper supports Wilson, 1916, 254, 256; becomes Democrat, 257; mentioned, 106
Murphy, Eva Morley (WCTU officer), 220, 231, 246

Nagel, Charles (U.S. secretary of commerce and labor), 154
Nation, James (state treasurer), 113
National Progressive Republican League, 181–82
Neeley, George (congressman), 238, 244
Negro vote in 1912, 198
Nelson, Col. William Rockhill (of *Kansas City Star*), 52, 153, 199, 215, 247
New Deal, 262
"New Freedom" platform of Wilson, 200
Nicholson, George (of Santa Fe), 60
Norris, George (Nebraska congressman), 142, 143
Norton, Thomas J. (of Santa Fe), 61
Nortoni, Albert (of St. Louis), 213

oil industry: Kansas output, 11; Hoch wants state oil refinery, 46–48, 72; Stubbs opposes state refinery, 48–49, 72; state refinery law passed, 49, declared unconstitutional, 50; its producers not tariff revisionists, 107; mentioned, 51
Orchestra Hall meeting, Chicago, 1912, 187
Osawatomie, Kansas, speech by Roosevelt, 229
overseas expansion, 25

Parker, Alton B. (presidential candidate), 201
Parker, John (of Louisiana), 253
Parker, Lyman (Frisco general solicitor), 26
Payne, Sereno (New York congressman), 149
Payne-Aldrich Act, 127, 136, 144, 153, 155, 172
Payne bill, 148–49
Peck, George (Santa Fe general solicitor), 16, 64, 65
Peffer, William A. (senator), 95
pensions: for veterans, 8; for widows, 231, 241
Perkins, George: and 1902 election, 26–27; and Roosevelt's 1912 campaign, 188–89, 198, 201, 207; Progressive national chairman, 232–33; and Roosevelt's 1916 campaign, 252, 253, 256; mentioned, 199
Peterson, Elmer (editor), 117–18
Pierce, Winslow S. (Union Pacific general counsel), 27
Pinchot, Amos (Progressive leader), 232–33
Pinchot, Gifford (chief forester): his controversy with Ballinger, 136, 145; and Roosevelt, 178, 194; and Perkins, 232–33
Pitney, Mahlon (justice), 191
Plumb, George (state representative), 77
Plumb, Preston B. (senator), 77
poll tax, 241
Polley, M. C. (banker), 93
Pollock, John (judge), 34, 126
Populists, 1, 2, 8, 13, 16, 51, 178
Porter, Silas (Leland ally), 20
postal services, 8, 155, 156
Price, Francis (state senator), 128, 129
primary, first senatorial, 107
primary, party, 261

315

primary, presidential preference, 128, 132, 241
primary election law: progressive Republicans support, 8; Hoch requests, 45, 46, 84, 85; Kansas Civic Voters League supports, 71; 1906 platform favors, 76, 77; Long opposes, 87, 90–91; Square Dealers support, 88; passed, 89–90, 92–95; first implemented in Kansas, 99; Madison supports, 145, rewritten, 1911, 134
Pringle, J. T. (Kansas Speaker), 28
Progressive party: supports reforms, 9; its 1912 National Convention, 188; its birth and development, 209–28; its 1914 Kansas platform, 231, 239–40; council, 240; and 1914 elections, 245–46; Chicago meeting, December 1914, 248; Chicago meeting, January 1916, 251; its 1916 conventions, 252–55; its final meeting, 257; joins Prohibition party, 257; mentioned, 230, 256
progressives, 1, 7–8
prohibition: as reform movement, 1; in Kansas, 3, 86; progressive Republicans favor, 5; Hoch supports, 35, 45, 72, 84; Stubbs, Dawson enforce, 113–15; its supporters favor initiative, 131–32; and 1912 Progressive platform, 188; Stubbs, Hodges, Capper favor, 203, 204, 205, 231; its supporters help Progressive party, 220; Murdock opposes, 235; in 1914, Republicans, Progressives support, 241; Progressive party joins Prohibition party, 257; enforcement of, 261, 277 n9
public utilities: commission established, 3; progressive Republicans seek to regulate, 8; Stubbs favors bill, 121–23, 127, 170; bill passed, 132–33; Public Utilities Act, 262
pure food and drug law, Kansas, 133

Quincy, Fred (state senator), 77

railroad brotherhoods, 193
Railroad Commissioners, Board of: Hoch and, 42; established, 53, 54; made elective, 54; advises I.C.C., 54; railroads oppose its decree, 55; its decision on passenger rates, 123; becomes Public Utilities Commission, 133; mentioned, 121
Railroad Improvement Agitation Association, 117
railroads: and rates, 4, 53, 56–58, 170; regulation of, 8, 43, 45, 269 n7; political influence of, 22–26, 34, 35, 52, 56, 60–61, 64, 85; and discriminatory rates, 47–48, 52, 103–4, 158; and passenger rates, 55, 76, 77, 84, 86, 92, 123, 127, 262; and free passes, 55, 61–62, 100; inadequate service of, 56, 59; and sidetracks, spurs, 60; control newspapers, 62–63; and banks, 64; lobby, 64–66; and anti-pass legislation, 76, 77, 84, 85; and maximum freight rates, 85, 262; and reassessment of assets, 85; and indebtedness limitation, 109; and mail charges, 138–39; and Madison, 145; and Mann-Elkins bill, 157–59; state-owned and -operated, 231, 240; abuses of, 261. See also, Missouri, Kansas and Texas Railway Co.; Missouri Pacific Railroad; Rock Island Railroad; Santa Fe Railroad; Union Pacific Railroad
reapportionment of Kansas congressional districts, 32, 45
recall. See initiative, referendum, and recall
Reed, Clyde (Kansas governor), 260
Reeder, William (congressman): and Cannonism, 143–44; and tariff, 151, 153; and postal issues, 151; and 1910 election, 171, 175; mentioned, 170
Rees, Rollin (congressman), 172, 174, 175, 186
referendum. See initiative, referendum, and recall
Reid, Albert T. (newspaperman), 4
Republican party: progressive movement influences, 2; factionalism, 2, 11, 13, 44, 89; 1898 Kansas nominating convention, 17; state convention, 20 (1900), 42–43 (1904), 71–72 (1906), 252 (1916); state platform, 43, 45 (1904), 76 (1906), 108–9 (1908), 127, 177 (1910), 239–41 (1914); and 1906 senatorial election, 80; national convention, 135 (1908), 185–87, 200 (1912), 252 (1916); 1910 primary,

316

163–84; its December 1913 National Committee meeting, 226
Republicans, progressive: oppose populism, 2; of Kansas, compared with those of other states, 5–7; compared to Populists, 8–10; as Kansas faction, 89
Resing, H. L. (of Wichita Chamber of Commerce), 59–60
Richards, J. R. (Missouri Pacific state solicitor), 16, 34
Ripley, E. P. (Santa Fe president): explains discriminatory rates for Kansas City, 56; and newspaper advertising, 63; and rate controversy with Stubbs, 119–20; White's comments on, 250
roads, rock and dirt, 127
Robbins, Raymond (Chicago reformer), 231
Robbins, Mrs. Raymond (social reformer), 213
Rock Island Railroad, 40, 55
Roosevelt, Theodore: speeches of, 2, 177–78, 186, 197, 229; and White, 3, 101; appoints Pollock, 34; and Kansas Republican League, 37; and Burton investigation, 39; and Square Deal, 51–52; and railroads, 67, 69, 139; and 1904 campaign slogan, 77; and Post Office investigation, 96–97; and Hepburn bill, 98; popular in Kansas, 99; and Long, 104; and "Armageddon," 134, 186; endorses Taft (1908), 135; and railroad mail charges, 139; and Cannon, 140; and tariff, 148; at Osawatomie, 177–78, 229; as presidential candidate, 183–84; his 1912 campaign, 185–207; Progressive National Convention nominates, 189; and struggle over Kansas electors, 193–97; and assassination attempt, 197; loses in Kansas (1912), 201; and 1912 vote, 209; calls December 1912 Chicago conference, 210–11; and trusts, 214; and Progressive party, 217, 221, 224; and 1914 progressive Republican candidates, 233, 242; opposes government ownership of utilities, 240–41; and 1912 vote, 245, 256; "suspends" Progressive party, 246–48, 250; as 1916 potential Republican presidential nominee, 251–53; refuses 1916 Progressive nomination, 254; endorses Hughes (1916), 254; and rise of progressivism, 261; endorses Taft (1906), 275 n40; mentioned, 181, 182
Roosevelt Clubs, 194, 197
Root, Elihu (New York senator), 135, 157, 186, 235
Ross, W. D. (state superintendent of public instruction), 210
"rotten borough" system, 216
Rowell, Chester (California editor), 248
Royce, John W. (state bank commissioner), 72
Ryan, Frank (gubernatorial candidate), 191–92
Ryan, W. H. (state Democratic chairman), 179

Sabbatarian legislation, 262
Santa Fe Railroad: and Leland, 16; and Kansas Republican League, 40; and rates, 48, 55, 119–20; and control of newspapers, 62, its spirit, 250
Sapp, Col. Bill (Democratic national committeeman), 199, 200, 204
Sartin, U. S.: at 1912 Republican National Convention, 187; chairman Kansas Progressive party, 213, 214, 215, 222, 225, 233, 240, 246; and withdrawal of Progressive electors (1916), 255
school-book commission, 133
schools, rural, 127
Scott, Charles F. (congressman): in 1910 election, 62, 166–67, 172–73, 175, 181; chairman Agricultural Committee, 144; on Cannon and Cannonism, 144; and tariff, 150, 153; and Postal Savings Bank Law, 155; and Stubbs, 166; on 1912 convention, 187; and Chautauqua debates with Allen, 219–20; on Bristow, 227; and 1914 election, 235; and his 1918 senatorial campaign, 257, 258; mentioned, 170
Scoville, C. C. K. (Kansas State Bankers Association president), 126
Securities Exchange Commission, 262
Senate Judiciary Committee (Kansas), 128–29
senators, direct election of: progressive Republicans support, 8; Stubbs supports, 128, 203; defeated, 1911, 132;

317

amendment to U.S. Constitution, 155; Bristow favors, 214; Bristow authors amendment, 237
Sessions, Charles (Kansas secretary of state), 81, 190, 195, 196, 223
Shaw, Dr. Anna (of New York), 213
Sheldon, the Rev. Charles Monroe, 51, 121
Sherman Antitrust Act, 43
short ballot, 9, 177, 241, 261
Silver Republicans, 13
Simmons, J. S. (Kansas Speaker), 82
Simpson, Jerry (congressman), 11, 25
Smith, A. W. ("Farmer") (Boss Buster), 17, 20, 160
Smith, Charles Blood (Topeka attorney), 34
Smith, F. Dumont (journalist), 82, 178, 198
Smith, W. R. (Santa Fe general attorney), 64, 76
Social Gospel, 51, 52
Southwestern Bell Telephone Co., 250
Southwestern Interstate Coal Operators Association, 115
"Square Deal": sentiment in Kansas, 51, 52; clubs formed, 76–77, 260; against convention system, 92; mentioned, 215
*Square Deal Hand Book*, 77, 78, 80, 84
Stahl, Frank M. (Kansas State Temperance Union superintendent), 132
Standard Oil Co., 46–50, 168, 169, 199
Stanley, Fred (Republican committeeman), 194, 252
Stanley, William E. (Kansas governor), 20, 29, 145
Stanley, Mrs. William E., 73
Stannard, C. A. (state representative), 77, 82
state printer, 32, 34–35, 46, 170
State Republican League (1912), 202, 203
State Tax Commission, 45, 46, 123, 134, 262
Stavely, J. H. (state senator), 128
Stewart, J. H. (state senator), 77, 128
Stich, A. C. (Wagstaff's campaign manager), 169
Stone, Robert (state representative), 129, 130, 171
Stuart, William I. (judge), 191–92

Stubbs, Walter Roscoe: 1905 Kansas University speech, 6; 1905 Topeka speech, 12; independent of factions, 35; state representative, 36; 1904 Republican state chairman, 36, 44, 77; encourages Hoch, 37–38; and Kansas Republican League, 40, 72; his senatorial ambitions, 41–42; declines Hoch's support, 43; 1904 Kansas Speaker, 45; opposes state oil refinery, 48–49; and railroads, 60, 118, 119–20; and Kansas Civic Voters League, 68, 70–71; attacks Long, 71; at 1906 state convention, 75; in 1906 senatorial election, 78, 80, 81; asks special session, 88; and progressive Republican faction, 89; and Bristow, 90; opposes convention system, 92; supports primary law, 93, 95; and White, 202; supports prohibition, 107, 113–16, 231; elected governor (1908), 107–8, 109, 260; and 1908 platform, 109; as governor, 111–34; his personality a drawback, 111–12; and labor, 115; supports employers' liability, 115–16; supports workmen's compensation, 116; acts against dairy trust, 117; his legislative program, 120–26; and 1910 election, 127, 166–69, 171, 173–77, 179–80, 182, 184; his 1911 proposals, 127–34; and Allen, 164; as senatorial hopeful, 166; and Roosevelt's Osawatomie speech, 178; heralds National Progressive Republican League, 181; and Roosevelt's 1912 campaign, 185, 189, 194, 195, 198; opposes 1912 bolt, 186; and 1912 National Convention, 187; his 1912 senatorial campaign, 191–93, 203, 204, 209, 213, 229, 236, 237; and 1912 vote, 202, 204, 207; attends Roosevelt's December 1912 conference, 210–11; and Progressive party, 215–17; 225–26, 228, 229–31; and 1914 election, 238, 243; and government ownership of utilities, 240; loses 1918 senatorial election, 257–58; loses 1922 gubernatorial nomination, 257; mentioned, 59, 62, 76, 99, 161, 199, 251

Taft, William Howard: Roosevelt supports (1908), 99; his acceptance speech, 104; and Bristow, 108; carries Kansas, 110; opposes bank deposit insurance, 124; his first months as president, 127; and Kansas insurgents, 135-64, 168, 280 n4, 283 n69; and Cannon, 140; and Ballinger-Pinchot affair, 146-48; and tariff revision, 148-54; supports corporation tax, 152; and Postal Savings Bank Law, 155; and postal service, 156; and Mann-Elkins bill, 159; and patronage, 159-61, 163; tours Japan and Korea, 173; disappointed in 1910 Kansas primary, 176; calls 1910 White House harmony meeting, 181; and Canadian Reciprocity, 182; vetoes Farmers' Free List, 182; renominated (1912), 185-86; nomination called "stolen," 189, 194-95, 205; and 1912 election, 190-92, 198, 200; and elector struggle, 193-97; loses Kansas, 201; mentioned, 94, 118, 134, 166, 177, 183, 187, 223, 235

Taft Clubs, 99

Taft Republican League, 202

tariffs and tariff revision: in 61st Congress, 4; progressive Republicans, Kansas Civic Voters League support downward revision, 8, 70; Republicans support reciprocity, 8; Long and, 25; Madison and, 145; Bristow on, 148-52, 214, 282 n42, 282 n52; Taft on, 148-52; La Follette and Beveridge on, 155; Stubbs and, 168; Hodges and, 206; Curtis and, 236; Republicans, Progressives on, in 1914, 241. See also Canadian Reciprocity; Cuban Reciprocity; Farmers' Free List; Payne-Aldrich Act; Payne bill; Underwood tariff

taxes. See corporation tax; income tax; inheritance tax

Taylor, W. Carr (vice-president Kansas Republican League), 38

Thompson, William (senator), 203, 204

trade reciprocity, 43

Troutman, James A.: 1902 gubernatorial candidate, 23-24; and Long, 70; and Square Deal Club, 77, 79; on Long-Bristow campaign, 105-6; calls 1913 harmony meeting, 215-17, 223; and 1914 platform, 239; mentioned, 222

Tucker, H. H. (senatorial candidate), 236-37

Underwood tariff, 248
Union Pacific Railroad, 55
United Commercial Travelers of America, 55, 86
United States Steel Corp., 183-84, 199
university and state colleges, reorganization of their governing boards, 133

Valentine, David (Kansas Supreme Court clerk), 172
Van Devanter, Willis (justice), 191
Van Sant, George (Minnesota governor), 68

*Wabash* case, 54
Waggener, Balie (of Missouri Pacific), 40-41, 43, 65, 126
Wagstaff, Tom (gubernatorial candidate), 168, 169
Walker, Paul (railroad lobbyist), 65
Wall Street, 199, 219
Warren, Fred (Kansas Socialist), 176-77
Webster, John L. (attorney), 126
West, J. S. (judge), 212
White, William Allen: his "What's the Matter with Kansas?" 3; his characterization of progressive Republican, 4; and Leland, 14, 15; and Roosevelt, 21, 101, 184-96; and Long, 28, 105; and 1903 scandals, 33; a Muckraker, 51; on railroads in politics, 60-61; on free passes, 62; supports Kansas Civic voters League, 70; supports Stubbs, 73, 111, 112; and *Square Deal Hand Book*, 78; and Hoch (1906), 79; and 1906 senatorial campaign, 82; and Curtis, 83, 259-60; requests special session, 88; and progressive Republicans, 89, 164-86; promotes Stubbs-Bristow unity, 90; opposes convention system, 92; supports primary, 93, 95; Bristow's 1908 campaign manager, 100-102; debates Long, 101-3; asks dairy antitrust action, 117-18; testifies in Kansas senate, 130-31; on Taft and insurgents, 154; and Taft, 163; and 1910 election, 166, 169-74, 176-77; and Roosevelt's Osawatomie speech, 178; and La Follette, 182-83; and 1912 election, 184-

319

89, 193–99, 203, 207; opposes bolt, third party, 186, 187, 209; and Progressive National Convention, 188; and 1912 electors, 193, 195–96; and Kansas Progressive party, 209–11, 213, 215, 217, 220–22, 224–28; calls Topeka conference, 213; and Troutman, 217; and 1914 Progressive campaign, 229, 234–36, 238, 242–46; compared to David Lloyd George, 231; and Perkins, 232–33; on 1914 Republican platform, 239–41; and suspension of Progressive party, 248; becomes increasingly conservative, 249–50; asked to rejoin Republicans, 251; works to reunite parties, 251; and Roosevelt's candidacy, 252–54; endorses Hughes, 255; on 1916 election, 256; prominent in Republican party, 257; supports Allen, 258–59; 1924 independent, anti-Ku Klux Klan gubernatorial candidate, 259; and reform, 294 n12; mentioned, 77

Wichita Chamber of Commerce, 68–69, 97

Wickersham, George (U.S. attorney general), 125, 136, 154, 155, 157–58

Williams, Al (Boss Buster), 202

Williams, William D. (Texas railroad commissioner), 118

Wilson, James (U.S. secretary of agriculture), 166

Wilson, Woodrow: and 1912 election, 197, 199, 200, 202; his "New Freedom" platform, 200, 218–19; and tariff, 201; appoints Murdock to FTC, 246; *Wichita Eagle* supports (1916), 254; some Progressives support, 255; and 1916 election, 256

woman suffrage: Hoch supports reluctantly, 45; amendment submitted (1912), 134; Hodges on, 204; Capper favors, 205; Progressive party and, 220, 241, 261; Bristow on, 234; Murdock opposes, 235; Republican party and, 241, 261; its effect on 1916 election, 295 n26

Women's Christian Temperance Union, 220, 241

Woods, Harry (delegate), 187

workmen's compensation, 116, 177, 203, 262

World War I, 256, 260

zinc, 11, 150

Zumwalt, Ermi (editor), 62–63

www.ingramcontent.com/pod-product-compliance
Lightning Source LLC
Chambersburg PA
CBHW070233240426
43673CB00044B/1774